NIETZSCHE AND BUL

Nietzsche once proclaimed himself the "Buddha of Europe," and throughout his life Buddhism held enormous interest for him. While he followed Buddhist thinking in demolishing what he regarded as the two-headed delusion of Being and Self, he saw himself as advocating a response to the ensuing nihilist crisis that was diametrically opposed to that of his Indian counterpart. In this book Antoine Panaïoti explores the deep and complex relations between Nietzsche's views and Buddhist philosophy. He discusses the psychological models and theories which underlie their supposedly opposing ethics of "great health," and explodes the apparent dichotomy between Nietzsche's Dionysian life-affirmation and Buddhist life-negation, arguing for a novel, hybrid response to the challenge of formulating a tenable post-nihilist ethics. His book will interest students and scholars of Nietzsche's philosophy, Buddhist thought, and the metaphysical, existential, and ethical issues that emerge with the demise of theism.

ANTOINE PANAÏOTI is Lecturer in Philosophy at McGill University and the University of Montreal, and a post-doctoral fellow at the Center of Research in Ethics, University of Montreal.

NIETZSCHE AND BUDDHIST PHILOSOPHY

ANTOINE PANAÏOTI

CAMBRIDGE
UNIVERSITY PRESS

CAMBRIDGE
UNIVERSITY PRESS

University Printing House, Cambridge CB2 8BS, United Kingdom

Cambridge University Press is part of the University of Cambridge.

It furthers the University's mission by disseminating knowledge in the pursuit of education, learning and research at the highest international levels of excellence.

www.cambridge.org
Information on this title: www.cambridge.org/9781107451490

First published 2013
First paperback edition 2014

A catalogue record for this publication is available from the British Library

Library of Congress Cataloguing in Publication data
Panaioti, Antoine, 1984– author.
Nietzsche and Buddhist philosophy / Antoine Panaioti.
pages cm
1. Nietzsche, Friedrich Wilhelm, 1844–1900. 2. Buddhist philosophy. I. Title
B3318.B83P36 2012
181'.043–dc23
2012019062

ISBN 978-1-107-03162-3 Hardback
ISBN 978-1-107-45149-0 Paperback

À Lhassa et Alexandre, mes enfants, mes amours

Contents

Acknowledgments

It would not have been possible for me to write this book without the help, encouragement, and guidance of Eivind Kahrs and Raymond Geuss, my two doctoral supervisors at the University of Cambridge, and Christine Tappolet, my postdoctoral supervisor at the Centre de recherche en éthique de l'Université de Montréal. Special thanks, also, to Margaret Cone, who read Pāli with me throughout my four years in the UK and with whom I engaged in several stimulating debates on Buddhist thought. I also have Vincenzo Vergiani to thank for giving me the opportunity to teach Sanskrit and Indian Intellectual History during my final year in Cambridge and to hold a seminar on Madhyamaka philosophy over the Lent, Easter, and Michaelmas terms of 2009. Teaching in the Faculty of Asian and Middle Eastern Studies helped me clarify many of my ideas on Buddhism, in particular. I also wish to thank Rupert Gethin and Martin Ruehl, my two doctoral examiners, for their constructive criticism of my dissertation and their ongoing support for the project of writing a monograph on the basis of my doctoral research.

The ideas set forth in this book took shape over a period of ten years. Countless people played a role in this process, as teachers, students, friends, adversaries, and family. I can mention but a few. At McGill University, I would particularly like to thank Alia Al-Saji, Katherine Young, Emily Carson, Lara Braitstien, Thubten Jinpa, Sanjay Kumar, Philippe Turenne, and Hasana Sharp. Many thanks, also, to Jonardon Ganeri and Jim Benson, my MPhil examiners, for their precious feedback on my thesis on Nāgārjuna's philosophy. At the Centre de recherche en éthique de l'Université de Montréal, I more recently received invaluable help from my colleagues, especially Sara Villa, Morgane Paris, Ryoa Chung, and Nathalie Maillard. I also wish to thank Hilary Gaskin of Cambridge University Press and my two anonymous external readers for their helpful feedback on the initial typescript of this work. Over the last decade, I have also benefited greatly from thought-provoking conversations and debates with a number of close friends, especially Lily Soucy, Oliver Moore, Nikolas Metaxas, Pierre-Antoine Tibéri, Fabrizio Biondi-Morra, Anna Elsner, Richard Armstrong, Pierre-Luc Déziel, and Sofia Bachouchi. Nikolas Metaxas is in fact responsible for first provoking me to think about the issues dealt with in this book. In a sense, the conception of the book took place on a cold winter night of February 2005 in a Montreal café where Nick and I locked horns over the opposition between Nietzschean life-affirmation and (presumed) Buddhist life-negation.

Ultimately, my family deserves the most thanks. I wish to express my gratitude to my parents, Hélène Panaïoti and Glen Williams, and my brother, Thomas Williams, for their unswerving support at every step on my tortuous path. Many thanks, also, to my grandparents, Constantin and Thérèse Panaïoti. My grandfather deserves much credit for teaching me how to reason from the age of five – and forcing me to do so before I even began studying in earnest (which took a while). My grandmother, with her insatiable *joie de vivre* through thick and thin, has likewise been a true inspiration since childhood. All my love and deepest gratitude, finally, to my two extraordinary children, Lhassa and Alexandre Panaïoti, and to their beautiful, outstanding mother, Lily Soucy. I owe everything valuable I have ever accomplished so far to Lily. And without Lhassa and Alexandre, this book would never have seen the light of day.

Note on translations, texts, and sources

All translations from French, German, Sanskrit, and Pāli texts in this book are my own. I have used standard abbreviations, listed below, to refer to most of the canonical Western and Indian texts cited. In the case of Indian texts, I have relied on critical editions of texts and/or editions of these texts that Indologists widely accept as authoritative. All citations from Schopenhauer's works are from the 1988 edition of A. Hübscher's critical edition of his works, *Sämtliche Werke* (Mannheim: F. A. Brockhaus). All citations from Nietzsche's letters are from G. Colli and M. Montinari's 1980 critical edition of his correspondence, *Nietzsche Briefwechsel* (Berlin: W. de Gruyter). All citations from Nietzsche's works, finally, are from G. Colli and M. Montinari's 1977 critical edition of his texts, *Nietzsche Werke* (Berlin: W. de Gruyter).

Given that I make liberal use of Nietzsche's notes and unpublished fragments, I should make my methodology clear concerning my use of such sources. The use (and abuse) of the fragments, after all, is something of a contentious issue in Nietzsche scholarship. My approach to the *NL* may be characterized as a type of middle way between Heidegger's emphasis on *WM* as the seat of Nietzsche's true philosophy, on the one hand, and the complete rejection of Nietzsche's unpublished material, on the other, e.g. J. Young's condemnation of "posthumous Nietzsche," in *The Death of God and the Meaning of Life* (London: Routledge, 2003), pp. 97–106.

Several of Nietzsche's fragments were grouped together by Nietzsche's sister, Elisabeth, and published under the title *Der Wille zur Macht* in 1901. Heidegger believed Nietzsche's published works were really a mere preamble to the work he was preparing and that Nietzsche's true contribution to philosophy can be found in *WM* alone, his "chief philosophical work." See M. Heidegger, *Nietzsche*, 4 vols. (Pfullingen: Neske, 1961), vol. 1, p. 12. Diametrically opposed to this extreme position is the view that *WM*, or any collection of Nietzsche's unpublished fragments for that matter, is little more than a "trash-bin of thoughts, doodles, day-dreams and (usually failed) thought experiments." See Young, *The Death of God*, p. 98; cf. B. Magnus, Nietzsche's Existential Imperative (Bloomington: Indiana University Press, 1990) and M. Clark, *Nietzsche on Truth and Philosophy* (Cambridge University Press, 1990) for more moderate versions of this view.

The plain, unexciting truth is that the fragments are neither gold nor rubbish. Most of them simply provide insights into what it is that Nietzsche was thinking when he was writing certain texts, and several of them are little more than prior versions of aphorisms that effectively appeared in his published works. I see no real risk in giving due consideration to what can be found in Nietzsche's notepads. The simple reason for this (contra Young) is that there is no bifurcation between Nietzsche qua wild, ranting, irrationalist note-taker and Nietzsche qua collected, scrupulous published author. This book makes use of the fragments, then, as a reliable (though by no means privileged) source for Nietzsche's thought.

Abbreviations

A	*Der Antichrist*, Friedrich Nietzsche
AK	*Abhidharmakośa*, Vasubandhu
AKBh	*Abhidharmakośabhāṣya*, Vasubandhu
AN	*Aṅgutarranikāya*
BA	*Bodhicāryāvatāra*, Śāntideva
BAP	*Bodhicāryāvatārapañjikā*, Prajñākaramati
BĀU	*Bṛhadāraṇyakopaniṣad*
ChU	*Chāndogyopaniṣad*
DBhS	*Daśabhūmikasūtra*
Dhp	*Dhammapadā*
DN	*Dīghanikāya*
DW	*Die dionysische Weltanschauung*, Friedrich Nietzsche
E	*Ethica*, Baruch Spinoza
EH	*Ecce Homo*, Friedrich Nietzsche
FM	*Über das Fundament der Moral*, Arthur Schopenhauer
FmW	*Über die Freiheit des menschlichen Willens*, Arthur Schopenhauer
FW	*Die fröhliche Wissenschaft*, Friedrich Nietzsche
GD	*Götzen-Dämmerung*, Friedrich Nietzsche
GM	*Zur Genealogie der Moral*, Friedrich Nietzsche
GT	*Die Geburt der Tragödie*, Friedrich Nietzsche
JGB	*Jenseits von Gut und Böse*, Friedrich Nietzsche
KrV	*Kritik der reinen Vernunft*, Immanuel Kant
KU	*Kenopaniṣad*
M	*Morgenröthe*, Friedrich Nietzsche
MA	*Madhyamakāvatāra*, Candrakīrti
MM	*Menschliches, Allzumenschliches*, Friedrich Nietzsche
MMK	*Mūlamadhyamakakārikā*, Nāgārjuna
MN	*Majjhimanikāya*
MP	*Milindapañha*

MSA	*Mahāyānasūtrālaṃkāra*, Asaṅga
MV	*Madhyamakavṛtti*, Candrakīrti
NB	*Nietzsche Briefwechsel*
NL	*Nachgelassene Fragmente*, Friedrich Nietzsche
NW	*Nietzsche contra Wagner*, Friedrich Nietzsche
Pm	*Paramatthamañjusā*, Dhammapāla
PP	*Parerga und Parapolimena*, Arthur Schopenhauer
Pp	*Prasannapadā*, Candrakīrti
PtZG	*Die Philosophie im tragischen Zeitalter der Griechen*, Friedrich Nietzsche
S	*Zu Schopenhauer*, Friedrich Nietzsche
SF	*Über das Sehen und die Farben*, Arthur Schopenhauer
SN	*Saṃyuttanikāya*
Sn	*Suttanipāta*
ThGA	*Therātherīgathāṭṭhakathā*, Dhammapāla
THN	*Treatise of Human Nature*, David Hume
TV	*Triṃśikāvijñapti*, Vasubandhu
UB	*Unzeitgemässe Betrachtungen*, Friedrich Nietzsche
V	*Vinaya*
VP	*Die vorplatonischen Philosophen*, Friedrich Nietzsche
Vsm	*Visuddhimagga*, Buddhaghosa
VV	*Vigrahavyāvartanī*, Nāgārjuna
WL	*Über Wahrheit und Lüge im aussermoralischen Sinne*, Friedrich Nietzsche
WM	*Der Wille zur Macht*, Friedrich Nietzsche (ed. E. Forster-Nietzsche and P. Gast)
WN	*Über den Willen in der Natur*, Arthur Schopenhauer
WSG	*Über die vierfache Wurzel des Satzes vom zureichenden Grunde*, Arthur Schopenhauer
WWV	*Die Welt als Wille und Vorstellung*, Arthur Schopenhauer
YṢK	*Yuktiṣaṣṭikākārikā*, Nāgārjuna

Introduction

Can there be any sense to existence once Being is recognized to be a fiction?[1] Is ethics possible without God? Is there any purpose to existence in this world, if this world is all there is? Is virtue possible without Transcendence? If nothing stands behind, let alone beyond, this world of becoming, can life still have meaning?

All these questions are variations on a single theme. This arresting theme will captivate anyone who has ears for Friedrich Nietzsche's philosophy, and, more generally, anyone who is not lulled by theism or one of its surrogates. It announces what I call the *challenge of nihilism.* The challenge of nihilism is the challenge of developing an ethics after the collapse of the fiction on which all prevalent ethical systems formerly relied. Nietzsche rightly identified this fiction. It is Being – "what is, but does not become."[2] The challenge of nihilism, accordingly, is the challenge of formulating a human ideal in and for a world of evanescent becoming.

From Parmenides and Plato onward, the edifice of Western thought has been built on the "empty fiction" of Being.[3] This fiction has many faces: God, Substance, the Absolute, the Transcendent, etc. Being is what underpins the metaphysical concept of the Real, the epistemological concept of the True, and the moral concept of the Good. Contrasted to Being, becoming is thus unreal, false, and evil. On one side is the fixed, reliable Truth of what is; on the other, the shifting, treacherous appearance of what becomes.[4]

A philosophical, existential, and ethical vacuum attends the sobering realization that becoming is all there is, that Being is a lie. Nothing, it

[1] All the names (e.g. Being, God, Truth) and properties (e.g. Permanence, Bliss, Transcendence) of the "*wahre Welt*" (Real/True World) rejected in both Nietzsche's thought and Buddhist philosophy will be capitalized throughout this book. This serves the purpose of underlining the robustly metaphysical character of such concepts. Cf. Rorty's capitalization of "Platonic notions" such as Truth, Goodness, Rationality, and Philosophy in R. Rorty, *Consequences of Pragmatism* (Minneapolis: University of Minnesota Press, 1991).

[2] *GD* v §1. [3] *Ibid.* §2.

[4] Cf. J.-P. Sartre, *L'être et le néant: essai d'ontologie phénoménologique* (Paris: Gallimard, 1943), p. 12.

nihilism

then seems, is real, true, or good. This vacuum Nietzsche calls nihilism. The crisis of nihilism follows on the heels of the death of God/Being. It is a crisis in so far as it threatens to undermine all value, meaning, and purpose. Hence the necessity of responding to the challenge of nihilism by formulating a genuinely post-theistic ethics. Without such an ethics, the world remains cloaked in valuelessness, any ground for evaluation is lacking, and all human beings are deemed equally worthless. No vision guides the way. Mediocrity and laissez-faire on every plane follow. Cultures decay, societies disintegrate, and people stagnate. The revival of mindless fanaticism and desperate religiosity we are witnessing today feeds off the ethical bareness of a culture (perhaps only temporarily) weaned off the soothing lies of theism. Lest a great opportunity should be wasted, the challenge of nihilism must therefore be met, though we have yet to begin really facing up to it, let alone understanding it. This is why Nietzsche remains the most relevant thinker of our day. He was indeed a posthumous philosopher. His time has now come.

nihilism as "great opportunity"

Nietzsche's attempt to respond to the challenge of nihilism takes the form of his ethics of life-affirmation. Stability, Peace, and Bliss are properties of Being. But Being is a fiction. A world of becoming is therefore a world of ceaseless instability, struggle, and suffering. Accordingly, the ideal of life-affirmation consists of a stance toward suffering. This stance comports two fundamental features, namely a distinctive attitude toward one's own suffering (*amor fati*) and a distinctive attitude toward the suffering of others (the "overcoming of compassion"). The end goal envisaged by the ethics of life-affirmation is a state of great health which involves not only accepting, but embracing, affirming, and celebrating life's limitless suffering.

does not this criticism w/ a plary action

As they are presented in Nietzsche's writing, however, both *amor fati* and the overcoming of compassion are astonishingly vague ethical concepts. Nietzsche's vision of great health, as a result, remains something of a mystery. The incisiveness and acuity of Nietzsche's negative and critical views find no parallel in his positive philosophy. This might very well have been deliberate. The ethics of life-affirmation Nietzsche began to formulate in his later years is a sketch, a rough *brouillon*, a project. Perhaps a preamble?

In developing his response to the challenge of nihilism, Nietzsche modeled himself on the counter-example of the man he regarded as his greatest predecessor. "I could become the Buddha of Europe," he writes in 1883, "though frankly I would be the antipode of the Indian Buddha."[5] By the time he collapsed in 1889, Nietzsche had gone a long way toward becoming both.

[5] *NL 1882–1884*, 4(2).

Nietzsche knew that Siddhārtha Gautama, the historical Buddha, had done two of the things he was now doing. First, the Buddha firmly rejected the myth of Being and admitted only of becoming. Second, he sought to formulate an ethics which did not rely on the fiction of an Abiding, Blissful Absolute – an ethics designed to address the fundamentally painful nature of life in a world of turbulent becoming and frustrating impermanence. The Buddha's ethics, accordingly, was also geared toward an ideal state of supreme wellbeing, or great health (*nirvāṇa*).

This is why Nietzsche proclaimed himself the Buddha of Europe. Like his Indian predecessor, he is a defiant thinker, honest enough to denounce Being as a lie and brave enough to formulate an ethics of great health founded on the reality of becoming alone. But Nietzsche also presents himself as an Anti-Buddha. To the Buddha's ethics of life-negation, which he regarded as fundamentally unhealthy, Nietzsche opposes that of life-affirmation. *Amor fati* is *nirvāṇa* turned inside out, the overcoming of compassion the opposite of the Buddhist cultivation of compassion. Already, the story of Nietzsche's attempt to respond to the nihilist crisis becomes richer.[6]

The heuristic gains in the interpretation of Nietzsche's thought secured through a closer examination of its relation to Buddhism are only the tip of the iceberg. Buddhist thought has much to offer the Western philosophical tradition in and of itself.[7] Considered in connection with Nietzsche's thought, however, it offers no less than an opportunity to begin overcoming humanity's debilitating addiction to Being without tumbling into an ethical void. Nietzsche and the great Buddhist philosophers of Classical India called a spade a spade: practically all of philosophy and religion – East and West – has been built on the two-headed delusion of soul/ego/self and God/Being/Substance.[8] Moreover, in the Buddhist tradition, as in Nietzsche's writing, there is a firm push to *psychologize* the universe not only of religious, but also

6 The relative scarcity of studies dealing with Nietzsche and Buddhism is entirely out of proportion with the significance of Nietzsche's engagement with Buddhism in the development of his thought. Such works exist, but tend to be ignored by the vast majority of Nietzsche scholars, sometimes with good reason. Be that as it may, failure to take Nietzsche's engagement with Buddhism seriously has resulted in a major blind spot in our understanding of both Nietzsche's thought and its broader philosophical significance.

7 Those who need to be convinced of this should turn to two recent volumes which clearly exhibit the pertinence of Buddhist ideas for both the analytic and continental traditions of contemporary Western thought, namely M. D'Amato, J. Garfield, and T. Tillemans (eds.), *Pointing at the Moon* (Oxford University Press, 2009) and M. Siderits, E. Thompson, and D. Zahavi (eds.), *Self, No Self? Perspectives from Analytical, Phenomenological and Indian Traditions* (Oxford University Press, 2011).

8 The juxtaposition of these two triads of concepts is not arbitrary. The soul is the personal, individual correlate of God – his *anima*, according to some. The "I" is supposedly "what is, but does not become," i.e. Being, qua ground of subjectivity. The self, finally, is the substance of which mental and physical events are attributes.

of abstract, theoretical thought. This psychological push is intimately tied to the broader medical discourse in which these philosophies are couched. Metaphysical thinking,[9] in particular, is interpreted in terms of the subject's specific (pathological) needs and desires. Drawing the relations between Nietzsche's thought and Buddhist philosophy, then, does not only add a significant measure of depth to our understanding of the implications of rejecting Being – at the metaphysical, epistemological, and ethical level – it also brings into relief a complex set of psychological considerations which point to a new, genuinely post-theistic conception of virtue.

Nietzsche believed the Buddha suffered from precisely that illness that he, Nietzsche, had diagnosed, namely *décadence*. He therefore opposed his ethics of life-affirmation to the Buddha's presumed *décadent* ethics of life-negation. But Nietzsche was wrong in believing the former and therefore misguided in doing the latter. As such, his response to the challenge of nihilism is no guiding light. Having said this, by dispelling Nietzsche's confusion and, in the process, enriching our understanding of both his thought and Buddhist philosophy, the road is paved toward a new ethical vision. Indeed, the psychological insights gained through the implosion of the life-negation/affirmation dichotomy point not only to something of a hybrid account of what is unhealthy about the common person's take on the world, but also toward something of a hybrid vision of great health. At stake, then, is a new response to the challenge of nihilism, which overcomes the limitations of Nietzsche's response. A new account of moral psychology, a new ethics, a new direction for human striving – this, ultimately, is what the present work aims to formulate.

The thrust of this enterprise is informed by clear methodological commitments. These include a particular method of interpreting Nietzsche's thought, a specific approach to Buddhism, and a distinctive hermeneutics for bringing Nietzsche's thought and Buddhist philosophy into dialog. A few words on each of these three points.

Nietzsche does not speak with one voice, but with a plurality of voices. Most philosophers strive for consistency and uniformity in their claims, arguments, and overall positions. This is not the case with Nietzsche. It is not that he reveled in inconsistency and contradiction, or that he cared nothing for consistency, as some of his less charitable readers might be

[9] Substance metaphysics is what Nietzsche and Buddhist philosophers had trouble with. It is not clear that they would have regarded so-called "process metaphysics" as meta-physics. Accordingly, except when otherwise stated, the terms "metaphysics" and "metaphysical" in this book refer to substance metaphysics.

inclined to believe. Rather, Nietzsche strove to give full expression to various viewpoints, or perspectives, and accepted that a consequence of doing so was the emergence of clashes, conflicts, and ambiguities among various perspectives.[10] Though it is inevitable to speak in this way, there is therefore always something slightly inaccurate about any statement beginning with "Nietzsche said/claimed/believed . . ." This is because there is no singular Nietzsche.[11]

Nietzsche's approach to writing philosophy is consistent with his broader theoretical positions. First, Nietzsche did not believe in a unified subject.[12] Instead he highlighted the "plurality" within the apparently singular subject. Nietzsche's polyphonic texts are consonant with the radical plurality of his own subjectivity.

Second, Nietzsche rejects the cognitive/emotive/conative trichotomy on which rests the very belief in the presumed impartiality of the philosopher.[13] Philosophical insight, for any of Plato's (or Aristotle's) successors, consists in a "knowing" untainted by what is considered lower in man, namely the deceptive senses, capricious emotions, and fickle volitions. Nietzsche has a different story to tell. He reduces both the cognitive and the emotive to the conative – all beliefs and feelings, he claims, have for their necessary condition and psychological ground certain desires and needs. Even abstract knowledge, which in effect falsifies reality – no true circle, triangle, or sphere exists in the actual world, numbers are mere empty place-holders, etc. – is a product of a primitive will to live and predominate in one's environment which leads the subject to ignore (irrelevant) particularities, to generalize, to generate universals, etc.[14] Nietzsche's view has important implications for

[10] In commenting on Nietzsche's method, P. Heller, *Studies on Nietzsche* (Bonn: Bouvier, 1980), and P. de Man, "Nietzsche's Theory of Rhetoric," *Symposium* 28(1), 1974: 33–51, emphasize the dynamics at play between the perspectives in Nietzsche's texts: the ways in which they supersede and overcome one another and thus mirror the mechanisms of the world's perpetual becoming. In contrast, my point here concerns the irreducible plurality of these perspectives, whose oppositions and dynamics, as we will see, are not always dialectical (contra Heller and de Man).

[11] This idea should not be confused with the standard view that there are, so to speak, three Nietzsches, corresponding to his so-called periods – early, middle, and late. See M. Clark, "Nietzsche, Friedrich," in *Concise Routledge Encyclopedia of Philosophy* (London: Routledge, 2000), pp. 630–1. In fact, the present study pays little attention to the distinction between the three periods, focusing instead on the plurality of Nietzsche's voices, several of which span two or three "periods," and some of which make fundamentally contradictory claims within the same period.

[12] See, for instance, *JGB* §19.

[13] On this point, see *JGB* §§3, 5, and 6, in particular. (Nietzsche does not use the terms "cognitive," "emotive," and "conative," but that is irrelevant.)

[14] See, on this point, Nietzsche's striking remarks at *JGB* §§3, 4, and 14. It could be argued that this feature of Nietzsche's thought anticipates contemporary developments in evolutionary psychology. It should be kept in mind, however, that Nietzsche regarded evolutionary theory's emphasis on adaptation as reflective of a reactive and thus unhealthy will (*GM* II §12).

the figure of the philosopher. In expounding a system or a view, a philosopher is just giving voice to some feature of his will(s). More often than not, Nietzsche claims, the works of artists and thinkers are the fruit of conflicts among the plural wills within them.[15] In Nietzsche's own case, various voices are given the opportunity to expound various perspectives expressive of various wills. Hence the plurality of Nietzsche's voices.

Third, the demise of the metaphysics of Being, and with it of the apparent/true world divide, implies that there is no determinate Absolute Truth about any matter – that there is no "view from nowhere," to use T. Nagel's phrase.[16] There is only a plurality of perspectives stemming from and expressive of a plurality of interests.[17] The theory of perspectivism which emerges from Nietzsche's critique of metaphysics and psychology is in effect put into practice in his use of polyphony.

Such are the theoretical underpinnings of Nietzsche's approach to writing philosophy as a Bhaktinian play of masks and voices. This approach should not be dismissed as immature and narcissistic obscurantism; it is, though Nietzsche would not like this turn of phrase, the "logical implication" of his views on the subject, on the human psyche, and on Truth and knowledge.

The effects of Nietzsche's approach are threefold. First, Nietzsche uses key terms or concepts in apparently contradictory, inconsistent, or at the very least ambiguous ways – e.g. the terms "nihilism" and "nihilistic." A good way to understand this rather frustrating feature of his writing is to accept it as an unhappy consequence of his use of distinct voices which confusingly use the same word in different senses. Second, Nietzsche makes apparently contradictory statements – e.g. "Buddhism is beyond good and evil" (*A*) and "the Buddha remains under the delusion of morality" (*JGB*). Again, such confusing contradictions are the result of the plurality of Nietzsche's voices. Third, some of Nietzsche's voices adopt extreme positions expressed in particularly shocking language – positions that clash with what appears to be the more nuanced thrust of his overall philosophical project (e.g. his polemical claim that compassion thwarts natural selection).

It may be objected that a thinker such as Nietzsche cannot have an "overall philosophical project," that his texts are just a mumbo-jumbo of contradictory views, and that there is no way to adjudicate between his voices. On this view, Nietzsche is a literary figure, not a true philosopher,

[15] Some examples are discussed in *GM* III.

[16] T. Nagel, *The View from Nowhere* (Oxford University Press, 1989).

[17] *NL 1885–1887*, 7(60).

because he fails to think systematically.[18] This is one of two extreme positions. The other is to treat Nietzsche's thought as a system, as J. Richardson does.[19] To do so, equal value and weight must be given to all of his voices so that all of his claims may be amenable to uniform treatment on the same discursive plane. This involves a veritable flattening out of Nietzsche's texts – a translation on a two-dimensional plane of what is three-dimensional – with various voices expressing perspectives from various angles, but also from various positions on the vertical reactive/active or unhealthy/healthy axes. Through formidable interpretative contortions, this approach makes for a relatively cogent albeit thoroughly unpersuasive "system." Most philosophers do their best to turn their thinking into a flat plane. Nietzsche's thinking is a harsh mountainous landscape and any attempt at turning it into a plane is bound to fail. This approach impoverishes Nietzsche's philosophy, which is no better than to dismiss it as "mere literature."

These two extreme positions are not exhaustive. Though Nietzsche very confusingly puts his perspectivism into practice, he can be read as a philosopher. He does not present a system, but there is nevertheless consistency and coherence in the overall attitude his thoughts give voice to, and in the overall direction in which it points. He might not have a system, but Nietzsche certainly has a project. The overarching ideal toward which his thought is geared is the great health of life-affirmation. This ideal finds its first articulation in Nietzsche's early discussion of Attic tragedy and remains the guiding star of his thinking until his collapse. The key hermeneutical principle at work in this book, accordingly, is to respect the irreducible plurality of Nietzsche's voices – to accept his playful practice of perspectivism – without losing track of what provides his thought with its overarching unity, namely the ideal of great health. This makes it possible to avoid despair before Nietzsche's contradictions and ambivalences without falling prey to the naivety of reading a fixed system into his writings.

This basic principle is manifested in two ways. First, it allows for an interpretative strategy which essentially consists in foaming the apparent inconsistencies, contradictions, and ambiguities in Nietzsche's texts with a view to arriving at the larger framework which makes sense of the various

[18] This seems to have been Russell's position in *History of Western Philosophy and its Connection with Political and Social Circumstances from the Earliest Times to the Present Day* (New York: Simon and Schuster, 1945) – a position uncritically accepted by almost an entire generation of Anglo-American early postwar scholars. Of course, Russell's assessment of Nietzsche was also (if not mainly) grounded in a harsh ad hominem assessment of Nietzsche's supposedly vile moral character.

[19] J. Richardson, *Nietzsche's System* (New York: Oxford University Press, 1996).

perspectives Nietzsche gives voice to. This larger framework almost invariably involves Nietzsche's foundational ideas on health (the active, creative, affirming drives) and sickness (the passive, reactive, negating drives). It is therefore through the resolution of apparent contradictions among Nietzsche's views that a deeper understanding of his overall project will be attained.

Second, the hermeneutical principle outlined above makes it possible to adjudicate between Nietzsche's various voices and attribute different weights to his diverse claims. The principle at play here is that of relative healthiness. Some of Nietzsche's voices are more reactive (less healthy), others more active/creative (healthier). Keeping this in mind, it is possible to downplay what (healthy/creative) Nietzsche himself would most likely have regarded as more reactive, less healthy positions.[20]

I suspect Nietzsche would have approved of this approach. Not only does the reading it allows for take the plurality of his voices seriously, but it is also creative in and of itself. Mummy-like impartiality is not what guides this inquiry;[21] some ideas in Nietzsche's text are intentionally (and consciously) emphasized, others paid less attention to, and all of those that are engaged with are treated as living, plastic, dynamic ideas, which can be utilized and learned from, not merely analyzed and commented on. More importantly, my reading is, so to speak, a direct expression of my will to "go somewhere" with Nietzsche's positive philosophy. M. Foucault once observed that the truly interesting question, when it comes to Nietzsche and Nietzscheisms, is not "what did Nietzsche say?" but rather "what serious use can Nietzsche be put to?"[22] Like B. Williams, I agree with Foucault, and I am convinced Nietzsche would have agreed as well. This book puts Nietzsche to use for a specific purpose, namely that of formulating a new, better, healthier response to the challenge of nihilism than that which we find in

[20] Examples of these include naive glorifications of violence and cruelty designed, more than anything, to provoke his bleeding-heart contemporaries – the desire to provoke is obviously reactive – or his misogynist views – clearly the result of Nietzsche's reaction to his unhappy upbringing and his traumatizing experiences with Lou Andreas-Salomé. It may be argued that this lets Nietzsche off the hook too easily: nay, that I am resuscitating Kaufmann's gentle Nietzsche in his *Nietzsche: Philosopher, Psychologist, Antichrist* (Princeton University Press, 1974). My response is that I am simply applying the (Nietzschean) principle of "relative health" to isolate and downplay particularly immature, resentful, and reactive voices in Nietzsche. This is required if we are to remain focused on the ideal of great health without being distracted by the relatively irrelevant squeals of Nietzsche's angrier, more resentful voices.

[21] On philosophers' unhappy tendency to turn everything they touch into mummies, see *GD* III §1.

[22] Cited in B. Williams, *The Sense of the Past* (Cambridge University Press, 2006), p. 300. Contra an objectivist critic, this approach to Nietzsche's texts in no way implies immunity from misinterpretation. Irrespective of its dynamism and creativity, my exegesis of Nietzsche's works remains as falsifiable as any other reading.

Nietzsche's work. In my opinion, it is time for Nietzsche himself to "go under" and thus, in a sense, to fulfill his destiny.[23]

Concerning Buddhism, it should be noted that this book engages with Buddhism as philosophy, not as religion. More specifically, in that the sources I draw from are exclusively South Asian, this book is about Nietzsche and Indian Buddhist thought.[24] From these sources are extracted, abstracted, and reconstructed a set of fundamental positions which taken as a whole is what I will call *Buddhist philosophy*. There is no doubt that Buddhism has played the role of a religion – i.e. a source of metaphysical consolation – for most of its followers since its inception, and that for millennia Buddhist institutions have played the social, cultural, economic, and political role that religious institutions have played the world over. Buddhist schools, moreover, began splintering up soon after Siddhārtha Gautama's death, which resulted in the rapid proliferation of opposed doctrinal positions on a number of philosophical points. Nevertheless, in its essence – i.e. in the teachings of its founder and a number of his erudite followers – Buddhism also bears a distinct philosophical core which is easily detachable from the culturally and historically contingent doctrinal components of various Buddhist schools. This core is what I am concerned with in this book.

There is no doubt that Buddhism is geared toward a specific practical goal, namely the attainment of a liberating wisdom which leads to radical qualitative change in one's experience of and relationship to the world. As M. Siderits has noted, however, the ethical character of Buddhism can be regarded as incompatible with the rationalism of Western philosophy "only when we assume that rationality is incapable of resolving soteriological or existential concerns."[25] The Buddha and his followers, however, never made this assumption. On the contrary, they thought resolving existential and ethical issues requires us to think clearly and to analyze the workings of the mind, the world we experience, the ways in which we engage with it, and so

[23] These turns of phrase are borrowed from *Z* (see *Z* I "Zarathustras Vorrede" §§9–10, especially).

[24] My sources are the Buddha's discourses as recorded in the Theravāda canon and the works of Indian Buddhist philosophers of the Classical period. When they are not translated, all Buddhist technical terms will appear in their Sanskrit form, even when I quote from a Pāli text; cf. A. K. Warder, *Indian Buddhism* (Delhi: Motilal Banarsidass, 1970).

[25] M. Siderits, *Buddhist Philosophy and Personal Identity: Empty Persons* (Aldershot: Ashgate, 2003), p. xiv. Hayes takes offence at the use of the term "soteriology" in discussions of Buddhism. As he rightly notes, there is no *sōtēr* ("savior") in Buddhism and thus no *sōtērion* ("salvation"). As a consequence, Hayes argues, it is inaccurate to speak of soteriology in the Buddhist context. R. P. Hayes, *Diṅnāga on the Interpretation of Signs* (London: Kluwer Academic Publishers, 1989), pp. 34–5. I am inclined to agree. This is why I speak of Buddhist ethics and Buddhist moral psychology in this book, not of Buddhist soteriology.

on.[26] As a result, there is nothing wrong with treating Buddhism philosophically, as philosophy.[27]

The controversial task of isolating an "ideal" Buddhist philosophy from Buddhism as religion and ideology involves identifying those features of Buddhist doctrine which are non-dogmatic, falsifiable, and logically independent of dogmatic positions.[28] On the level of metaphysics, the Buddhist philosophy thus arrived at firmly rejects the existence of an abiding ego and is committed to a radical critique of substance metaphysics. In the ethical domain, Buddhist philosophy advances a set of claims about what makes people psychologically unhealthy and thus also about what striving towards the great health of *nirvāṇa* involves. When it comes to epistemology, it espouses a position which in today's parlance may be described as pragmatic contextualism. In the philosophy of language, finally, it subscribes to a form of nominalism. Things are far more complicated in the details, but in essence this is what the Buddhist philosophy at play in this book comprises.

There are two things about this approach to Buddhism which might prove particularly irritating for Buddhists and Buddhologists alike. The first is that no attention whatsoever will be paid to the scholastic metaphysical themes to which Buddhist authors throughout the ages have devoted much attention and which Buddhists have always regarded as central to their belief system. Principal among these are rebirth, natural moral retribution, and the status of such a perfected being as the Buddha after death. As important as these themes were in Classical Indian discussions, the fundamental philosophical (i.e. non-dogmatic, falsifiable) positions that form the core

[26] As Siderits notes, the supposed ideological gulf between Western philosophy and Eastern "wisdom" is the heritage of the nineteenth-century Romantic construction of Asian cultures as purely "spiritual" in opposition to a crudely positivist and rationalist West (*Buddhist Philosophy*, p. xiv). On the Romantic reception of Eastern texts in Europe and its enormous impact on contemporary attitudes to India and to Indian thought, see the excellent works of R. Schwab, *La Renaissance orientale* (Paris: Payot, 1950), R. Gérard, *L'Orient et la pensée romantique allemande* (Nancy: Thomas, 1963), R.-P. Droit, *L'oubli de l'Inde: une amnésie philosophique* (Paris: Presses Universitaires de France, 1989), and W. Halbfass, *India and Europe: An Essay in Understanding* (State University of New York Press, 1988). In reality, reasoning is not so foreign to Asia and Western rationality is not as detached from more practical and ethical concerns as some might think. As a result, it is not possible to develop a coherent argument to justify what Halbfass calls the "the exclusion of the Orient from the domain to which the concept of philosophy is applicable" (*India and Europe*, p. 155). For a more detailed discussion of the "Euro-contemporocentrism" characteristic of the mainstream Western philosophical attitude to Indian thought, see R. King's excellent *Introduction to Hindu and Buddhist Philosophy* (Edinburgh University Press, 1999), especially pp. 1–41.

[27] *Nirvāṇa*, the *summum bonum* of Buddhist ethics, is said to be accompanied by "wisdom/insight" (*prajñā*). Indeed, developing wisdom is essential to attaining *nirvāṇa*. As such, for all its emphasis on a practical, ethical goal, there is no doubt that Buddhism is, nominally at least, a form of "love of wisdom" (*philō-sōphia*).

[28] Cf. M. Siderits, *Buddhism as Philosophy: An Introduction* (Aldershot: Ashgate, 2007).

of Buddhist philosophy are logically independent of these issues. Whether or not reincarnation and natural moral retribution actually occur has no bearing whatsoever on whether or not Being is a coherent concept, or whether or not there is a permanent ego at the heart of the subject. Similarly, my account of *nirvāṇa* as the great health which attends the going out of the fiery fever of thirsting (*tṛṣṇā*) bears no necessary relation to one's position on persons' fate after death, whether or not they are enlightened. In short, my ideal Buddhist philosophy is entirely independent of the historically, culturally, and ideologically contingent features of Buddhist religious doctrine. This distinction between the necessary and the contingent might be interpreted as a form of arrogance characteristic of philosophers, but it is hard to deny its value or to resist the greater focus it allows for.

The other major irritant in my approach involves not what it excludes by way of doctrine, but by way of schools. In short, I take any version of Buddhism which (1) defends the existence of an irreducible self (e.g. Pudgalavāda), (2) propounds the existence of a Transcendent Absolute (e.g. Cittamātra), or (3) endorses a form of realist, substance metaphysics (e.g. Vaibhāṣika Sarvāstivāda)[29] as fundamentally inconsistent with the basic tenets of the Buddha's thought.[30] Everything in the world, according to the early discourses, is dependent on causes and conditions and, as a result, is impermanent. As later Buddhist philosophers rightly saw, this is true both of the various elements that make up the "person" – hence the "selflessness" of persons – and of the constitutive elements of anything at all in world – hence the universal "substancelessness" of all things. On this view, Nāgārjuna, the second–third century CE founder of the Madhyamaka school, did little more than draw the logical conclusions of the Buddha's fundamental philosophical views. What is known as the dependent

[29] Contrary to what many scholars of Buddhism seem to believe, (3) does not include all of the schools that engaged in the Abhidharma taxonomic project. Of those schools whose texts are extant, only the Vaibhāṣika Sarvāstivādin Ābhidharmikas explicitly regarded the "elements" (*dharma*) that make up the world as substantially existent rather than as fleeting processes. As Gethin rightly notes, the ontological status of the elements was not specified in the early Abhidharma found in Theravāda sources. R. Gethin, "He Who Sees *Dhamma* Sees *Dhammas*: *Dhamma* in Early Buddhism," *Journal of Indian Philosophy* 32(4), 2004: 513–42, at pp. 541–2. For a detailed exploration of the transition from ontologically non-committal taxonomy to realist ontology in Sarvāstivādin circles, see C. Cox, "From Category to Ontology: The Changing Role of *Dharma* in Sarvāstivāda Abhidharma," *Journal of Indian Philosophy* 32(5–6), 2004: 543–97.

[30] It goes without saying, then, that I will disregard the now-defunct transcendentalist strand of Buddhist scholarship, which claimed that the Buddhist critique of the self really only points to a "super-personal self." E. Conze, "Spurious Parallels to Buddhist Philosophy," *Philosophy East and West* 13(2), 1963: 105–15, at p. 114. On this Buddhological current and its grave shortcomings, see S. Collins, *Selfless Persons: Imagery and Thought in Theravāda Buddhism* (Cambridge University Press), pp. 7–12.

dependent co-arising of all things (handwritten marginal note at top)

co-arising of all things is the essence of Buddhist thought, and it is from this critical point that almost everything else in Buddhist philosophy follows.[31]

It should be noted that my verdict on the other principal Buddhist schools whose texts are extant is pronounced from within the Buddhist tradition. It is on a Buddhist rather than on some external view that strands of Buddhism that continue to express a belief in Being – be it in terms of a self, an Absolute, or a Substance – are denounced as exhibiting precisely that fundamental psychological defect that Buddhism is meant to fight, namely a lingering attachment to Permanence, or the need for the firmness of an "It Is." In other words, there is a story to be told from within the Buddhist tradition for why schools such as Pudgalavāda, Cittamātra, and Vaibhāṣika Sarvāstivāda thwart the Buddha's message.

Certain schools of Buddhist thought thwart the central message (handwritten marginal note at left)

It may also be objected that there is something artificial, unfair, uncharitable, and intellectually arrogant about distinguishing between pure, or ideal, Buddhist philosophy and Buddhism as religion. I am willing to bite this bullet. What I do is artificial and it is in a sense uncharitable to all of those who hold that you need to believe in reincarnation and *karman* to be a proper Buddhist. But all that matters for my purposes is that it be philosophically legitimate.

It should be noted, in this connection, that my approach is consonant with two ideas highlighted in even the most traditional presentations of Buddhism. First, Buddhism's self-understanding as a form of therapy is taken very seriously. Second, the construction of an ideal Buddhist philosophy may be regarded as an application of the Buddhist principle of "skillfulness in means" (*upāyakauśalya*).

These two points are in fact closely related. The Buddha should first and foremost be looked upon as a therapist, not a theoretical thinker. His message aimed to alleviate human suffering. As such, it is geared toward a distinctive ideal of great health, namely *nirvāna*. Buddhist philosophy as it is presented in this book retains the fundamentally therapeutic character of more traditional formulations of Buddhist thought. As a physician of mankind, the Buddha pragmatically tailored his teaching to his public, depending on its degree of intellectual and ethical

---

[31] Just as this study pays scant attention to the distinction between Nietzsche's three periods, it also underplays the distinction between "early Buddhist" views and those of thinkers associated with the later, so-called Mahāyāna movement in Buddhism (namely, Nāgārjuna, Candrakīrti, or Śāntideva). As with Nietzsche's periods, the idea is that there really is far more continuity than discontinuity between the various periods in the development of Buddhist philosophy and that there is thus no justification for treating these presumed "periods" in isolation.

maturity.[32] Absolute, determinate truth seemed to be far less important to him than the effect his words and ideas would have on his audience. To him, the "what?" was apparently of far less relevance than the "how?" and the "to what end?"[33] So my use and formulation of Buddhist philosophy does not only respect the fundamental idea of Buddhism as a philosophy of great health, it may also be regarded as the "skillful" presentation/adaptation of Buddhist ideas for a specific audience.

This book is addressed first and foremost to those interested in philosophical and ethical issues as they are framed in the Western tradition. My presentation of Buddhism as philosophy reflects this. Not only do I sincerely take it to reach the heart of what is essential about the intellectual movement the historical Buddha started, but my presentation of Buddhism also purports to be a "skillful" way of presenting Buddhist ideas to a Western philosophical public. As a result, my deferral to the conservative contemporary Western convention of regarding only non-dogmatic and falsifiable positions as "philosophical" need not be seen as unreflective positivist Eurocentrism. The Buddhist tradition itself allows for such an adaptation of the Buddha's teaching. Skillfulness in means trumps all dogmatic intransigence.

A few words, finally, on the hermeneutical strategy this book deploys to bring Nietzsche's thought and Buddhist philosophy into dialog. The hermeneutics at the heart of this book proceeds through a "fusion of horizons"[34] on the discursive plane of the medical discourse. Ethics, in particular, will be discussed in terms of a typology central to both philosophies, namely that of healthy vs. sick types.[35]

Of course, my decision to emphasize the ideal of great health in both Nietzsche's thought and Buddhist philosophy is far from an arbitrary

[32] As Burton writes, "a good doctor varies the medicine in relation to the precise nature of the disease, and a similar flexibility is found in most Buddhist traditions. It is believed that the Buddha did not teach the same thing to all people but adapted his message depending on the specific needs, capacities and interests of his audience." D. Burton, "Curing Diseases of Belief and Desire: Buddhist Philosophical Therapy," in C. Carlisle and J. Ganeri (eds.), *Philosophy as Therapeia*, special issue of *Royal Institute of Philosophy Supplement* 66: 187–217, at p. 203.

[33] On this point, see also the introduction to S. Hamilton, *Early Buddhism: A New Approach: The I of the Beholder* (Richmond, CA: Curzon Press, 2000).

[34] This form of "fusion of horizons" is not the same as that described by Gadamer, who coined the phrase. H.-G. Gadamer, *Wahrheit und Methode: Grundzüge einer philosophischen Hermeneutik* (Tübingen: Mohr, 1972). Rather than fusing the interpreter's and the interpreted text's horizons, my aim is to fuse the horizons of two different types of texts, or philosophies.

[35] In Nietzsche's thought, this distinction can also be described in terms of the strong vs. weak type. As I will explain in Chapter 1, strength/health and sickness/weakness in the context of Nietzsche's thought (and Buddhist philosophy for that matter), are not to be understood literally, as corresponding to physiological fitness/illness in the standard biological sense.

decision. In one way or another, practically every extant Indian Buddhist text underscores the centrality of the medical discourse in Buddhist thought and practice. Simply put, the great health of *nirvāṇa* is what Buddhism is ultimately all about. Nietzsche's positive thought is similarly geared toward an ideal of great health.[36] What is more, the very notion of great health is already central to Nietzsche's engagement with Buddhism. As the antipodal "Buddha of Europe," after all, Nietzsche saw himself as propounding a life-affirming "great health" diametrically opposed to what he regarded as the Indian Buddha's life-negating "great sickness." The hermeneutics of fusing the Buddhist and Nietzschean horizons over the discursive plane of great health, in short, has its roots in Nietzsche's writing. In fact, it is really just a matter of taking Nietzsche seriously.

[36] It should be noted, in this connection, that the infamous figure of the *Übermensch* is conspicuously absent from the present book. Indeed, it seems to me (and to a growing number of scholars) that unlike the figure of the "healthy type," the figure of the *Übermensch* belongs more to the world of Zarathustra's wisdom than to that of Nietzsche's thought. Nietzsche's ironic relation to Zarathustra's proclamations has recently been highlighted by Pippin, "Introduction," in R. B. Pippin (ed.), *Thus Spoke Zarathustra: A Book for All and None*, trans. A. Del Caro (Cambridge University Press, 2006), pp. viii–xxxv. More generally, *Z* is the text I least draw from in my discussion of Nietzsche's philosophy.

PART I

Nihilism and Buddhism

CHAPTER I

Nietzsche as Buddha

The key concept in Nietzsche's relationship to Buddhism is nihilism. Buddhism, Nietzsche claims, is a form of nihilism, as is his own thought.[1] But what exactly does Nietzsche understand by this term? Answering this apparently simple question is not as easy a task as might first appear. In fact, "nihilism" cannot coherently stand for one concept in Nietzsche's works. To wit: if nihilism is the disorienting sense of valuelessness and aimlessness that attends the death of God,[2] then what does Nietzsche mean when he describes Christianity as "nihilistic,"[3] or Christians, followers of Plato, and German Idealists as "nihilists"?[4] Certainly, Nietzsche did not mean to say that Christians, Platonists, and Idealists developed their worldviews against the backdrop of God's death. Nor could he have been saying that they were all crypto-atheists. Nihilism looks like an incoherent concept. Yet Nietzsche's views on nihilism are central to his relationship to Buddhism. The first step toward understanding this relationship, then, is to clarify the distinct meanings of the term "nihilism" in Nietzsche's writing.

For all the ambiguity in Nietzsche's nihilism(s), at least one thing is clear. When Nietzsche uses words such as "nihilism," "nihilist," and "nihilistic" he is not referring to what philosophers now understand by the term nihilism. This term is primarily used in discussions of metaphysics and ethics. Metaphysical nihilism is the position that nothing really exists, and

[1] *NL 1885–1887*, 9(35).

[2] *Ibid.*, 5(71): "Belief in aim- and senselessness [i.e., nihilism] is the psychologically necessary *affect* once the belief in God . . . is no longer tenable." See also *ibid. 1888–1889*, 17(3). Most scholars, even those who offer sophisticated and careful analyses of nihilism in Nietzsche's thought, seem content to work under this definition of nihilism alone – namely, M. Heidegger, *Nietzsche*, 4 vols. (Pfullingen: Neske, 1961), R. G. Morrison, *Nietzsche and Buddhism: A Study in Nihilism and Ironic Affinities* (Oxford University Press, 1997), B. Williams, "Introduction," in B. Williams (ed.), *The Gay Science*, trans. J. Nauckhoff and A. del Caro (Cambridge University Press, 2005), pp. vii–xxii, and B. Reginster, *The Affirmation of Life: Nietzsche on Overcoming Nihilism* (Cambridge, MA: Harvard University Press, 2006).

[3] *A* §20. [4] *EH* "Warum ich so gute Bücher schreibe"; *GT* §2.

that the universe actually amounts to an absolute void. This is a position some scholars (wrongly) attribute to the philosophy of Nāgārjuna and his followers.[5] It might also be argued that this is the logical implication of Nietzsche's critique of the metaphysics of Being. Be that as it may, metaphysical nihilism is not what Nietzsche understood by nihilism.

Meta-ethical nihilism, for its part, is the view that no moral facts exist – that the set of "moral entities" is an empty set.[6] And while Nietzsche is sometimes characterized as a meta-ethical nihilist,[7] such nihilism is only tangentially related to one of the ways Nietzsche himself uses the term. In a number of passages, Nietzsche describes nihilism as a consequence of the realization that the metaphysics on which Judeo-Christian morals is grounded is hopelessly *dépassé*. Such nihilism is thus subsequent to the realization that no "moral facts" (as previously envisaged) exist, i.e. to meta-ethical nihilism.[8] It is obvious, then, that the nihilism discussed by Nietzsche cannot be that of contemporary meta-ethicists.

So much for what nihilism is not. The question "what is nihilism?" remains. Ultimately, two principal nihilisms[9] need to be distinguished in Nietzsche's writing.[10] At the heart of such "nihilistic" ideologies as Christianity, Platonism, and Idealism is a nihilism which lies at the root of all traditional worldviews based on theism or, more generally, of any faith in Being. I call this the *nihilist mentality*. In contrast, the existential vertigo attendant upon the death of God refers to a historical and cultural crisis

[5] See D. Burton, *Emptiness Appraised: A Critical Study of Nāgārjuna's Philosophy* (Richmond CA: Curzon, 1999); C. Oetke, "Remarks on the Interpretation of Nāgārjuna's Philosophy," *Journal of Indian Philosophy* 19(3), 1991: 315–23, and "'Nihilist' and 'Non-Nihilist' Interpretations of Madhyamaka," *Acta Orientalia* 57(1), 1996: 57–103; and T. Wood, *Nagarjunian Disputations: A Philosophical Journey through an Indian Looking-glass* (University of Hawaii Press, 1994).

[6] See G. Harman, "Ethics and Observation," in S. Darwall, A. Gibbard, and P. Railton (eds.), *Moral Discourse and Practice* (Oxford University Press, 1997), pp. 83–8, and *Explaining Value and Other Essays in Moral Philosophy* (Oxford University Press, 2000), as well as Mackie's error theory in "*Ethics: Inventing Right and Wrong,*" in Darwall, Gibbard, and Railton, *Moral Discourse and Practice*, pp. 89–100.

[7] Consider, for instance, *JGB* §108: "There are no moral phenomena, only a moral interpretation of phenomena" (Cf. *GD* VII §1). However, on Mackie's error theory, meta-ethical nihilism only holds in so far as one endorses meta-ethical cognitivism, which Nietzsche certainly did not. For Nietzsche moral propositions are a question of how one feels, not what one knows.

[8] On this point, see Reginster, *The Affirmation of Life*, pp. 25–6.

[9] I say "principal nihilisms" because there are also two other, relatively minor, nihilisms which appear in Nietzsche's unpublished notes, namely active/passive nihilism (*NL 1885–1887*, 9(35)). These will be discussed in Chapter 2.

[10] This distinction is far more fundamental than those previously discussed in commentarial literature – namely Morrison on active/passive nihilism (*Nietzsche and Buddhism*, pp. 22–3), Reginster on nihilist disorientation/despair (*The Affirmation of Life*, pp. 33–4), and Heidegger's "three forms of nihilism" (*Nietzsche*, vol. II, pp. 63–71).

precipitated by the breakdown of systems of valuation based on such metaphysics. I call this the *nihilist crisis*. Both of these require a detailed discussion.

The nihilist mentality is what stands behind the fiction of Being. More specifically, it is what gives birth to what Nietzsche calls the *wahre Welt* ("True/Real World"),[11] the principal posit behind practically all religious, philosophical, and even scientific thinking.[12] In short, the nihilist mentality is responsible for generating the delusion of a realm of Being that is somehow more fundamental, more real, and truer than the world of transient becoming which is given to us in experience.[13]

What, one might ask, is nihilist about that? The metaphysics of Being is nihilist in that it begins with a resounding "no." Central to the narrative through which the fiction of Being is devised is a denial of the key properties of the world we see and experience. In short, the nihilist mentality produces Being through a negation of becoming. Nietzsche explains how the fiction of the *wahre Welt* is generated through a specific type of reasoning which infers the *wahre Welt*'s negative properties through a contradiction of the properties of the actual world:

> This world is apparent – *therefore* there is a true world. This world is conditioned – *therefore* there is an unconditioned world. This world is full of contradictions – *therefore* there is a world free of contradictions. This world becomes – *therefore* there is a world which is.[14]

It is through a reactive procedure that negates and denies validity to the very real qualities of the world as it is presented to us by our senses that the fictitious, supra-sensuous domain of the Real is generated. In brief, "the '*wahre Welt*' has been constructed out of contradiction to the actual world (*wirkliche Welt*)."[15] The nay-saying at the root of the metaphysics of Being is what discloses the fundamentally nihilistic character of such metaphysics.

The metaphysics of Being, however, is nihilist not only by virtue of its source in and through nay-saying, but also of its implications at the level of

[11] The term *wahre Welt* is not translated because the German "*wahr*" implies not only that something is true, but also that it is real. If anything, the *wahre Welt* is a metaphysical concept more than an epistemological one (Truth is a property of Being – the Real – not vice versa). *Wahre Welt* metaphysics, indeed, is a "metaphysics of Being," to borrow Heidegger's phrase.

[12] *FW* §344. See also *GM* III §24.

[13] At *GD* III §2, Nietzsche speaks of the *wahre Welt* as the product of the "falsification of the testimony or our senses." As will soon be clear, however, his critique of the metaphysics of Being is less of a positivist attack on theism than a harsh verdict on what weak, irritable people invented to provide for themselves the consoling illusion of stability in a world they found too hostile to engage with at face value, and, in the same stroke, to take vengeance on life.

[14] *NL 1885–1887*, 8(2). [15] *GD* III §6.

ideology – implications which follow quite naturally from its genesis in negation. Consider its two key features. First, it is primordial *substance metaphysics* in that it posits a Fundamental, Real Substance (Being) that underlies all merely contingent, or accidental, phenomenal change (becoming). Second, it is the primordial *metaphysics of transcendence* in that it posits a realm of Being and Truth that transcends the immanent world of becoming and mere appearance. The "Real/True World" of Being is both *behind* the world we see (as Truth is "behind" the veil of appearance/illusion, Substance "behind/under" its attributes) and *beyond* it (as the Transcendent is "beyond" the immanent, Heaven "beyond" Earth, etc.). The implication, of course, is that this world of becoming is "nothing" (*nihil*).[16] The actual world, compared to the Substantial, Transcendent *wahre Welt*, is mere surface and mere immanence – metaphysically speaking, it is no-thing. The nihilist mentality thus delivers a True and Real World of Being at the cost of reducing the world of becoming to nil.

Metaphysical nihilism regarding the ontological value of "what becomes" has for its corollary a meta-ethical nihilism concerning its moral worth which then serves as ground for the moral condemnation of the actual world. As Nietzsche emphasizes in *A*, the *wahre Welt*'s transcendence finds its strongest expression in a set of moral ideas closely connected to the notion of Reality/Truth (*Wahrheit*), namely the Good, Justice, Peace, Bliss, etc. Implicit in the very postulation of a *wahre Welt* endowed with such attributes is a complete devaluation of the world we live in.[17] The world of becoming is not only untrue and unreal, it is also a realm to which the Good is fundamentally foreign. The result is meta-ethical nihilism concerning the world we live in – an attribution of the "value of nil" to the actual world.[18] Deleuze explains: "Values superior to life cannot be separated from their effect: the depreciation of life, the negation of this world."[19] But the negation of the actual world's value implicit in the invention of a *wahre Welt* is only foreground for the nihilist's moral condemnation of this world. The world of becoming is not simply morally worthless or valueless; it has a positively negative moral value. As Nietzsche explains, "once the concept of 'nature' had been devised as the concept antithetical to 'God,' 'natural' had to be the word for 'reprehensible.'"[20] The

[16] See, in this connection, *GD* III and IV. [17] *A* §15.

[18] G. Deleuze, *Nietzsche et la philosophie* (Paris: Presses Universitaires de France, 1962), p. 170.

[19] *Ibid.*, p. 169.

[20] *A* §15. Cf. *EH* "Warum ich so klug bin" §3: "What is the greatest objection to existence so far? *God*"; and *GD* VIII §34: "The 'beyond' – why a beyond, if not as a means to besmirch this world?" Though Nietzsche is specifically targeting Christianity in such passages, his claims apply *mutatis mutandis* to all forms of *wahre Welt* ideology. Texts such as *GD* II–IV make this very clear.

nihilist mentality thus delivers the domain of the Good at the price of reducing the actual world to a moral wasteland.

At the root of the nihilist mentality's ideology, then, are two twin claims: "no, the world of becoming is not real!" and "no, the world of becoming is not good!" The result is a realm of Being which is Real and Good, opposed to a devalued, deflated, nihilized realm of becoming which is unreal and evil. But it is obvious that what nihilists thus arrive at is precisely what fueled their thinking from the start. The metaphysics of Being begins with a series of no's concerning the actual world and delivers an actual world reduced to no-thing – no 'Real thing' in this sea of becoming and no 'Good thing' in this sea of change, struggle, and contradiction.

Such suspicious circularity prompts Nietzsche to enquire as to the psychological ground of such thinking.[21] What does it betray to begin by saying no? Of what is the nihilist's depreciation of life indicative, or symptomatic? These are the questions Nietzsche wants to answer. And on this point Nietzsche is unambiguous. The thinking behind the fiction of Being/God "has its root in *hatred* of the natural (– reality! –), it is the expression of a profound discontent with what is real."[22] At the root of the nihilist mentality's invention of Being, then, is spite against existence itself.

Unpacking this psychological claim requires an examination of a key concept of Nietzsche's philosophy, namely *décadence*. *Décadence* is a form of physical and emotional weakness, which manifests primarily as weariness[23] and irritability.[24] This irritability is what provides *décadence* with its "formula," namely "the preponderance of feelings of displeasure over feelings of pleasure."[25] Weary and irritable as they are, *décadents* are continually exasperated by life.

The *décadent* is the quintessential sick type of Nietzsche's philosophy. And indeed, *décadence* is best understood as an illness. Most people are certainly familiar with the aversion from contact which is experienced when one's health and vitality are in "decline" (the literal meaning of *décadence*).

[21] This psychological turn in Nietzsche's enquiry into the origins of the *wahre Welt* reflects his broader theoretical commitment to the view that the function of metaphysics is to substantiate and justify a primary moral outlook (*JGB* §6). According to Nietzsche, the relationship between a metaphysical system and the morals it "delivers" is always circular, in so far as all kinds of metaphysics both bolster and find their ground in an (often pre-reflective) moral/ethical attitude. Accordingly, Nietzsche's account of the genesis of the metaphysics of Being is not supposed to be historical. Its focus, rather, is on the psychology that underpins it.

[22] *A* §15. See also *EH* "Warum ich ein Schicksal bin" §8.

[23] At *EH* "Warum ich ein Schicksal bin" §7, Nietzsche refers to *décadents* as "the exhausted." See also *NL 1888–1889*, 14(174). The connection between *décadence* and existential fatigue recurs throughout his late texts.

[24] *JGB* §293 and *A* §§20 and 22. [25] *A* §15.

When I am sick, all but the dimmest lights seem too bright, all but the softest sounds seem too loud, everything unexpected seems unpleasant, etc. I find myself longing for things to be still, quiet, stable, and predictable. It is this commonly experienced attitude that Nietzsche attributes to *décadents*.

The primary consequence (and thus symptom) of *décadence* is what Nietzsche calls *ressentiment*.[26] Among the affects of *ressentiment* are "anger, pathological vulnerability ... and thirst for revenge."[27] Again, Nietzsche seems to be pointing to a psychological state anyone who has ever been sick, worn out, stressed, or just exceedingly hungry will easily recognize. The increased sensitivity and vulnerability at both a physical and an emotional level that I experience when I am sick or very tired makes me more irritable and less patient (with people *and* objects – as though I felt "targeted'" by everything that happened to me), harsher in my judgments (as though looking down on a stranger, say, "lifted me up"), more prone to anger, to disappointment, to knee-jerk reactions (of body, speech, and mind), to passive-aggressive, or just plain aggressive, behavior, etc. Nietzsche's *ressentiment* refers to this general propensity to exhibit vengeful, self-defensive aggressiveness which in most of us accompanies states of sickness and exhaustion. This is why he describes it as the primary effect of *décadence*. In so far as the *décadent* is a fundamentally weak type, moreover, *ressentiment* is intimately connected to impotence. *Décadents* are too weak to actively engage with the world or enter any form of genuine struggle. Instead, they seethe with reactive rancor and let their *ressentiment* swell.

From the swollen bosom of *décadent ressentiment* is eventually born the *wahre Welt*. Nietzsche's contention is that the thirst for a *wahre Welt* is the product of the *décadents*' deep insecurity vis-à-vis the world and its endless instability. The turbulent tumult of becoming is deeply unnerving for hyper-sensitive *décadents*. As a result, they construe life itself as a problem: hence the "hatred of reality" that fuels the nihilist mentality and its metaphysics. But what really does the work of constructing *wahre Welt* metaphysics is *ressentiment*, more precisely "*ressentiment* against reality."[28] Nietzsche's contention is that the "nihilization" of the actual world in and through the fable of a Real World is a gesture of resentful revenge. It is this desire for revenge that gives the *décadents*' hatred its potency, its capacity to

[26] At *EH* "Warum ich so weise bin" §6, Nietzsche explains that *ressentiment* is the sickly *décadents*' "most natural inclination."

[27] *A* §15. [28] *NL 1885–1887*, 8(2); *ibid. 1888–1889*, 15(30).

create an ideology which takes its toll on life. The negation of the world's value – both ontological and ethical – is an act of retribution on the part of the *décadents* for the suffering they endure at the hands of unwieldy becoming. The life-negation at the core of the metaphysics of Being is the ultimate fruit of their *ressentiment*. It is through this affect that the *décadents'* reactivity becomes *creative*. Their creation is Being.

The first step in the cooking up of the *wahre Welt*, then, is not the intellectual postulation of a Real World of Being, Truth, Stillness, and Bliss. It is something pre-cognitive and pre-reflective; it is an attitude of distrust and frustration toward the world which results in a knee-jerk rejection of the world.[29] This attitude, according to Nietzsche, is the primordial moral(izing) attitude – "this world of becoming harms me, it is evil!," thinks the *décadent*. The sickness that underlies the fiction of Being, then, involves feeling targeted by life and thus construing existence as morally problematic and the world as guilty.[30] If the nihilist mentality's end result is a worldview in which the world as we see and experience it is worthless, valueless, meaningless, deceptive, and evil, it is because the nihilist has already decided, in advance, that the world is despicable.

leading to creation of world of Being

Nevertheless, though the *décadents'* invention of Being is primarily a destructive gesture of vengeance, there is also an element of creation in it. This connects to the last, perhaps most subtle, sense in which *wahre Welt* metaphysics is nihilist. With the fable of Being, the *décadents* equip themselves with exactly what they most deeply long for, namely a realm of Permanence, Stillness, and Bliss. Peace and quiet, after all, is "the Good" par excellence for the exhausted sick type.[31] Cooking up the *wahre Welt*, then, is not only an act of revenge, but also of soothing self-consolation and comforting. "Fear not, my brethren, Being, our final abode, awaits us, should we only succeed in extricating ourselves from this wretched world," say the *décadents*. Nietzsche's claim is that this is *nihil*ism in its purest form. Being is constructed through a contradiction of everything real – becoming, conditionality, impermanence, irreducible plurality, contradiction, uncertainty, instability, struggle, etc. – and, as such, it is the greatest nothing ever devised by humankind. Nietzsche explains: "The criteria which have been

[29] As Nehamas reports, "Nietzsche does not simply attack the distinction between appearance and reality. He also offers . . . a psychological account of its origin." A. Nehamas, *Nietzsche: Life as Literature* (Cambridge, MA: Harvard University Press, 1985), p. 171. See also G. T. Martin, "Deconstruction and Breakthrough in Nietzsche and Nāgārjuna," in G. Parkes (ed.), *Nietzsche and Asian Thought* (Chicago University Press, 1991), pp. 91–111.

[30] As Nietzsche explains at *GM* III §15, people who suffer instinctively look for the guilty party responsible for their suffering.

[31] *GM* III §17; *NL 1888–1889*, 14(174).

bestowed on the 'True Being' of things are the criteria of non-being, of *nothingness*."[32] Another way of putting it is that *décadent* nihilists have throughout the ages "call[ed] nothingness God."[33] The outcome of the *décadents*' nihilist mentality, then, is the unwitting worship of *nihil* under the guise of Being/God. This deification of nothingness is the fruit of the sickly *décadents*' quest for shelter from the precarious world of becoming. What Schopenhauer had called the "metaphysical need"[34] is really a cowardly will to nothingness.

The second nihilism discussed by Nietzsche is not a "mentality," but an event. This is the nihilist crisis. Here, Nietzsche's primary focus is on the nihilist crisis which had begun in the Europe of his day and in which we in the West arguably remain ensnared. Nihilism, in this context, is expressive of the radical valuelessness that overshadows all of existence once the only thing that was believed to give it value – the *wahre Welt*, or God – is revealed to be a lie. Nietzsche explains:

> Extreme positions are not succeeded by moderate ones, but by extreme positions of the *opposite* kind. And thus the belief in the absolute immorality of nature, in aim- and senselessness, is the psychologically necessary *affect* once the belief in God and in an essentially moral order is no longer tenable. Nihilism appears at that point . . . because we have become distrustful of any "meaning" in suffering, indeed in existence. One interpretation has collapsed; but because it was considered the [only] interpretation it seems as if there were no meaning at all in existence, as if everything were *in vain*.[35]

Life after the intoxication of theistic and metaphysical lies has worn out seems worthless, valueless, meaningless, and directionless.[36] The nihilism that ensues is a harrowing reality check which delivers a reality bereft of any value.

32 *GD* III §6. 33 *Ibid.* §17.

34 *WWV* II XVII. It should be noted that Nietzsche's earlier view on Schopenhauer's "metaphysical need" was that it actually manifests itself after the demise of religion, rather than being the source of religion, as Schopenhauer had claimed. See *FW* §151; *NL 1880–1881*, 6(290). At this stage, Nietzsche seems to have been thinking specifically of the "need" for a metaphysics of the thing-in-itself such as Kant's or Schopenhauer's. Later texts such as *JGB* §12 or *NL 1885–1887*, 8(2), however, make it clear that Nietzsche eventually realigned himself with Schopenhauer. Theology and religion, in the later works, are expressive of the *décadents*' primeval metaphysical need.

35 *NL 1885–1887*, 5(71). Consider, in this connection, Deleuze's description of this crisis: "Formerly life was depreciated from the height of superior values, it was denied in the name of these values. Here, on the contrary, only life remains, but it is still a depreciated life which now continues in a world without values, stripped of meaning and purpose" (*Nietzsche*, p. 170).

36 Heidegger aptly explains the connection between the world's value/worth and life's meaning/purpose in Nietzsche's thought. Simply put, the latter is dependent on the "ethical world order" provided by the former (*Nietzsche*, vol. II, p. 65).

The nihilist crisis is related to the nihilist mentality in two ways. First, it is on account of the nihilist mentality that God (the Christian *wahre Welt*) was seen as the sole seat of value, moral worth, and meaning in this allegedly lowly, corrupt world. With God's death, all we are left with is this devalued, deprecated life; there is, in Nietzsche's words, "a rebound from 'God is truth' to . . . 'all is false.'"[37] The world had been valued in and through its relation to a Divine, Transcendent, Supra-Natural Absolute. Once the intoxicating fiction of theism subsides, the symptoms of withdrawal appear – history seems aimless, the universe lacks any unity of purpose or sense, and truth seems a mirage.[38] The nihilist crisis, then, may be best described as a harsh hangover, which afflicts Europe after a long period of inebriation during which the world was given meaning through a great intoxicating lie. If the death of God precipitates the nihilist crisis by robbing the world of its fictional value, it is precisely because the nihilist mentality held sway over Europe for such a long time.[39] Its meta-ethical nihilism concerning the value of the world of becoming (as opposed to that of Being) turns into a final statement of the world's value, once it is seen that becoming is all there is.

The second sense in which the nihilist mentality prepares the terrain for the nihilist crisis relates to a specific nihilistic fiction, namely that of Truth. Nietzsche's contention is that the insistence on truthfulness (*Wahrhaftigkeit*) that does away with the fiction of God is a product of nihilistic morals. It is modern scientific probity that kills God by "prohibit[ing] the lie implicit in the belief in God," yet such probity is really an outgrowth of Christian truthfulness.[40] As such, it finds its historical and ideological ground in *wahre Welt* metaphysics.[41] The "Truth vs. lie" dichotomy, after all, is one of the foundational oppositions at the root of the *décadent* nihilists' distinction between Being and becoming, the Real and the merely apparent. In its incarnation as scientific probity, however, truthfulness is precisely what ends up denouncing the *wahre Welt* itself as a lie. The result is the death of God.

The demise of the Christian faith through and by its own truthfulness is an instance of what Nietzsche calls self-overcoming (*Selbstüberwindung*/

[37] *NL 1885–1887*, 2(127). [38] *Ibid. 1887–1888*, 11(99).

[39] At *A* §47, Nietzsche explains that "when one places life's center of gravity not in life but in the 'beyond' – *in nothingness* – one deprives life of its center of gravity altogether." The nihilist crisis occurs when the "beyond" is finally recognized to be nothing more than nothingness and life itself is left behind, devoid of any "center of gravity."

[40] *FW* §357. See also Nietzsche's discussion of modern science and its atheism as a new embodiment of nihilist morals at *GM* III §§24–5.

[41] On the "metaphysical faith" which remains at the root of "faith in science," see *FW* §344.

Selbstaufhebung).[42] Christian truthfulness prevails over what originally nurtured it, and destroys it: "Christianity *as dogma* was destroyed by its own morality."[43] The nihilist mentality, in this sense, is responsible for the debunking of its own foundational myth. The nihilist crisis in Europe is, in this sense, a result of the nihilist mentality's self-overcoming.

This discloses the "nihilism" at work in the nihilist crisis. The self-overcoming of the nihilist mentality operates through a new series of negations. No, God does not exist. No, Being is in no way attested to. No, there is no Heaven. No, there is no Good, no ground for Certainty, no Permanence and Stability, etc. In short, it is now the fictions of the nihilist mentality and its metaphysics that are negated. There is thus at the heart of the nihilist crisis a nihilism as activity – a project of demolition.[44] This activity of nihilizing the *wahre Welt* is what delivers nihilism as an ideological state of affairs; its result is the nihilist crisis, in which the world's previous (fictional) value and worth have been reduced to nil.

Now that the two principal meanings of nihilism in Nietzsche's texts have been clarified, it is possible to begin examining Nietzsche's complex relationship to Buddhism in earnest. Most fundamentally, Nietzsche is animated by the conviction that both he and the Buddha propounded the same no's in the context of very similar nihilist crises. It is by virtue of this common nihilist ground that Nietzsche identifies himself as "the Buddha of Europe."[45]

Nietzsche regarded himself as standing at a similar juncture in the history of European ideas as the Buddha did in the history of Indian ideas.[46] Perusing Nietzsche's notes on Ancient India and the rise of Buddhism,[47]

[42] *Ibid.* §357. See also *GM* III §27. [43] *GM* III §27. [44] *NL 1885–1887*, 9(35).

[45] *Ibid. 1882–1884*, 4(2).

[46] As Morrison writes, Nietzsche's "interest [in Buddhism] was centered upon what he considered to be a direct historical parallel between India at the time of the Buddha and the Europe of his own milieu" (*Nietzsche and Buddhism*, p. 8). Cf. F. Mistry, *Nietzsche and Buddhism: Prolegomenon to a Comparative Study* (New York: W. de Gruyter, 1981), p. 35; J. Figl, "Nietzsche's Encounter with Buddhism," in B. Bäumer and J. R. Dupuche (eds.), *Void and Fullness in the Buddhist, Hindu and Christian Traditions: Śūnya-Pūrṇa-Pleroma* (New Delhi: D. K. Printworld, 2005), pp. 225–37; and A. M. Frazier, "A European Buddhism," *Philosophy East and West* 25(2), 1975: 145–60.

[47] Other than Schopenhauer's works, the two principal Buddhological sources Nietzsche drew from in developing his ideas on Buddhism are C. F. Koeppen, *Die Religion des Buddhas* (Berlin: F. Schneider, 1857–9), and H. Oldenberg, *Buddha: sein Leben, seine Lehre, seine Gemeinde* (Berlin: W. Hertz, 1881). Other Indological sources he had access to include J. Wackernagel, *Über den Ursprung des Brahmanismus* (Basel: H. Richter, 1877), M. Müller, *Beiträge zur vergleichenden Mythologie und Ethnologie* (Leipzig: Englemann, 1879), and H. Kern, *Der Buddhismus und seine Geschichte in Indien* (Leipzig: O. Schulze, 1882). There is wide disagreement among intellectual historians on which texts Nietzsche read, when he read them, and how carefully (or selectively) he read them. On these issues, see Frazier, "A European Buddhism"; Halbfass, *India and Europe*; J. Figl, "Nietzsche's Early Encounters with Asian Thought," in Parkes, *Nietzsche and Asian Thought*, pp. 51–63, and

it becomes obvious that Nietzsche saw a clear "historical parallel"[48] between the Europe of his day and the charged spiritual and philosophical landscape in which the Buddha appeared.[49] Buddhism, Nietzsche writes in *A*, "arrives *after* a philosophical movement lasting hundreds of years; the concept of God is already abolished by the time it arrives. Buddhism is the only truly *positivistic* religion history has to show us."[50]

Of course, Nietzsche was well aware that Buddhist cosmology actually leaves the traditional Indian pantheon of gods and half-gods intact. But he also knew the Buddha denied any of these deities immortality. No being, according to Buddhism, is immune from decay. In this sense, Buddhism is indeed atheistic.[51] Indeed, it is the illusion of a *wahre Welt* – of Being, Permanence, and Stability – that the Buddha had seen through, and that is what mattered to Nietzsche. Moreover, Nietzsche interpreted the unraveling of Indian theism that preceded the Buddha as analogous to the process of nihilistic truthfulness undermining the fiction of (True) Being that had prompted the death of God in Europe. Commenting on modern European scientific truthfulness, which "now *forbids the lie implicit in the belief in God*," Nietzsche explains that "the same development occurred completely independently in India ... The same ideal

"Nietzsche's Encounter with Buddhism"; M. Sprung, "Nietzsche's Trans-European Eye," in Parkes, *Nietzsche and Asian Thought*, pp. 76–90; A. Vanderheyde, *Nietzsche et la pensée bouddhiste* (Paris: Harmattan, 2007); and R.-P. Droit, *Le culte du néant: les philosophes et le Bouddha* (Paris: Seuil, 1997). For two interesting, though by no means definitive, accounts of how these sources shaped Nietzsche's ideas, see Morrison, *Nietzsche and Buddhism*, pp. 6–29, and Halbfass, *India and Europe*, pp. 141–7. These are by far the most complete treatments of this question. Since its focus is on philosophy rather than intellectual history, a complete reconstruction of the genesis of Nietzsche's ideas on Buddhism, and of the cultural and intellectual context in which they took shape, falls beyond the scope of this book. The interested reader is referred to the above-mentioned sources.

48 This phrase is Morrison's in *Nietzsche and Buddhism*, and "Nietzsche and Nirvana," in W. Santaniello (ed.), *Nietzsche and the Gods* (State University of New York Press, 2001).

49 The period in which the Buddha arose, Nietzsche writes, was "more thoughtful and thought-addicted than ours"; it was a period in which "the people found themselves as deeply lost in the ravines of philosophical doctrines as European nations were at times in the subtleties of religious dogma" (*NL 1884*, 25(16)). See also *NL 1886–1887*, 5(72).13. Some Buddhist sources do attest to such a state of affairs, namely, the *Brahmajālasutta* (*DN* 1.12–46) and the *Sāmaññaphalasutta* (*DN* 1.47–86). In fact, it is the consensus among Indologists today that India at that time was indeed the scene of formidable intellectual and philosophical activity. On this point, see Thapar's outstanding work on Ancient Indian social history, *Ancient Indian Social History: Some Interpretations* (London: Sangam Books, 1984). See also R. F. Gombrich, *What the Buddha Thought* (London: Equinox Publishers, 2009).

50 *A* §20. It should be noted that, as early as 1881, Nietzsche had been urging Europe to rid itself of God by "undertaking what was done several thousand years ago in India, among the nation of thinkers, as an imperative of thought" (*M* §96).

51 For a succinct discussion of atheism in Buddhism, see A. K. Warder, *Outline of Indian Philosophy* (Delhi: Motilal Banarsidass, 1971), pp. 60–1. See also G. Wallis, "The Buddha Counsels a Theist: A Reading of the *Tejjivasutta* (*Dīghanikāya* 13)," *Religion* 38(1), 2008: 54–67, for a more detailed discussion of the Buddha's rejection of theism.

compelled the same conclusion. The decisive point was reached five centuries before the European calendar, with the Buddha."[52] The Buddha, in short, was the seminal figure of an Indian nihilist crisis precipitated by an Indian death of God.

Nietzsche's claim might not be very compelling from the standpoint of history. After all, theism certainly survived whatever death of God might have occurred in India. But from a philosophical standpoint his claim is of crucial importance. Nietzsche was right to think he and the Buddha were similar in that both attacked the prevalent ideologies of their time and that these ideologies were both predicated on the fiction of Being. Translated into Nietzschean jargon, Nietzsche and the Buddha both practiced the nihilism (as activity) at the heart of nihilist crises. By espousing a very similar set of negative views, they said no to the same things, for the same reasons. This is true irrespective of the fact that the two thinkers arose in markedly different historical and cultural contexts.

Nietzsche echoed the three major no's of his Indian counterpart. The first myth he joins the Buddha in exploding is that suffering is an accidental, or unnecessary, feature of existence. As Nietzsche was well aware, the very starting point of Buddhist philosophy and practice is the claim that suffering (*duḥkha*) is an essential feature of all, even the most comfortable, forms of life.[53] The Upaniṣadic Brahmins of Ancient India claimed that, contrary to appearances, Bliss is of the nature of everything.[54] The Buddha rejected this lie; he said no to this fiction. On the contrary, he claimed, suffering is of the nature of everything.[55] Indeed, overcoming the delusion that struggle and pain can ever be escaped through access to a realm of Peace, Serenity, and Permanence is the necessary condition for embarking on the path of Buddhist ethics.

This emphasis on suffering as a fundamental feature of existence, and on the lie implicit in any denial of this fact, finds a parallel in Nietzsche's

[52] *GM* III §27.

[53] This is the fundamental message of what tradition regards as the Buddha's first teaching, an account of which can be found at *V* I.10. *Duḥkha* (or *duḥkhatā*, a more straightforwardly nominal form) is a technical Buddhist term with no precise equivalent in English. In itself, the word stands for a wide spectrum of sensations ranging from acute physical pain or psychological torment to mere restlessness. Of course, the Buddha and his followers admitted of various forms and degrees of *duḥkha*. The early discourses speak of three major types of suffering: *duḥkhaduḥkhatā*, which is what we generally think of as physical pain and mental anguish; *vipariṇāmaduḥkhatā*, or the suffering caused by the fact that all things change and eventually fall apart; and the enigmatic *saṃskāraduḥkhatā*, which refers both to the suffering caused by our having inappropriate attitudes/beliefs (*saṃskāra*) and to the suffering invariably involved in our being composite (*saṃskṛta*) and therefore subject to decay (*SN* IV.259; see also *DN* III.216 and *SN* V.56).

[54] See, for instance, *BĀU* III.9.28. [55] *SN* IV.28.

thought.[56] One of the things Nietzsche inherited from Arthur Schopenhauer's philosophy is the view that life is pervaded with suffering.[57] Though he might not have subscribed to his philosophical mentor's radical view that suffering alone is positive and pleasure negative – pleasure being nothing but the absence of suffering[58] – Nietzsche certainly did have the more moderate view that life is full of sorrow and that the few pleasures we do experience are fleeting and short-lived.[59] In fact, for Nietzsche it is the Schopenhauerian "honesty" involved in recognizing the profound "ungodliness" of the world – i.e. its brutality and limitless suffering – that finally denounces theism as a lie.[60]

In short, Nietzsche remained a pessimist throughout his active life. By this I mean that what I will call *descriptive pessimism* – the view that living and suffering cannot be dissociated – is the unifying background of Nietzsche's work, spanning his so-called early, middle, and late periods. This claim is somewhat controversial. While there is no doubt that suffering – the contradictoriness, violence, and apparently senseless pains of existence – is the central "given" in so-called early Nietzsche,[61] the standard story is that he eventually grew out of his youthful enthusiasm for Schopenhauer's philosophy and thereupon relinquished his early concern with universal suffering, turning instead to the critique of morality, cultural criticism, and so on.[62]

56 Cf. M. Conche, "Nietzsche et le bouddhisme," *Cahier du Collège International de Philosophie*, vol. IV (Paris: Osiris, 1989), 125–44, at p. 125.

57 For a detailed discussion of Schopenhauer's influence on Nietzsche in this regard, see D. Berman, "Schopenhauer and Nietzsche: Honest Atheism, Dishonest Pessimism," in C. Janaway (ed.), *Willing and Nothingness: Schopenhauer as Nietzsche's Educator* (Oxford University Press, 1998), pp. 178–96, especially pp. 180f.

58 See *WWV I* §88, *WWV II* XLVI, pp. 657–8, and *PP II* §149. For an analogous view in Indian philosophy, see the position Maṇḍanamiśra attributes to his Naiyāyika opponent in the opening lines of his *Brahmasiddhi*.

59 In *FW*, he claims that if there is one thing every art and every philosophy presupposes, it is "suffering and sufferers" (§370); at *GM* III §28 he describes man as an "*ailing* animal"; and in a key fragment he uses the terms "existence" and "suffering" interchangeably (*NL 1886–1887*, 5(72).13).

60 *FW* §357. This passage makes it obvious that while it is truthfulness, for Nietzsche, that kills God, it is in large part truthfulness about suffering which fells the colossus. If truthfulness is God's executioner, the "problem of evil" is his sharp axe.

61 Consider, for instance, *PtZG* (1873), Nietzsche's unpublished text on "pre-Platonic" Greek thought, in which Anaximander and Heraclitus are praised for being the only ancient philosophers capable of recognizing the world for the great tumult of suffering it is (§§4–5). *GT*, for its part, is concerned with the Attic tragedy as a form of theodicy in the face of the world's limitless suffering. Nietzsche's defense of Schopenhauer's pessimism and harsh critique of Strauss's optimism at *UB* I §6 is also telling.

62 On this point, see D. Breazeale, "Introduction," in D. Breazeale (ed.), *Untimely Meditations*, trans. R. J. Hollingdale (Cambridge University Press, 1997), pp. vii–xxxii. The interested reader should turn to Janaway's *Willing and Nothingness* for further discussions of the relation between the philosophy of Schopenhauer and Nietzsche's thought.

The story is actually more complicated than this. To begin with, though there is no doubt that the young Nietzsche was very much impressed with Schopenhauer's thought,[63] he seems to have had some important reservations about his philosophical mentor's doctrine from the start.[64] Moreover, the view that Nietzsche ever rejected pessimism *in toto* is too crude. Nietzsche's early qualms about and later rejection of Schopenhauer's pessimism concerned not its descriptive element – i.e. the view that the world is full of suffering – but its normative element – i.e. the view that the world is so full of suffering that it ought not to exist.[65] It is this normative feature of pessimism that distinguishes what Nietzsche would later call "pessimism of the weak"[66] (i.e. Schopenhauer's) from "pessimism of strength" (i.e. the tragic Greeks').[67] As a strong pessimist, Nietzsche never stopped agreeing with the descriptive element of Schopenhauer's pessimism.[68] He never stopped thinking that life is fundamentally painful and that theistic optimism (or any optimism for that matter) is naive and deluded. This commitment to descriptive pessimism is part of what allowed him to proclaim himself the Buddha of Europe.[69]

The second area of overlap between Nietzsche's thought and the Buddha's teaching concerns a particular notion common to all traditional systems built on the fiction of Being. The object of negation, in this case, is a

[63] Schopenhauer's works are one of the reasons Nietzsche moved from classical philology to philosophy. Nietzsche discovered Schopenhauer as a young man, and even when he turned against his mentor and ultimately rejected the ideas put forth in *WWV*, Schopenhauer was in a sense always at the back of Nietzsche's mind. As Berman aptly notes, "Schopenhauer remained Nietzsche's main philosophical influence, even when he turned against him and Wagner ... Schopenhauer was probably more important to Nietzsche as a 'good enemy' than as a mentor or ally" ("Schopenhauer and Nietzsche," p. 187). My discussion of Nietzsche as Anti-Buddha in Chapter 2 lends further credence to Berman's claim.

[64] Breazeale, "Introduction," p. xvii. In note 13 of his text (pp. xxx–xxxi), Breazeale provides ample evidence of Nietzsche's early uneasiness with Schopenhauer's thought. See, in this connection, *S*, Nietzsche's 1868 unfinished critical essay on Schopenhauer's system.

[65] See I. Soll, "Pessimism and the Tragic View of Life: Reconsiderations of Nietzsche's *Birth of Tragedy*," in R. C. Solomon and K. M. Higgins (eds.), *Reading Nietzsche* (Oxford University Press, 1988), pp. 104–33, at pp. 124–5.

[66] *NL 1887–1888*, 11(294). See also *ibid. 1888–1889*, 14(25).

[67] *GT* "Versuch einer Selbstkritik" §1. See also *NL 1885–1887* 10(21) and *ibid. 1888–1889*, 14(25). What Nietzsche means when he confusingly writes that the Greeks were not pessimists at *EH* "Warum ich solche gute Bücher schreibe" *GT* §1 is that they were not weak pessimists, or normative pessimists. Cf. Soll, "Pessimism and the Tragic View of Life," p. 125.

[68] Though he does not use the terms "descriptive pessimism" and "normative pessimism," this is a point that Berman convincingly argues for in his discussion of Nietzsche's atheism ("Schopenhauer and Nietzsche," pp. 189f.).

[69] In this sense, Nietzsche follows in Schopenhauer's footsteps. After all, Schopenhauer placed a particular emphasis on the agreement between his thought and Buddhism, in no small part because of the latter's presumed pessimism. See, in this connection *WWV II* xvii, p. 186.

more local notion of Being, as it were. At stake is "what is, but does not become" at the personal, individual level, namely the soul, self, or ego. In Buddhist philosophy, as in Nietzsche's thought, the self is denounced as a misleading fiction. In technical terms, the idea is that both synchronic personal unity and diachronic personal identity are conceptually constructed, rather than real. This key point requires a detailed discussion.

The doctrine of "lack of self" is the bedrock of Buddhist philosophy.[70] If the Buddha's first teaching concerns the all-pervasive nature of suffering, his second concerns the inexistence of the self.[71] There is a good reason for this. According to the discourses, what characterizes the Buddhist sage is precisely the absence of the imputation of self or "mine" in any form to any physical or mental event.[72] Attaining the ethical goal at the heart of Buddhist philosophy and practice requires the complete overcoming of the "self" fiction.

Given its direct relation to ethics, it is obvious that the Buddhist critique of the self cannot be concerned with just any idea or notion of self or soul. Attaining *nirvāṇa* is not merely a matter of abandoning the idea of an immortal soul or some other abstraction of this sort.[73] The object of the Buddhist critique, rather, corresponds to the common-sense notion of "self" that is presupposed in everyday living and thinking.[74] The uncontroversial Buddhist claim is that all normal humans[75] share a pre-reflective belief in their own existence as a discrete, unitary, and enduring self.[76] It is by virtue

[70] Cf. D. Arnold, *Buddhists, Brahmins and Belief* (New York: Columbia University Press, 2005), p. 118.

[71] *V* I.10–11. This account of the order of the Buddha's teaching is common to all schools of Buddhism whose texts are extant.

[72] *SN* III.44. This feature of Buddhist moral psychology will receive a detailed discussion in Chapter 4.

[73] On this point, see M. Alhabari, "Nirvana and Ownerless Consciousness," in Siderits, Thompson, and Zahavi, *Self, No Self?*, pp. 79–113, at pp. 82f.

[74] This is why the fact that there exists a wide range of notions of self in philosophy, both ancient and contemporary, is not a problem for Buddhist thought. In fact, Buddhist philosophy is quite in line with Strawson's insistence that any enquiry into the nature of the self be related to the way in which we effectively think of ourselves:

> Metaphysical investigation of the nature of the self is subordinate to phenomenological investigation of the sense of self. There is a strong phenomenological constraint on any acceptable answer to the metaphysical question which can be expressed by saying that the factual "Is there such a thing as a mental self?" is equivalent to the question "Is any (genuine) sense of self an accurate representation of anything that exists?" (D. Strawson, "The Self," *Journal of Consciousness Studies* 6(5–6), 1997: 405–28, at p. 409)

[75] Those suffering from specific pathologies resulting in depersonalization are obviously excluded.

[76] Zahavi calls into doubt whether the self targeted by Buddhist philosophy really does capture our "pre-philosophical, everyday understanding of who we are." D. Zahavi, "The Experiential Self: Objections

of this intuitive and therefore often unarticulated belief in the "I" that we bestow unto ourselves both synchronic unity – it is the same "me" who has brown hair, loves my children, feels hunger, and is typing – and diachronic identity – it is the same "me" who wrote the doctoral dissertation currently being rewritten, by me, as a monographic typescript. The self, then, is both the unitary "owner" of the various physical and mental properties that make up an individual and the "core person" who is always there, "inside," as it were, from birth to death, if not before and after as well. If asked to describe what counts as our "deep self," finally, most of us will allude, in one way or another, to the enduring witness-subject at the heart of our being and to the agent of thought and action who exerts a large measure of control over body and mind. It is to this universal notion of self that the Buddha refers when he claims that there is no self.

Instead, the Buddhist view of the person is that of a functionally integrated system of psycho-physical processes devoid of a central, unchanging core.[77] Under analysis, what is found are various physical events and four types of mental events, namely sensations, conceptualizations, volitions, and cognitions.[78] No irreducible being or person is found as the "owner" or "bearer" of these five constituents; only the constituents are found.[79] The illusion of agential/personal (synchronic) unity is generated by the ways in which the manifold psycho-physical streams that make up a human being are functionally integrated. That of (diachronic) identity is generated by what Parfit, in his discussion of personal identity, calls relations of "connectedness" and "continuity" among these psycho-physical

and Clarifications" in Siderits, Thompson, and Zahavi, *Self, No Self?*, pp. 56–78, at p. 66. Alhabari does an excellent job of putting Zahavi's worries to rest in "Nirvana and Ownerless Consciousness," pp. 82–8.

77 This view, I note in passing, seems to be in perfect agreement with recent work in neuroscience. On this point, see F. J. Varela, *Ethical Know-How: Action, Wisdom, and Cognition* (Stanford University Press, 1999), p. 36; J. Westerhoff, *Nāgārjuna's Madhyamaka: A Philosophical Introduction* (Oxford University Press, 2009), pp. 208–10; and O. Flanagan, *The Bodhisattva's Brain: Buddhism Naturalized* (Cambridge, MA: MIT Press, 2011), pp. 95f.

78 This is the doctrine of the five constituents, or aggregates. It first appears in the Buddha's second teaching (*V* I.11) and recurs throughout the discourses. MacKenzie provides an excellent summary of what each of the constituents stands for in M. MacKenzie, "Enacting the Self: Buddhist and Enactivist Approaches to the Emergence of the Self," in Siderits, Thompson, and Zahavi, *Self, No Self?*, pp. 239–73, at pp. 242–3.

79 This position is widely held to be analogous to the bundle theory of the self propounded by thinkers such as Locke and Hume in the Western tradition. R. Sorabji, *Self: Ancient and Modern Insights about Individuality, Life, and Death* (Oxford University Press, 2006), pp. 278f. However, Alhabari has recently called into question whether this is an accurate description of the view expressed by the Buddha in the discourses (*Analytical Buddhism* and "Nirvana and Ownerless Consciousness"). This is a debate I need not enter. What matters for my immediate purposes is that Buddhist philosophy denies the existence of an enduring subject. How to qualify, with precision, the account of the person that emerges from this critique is beyond the scope of the present discussion.

streams.[80] In reality, however, there is no self to which such personal unity and identity may pertain. Just as the term "chariot" does not refer to anything other than a certain number of objects assembled in a particular way, the term "person" does not refer to anything other than a certain set of physical and mental processes functioning together in a particular way.[81] Strictly speaking, there is no unified subject who has brown hair, loves his children, feels hunger, is writing this sentence, etc.; there is only brown hair, a set of affectionate emotions directed towards two children, a feeling of hunger, a brain and body at work typing these words, etc. Similarly, there is no "core Antoine Panaïoti" who wrote a dissertation between 2007 and 2010 and who is now writing a book based on this dissertation; there is just a nexus of functionally integrated streams of psycho-physical events bearing high degrees of continuity, between 2007 and the present day at least.

Stated in more abstract terms, the Buddhist claim is that while we are all pre-reflectively committed to the view that our "self" is a fixed entity, or "thing" – a substance, as later Buddhist authors would refer to it – whatever we may point to when we say "this is my self" are really fleeting processes related in certain ways. The substance view of the self implicit in our common experience of the world is, under analysis, shown to be untenable.[82]

no 'self', just traits

idea of self is really...

[80] D. Parfit, *Reasons and Persons* (Oxford University Press, 1984), p. 206. Parfit himself recognizes the parallels between his views and the Buddha's (*ibid.*, pp. 273, 280, and 502–3). More recently, Parfit has attempted to distance himself from what he calls "the Buddhist View," by which he means a form of eliminationism concerning persons. See "Experiences, Subjects, and Conceptual Schemes," *Philosophical Topics* 26(1/2), 1999): 217–70, at p. 260. As is made clear in Ganeri's discussion of the topic (*The Concealed Art of the Soul*, pp. 161f.), however, the Buddhist position concerning persons is not as clear-cut as the Buddhist position vis-à-vis the self. A common position (Vasubandhu) is that persons are "real as conventional designata" (*prajñaptisat*), but lack substantial reality. On the Mādhyamika view, which denies substantial reality to all things, however, the "person" is no more of a reality/fiction than anything else. Though the issue is endlessly complicated, then, it can at least be said, contra Parfit, that Buddhist philosophy is not eliminationist with regard to persons.

[81] *SN* I.135. See also *MP* 27–8. The chariot analogy is a very popular one throughout Buddhist literature. On the mereological reductionism allegedly presupposed by such a view, see Siderits, *Buddhist Philosophy*, pp. 76–80. In Chapter 4, I will explain why, contra Siderits (and many others), not all early Buddhist schools were reductionist. I will also argue that the Buddha was not strictly speaking a reductionist.

[82] As Gethin explains, the Buddhist idea is that we should conceive of persons "in terms of sequences of causally connected physical and mental events rather than enduring substances." R. Gethin, *The Foundations of Buddhism* (Oxford University Press, 1998), p. 160. The implication, of course, is that we are all pre-reflectively committed to the substance view. In my opinion, this phenomenological claim is warranted, even though few people, unless trained in philosophy, would use the word "substance" to describe their core self.

inexistence of
self justified
by:

① Lack of control over changing of bodily ideas)

② Lack of permanence
events that make up a person are all fleeting
idea of conditionality

It is possible to reconstruct four main arguments for the inexistence of the self on the basis of Buddhist sources.[83] We may begin with the argument from lack of control. This capitalizes on the very limited control we have over "ourselves." Our bodies change and eventually decay and stop functioning whether we want them to or not. Likewise, our feelings, perceptions, desires, states of consciousness, etc., all seem to fluctuate without our being able to exert very much control over them. How appropriate is it, asks the Buddha, to consider as my "self" that over which I have so little control?[84] As I see it, this argument appeals to a very intuitive way of thinking of personal identity. One of the reasons I speak of my hand as mine and another person's hand as hers is that I can move my hand at will, but cannot move hers "from within," as it were, and vice versa. The Buddha's claim is that even the intention to move "my" hand is not mine in any significant sense. There is just an intention, a hand, and a motion. Positing an agent who intends and is also the possessor of the hand is superfluous.

The second argument relates to the transient nature of all physical and mental processes. The idea, in its barest form, is that whatever I might consider to be my "self" – i.e. any of the five constituents, the "whole" which they form, etc. – has no permanence whatsoever. There is nothing according to Buddhist philosophy that does not arise through certain chains of conditionality, and therefore that does not also pass away through other chains of conditionality. The physical and mental events that make up "me" are all fleeting.[85] Whatever I may grasp as "my self" eventually perishes. But the self is supposed to be something that endures. Personal identity over time implies more than mere continuity; it seems to refer to some sort of abiding entity. Otherwise, what would I mean when I say so-and-so is the same person I met as a child?

This, in itself, could stand as an 'argument from impermanence' against the everyday notion of the self. But the Buddha takes this criterial argument one step further, and in doing so it becomes clear that he was particularly concerned with the prevalent view of the self propounded in the Upaniṣads.[86] What is impermanent, the Buddha claims, cannot be a source of lasting felicity. It is, in this sense, unsatisfactory. In so far as nothing in

[83] For further discussion of the three first arguments – those met with in the Theravāda canon – see S. Collins, *Selfless Persons: Imagery and Thought in Theravāda Buddhism* (Cambridge University Press, 1982), pp. 97–103, and Gethin, *The Foundations of Buddhism*, pp. 136–8. MacKenzie provides a more detailed outline of the fourth argument at "Enacting the Self," p. 244.
[84] *SN* III.66–7.   [85] *SN* I.125.
[86] He presumably has the "charioteer analogy" presented at *KU* 3.3–4 in mind. On this point, see K. R. Norman, "A Note on *Attā* in the *Alagaddūpama-sutta*," in *Collected Papers II* (Oxford, Pāli Text Society), pp. 100–9.

the world of experience can ensure lasting satisfaction, then, nothing can qualify as the Upaniṣads' self, the nature of which is Bliss. The Buddha's conclusion is that in so far as everything, in one way or another, ultimately turns out to be a ground for disappointment, frustration, or pain, nothing counts as "self."[87]

The third argument hinges on the notion of superfluity. The initial idea is that no coherent account can be given of the relation between the self and five psycho-physical constituents. The self cannot be the same as these constituents, because they are impermanent, and the self, by definition, must be permanent. The self cannot be entirely separated from the constituents either, because they delimit the scope of experience and it is senseless to speak of anything that is "beyond experience." Finally, the self cannot "have" or "have the attribute of" any particular experience, because it then becomes unclear why we should even distinguish the "self" from "its" experiences to begin with.[88] The self, in short, is a superfluous concept. Experience can very well be accounted for without reference to an underlying ego and it is therefore entirely superfluous to posit this additional entity "I." The self plays no explanatory role and nothing is lacking in a description of the world that does without it.[89] As a result, there is no reason to believe it exists.

The fourth argument, finally, is not met with in the discourses but in a later Buddhist text, namely Vasubandhu's fourth-century CE *AKBh*. Like many of his Buddhist contemporaries, Vasubandhu admitted of only two valid means of knowledge, namely perception and inference. His claim is that neither of these affords knowledge of the self.[90] The self is neither experienced through sight, smell, hearing, taste, or touch, nor is it "seen" in introspection.[91] There might be a "sense" of self, then, but there is no

(3) Self as superflous concept

does not provide any new insight

[87] *SN* I.125. The connection between the True Self and felicity might seem peculiar to a Western philosophical audience, but one need only turn to the works of the Ancients (see Sorabji, *Self*) or, more recently, to Taylor's discussion of the self and morals to see that this is also a common idea in the Western tradition. C. Taylor, *Sources of the Self* (Cambridge, MA: Harvard University Press, 1989).

[88] *DN* II.66–8.

[89] Many thinkers in India and in the West have resisted this thesis. It is argued that subjectivity, agency, memory, time-consciousness, etc. – not to mention moral concepts such as responsibility and rational self-interest – require that there be a robust, unitary, enduring self. Most of these issues are discussed in Siderits, Thompson, and Zahavi, *Self, No Self?* This is unfortunately not the place to defend the no-self view from its many critics.

[90] *AKBh*, p. 461.

[91] Cf. Hume's search for the self at *THN* I.4 §4. On the affinities between Hume's and the Buddha's views, see A. H. Lesser, "Eastern and Western Empiricism and the No-Self Theory," *Religious Studies* 15(1), 1979: 55–64, but cf. Conze, who, given his (now thought to be misguided) transcendentalist interpretation of Buddhism, dismisses the parallel as "spurious" ("Spurious Parallels to Buddhist Philosophy," p. 114). It should be noted that Ganeri has presented a controversial

perceptual acquaintance with an enduring, substantial self. Vasubandhu goes on to claim that any inference produced to establish that the self exists is either invalid or based on unsound premises. The conclusion of this epistemic argument is that the statement that a self exists cannot be supported by valid means. Belief in the self should be discarded.

Of course, while Buddhist philosophy is intransigent in its critique of our everyday notion of self, in no way is it suggested that we stop speaking of selves, persons, beings, individuals, and so on. It is highly efficient to use personal pronouns to refer to people and, more general, to use various linguistic conventions which, taken literally, would seem to imply there is unity and identity where really there is none.[92] As the Buddha emphasizes, however, such words as "self" and "being" "are merely names, expressions, turns of phrase, designations in common use in the world."[93] In this way, though I can say "I am walking," I should not be misled into thinking there is really an agent ("I") and an action ("the walking done by me"), because really there is only activity (walking).[94] Indeed, though nothing would be lacking in a description of the world that makes no use of the concept of "self" and of all the idioms that rely on this fiction, it remains eminently practical to continue expressing ourselves as though the "I" (and personal pronouns) actually referred to an enduring entity rather than to a self-less collection of psycho-physical constituents in constant flux. To account for this, early Buddhist exegetes developed the hermeneutical device of distinguishing between the ultimate truth of "lack of self" and the conventional truth of statements regarding the "self," or the "I."[95]

Though Nietzsche develops and defends this idea somewhat less systematically, the Buddhist view that the unitary, enduring self is a fiction finds a close parallel in his writing. Nietzsche's view that "there is no ego at all"[96] is based on the fundamental insight, also found in Buddhism, that the "I" is little more that a "synthetic concept."[97] The idea here is that personal

historiographic case in favor of the view that Hume's views were in fact directly inspired by Buddhist ideas, via Bayle's 1702 (second edition) *Dictionnaire historique et critique* (*The Concealed Art of the Soul*, pp. 228–31).

[92] Cf. Gethin, *The Foundations of Buddhism*, pp. 145–6. [93] *DN* I.202.

[94] I borrow this example from Nāgārjuna (*MMK* II).

[95] It is important to see how the distinction between ultimate and conventional truth in Buddhist philosophy is not, as is commonly assumed, an ontological appearance/reality distinction (see, on this point, Ganeri, *The Concealed Art of the Soul*, p. 59). Rather, it is a hermeneutical device initially developed to distinguish between the "literal statements" uttered by the Buddha – e.g. "there is no self" – and "statements requiring interpretation" – e.g. statements that seem to refer to the self. Among the realist Vaibhāṣika Sarvāstivadins, however, the distinction became ontological – "*satya*" can mean both "truth" and "reality" – namely between conventional existence, or appearance, and substantial existence, or reality. This is a trend Nāgārjuna would energetically combat.

[96] *NL 1887–1888*, 9(108). See also *NL ibid.*, 40(42). [97] *JGB* §19; see also *ibid. 1885–1887*, 1(87).

identity – both synchronic and diachronic – is the product of a pre-reflective conceptual synthesis of the various mental and physical processes that make up a person. Of course, Nietzsche knew that the "I" is not a mere concept, but something "felt."[98] This feeling is what stands behind the "soul superstition."[99] Like the Buddha, Nietzsche both recognized that the notion of "self" or "I" is the product of pre-reflective psychological mechanisms and looked upon the concept of a unitary, enduring self as deeply problematic.

The self critiqued by Nietzsche shares many features with the self rejected by Buddhists. To begin, it is supposed to be something irreducible and permanent, which endures unchanged through time. It is like a nugget of fixed Being in a sea of becoming. Nietzsche calls this the "*atomism of the soul*," by which he means "the belief that holds the soul to be something ineradicable, eternal, and indivisible, a monad, or atom."[100] Second, the notion of self for Nietzsche is most fundamentally that of an agent, or doer. It is by virtue of a belief in the self as a discrete entity, which possesses and controls the body and mind, that activity – which, strictly speaking, is impersonal – can be bifurcated between an agent (the person) and an action (done by the person).[101] The third feature of Nietzsche's self is closely related to its role as agent. In short, it is supposed to be a unitary, singular subject responsible for thinking and willing.[102] The self, in this sense, is supposed to be the irreducible "I," which acts as the "cause of thoughts" and the source of "motives."[103]

Nietzsche argues that this concept of self is entirely unfounded. There is, to begin with, nothing permanent or enduring at the core of the subject. Nietzsche, on this point, presents an argument very similar to that found in the Buddha's discourses. The impermanence of all physical and mental events, he claims, prevents us from speaking of a person with robust diachronic identity: "Continual transition does not allow us to speak of the 'individual.'"[104]

Concerning the self qua agent, Nietzsche's claim also echoes that of Buddhist thinkers throughout the ages. All of human activity, on this view, is similar to an event such as "raining." Though we may say "it is raining," it is

[98] *NL 1887–1888*, 10(19).

[99] *JGB* §19. Nietzsche, in this connection, describes belief in the self, or soul, as "some piece of folk superstition from time immemorial . . . that still today has not stopped causing trouble as the superstition of the subject, or I" (*ibid.* "Vorrede").

[100] *Ibid.* §12. Nietzsche is clearly targeting Leibniz here, and in particular the concept of monad Leibniz puts forth in his 1714 *Monadology*. See G. F. Leibniz, *The Monadology and Other Philosophical Essays*, ed. and trans. P. and A. M. Schrecker (Indianapolis, IN: Bobbs-Merrill).

[101] *JGB* §16–17; *GM* I §13. [102] *JGB* §19. [103] *Ibid.* §17f. See also *GD* VI §3.

[104] *NL 1884– 1885*, 36(23).

clear that there is no 'it' qua agent that "rains," but only impersonal raining.[105] Similarly, when I say "I eat," there is really only eating.

Nietzsche's critique of the "I" as the singular seat of willing and thinking, however, finds no direct parallel in Buddhist thought. He argues that the very complexity of willing, in particular, indicates that what is really at stake is a multiplicity of wills, feelings, and other "mental events"[106] rather than a unitary self, or soul, which deliberates and decides on a course of action. Hence the subject as a "*multiplicity*,"[107] or a "social structure of many souls."[108] One should not misinterpret these phrases by inferring that Nietzsche thought that many discrete "selves" somehow "inhabit" each person. After all, it is clear that he thought the very notion of a discrete self as a simple enduring "thing" is nonsensical in and of itself, not only in so far as individuals have many of them. Though phrased in a peculiar way, his idea is essentially the same as the Buddha's. There is no singular core self that holds the reins of the mind–body complex; even those mental and physical processes which seem to proceed from the activities of a "self" – namely, willing, deciding, deliberating, remembering, lifting one's arm, etc. – are incredibly complex events which bring into play a multiplicity of processes and involve no "core being" who might be regarded as being "in charge." Synchronic personal unity, on Nietzsche's view, as in the Buddha's, is a mental construction.

The third point of overlap between Nietzsche's negative thought and Buddhist philosophy concerns their common rejection of what is now referred to as substance metaphysics. The central tenet of such metaphysics is that the world consists of things or entities (substances) which bear properties, or qualities (attributes). For instance, a substance metaphysician will hold that there are various types of "rocks" that bear the property of "hardness" to different degrees. The rock, on this type of view, possesses the property/quality of hardness. From the standpoint of the so-called attribute, hardness is said to *inhere* in the rock, which is the substratum for the property of hardness. This highly intuitive view is rejected in both Nietzsche's thought and Buddhist philosophy on the ground that it exhibits a commitment to the staticity of Being, i.e. to the enduring

[105] *GM* I §13. Nietzsche actually uses the example of lightning, but this does not translate well into contemporary English, which does not contain a verbal form referring to the "activity" of lightning – see King James Bible's "lightneth" (Luke 17:24).

[106] I put the term "mental events" in quotation marks because Nietzsche, unlike the Buddha, made himself quite clear on the mind–body question by espousing a clear non-dualist view, namely that of the world as will to power (*JGB* §36). This topic will be discussed in detail in Chapter 3.

[107] *NL 1884–1885*, 36(23). [108] *JGB* §19.

existence of substances which persist, unchanged and immutable, while their inessential, merely contingent attributes vary over time.

To fully appreciate the Buddhist view, it is important to set it in the religious and philosophical context in which Buddhism arose. The dominant Indian ideology in the Buddha's age was centered on a robust metaphysics of Being which found expression, most prominently, in the early Brahmanical Upaniṣads.[109] For the Upaniṣadic Brahmins, the entire universe reduces to the primordial Being (*brahman*) out of which it originally emanated.[110] *Brahman*, on this view, is the Primordial Substance underlying "everything there is" (*sarvam idam*). The Buddha offered an empiricist rebuke to this view:

> *Bhikṣus*, I will instruct you about "everything." Listen to this: what is "everything"? It is the eye and shapes, the ear and sounds, the nose and smells, the tongue and flavors, the body and tangible things, the mind and representations. That, *bhikṣus*, is called "everything." *Bhikṣus*, he who says: "Rejecting this 'everything,' I will proclaim another 'everything'!" is engaging in mere talk.[111]

The senses and their objects[112] is all that the Buddha admitted in his description of the world.

In short, the worldview that finds expression in the discourses is one that leaves no room for the concept of substance, or, more generally of "existence."[113] Indeed, when looking at a particular "thing," the questions the Buddha asks are not "what is it, what are its properties, etc.?," but rather "how does this arise/cease, under what conditions does this arise/cease, etc.?" In other words, he is not interested in what kind of thing *x* is, but in what kind(s) of process(es), or event(s), is (are) involved when we speak of *x*. The principle of universal impermanence is a direct consequence of this focus on conditional arising rather than existence. After all, as a disciple of the Buddha proclaims, "everything that arises also ceases."[114]

[109] This is by far the majority view among Buddhologists – most notably Warder (*Indian Buddhism* and *Outline of Indian Philosophy*), Gethin (*The Foundations of Buddhism*), and Gombrich (*What the Buddha Thought*) – though it has recently been called in question by J. Bronkhorst, *Greater Magadha: Studies in the Culture of Early India*, vol. II (Leiden: Koninklijke Brill NV, 2007). However, the evidence adduced by Bronkhorst does not justify abandoning the view that the Buddha's critique of self and Being targets Upaniṣadic doctrines. At any rate, this is certainly how he was interpreted by both his followers and their Brahmanical opponents in the Classical period.

[110] *BĀU* I.4.1f.

[111] *SN* IV.15. The recurrent vocative "*bhikṣus*" refers to the Buddha's public, namely an assembly of monastic followers (*bhikṣus*, literally "mendicants").

[112] Indeed, in the Indian context, the mind is treated, on a par with the five senses recognized in the West, as a sixth sense.

[113] On this point, see Warder, *Outline of Indian Philosophy*, pp. 58–61.

[114] *V* I.181.

In the works of Nāgārjuna and his followers the Buddhist critique of substance metaphysics becomes explicit. All things, Nāgārjuna argues, are empty of inherent existence, or "own-being." Nāgarjuna's view, in short, is that all things are lacking in substance. This is the principle known as emptiness (*śūnyatā*) – which is really shorthand for "emptiness of substance" (*svabhāva*).[115]

To establish his point, Nāgārjuna redeploys and redefines the foundational Buddhist teaching of dependent co-arising.[116] In the discourses, dependent co-arising – said to correspond to the cognitive content of the Buddha's enlightenment[117] – is quite narrowly applied to the person to show that what we call an "individual" is really a dependently co-arisen nexus of fleeting, fluctuating factors entirely devoid of a substantial "self." Nāgārjuna takes this a step further and claims that all things in the world are dependently co-arisen and therefore entirely void of robust, intrinsic existence, or substance: "Since there is nothing which is not dependently co-arisen, there is nothing that is not empty [of substance]."[118] One of Nāgārjuna's main ideas is that the very notion of a substance is incoherent. Substance is supposed to be uncaused. As such, it corresponds to nothing in a world of universal conditionality. What is more, even if a substance were to exist, the very fact that it is uncaused would prevent it from partaking in this world of conditionality – being uncaused, it could have no causal efficacy itself.[119] As such, substances are redundant entities – they play no explanatory role.

What is more, on Nāgārjuna's view, substance is not only an incoherent and/or redundant concept, it is also fundamentally incompatible with the world as we actually experience it. Relatively simple analyses of "things"[120]

[115] On this point, see Westerhoff, *Nāgārjuna's Madhyamaka*, pp. 23f.

[116] The two propitiating verses at the beginning of the *MMK*, though probably interpolated, have the virtue of making it clear from the very outset that Nāgārjuna is revising the teaching of dependent co-arising (*pratītyasamutpāda*) to claim that all things, not just persons, lack a substantial nature (*-bhāva*) of their own (*sva-*).

[117] See *V* I.1–2. [118] *MMK* XXIV.19. [119] On this point, see *MMK* XV and XXIV.

[120] These "things" include all of the primary elements to which earlier Indian metaphysical schools (including the Buddhist Vaibhāṣika Sarvāstivāda) had sought to reduce reality. Nāgārjuna passes under review all such concepts – such as the senses (*MMK* III), the traditional elements of Indian cosmology (*MMK* IV), the constituents (*MMK* V), the factors of existence (*MMK* VI), etc. – to show that all of these can only ever exist/occur as processes devoid of intrinsic, non-contingent existence, rather than as static entities possessed of substance. He also examines various relations – such as that between cause and effect (*MMK* I), going and goer (*MMK* II), action and agent (*MMK* VIII), fire and fuel (*MMK* X), etc. – to show that these can only involve contingent, mutually co-dependent processes rather than actual entities. Nāgārjuna's preferred strategy to argue for these results is to highlight the "undesired consequence" (*prasaṅga*) of attributing a substantial essence to whatever *x* is under discussion. He proceeds, in short, through series of *reductiones ad absurdum*.

and of the relations between them lead to the conclusion that our world must be made up of processes alone, not of property-bearing "objects." If things occur the way they do, he claims, it is precisely because they are empty of substance.[121] Moreover, a world of Substance, or Being, would in no way resemble the world we live in. There would be no arising, no passing away, and the universe would be immutable and free from all of the diversified states that can be witnessed.[122] Between a world of immutable Being and one of constant flux and turbulent becoming, Nāgārjuna takes a position diametrically opposed to Parmenides', Zeno's, or Plato's – Being is unreal, or fictional, and becoming alone is real.

Indeed, Nāgārjuna calls the very notion of Being, or existence, into question: "There is no such thing as existence (*sattā*) when it comes to entities devoid of own-being."[123] With universal conditionality, falls Substance – the world is made up of processes that arise in mutual dependence so that everything lacks substantial, intrinsic existence. With Substance, in turn, falls existence itself, for only substances could be said to really exist. Nothing ever "is," for Nāgārjuna, events just "take place," or "occur." Nāgārjuna, in short, rejects any metaphysics of Being and, more generally, any thought system that posits a realm of Ultimate Reality or Absolute Truth over and above a realm of "mere" conventions or transactional practices. This is because, on his view, the notion of "own-being" on which any metaphysics of this sort relies is little more than a fiction.

Universal emptiness of own-being thus constitutes a robust rejection of the metaphysics of Being in favor of "universal becoming."[124] Instead of Being and beings, what we have is a world of interdependence, interrelatedness, and contingency – a world of dynamic processes rather than discrete entities. Instead of a world of entities (substances) bearing properties (attributes), what we have is a world of fleeting "qualities" – to

[121] This is the conclusion of *MMK* xxiv, arguably the clearest expression of Madhyamaka philosophy on offer. At *MMK* xxiv.15, Nāgārjuna declares: "Everything makes sense for him who accepts emptiness. Nothing makes sense for him who does not accept that things are empty." Cf. *VV* 70: "Everything prevails for him for whom emptiness prevails. Nothing prevails for him for whom emptiness does not prevail." The auto-commentary to this verse makes it clear that "everything" stands, among other things, for all conventions about how the world operates. On this key point, see in particular Arnold, *Buddhists, Brahmins and Belief*, pp. 140f. and G. Priest, *Beyond the Limits of Thought* (Oxford University Press, 2002), pp. 266f.

[122] *MMK* xxiv.38. [123] *MMK* i.10a–b.

[124] This is the interpretation of Nāgārjuna's philosophy that best fits the texts. Nāgārjuna interpretation, it should be mentioned, is a very controversial subfield in Buddhology. The philosopher has been presented as a metaphysical nihilist, a monist–absolutist relying on something like Kant's transcendental idealism, and, more recently, a metaphysical idealist *à la* Berkeley. Nāgārjuna has also been presented as a radical skeptic, as a proto-Wittgenstein, and as anticipator of Rorty and Derrida.

retain the substantialist term – in which a "thing" is nothing more than "the sum of its effects."[125]

Nietzsche holds the same view.[126] In a wealth of passages, Nietzsche ridicules the ideas of rigid existence (as opposed to arising), of Substance (as opposed to force), and of Being (as opposed to becoming).[127] For Nietzsche, Parmenides and his Eleatic followers were wrong and Heraclitus was right[128] – one never steps in the same river twice. "The lie of thinghood, the lie of substance, of permanence," writes Nietzsche, all result from the "falsification of the testimony of the senses."[129] As in Buddhist thought, the world as Nietzsche sees it is composed of evanescent processes and events alone, not of things. There is no object, or entity, that endures phenomenal change and "bears" attributes; there are only dynamic processes.[130] In short, Nietzsche rejects substance metaphysics on grounds very similar to Nāgārjuna's. For him, ours is a world of perpetual becoming and impermanence in which there is no place for the staticity of Being, or substance. This is what Nietzsche has in mind when he claims that Buddhism has the illusion of God behind it.[131] As he rightly saw, Buddhism entirely rejects Substance, which, for Nietzsche, is a just another form of the *wahre Welt* fiction.

processes not things

But Nietzsche has more to say on this point. In connection with the Buddhist critique of metaphysics, he writes: "The Buddhist negation of Reality . . . is perfectly consistent: not only undemonstrability, inaccessibility, absence of categories for a 'world-in-itself,' but also an *insight into the erroneous procedures* by means of which this whole concept is arrived at."[132] What, one may ask, could Nietzsche have been referring to in this passage?

As Nietzsche had obviously realized, the Buddhist critique of Being, and with it of substance metaphysics as a whole, is, more than anything, a psychological critique. This is not to say that Buddhist thought, like Nietzsche's, attributes the "nihilistic" invention of the *wahre Welt* to *décadence* and *ressentiment*. Rather, the Buddhist insight is that to look

125 Nehamas, *Nietzsche*, p. 74. This phrase appears in Nehamas's discussion of Nietzche's critique of substance metaphysics, but unsurprisingly it is perfectly suited to Buddhist philosophy as well.

126 Cf. Conze, who rejects the parallel between the doctrine of emptiness and Nietzsche's nihilism as a "spurious parellel" owing to a fundamental misunderstanding of Buddhist ideas ("Spurious Parallel to Buddhist Philosophy," p. 106). But Conze held the view, which is now considered to be incorrect, that Buddhism is geared toward the realization of a Transcendental Reality. Combined with Conze's partial and somewhat uncharitable reading of Nietzsche's critique of the *wahre Welt*, this makes for quite an unsatisfactory assessment of the parallels between Nietzsche's thought and Buddhist philosophy.

127 These include a number of passages from his early lectures (*VP*) and unpublished texts (namely, *PtZG*), from his notes, and from published texts such as *JGB* and *GD*.

128 *GD* III §2. 129 *Ibid.* 130 On this key point, see Nehamas, *Nietzsche*, pp. 74–105.

131 *A* §20. 132 *NL 1887–1888*, 9(62).

upon the world as composed of enduring substances underlying fleeting properties – to see Being where there is only becoming – is the outcome of a grand personification of the universe. The illusion of Being, in short, is really a cosmic version of the illusion of the self. It is generated through the same psychological process, applied to the entire world and its myriad fleeting phenomena, as that on account of which the flux of fleeting psycho-physical events is unified into a unitary, permanent, and substantial "I" which is then assumed to act as a substratum for physical and mental events. The fiction of the I, in this sense, is the model for the fiction of Being as a whole. The self, otherwise stated, is the prototypical Substance. Just as it abides, unchanged and fixed, behind/under the rise and fall of physical and mental events, whatever "is" endures through time, untouched and unmoved by everything that arises and passes away.

This analysis of the psychology at the root of the metaphysics of Being is evinced by the case of the early Brahmanical metaphysics which served as the Buddha's foil. For the authors of the Upaniṣads, the primordial Being of which the entire universe is an emanation is none other than *ātman*, or "self."[133] The unitary cosmic principle, or Substance, is none other than a Universal Self. The upshot is that the core of my person – my "self" (i.e. *ātman*) – is identical with the primary Being that underlies all of reality (i.e. *brahman*). It is this doctrine concerning the fundamental identity between the personal self and the Cosmic Self that the sage Uddālaka Aruṇi imparted to his son with the famous lines: "This very subtle thing is the essence of everything there is. It is the Truth. It is the Self. It is what you are (*tat tvam asi*), Śvetaketu."[134] Such metaphysics also underlies the sage Yājñavalkya's injunction to his wife: "Verily, Maitreyī my dear, the self is what should be seen, heard, thought about and concentrated upon. When one has seen, heard, thought about and concentrated upon the self, this entire universe is known."[135] Of course, "knowing everything there is" for mystics such as Yājñavalkya and Uddālaka Aruṇi does not involve acquiring exhaustive empirical knowledge of the world. Rather, it is attaining knowledge of the Absolute, of the undying essence of all things.[136] It is attaining, in Nietzsche's words, the *wahre Welt*.

[133] Consider, for instance the cosmogonical account at *BĀU* I.4.1f.

[134] *ChU* VI.8.7. These famous lines are repeated at the end of VI.9–16.

[135] *Ibid.* IV.5.6. Cf. the closing line of the *BĀU* cosmogony referred to above: "The self is the path to everything there is. For, through it, one knows everything there is" (I.4.7).

[136] The Upaniṣadic self, indeed, is described as being entirely intangible and unthinkable (*KU* 3.15.a–b and 6.12) and "free from old age and death, free from sorrow, free from hunger and thirst" (*ChU* 8.1.5). In short, it seems to have been arrived at through the metaphysician's traditional *via negativa*.

The *wahre Welt* as Cosmic Self – this is the grand delusion the Buddha and his followers saw through. The Upaniṣadic authors, in short, delivered the Buddha his "*insight into the erroneous procedures* by the means of which this whole concept [the *wahre Welt*] is arrived at"[137] on a platter. Indeed, a key (and under-appreciated) point of Buddhist philosophy is that there is nothing coincidental about the Upaniṣadic Brahmans' case. The self that we pre-reflectively construct as a permanent substance, or enduring substratum, really is the model for Being, Substance, or God. Behind the twin Buddhist critique of Self and Substance is the view that the "I" is the primordial "substance," the first being, the first thing that "is, but does not become." The Brahmins' speculations on the underlying identity of one's true self and *brahman* qua World Soul were not a mere accident. In fact, the Upaniṣadic reasoning is particularly revealing. It is arguably one of the most transparent cases of what Nietzsche, more than two millennia later, would call *wahre Welt* metaphysics.[138]

Self as a model for construction of Being / Substance / God

The fundamental connection between the fiction of the self and the fiction of Being is brought out most clearly in the works of Nāgārjuna and his followers. In claiming that all things lack intrinsic existence, or substance, he is essentially claiming that all things lack a self:[139] indeed, that the principle of the "selflessness of [all] factors of existence" (*dharmanairātmya*) is simply an extension of the principle of the "selflessness of persons" (*pudgalanairātmya*).[140] This extension is founded on the fundamental insight that what underlies the fiction of Being is the illusion of selfhood itself. Indeed, Nāgārjuna and his Mādhyamika followers located the effects of what the Indian philosophers of the Classical period called the ego-principle (*ahaṃkāra*) well beyond the ego itself. The ego-principle is what is originally responsible for pre-reflectively generating the sense of an enduring ego as the owner of the mind–body complex;

137 *NL 1887–1888*, 9(62).

138 In the Western tradition, such transparency can be found in the work of Leibniz. In his *Monadology*, pp. 213–25, Leibniz posits irreducible soul-like entities as the foundational simple, primary substance out of which the world is composed. For Nietzsche's tongue-in-cheek critique of such "atomism," see *JGB* §12.

139 In pointing to the roots of his critique of substance, Nāgārjuna specifically refers to one of Buddha's teachings on the twin illusions of a presumed person's existence and non-existence (*MMK* xv.7). The text Nāgārjuna cites is the *Kaccāyanasutta* (*SN* II.16–17). In this discourse, the Buddha claims that to speak of a person as "existing" or "not existing" makes no sense because there is no person to begin with. He presents his doctrine of dependent co-arising as an alternative, or middle way. The upshot is that talk of being/non-being, or existence/non-existence, should be abandoned in favor of a focus on becoming, or (impersonal) arising and cessation. Nāgārjuna's point is that this applies to all and any talk of being/non-being, not only that which pertains to persons.

140 On this point, and the ample discussion it received among Nāgārjuna's followers, see D. S. López Jr., "Do *Śrāvakas* Understand Emptiness?," *Journal of Indian Philosophy* 16(1), 1988: 65–105.

it is the maker (*-kāra*) of the "I" (*ahaṃ*).[141] Underlying the Madhyamaka extension of the doctrine of selflessness to all entities is the insight that the ego-principle actually affects our entire pre-reflective cognitive take on the world. The ego-principle does not only "make" the self, it also projects the permanence and stability of the "I" qua owner out into the world in the guise of a pre-reflective commitment to "things" as property-bearing substances. We thus assume that things "actually exist," that the world is made up of "really existing" entities related in specific, rigid ways. Our pre-reflective commitment to substance metaphysics, on the Buddhist account, is an outgrowth of our pre-reflective commitment to a substance view of the self.[142] We are continually personifying the impersonal in the process of reification – which, after all, is what we do with our own mind–body complexes.

In this way, Madhyamka thought goes beyond a critique of the mystical worship of Being/God that may follow from the "self"-delusion. Its claim is that naive common sense itself – which sees a world of beings and selves, of agents performing actions, of substance and attribute, etc. – exhibits the most pernicious and insidious effect of the ego-principle. As such, "common sense" involves an implicit commitment to a metaphysics of Being predicated on things' substantial existence which already paves the way towards explicit theism, or absolutism, or some other, soberer version of substance metaphysics. All of these, on the Buddhist view, are really only grand self-worship (e.g. the case of the Upaniṣadic Brahmins). In contrast, the Mādhyamika view insists that careful analyses reveal that trying to make sense of the world in terms of things/entities, substances and attributes, etc., requires a colossal falsification of experience. Becoming alone has a place in a truly "realistic" worldview. There are only insubstantial processes and relations, no "things" whatsoever, let alone persons. In this way, Buddhism seeks to undermine humanity's greatest fictions at their root. This is because, according to Buddhist philosophy, Being/Substance has no

[141] On this point, see M. Hulin, *Le principe d'égo dans la pensée indienne classique: la notion d'ahaṃkāra* (Paris: Collège de France, 1978), p. 3f.

[142] Buddhist philosophy thus finds itself fundamentally opposed to the type of view espoused by P. Ricœur, *Soi même comme un autre* (Paris: Seuil, 1990), who distinguishes between the identity we attribute to enduring things, sameness (*mêmeté*), and the identity we attribute to ourselves, selfhood (*ipséité*). Ricœur believes only the former involves the idea of an enduring substance, while the latter has little to do with the persistence of an enduring core self. On the Buddhist view, which I take to be phenomenologically warranted, we are all pre-reflectively committed to a "substance view of self" when it comes to our experience of selfhood. This implicit substantialism, which reifies the hypostasized self, is also present in our take on the external world so that events and processes, like those that make up the supposedly self-identical "me," are also reified as hypostasized things. This topic will be discussed in greater detail in Chapter 4.

ground outside flawed human psychology. Its only ground is our delusional sense of personal identity.[143]

It is in adopting this very same view that Nietzsche finds himself in closest agreement with Buddhist philosophy. Substance metaphysics, the fiction of Being, the "lies" of unity, thinghood, and permanence, etc. – all these things are secreted out of the ego according to Nietzsche. Discussing what he calls "the metaphysics of language" in *GD*, he writes:

> It is *this* [the metaphysics of language] which sees everywhere deed and doer . . . this which believes in the "I," in the "I" as being, in the "I" as substance, and which *projects* the belief in the I-substance onto all things – only thus does it *create* the concept "thing" . . . Being is everywhere thought in, *foisted on* . . . it is only out of the conception "I" that there follows, as a consequence, the concept of "being" . . . I fear we will not get rid of God because we still believe in grammar.[144]

The metaphysics of language which so believes in the "I," of course, is itself rooted in the very notion of the self. Consider the following passage:

> The concept of *substance* [is] a consequence of the concept of the *subject*: *not* vice versa! If we reject the soul, "the subject," we then completely lack the precondition for "substance" . . . The "subject" is the fiction that many similar states in us belong to one substratum.[145]

The primary "substance," the prototype for anything that "is" rather than becomes, knows permanence, stability, etc., is none other than the self. The "I" is the illusory unitary substratum of all our feelings, the illusory unitary

143 Westerhoff, in this connection, is wrong to claim that the notion of substance in Nāgārjuna's works is unlike any Western notion of substance in so far as it involves a "cognitive component," which Western notions of substances universally lack. According to Westerhoff, Nāgārjuna's notion of substance is unique, in that it is "not just a theoretical concept of ontology but rather a cognitive default, an addition that the mind unwittingly makes when trying to make sense of the world" (*Nāgārjuna's Madhyamaka*, p. 13). But the fact that Nāgārjuna regards substance as a "conceptual superimposition" (*ibid.*) does not imply that his concept of substance is in any way different from the West's. Rather, what we find in Nāgārjuna is an additional, psychological claim about the roots of substance metaphysics. The term "*svabhāva*" has the same overall meaning as "substance" in Western metaphysics – it is the "really existent" substratum that underlies contingent "accidents" and phenomenal change. What is unique to Nāgārjuna's philosophy – and puts it in a category apart from any Western discussion of metaphysics (other than Nietzsche's) – is that it goes beyond the claim that there is no room for substance in our picture of the world, and adds that the attribution of "own-existence," which characterizes our intuitive take on the world, has deep roots in human psychology.

144 *GD* III §5. See also *ibid.* §2. As Nietzsche's comments make clear, it is obvious that language structures the world in terms of substance and attribute. This is something Buddhist philosophers were also aware of. This is why they regarded language as the domain of conventions (*saṃvṛti*) or transactional practices (*vyāvahara*), and argued that it should not be taken to capture extra-linguistic reality (i.e. flux and process) transparently. These issues will be discussed at greater length in Chapters 3 and 4.

145 *NL 1887–1888*, 10(19).

ground of all of our actions. It is that which is supposedly fixed and survives the "multiplicity of change." As such, the "I" is the prototypical substance; it is the psychological model for and the experiential ground of the metaphysics of Being.[146] As the source of our conception of substance, it is only natural that "our *belief in the ego* as a substance, as the only reality on the basis of which we ascribe reality to things in general"[147] should also be the basis of all major world religions. "The entire religious history of mankind," Nietzsche concludes, "is recognized as the history of the soul superstition."[148] All of metaphysics and religion, in short, is a fruit of the "self"-delusion.

It is perhaps in the following fragment that Nietzsche expresses his view most clearly:

> The concept of "reality" and "existence" is derived from "subject"-feeling. The "subject": interpreted from inside ourselves, so that the "I" appears to be a substance, as the source of all actions, as the agent. The logical-metaphysical postulates, the belief in substance, accident, attribute, etc., have their power of persuasion through the habit to regard all of our actions as consequences of our will – so that the I, as a substance, does not vanish in the multiplicity of change.[149]

The key terms in this fragment are "feeling" ("subject"-feeling) and "habit." Ultimately, that to which Nietzsche attributes the prevalence of substance metaphysics is not the *concept* "self/ego/subject," but the pre-reflective *feeling* of being a substantial self and the mental, cognitive, and therefore also linguistic habits that follow from this. The "I" that is bloated into God/Universal Spirit, into Cause, into Substance, into a *wahre Welt*, etc., is *not* an idea or concept, but something pre-reflective and pre-philosophical.[150]

In sum, when it comes to the relation between the "I" as the product of pre-reflective synthesis, the self/soul as dogma, and the fiction of Being, the story in Nietzsche's thought and in Buddhist philosophy is very similar. The flux of mental and physical events that make up an "individual" are pre-reflectively synthesized. The product of this synthesis is then reified, which

entire religious history based on belief in the ego (self-delusion)

[146] Nietzsche, in this connection, speaks of belief in the self as the "oldest realism" (*ibid. 1885–1887*, 7(63)).

[147] *Ibid. 1887–1888*, 10(19) [148] *Ibid.* [149] *Ibid.* 9(98). See also *GM* I §13.

[150] Emphasizing the role of the "subject-feeling" as opposed to the *concept* of the subject, or ego, makes it possible to reply to Nehamas's important critique of Nietzsche's view. Nehamas finds the view that the prototypical substance is the ego "deeply unsatisfactory" and seeks to provide evidence to show that this could not really have been Nietzsche's view (*Nietzsche*, pp. 85–6). As it turns out, however, the three arguments he adduces to support this judgment presuppose that Nietzsche's view is about the *concepts* of "ego" and "substance," when really what it concerns is the *sense* of substantial, abiding existence that is first experienced within, as pertaining to the "self," and then projected outward.

gives rise to the sense of a substantial "I" which confers both illusory synchronic unity (where there is really only multiplicity) and illusory diachronic identity (where there is really only continuity) to the so-called subject. It is this sense of self that is "exploited," as Nietzsche says at *GM* I §13, by metaphysicians and religious types to construct the concept of "soul." Of course, due to its origins, belief in the soul is a very natural, not to say intuitive, belief. The fiction of Being, for its part, also finds its origin in the psychological mechanisms that produce the "I." It is on pre-reflective analogy with oneself, as it were, that anything we encounter in the world is immediately assumed to consist, most fundamentally, of an enduring substance underlying fleeting attributes. One step further and we arrive at the Primordial Substance that stands behind "the world" taken as one thing, at the Creator God from which it originated, at the noumenal thing-in-itself (*Ding an sich*) behind all appearances, and so on. The *wahre Welt*, God, *brahman*, Being, etc., is thus to the evanescent and deceptive world of becoming what the permanent, abiding and real "I" is to the fleeting physical and mental events that constitute the person – alternatively, it stands in the same relation to the world of becoming as the pure, immortal soul stands to the corrupt, decaying body. In this way, the fiction of Being derives from the fiction of the self. The same principle of individuation is at work at both the microcosmic level of the person and the macrocosmic level of the entire world.

Finally, there is also a connection between Nietzsche's and the Buddha's rejection of the twin illusions of God/Being/Substance and soul/ego/self, on the one hand, and their insistence on the universality of suffering, on the other. If suffering is a necessary, not accidental, feature of existence and no abiding Peace, Stillness, and Bliss can ever be attained, it is because the latter are properties of a Transcendent Absolute that does not exist. Both Nietzsche and the Buddha reject the idea that there is a pure soul which may experience some sort of final homecoming to the blissful abode of Being. For them, there is nowhere to hide from the constant, turbulent flux of fleeting becoming. There is no Being or soul, and thus no lasting Bliss.

In both Nietzsche's thought and Buddhist philosophy, then, all three of the principal myths at the heart of what Nietzsche calls nihilist metaphysics – the myth of Bliss, of the I, and of Being – are not only rejected on similar grounds, but related in the same way. As a result, they fall in the very same domino-like fashion – the "I"–Being–Bliss. To reject these myths, for Nietzsche, is to espouse nihilism. And he felt this is what the Buddha had done. After the Buddhist critique of self (*ātman*), Being (*brahman*), and Bliss (*ānanda*), life is bereft of the worth it formerly had. As a harbinger of nihilism, the Buddha destroyed the value and meaning previously attributed to life through nihilist myths by exploding those myths. It is by exploding those same myths in their European form (soul, God, Heaven) that Nietzsche assumes the role of Europe's Buddha.

The affinity between Nietzsche and the Buddha goes beyond the critical elements of their thought. The nihilist crisis is the crisis of valuelessness, worthlessness, meaninglessness, and purposelessness. But this is only a transitional stage. The ethical void left by the critiques of thinkers such as Nietzsche or the Buddha must be filled – it cannot but be filled.[151] The challenge of nihilism, as I explained above, is the challenge of developing a post-nihilist ethics without relapsing into the delusional thinking at the basis of former modes of valuation. It is important to note, moreover, that the form of such ethics is the same in both Nietzsche's thought and Buddhist philosophy. Indeed, their ethical visions are visions of *great health*.

There is a deep relation, in this connection, between Nietzsche as Buddha and Nietzsche as Antichrist. Other than the fact that Buddhism is "a hundred times more realistic than Christianity" in that it is atheistic, positivistic, phenomenalistic, and anti-metaphysical,[152] what radically sets it apart from the Christian faith is that its ethics is not moralistic, but hygienic. In *EH*, Nietzsche writes: "[the Buddha's] 'religion' should rather be called a kind of hygiene, lest it be confused with so pitiable a phenomenon as Christianity."[153] Contrary to Christianity, which claims that suffering is the result of sin and founds its ethics on a moralizing guilt complex, the Buddha recognizes that suffering is rooted in human psychology and physiology and therefore takes "hygienic measures" against it.[154] Good acts, attitudes, states of mind, etc., are prescribed in so far as they are healthy, and bad ones are condemned in so far as they are unhealthy, all in view of Buddhism's "fundamental hygienic purpose."[155] This is in stark contrast to Christianity, which adopts a typically nihilistic moral attitude whereby goodness flows from one source alone – God, or Heaven – and everything related to the world here below – the body, worldly pleasures, etc. – is regarded as evil and corrupting. In this sense, Nietzsche explains, "Buddhism is profoundly distinguished from Christianity by the fact that

---

[151] This is because the attribution of value, worth, meaning, and purpose is, according to Nietzsche, a fundamental activity, which any living creature engages in by necessity, whether consciously or not (see, in this connection, *JGB* §9).

[152] *A* §20. Cf. *ibid.* §23: "Buddhism, to say it again, is a hundred times colder, more veracious, more objective [than Christianity]."

[153] *EH* "Warum ich so weise bin" §6.   [154] *A* §20.   [155] *Ibid.*

Europe's Buddha:
- destroying myths of
  Being, + Bliss
    – idea of "great"
         health

the self-deception of moral concepts lies far behind it. In my terms, it stands *beyond* good and evil."[156]

Of course, the traditional notions of "good" and "evil" cannot survive the demise of the metaphysics of Being, which destroys the very ground of the Good. Nietzsche's idea is that the Buddha had to replace such moral concepts with ethical concepts of another kind, and that he selected the concepts of "healthy" and "unhealthy" instead. It is obvious from Nietzsche's comments on Buddhism that he was well aware of the medical discourse in which Buddhist teachings are couched. Buddhists across the ages have regarded the historical Buddha, Siddhārtha Gautama, as the supreme physician[157] and his teaching as a form of therapeutic practice.[158] Accordingly, Buddhist philosophy and practice are geared toward a distinctive ideal of great health, or supreme wellbeing, namely *nirvāṇa*.[159] Those who have not attained this state are described as sick, deluded, and/or impaired.[160] Among those things to which the Buddha's teaching acts as an antidote are the so-called secretions (*āsrava*), fluid-like toxins that seep into the subconscious strands of the psycho-physical apparatus, thereby infecting it with latent psychological proclivities (*abhiniveśa*) and biases (*anuśaya*). His teaching is also described as washing away the defilements (*kleśa*) that taint the common person's mind. In short, Buddhist ethics hinges on a distinctive notion of the "healthy type" which stands opposed to the "sick type." In replicating this, Nietzsche follows his Indian predecessor's example. His ethics also concerns the fundamental opposition between healthy/strong types and sick/weak types. Standing, like the Buddha, beyond the nihilist myths of Good and evil, his ethics is one of great health and his target is also a form of illness, namely *décadence*.[161]

extreme health

[156] *Ibid.*

[157] This epithet is widely used in the Pāli canon. See, for instance, *AN* IV.340 and *MN* I.156–60, II.256–60. It has survived into the present, across the millennia.

[158] This idea is so common in Buddhism that practically any text in Indian Buddhist literature will include a reference to medical practice or use a medical analogy to illustrate a point. For a useful survey of the so-called "medical analogy" in Buddhist texts, see C. W. Gowans, "Medical Analogies in Buddhist and Hellenistic Thought: Tranquility and Anger," in Carlisle and Ganeri, *Philosophy as Therapiea*, pp. 11–33, at pp. 16–19.

[159] In the Pāli canon, *nirvāṇa* is described as health (*ārogya*) at *MN* I.508–11 and *Sn* 749. Cf. *SN* IV.371's and *MN* I.173's *abhyādhi* and *ibid.* 511's *anītika*. All these negative constructions literally mean "lack of illness," but negative terms in Indian languages frequently have a positive meaning. Accordingly, *ārogya, abhyādhi*, and *anītika* all have the sense of "wellbeing."

[160] Consider, for instance, *Dhp* 198: "Verily, we live pleasantly, without sickness among the sick. Among the sick, we dwell without sickness."

[161] Nietzsche only begins to present himself as a physician of mankind in his later works. Though a growing body of scholarship – namely, K. A. Pearson, "For Mortal Souls: Philosophy and Therapiea

It would seem, then, that responses to nihilist crises invariably involve an ethics couched in medical terms. Rid of the fictional triad Self–Being–Bliss and presented with this world of suffering and becoming alone, Buddhist philosophy develops an ethical ideal founded on a distinctive notion of health. Following a similar critique, Nietzsche, qua Buddha of Europe, also formulates an ethics of great health. Irrespective of the content of this post-nihilist ethics (on which I will dwell at length in the following chapters), a series of questions regarding their very form presents itself. Why must ethics after the death of God be couched in medical terms? Why does the distinctive notion of a healthy type play such an important role in Nietzsche's positive thought and in Buddhist ethics? Is this just a stylistic convention, an arbitrary choice, or is there some deeper connection between the demise of *wahre Welt* fictions and the ideal of great health?

The distinction between immanence and Transcendence is the key to addressing this difficult issue. Under the sway of what Nietzsche calls nihilist *wahre Welt* fictions – be they Christian, Brahmanical, or of some other type – a clear distinction is drawn between the immanent (this natural, "apparent world" of becoming) and the Transcendent (the Supra-Natural, 'True/Real World' of Being). The Good is located in the realm of the Transcendent. In contrast, the immanent, apparent world is corrupt and immoral. Its lowly, brutish inhabitants can only be saved by turning away from it and toward its Transcendent counterpart. It is on this essential structure that traditional, so-called nihilist morality rests. Such morals are rooted in the Transcendent.

With the collapse of the distinction between the immanent and the Transcendent, however, the metaphysical carpet is pulled from under morality's feet. Hence the nihilist crisis. On what basis can an ethics then be formulated? Note that when it comes to the domain of evaluation, if there is anything that survives the demise of the Transcendent, it is precisely those purely descriptive categories in which humans always compared and contrasted various individuals or organisms down here in the (formerly merely immanent) world. These are the categories of relative

in Nietzsche's *Dawn*," in Carlisle and Ganeri, *Philosophy as Therapiea*, pp. 137–63; H. Hutter, *Shaping the Future: Nietzsche's New Regime of the Soul and its Ascetic Practices* (Lanham: Lexington Books, 2006); and M. Ure, *Nietzsche's Therapy: Self-Cultivation in the Middle Works* (Lanham: Lexington Press, 2008) – indicates that Nietzsche had a sustained interest in philosophy as therapy from the late 1870s onward, it is only in the early 1880s that Nietzsche takes the resolute "physiological turn" that would lead up to his diagnosis of *décadence* in his late works. In fact, Nietzsche's declaration that he could be "the Buddha of Europe" in 1883 marks the beginning of this project. This is no coincidence: Kern's manual on Buddhism, which lays particular emphasis on the figure of the Buddha as therapist, appeared in 1882 and quickly found its way into Nietzsche's library.

health and sickness. This is why ethics becomes a matter of health after the nihilist crisis.

Morals turn into hygiene, the ethicist becomes physician, and a person's ethical worth becomes a function of his or her healthiness. The purely phenomenal, empirical world that survives the death of God/Being reduces to the body, its senses, various sense objects, and mental events. This exclusive focus on our natural, all too natural, psycho-physical apparatus and its interaction with its environment leaves few candidates other than the categories of health and illness to articulate an ethical ideal.[162] In the absence of a Transcendent *wahre Welt*, the immanent realm of the sentient body alone can provide a basis for any discussion of virtue. And health is clearly what has always had value and meaning "down here," as it were. Once there is no "above" or "beyond," health thus becomes the paradigm for value, worth, and meaning, i.e. for ethics. Hence the medical discourse that pervades Buddhist literature and Nietzsche's parallel concern with health and sickness.[163]

It may be objected that medical metaphors in general and the therapeutic discourse in particular are in no way limited to the articulation of Buddhist philosophy and Nietzsche's positive thought. For instance, Plato often compares Socrates to a physician, the philosophers of Antiquity often described themselves as therapists who cure the illnesses of the soul, and Christian texts also make use of analogies drawn from the medical discourse, if they are not directly praising Jesus for the miraculous healings he performs.[164] In the Indian context, Classical Brahmanical schools (foremost among them the Vedānta) also employ the medical paradigm to express their ethical views in spite of their theism and metaphysical absolutism.[165] In light of this, it seems questionable whether there really is any connection

[162] This thesis is somewhat controversial. It could be argued that there are other candidates for "goodness" after the death of God, such as creativity, beauty, greatness, the sublime, or authenticity. My basic point, however, is that "health/healthy" is the most primitive "good" and "illness/ill" the most primitive "bad" when it comes to evaluating creatures in this world, and in this world's terms. When this world is all we are left with, it is only natural that they should become the terms in which ethics is discussed. If they have not done so in most secular contemporary discussions of ethics, it is because, consciously or not, secular ethicists are still committed to some form of *wahre Welt*. I will have more to say on this point in the conclusion.

[163] A similar development can be observed in some strands of Hellenistic philosophy, particularly among naturalist Epicureans (see Gowans, "Medical Analogies in Buddhist and Hellenistic Thought," pp. 19f.) and atheist skeptics (see Ganeri, *The Concealed Art of the Soul*, pp. 106f.).

[164] On this point, see F. Bonardel's detailed discussion of the distinction between Buddhist and traditional Western uses of the medical discourse in relation to ethics in *Bouddhisme et philosophie: en quête d'une sagesse commune* (Paris: Harmattan, 2008), pp. 26f.

[165] On this point, see W. Halbfass, *Tradition and Reflection: Explorations in Indian Thought* (State University of New York Press, 1991), pp. 243–63.

between great health ideals and the rejection of the metaphysics of Being. Metaphors of illness and therapy appear to be commonly used even in robustly metaphysical systems.

However, it is important to see that such religious and metaphysical systems make a strictly metaphorical use of the language of health. References to health in these contexts are entirely figurative. They stand in for something whose literal description would require a robust metaphysical account – such as, say, the soul reaching Heaven, or *ātman* uniting with *brahman*. Using Nietzsche's terminology, the medical discourse in such contexts is metaphorical in that it borrows the categories of the "apparent world" (health/illness) to express something that supposedly happens at the level of the "True/Real World." But when the *wahre Welt* is rejected, the medical discourse in which ethics is couched is no longer metaphorical or figurative in the same sense. Health does not stand in for something that would allow of a more accurate, more literal, metaphysical description. The simile implicit in the metaphor is now absent; goodness is no longer *like* health, goodness just *is* health.

Though the notion of health is to be taken more literally in the context of Nietzsche's thought or Buddhist philosophy, it is nevertheless important to note that such notions are not supposed to correspond to or imply a state of physical health as understood in modern medicine. In 1889, Nietzsche was writing of the great health that he had attained[166] in spite of the fact that he was on the verge of physical and psychic collapse. Similarly, *nirvāṇa* does not imply a state of physical fitness as conventionally understood. These notions of great health are new notions of health. Accordingly, this book's discussion of health and illness is not to be taken as referring to physiological fitness. It is not that, according to Nietzsche or the Buddha, I am actually less virtuous when I catch a cold. The idea, rather, is that the notion of illness removal, for instance, is particularly elucidating when it comes to formulating post-theistic, post-metaphysical conceptions of virtue.

There is another important difference between the way health is talked and thought about in systems that remain committed to metaphysics of Being and those that reject them. This concerns the fiction of the rational soul. In Christianity or Platonic philosophy, morals (and philosophy in general) are meant to heal the soul of the sicknesses that afflict it through association with the body, i.e. passions, desires, instincts, etc. What is more, it is the rational soul that can see the Good and the other Forms, fight the passions, and aim for the realm of Being. In the ethics of a Buddha or a

[166] See, in particular, *NW* "Epilog" §1.

Nietzsche, however, this entire framework is rejected. No soul or self, let alone a rational soul or self, stands apart from the body, desires, passions, feelings, etc. It is not the soul that must regain health through faith (Christianity) or the operation of reason (Plato), but the entire mind–body apparatus. In contrast to Plato's idea in particular, great health cannot be attained through the operation of reason alone – the supposed soul's highest faculty – but through an engagement of the entire mind–body complex, which involves more than mere reasoning. The idea of great health for Nietzsche or the Buddha, then, is not only taken more literally, it also stands for something different. It pertains to the entire "person," not just to its deep self/soul. As such, it cannot just be a matter of "having faith" or "being rational."

I would argue, in this connection, that if contemporary secular ethics has failed to take the Nietzschean or Buddhist "physiological turn," it is precisely because, with its rationalism, it remains unwittingly committed to a lingering mind–body dualism. Certainly, talk of the soul, and now even of the self, is waning. But Reason, or the cognitive faculty, as something firmly set apart from our more "animal" (natural) side – emotions, volitions, feelings, etc. – remains what most philosophers still count on to guide us through the thorny world of ethics. In this sense, Western philosophy is still very much Platonic. It believes in the rational soul, even as it rejects its ontology. It is naturalist, yet still infected with a vestige of apparent/True world dualism. When Reason will finally be fully naturalized, ethics and psychology (not to say psychiatry) will become one. Ethics will become, as it is in Nietzsche's thought and in Buddhist philosophy, a matter of great health.[167]

Nietzsche as Buddha. This phrase is the key to understanding a central aspect of Nietzsche's self-understanding. It is also the key to understanding central aspects of Nietzsche's thought. He is the Buddha of Europe in so far as he rejects the three *décadent* nihilist myths of self, Being, and Bliss, thereby assuming an active role in the midst of the European nihilist crisis. He is also the Buddha of Europe in that he responds to the challenge of nihilism by envisioning an ethical ideal of great health. It is in doing just this, however, that Nietzsche claims to diagnose the *décadence* at the core of Buddhist ethics. From Buddha, Nietzsche turns Anti-Buddha.

[167] In fact, it may be claimed that a renewed interest in "philosophy as therapy" is already on the horizon. See, in this connection, Ganeri and Carlisle's recent *Philosophy as Therapiea*.

CHAPTER 2

Nietzsche as Anti-Buddha

Prima facie, Nietzsche's central claim as Anti-Buddha directly contradicts his view qua Buddha. Siddhārtha Gautama, the historical Buddha, is *not* beyond good and evil; on the contrary, he remains "under the spell and delusion of morality."[1] This is because the Buddha's ethics remains rooted in a resentful condemnation of the world. The Buddha continues to evaluate life and nature as evil and deceptive even though he rejects the *wahre Welt* in opposition to which the actual world typically suffers such bad press. In propounding a great health which effectively consists in non-existence – *nirvāṇa*, here understood literally as "going out," or "extinction"[2] – the Buddha shows himself to be a sickly *décadent*, a prophet of life-negation.

How can Nietzsche's claims as Buddha and as Anti-Buddha be reconciled? Is Nietzsche just contradicting himself? Surely the Indian Buddha cannot both be and not be "beyond good and evil"?[3] To begin resolving this issue, it will be helpful to couch Nietzsche's views on the Buddha's *décadence* in terms of the distinction between the nihilist mentality and the nihilist crisis.

On Nietzsche's view, the Buddhist response to the nihilist crisis remains an expression of the *décadent* nihilism at the core of the nihilist mentality. As

[1] *JGB* §56. See also *NL 1885–1887*, 2(127). I should make it very clear from the outset that everything I write about Buddhism in this chapter concerns Nietzsche's interpretation of Buddhism. Unlike Chapter 4, the present chapter is not concerned with Buddhist doctrine as such; it merely reports and reconstructs Nietzsche's views.

[2] Morrison examines some of the reasons why Nietzsche retained the "annihilationist" interpretation of the Buddhist goal of *nirvāṇa* promulgated in early Buddhological works (e.g. Koeppen's work, *Die Religion des Buddhas*, and Müller's early essays on Buddhism) in spite of the fact that this interpretation had been called into question by the later Buddhologists he had read (Morrison, *Nietzsche and Buddhism*, pp. 52–9). But the problem Morrison sees here is really not a problem at all. Indeed, the fact that Oldenberg, the late Müller, and even Schopenhauer resist the annihilationist interpretation by suggesting that *nirvāṇa* really involves a return to "pure being" (*ibid.*, p. 56) directly confirms Nietzsche's suspicion that the ethical ideal of *nirvāṇa* is one of utter life-negation. As seen in Chapter 1, "pure being," for Nietzsche, is really nothing more than "pure no-thing."

[3] Nietzsche's inconsistency cannot be attributed to a change of opinion over time – both contradictory views are put forward in texts from the same "period."

such, the Buddha continues to evaluate life in moral terms. Nietzsche explains: "With [Buddhism] there is in nihilism a morality that is not overcome: existence as punishment, existence construed as an error, error thus as punishment – a moral valuation."[4] Buddhism, in this sense, is just as much of a "nihilistic religion" as Christianity; both are "religions of *décadence*."[5] Buddhism certainly stands beyond good and evil in that its concrete ethics is a hygiene focused on healthy/unhealthy rather than good/evil acts, states of mind, and behaviors, but it nevertheless continues to regard existence as evil. As such, though Buddhism rejects the metaphysics that stands at the basis of the explicit moral distinction between Good and evil, it remains committed to the implicit moral condemnation of the world that stands at the root of the *décadents*' nihilist mentality.

Buddhism, in this sense, is a form of what Nietzsche calls "passive nihilism."[6] Passive nihilism is a form of response to the nihilist crisis. In Chapter 1, I explained how nihilist crises are precipitated by an active nihilizing of the metaphysical myths invented by *décadents*. Nietzsche and the Buddha are two such nihilizers, as it were. The Buddha's "weary nihilism,"[7] however, fails to go beyond the negation of life's (former, metaphysics/religion-based) value. The valuelessness at the heart of the nihilist crisis is thus taken be a final verdict.[8] The Buddha, in short, is one of those nihilists who "judges of the world as it is that it ought *not* to be and judges of the world as it ought to be that it does not exist."[9] In short, he continues to regard the value of this world as *nil* after the demise of metaphysics which had, precisely, reduced it to *nil*, and fails to rehabilitate this world by creating new, positive values for it. Such passive nihilism is a "sign of weakness,"[10] i.e. a sign of *décadence*.

Indeed, the Buddhist is too weak to will a positive "good" other than the Peace, Stillness, and Bliss of Being. His reaction to the realization that such a Good does not exist is to despair of life. As a result, to the Buddha "the good" becomes an absolute negative, namely non-existence. This is why Buddhists, in striving toward *nirvāṇa*, actively and consciously "seek a way toward non-being."[11] Existence is judged to be so bad that, in the absence of a metaphysical anti-world as a goal for human striving, non-existence becomes the highest desideratum. The Buddhist response to the challenge of nihilism, Nietzsche explains, consists in a "nihilistic turning away from life, a longing for nothingness, or for [existence]'s opposite, for a different

[4] *NL 1885–1887*, 2(127) and 9(35). [5] *A* §20. [6] *NL 1887–1888*, 9(35). [7] *Ibid.*
[8] On this point, see Morrison, *Nietzsche and Buddhism*, pp. 22f. [9] *NL 1887–1888*, 9(60).
[10] *Ibid.* (35). [11] *Ibid.* 10(190).

sort of being."[12] The Buddha's goal, in short, is explicitly nihilistic. To end suffering – to put an end to the "evil" of suffering – he wants to terminate existence and he calls this termination "good." He might be a "profound physiologist,"[13] then, but the pathological condition he aims to fight against is life itself. This is because, contrary to appearances, the Buddha is not really beyond good and evil. Even after rejecting the myth of Being, his *décadence* continues to manifest itself as a life-negation which is now explicit.

In light of this, it seems clear that Nietzsche's positive assessment of Buddhism in texts such as *A* and *EH* is not entirely sincere. Nietzsche's praise of Buddhism in these texts serves the purposes of his anti-Christian diatribes.[14] This of course is not the only source of Nietzsche's affinity with Buddhism. As I showed in Chapter 1, when it comes to several of his negative views and his formulation of a post-theistic ideal of great health, Nietzsche genuinely regarded himself as the "Buddha of Europe." Nevertheless, there is no doubt that when Nietzsche tells us that Buddhism stands beyond good and evil, he does so exclusively from the standpoint of his polemics against Christianity.[15]

One should also be wary of taking Nietzsche's comments on the relation between Buddhism and *ressentiment* at face value. In the texts in which he extols the Buddha's virtues, an important part of Nietzsche's praise concerns the *décadent* physician's attitude toward *ressentiment*. "There is nothing to which [the Buddha's] doctrine is more opposed," Nietzsche tells us, "than the feeling of revenge, antipathy, *ressentiment*."[16] And because *ressentiment* is indeed what most weakens and extenuates the *décadent*,[17] the Buddha's prescription actually has the desired effect. This is why, in contrast to

[12] *GM* II §21. See also *NL 1887–1888*, 10(190). [13] *EH* "Warum ich so weise bin" §6.

[14] Conche expresses this idea very clearly: "Nietzsche casts a positive or negative judgment on Buddhism depending on whether he looks at it obliquely or indirectly, that is to say through reflection on Christianity . . . or directly, as being, ultimately, a nihilism, a symptom of being exhausted by life" ("Nietzsche et le bouddhisme," p. 127).

[15] Purushottama, in this connection, speaks of Nietzsche's "'instrumentalist' involvement with the philosophies of Europe's Other, using Asian thinking to challenge Christianity and the 'décadence' of the Western intellectual tradition." B. Purushottama, "Nietzsche as 'Europe's Buddha' and 'Asia's Superman'," *Sophia* 47(3), 2008: 359–76, at p. 375. See also Mistry, *Nietzsche and Buddhism*, p. 44; Figl, "Nietzsche's Encounter with Buddhism," p. 234; E. Scheiffele, "Questioning One's 'Own' from the Perspective of the Foreign," in Parkes, *Nietzsche and Asian Thought*, pp. 31–47, at p. 42; Frazier, "A European Buddhism," pp. 146–7; Vanderheyde, *Nietzsche*, pp. 169ff.; and Droit, *L'oubli de l'Inde*, pp. 188–9.

[16] *EH* "Warum ich so weise bin" §6. See also *A* §15.

[17] *EH* "Warum ich so weise bin" §6: "No reaction could be more disadvantageous for the exhausted: such affects [the affects of *ressentiment*] involve a rapid consumption of nervous energy, a pathological increase of harmful excretions."

Christianity's, Buddhism's goal is actually attainable: "They claim cheerfulness, stillness, absence of desire to be the highest goal, and they *attain* this goal. Buddhism is not a religion in which one merely aspires for perfection: perfection is the normal case."[18] What are we to think of such hyperbolic enthusiasm in light of the distinction between Nietzsche qua pro-Buddhist anti-Christian polemicist and a soberer Nietzsche concerned with life-negation in all of its forms?

To begin with, it is important to recognize that Nietzsche did indeed take the Buddhist fight against *ressentiment* to be far healthier for *décadents* than the moralizing Christian crusade against sin.[19] In the same way as he genuinely thinks Buddhism, as a soberly anti-metaphysical religion, "is a hundred times colder, more veracious, more objective" than Christianity,[20] Nietzsche does see great value in Buddhism's condemnation of *ressentiment* as an unhealthy affect. At the same time, it is obvious that Nietzsche can only be telling half the story here. In so far as his ethics is an expression of life-negation, the Buddha must still be harboring what Nietzsche calls "*ressentiment* against reality."[21] This, after all, is what lies behind the *décadents*' moral condemnation of the actual world, i.e. the realm of becoming. Behind any judgment "life is evil," or "becoming is no good," lurks a hidden *ressentiment*. As a *décadent* movement, Buddhism is a religion of *ressentiment* against reality and, as a plain nihilist, the Buddhist's will to nothingness exhibits an underlying desire for revenge against life. We are faced with a second apparent contradiction, then. Though the accomplished Buddhist is "beyond *ressentiment*," he is also still ensnared in *ressentiment*.

How could Nietzsche both praise Buddhism for fighting *ressentiment* and condemn it for harboring *ressentiment*? What is required is a distinction between two levels, or layers, of *ressentiment*. *Ressentiment*$_1$ operates at the surface level of conscious intention. It is explicitly directed toward certain persons and manifests itself as envy, hatred, resentment, aversion, vengefulness, etc. *Ressentiment*$_2$, in contrast, is subconscious and attitudinal. It grows out of the *décadent*'s general feeling of discontent, discomfort, and dissatisfaction with this painful world of flux, contradiction, and becoming. It is a pre-reflective, unarticulated, and subliminal will to take revenge on life.

[18] *A* §21.

[19] At *EH* "Warum ich so weise bin" §6, Nietzsche makes it clear that he himself applied the Buddha's method in periods of deep agony. He is not entirely insincere, then, when he writes that the Buddha is a "profound physiologist" (*ibid.*).

[20] *A* §23. [21] *NL 1885–1887*, 2(127).

The nihilist *décadents'* invention of the *wahre Welt* – indeed, their very "metaphysical need" – is fueled by this more insidious *ressentiment.*[22]

Now, the example of Buddhism shows that *ressentiment*$_2$ can survive the destruction of the metaphysical fictions that initially grew out of it. What is more, the example of the Buddhist type shows that "*ressentiment* against reality," or *ressentiment*$_2$, can remain even when *ressentiment*$_1$ – the affect responsible for hating specific people and situations, seeking active revenge, etc. – is fought against and even removed. The contradiction in Nietzsche's view thus fades away. The accomplished, serene Buddhist is both beyond *ressentiment*$_1$ and still animated by *ressentiment*$_2$.

This distinction also makes it possible to gain a better understanding of what happens to passive nihilists in the midst of the nihilist crisis. Their inability to imagine a *summum bonum* other than non-existence after the death of God, or *brahman* – their inability to see any worth in becoming once the myth of Being has been debunked – is not due to a simple lack of imagination. Nor is it just a matter of laziness (as *décadents*, after all, exhaustion and weariness is their distinguishing feature). No, what lies behind the Buddhist worship of non-being qua ethical goal is exactly what lies behind the nihilist mentality's worship of God qua glorified *nihil.*[23] *Ressentiment*$_2$ remains the psychological ground of the passive nihilists' ideology. Buddhist ethics begins with a reaction; it begins with a vengeful, resentful "no" in the face of life. In fact, Buddhism's quest for "extinction" in non-being is really a laying bare of the life-negation that has always stood behind the nihilist mentality. It is life-negation in its purest, most honest form. Nothingness is no longer cloaked with a metaphysical garb and called God, Heaven, *brahman*, or the *Ding an sich*; instead, nothingness is explicitly and transparently aimed for.[24] As with all such life-negation, this longing for nothingness is a consequence of the weariness and irritability of *décadence.* And in spreading the doctrine of a "good life" geared toward non-existence, or death, the Buddha shows he is committed to the *décadent* program of revenge against life. *Ressentiment*$_2$ is what animates him.

[22] Of course the revaluation of the so-called "master morals," which in the Judeo-Christian context accompanied this metaphysical development, also brought the more conscious, intentional *ressentiment*$_1$ into play (see, on this point, *GM* I), but this should not prevent us from distinguishing *ressentiment*$_1$ from *ressentiment*$_2$.

[23] As I explained in Chapter I, the *wahre Welt* is arrived at through a pure and simple contradiction of the "actual world." As such, it is a grand nothing.

[24] Discussing the *décadent's* perennial desire for *unio mystica*, Nietzsche explains that it has really always been "the desire of the Buddhist for nothingness, *nirvāṇa* – and nothing more!" (*GM* I §6).

Nietzsche knew that the starting point for the "good life" in Buddhism is the realization that suffering is intrinsic to life. And, as I explain in Chapter 1, on this point he agrees with the Buddha. Living without suffering is a contradiction in terms, and to realize this is an essential step in any coherent response to the challenge of nihilism. As a post-theistic ethics, Buddhist ethics focuses on the very real phenomenon of suffering, on the psychology that underpins it, on appropriate responses to it, and so on. And while Nietzsche believes that Buddhism's focus on suffering, in and of itself, was quite apropos (not to mention refreshingly realistic and sober, in comparison to Christian morals), he nevertheless feels that Buddhism's attitude toward suffering is fundamentally unhealthy. As such, the great health envisioned by the Buddha is actually a state of great illness.

On Nietzsche's diagnosis, Buddhist ethics comports two fundamental features, both of which exhibit an unhealthy, typically *décadent* stance toward suffering. The Buddhist ideal of *nirvāṇa* concerns one's own suffering – the state of "extinction," after all, involves removing the very condition for experiencing pain. The Buddhist ideal of cultivating compassion, for its part, concerns the other's suffering. Nietzsche's assessment of each of these requires further discussion.

The Buddhist *summum bonum*, *nirvāṇa*, is expressive of a sober will to end suffering. As Nietzsche notes, "the question 'how can *you* escape from suffering?' regulates and limits the whole spiritual diet" in Buddhism.[25] *Nirvāṇa*, this "deepest sleep,"[26] is envisioned as a state of painlessness. In cosmological terms, it therefore stands for the end of the cycle of rebirth in a world of boundless suffering. On Nietzsche's analysis, bereft of the positive promise of Bliss in the realm of a Transcendent Being, the *décadent* Buddhist turns to the second-best thing, namely the negative promise of "not suffering" in the state of *nirvāṇa*, or nothingness. And in seeking to escape from the struggle of becoming to the peace and quiet of non-being, the Buddhist engages not only in life-negation, but also, and most fundamentally, in self-negation.

This comes out very clearly in the Buddha's four noble truths, which Nietzsche first read about in Schopenhauer's works.[27] Here, the great physician of Ancient India provides: (1) a statement of the condition to alleviate, namely suffering; (2) a diagnosis of what causes this condition, namely desire; (3) a prognosis asserting that suffering will effectively end if

[25] *A* §20. [26] *GM* III §17. See also *ibid.* §27.

[27] Schopenhauer discusses this central Buddhist teaching at *WWV II* L, pp. 716f. Nietzsche would also have been familiar with it from the works of early German Indologists and Buddhologists.

(and only if) desire is brought to cessation; (4) a prescription outlining what must be done in order to heal, i.e. to bring desire to an end, and with it suffering itself. It follows from (2) and (3) that the state of *nirvāṇa*, which (in psychological rather than cosmological terms) involves the total absence of suffering, can only be brought about through the destruction of desire. If step (1) relates closely to *décadent* life-negation, then, steps (2) to (4) relate to its practical corollary, namely self-negation.

Concerning step (1), it is important to see that the Buddhist desire to end suffering is already an expression of the Buddhist type's fundamental *décadence*. As an irritable *décadent*, the Buddhist suffers from an excessive susceptibility to suffering.[28] His weariness is such that he cannot but experience resistance – not to say contact in general – as painful. Nietzsche, in this connection, speaks of the *décadents*' "*instinctive hatred of reality*," which is "a consequence of an extreme capacity for suffering and excitement which no longer wants any contact because it feels every contact too deeply."[29] The consequence is the fundamental hedonism implicit in any form of *décadent* flight from suffering[30] and made explicit in Buddhism which, with its ethics, elevates "the hedonism of the weary" into "the highest measure of value."[31] It is as a *décadent* hedonist, then, that the Buddhist construes suffering as a problem to begin with and seeks to attain a state of painlessness. Nietzsche explains: "The only pleasure which anyone will still feel in the condition of exhaustion [i.e. *décadence*] is falling asleep . . . The exhausted want rest, relaxation, peace, calm – this is the happiness of the nihilistic religions and philosophies."[32] In this sense, the Buddhist quest for the painlessness of *nirvāṇa* remains, like practically all the ethical doctrines promulgated over the course of history, an expression of "the idiosyncrasy of *décadents*."[33] What all *décadents* want is no longer to suffer, and this is exactly what the Buddha offers. Of course, in constituting pain as something to be removed, he is already committed to life-negation. If there is no living without suffering, there is no absence of suffering without absence of life.

The fight against desire which aims to bring suffering to an end, accordingly, is a fight against life. In this way, from life-negation one gets to self-negation. This finds its clearest expression in steps (2) and (3) of the Buddha's foundational teaching. Suffering has its origin in desire, claims the Buddha. It follows from this that desire must end if suffering is to end. The strategy employed to attain *nirvāṇa* is therefore comparable to that of

28 *A* §20. 29 *Ibid.* §30. 30 *Ibid.* 31 *NL 1887–1888*, 10(190). See also *ibid.*, 9(35).
32 *NL 1888–1889*, 14(174). 33 *EH* "Warum ich ein Schicksal bin" §7; *GD* v §6.

the Russian fatalist[34] who lies down in the snow and allows his instinct to freeze, as it were, so as to expend as little of the scarce energy he has left. The fight against desires, passions, and instincts found in Buddhism is a natural, not to say instinctive, response typical of *décadence*.[35] The *décadents* suffer continually because of their extreme weariness; their energy levels are so low, so to speak, that any form of contact, any encountering of resistance, is experienced as painful. It follows that terminating suffering involves removing the very conditions for entering into conflictory (and thus by definition painful) contact with people, things, and situations. Rid of desire, will, ambition, determination, vision, aspiration, hope, etc., Buddhists lie down in the snow and allow themselves to go numb. Without desire, there is no struggle, no resisting and resistance, no disappointment. In short, there is no suffering. Free of desire, the *décadent* Buddhists put up no resistance. Frozen in the snow of passionlessness, they enter the "deepest sleep"[36] of *nirvāṇa*.

This ideal of "destroying desire" in order to bring suffering to cessation falls squarely within the framework of what Nietzsche calls unselving morals (*Entselbstungsmoral*). "Unselving" is the essence of life-negating ethics.[37] The ethics of unselving involves a battle against one's passions, instincts, and desires – against one's very *will*, in short.[38] As such, unselving is life-negation in its most concrete articulation, i.e. as *self*-negation. Will, desire, passion, the instincts of growth and expansion, etc. – these are what are most fundamental to the human being. Living implies willing.[39] Consequently, fighting one's will is tantamount to fighting one's own vitality. It is life-negation through self-negation. In the Buddhist's case, it is thus the praxis of unselving that delivers the stated goal of ending suffering. Through self-negation – the destruction of desire – Buddhists attain their fundamentally life-negating goal – the cessation of suffering. Of course, in applying the method of unselving to numb *décadents* in this way, the Buddha is, once more, elevating the "idiosyncrasy of the *décadents*" into an imperative.[40] He is delivering to the weary their happiness, i.e. painlessness, by encouraging

nirvana as "deepest sleep"

[34] See *EH* "Warum ich so weise bin" §6 for Nietzsche's rapprochement between Russian fatalism and the Buddha's medicine.

[35] See, in this connection, *GD* II §11: "To *have* to fight the instincts – that is the formula of *décadence*."

[36] *GM* III §17. [37] *EH* "Warum ich so weise bin" §6.

[38] *Ibid.* "Warum ich solche gute Bücher schreibe" *M* §2; *ibid.* "Warum ich ein Schicksal bin" §7; and *GD* V §1.

[39] *JGB* §259. See also *ibid.* §13. Nietzsche's views on the primacy of willing in human psychology and on the will to power more generally will receive a detailed discussion in Chapter 3.

[40] *EH* "Warum ich so weise bin" §6.

them to put their instincts and passions to sleep, to become numb and offer no resistance – in short, to unselve themselves. Thus is reached the great sleep, the nothingness, the anti-life, of *nirvāṇa*.

For Nietzsche, the supreme life- and self-negation of desirelessness is not great health, it is great sickness. The ethics of unselving both grows out of and accentuates the illness of *décadence*. Having said this, as a component of a genuinely post-theistic ethics, Nietzsche also distinguishes Buddhist unselving from previous unselving morals. The traditional forms of such morals rely on a strict dichotomy between the pure soul as the abode of reason and source of goodness, on the one hand, and the corrupt body, seat of desires, passions, and instincts, on the other.[41] Such dualism is rejected in Buddhism, which gets rid of the very notion of a soul. Nevertheless, though this is no longer done from the standpoint of the pure soul – let alone of a Transcendent Good – the Buddha continues to regard desires, passions, and instincts as something to be fought against and eventually destroyed. His is no longer a moral fight, which construes suffering as the result of corporeal sin encroaching upon the divine soul and miring it in this corrupt world. Nevertheless, in so far as it seeks to end suffering, the Buddha's fight remains a fight against what is most essential to living, i.e. desiring. Rid of its "core self," the empty shell of the pain-ridden psycho-physical apparatus is declared harmful and evil. The ethical goal is to bring it to cessation – to "put it out" in *nirvāṇa*. This requires the unselving, or destruction, of whatever survives the disappearance of the self/soul.

Accordingly, Nietzsche's comments on Buddhism's healthy "egoism" in his anti-Christian polemics must be taken with a grain of salt. At *A* §20, Nietzsche presents the Buddha as combating the prevalent trend in the Indian ideology of his day, which had "damaged the instinct of personality by subordinating it to the 'impersonal'" and had thereby led to "the loss of the individual's interest in himself."[42] The Buddha, on this version of events, fought this trend "with a rigorous attempt to lead even the most spiritual interests back to the *person*. In the Buddha's doctrine, egoism becomes a duty."[43] On the face of it, Nietzsche seems to be saying that the Buddha combated unselving and reinstituted a healthy self-concern. As in prior cases of contradictions between Nietzsche as Antichrist and Nietzsche as Anti-Buddha, the pro-Buddhist claim is not entirely insincere. Nietzsche does indeed think that *décadent* Buddhists' concern with their

41 See, in this connection, *EH* "Warum ich solche gute Bücher schreibe" *M* §2 and *ibid.* "Warum ich ein Schicksal bin" §8.

42 *A* §20. 43 *Ibid.*

own suffering constitutes a relatively enlightened focus on oneself, one's psychology, one's physiology, etc., especially when contrasted to the Christian focus on sin and guilt, or systems aimed toward an impersonal merging with the Cosmic Whole, such as Upaniṣadic Brahmanism. At the same time, irrespective of the relative healthiness of Buddhists' egoistic concern with their own suffering, it is clear that Nietzsche regarded the method which the Buddha developed to combat suffering as involving the very same unselving as that which lies at the heart of all nihilistic morals. The Buddhist's self-concern might be less deluded than the metaphysical basis of more traditional ethics, but it nevertheless delivers an unhealthy, self- and life-negating ethics of unselving. One must be sick and weary to long for *nirvāṇa*, and progressing toward *nirvāṇa* makes one sicker and wearier.

The *décadence* at the heart of Buddhism is also disclosed in the second major feature of its ethics. When it comes to the suffering of others, Buddhism prescribes the "cultivation of compassion." Nietzsche had not failed to notice how important compassion, equanimity, and altruism are to the Buddhist path. He sees a profound connection between Buddhism and compassion in particular.[44] And indeed, if Buddhists espouse the quintessentially unhealthy attitude to their own suffering – i.e. the desire to end it – it makes perfect sense that they should also adopt the quintessentially unhealthy attitude to the other's suffering – i.e. compassion.

Why does Nietzsche think compassion is so unhealthy? At the most superficial level of analysis, we find Nietzsche's simple claim that the glorification of compassion found in Buddhism exhibits a "deadly hatred for all suffering in general."[45] The Buddhist dreads suffering. This dread extends beyond self-concern into a refusal to accept the other's suffering as well. Of course, since suffering is of the essence of life – so that a "hatred of suffering" is really tantamount to "a hatred of life" – Buddhists' cultivation of compassion is really just an extension of their underlying life-negation.[46]

[44] Nietzsche makes frequent reference to the preeminence of compassion in European moral discourse as a "Buddhistic pre-movement." *NL 1887–1888*, 9(126). See also *ibid.* 1885–1887, 9(126), *GM* "Vorrede" §5, and *JGB* §202. Nietzsche's views on compassion will be discussed in detail in Chapter 5. In the present context, my concern is with his views on compassion as they relate to his views on Buddhist ethics.

[45] *JGB* §202.

[46] See, in this connection, *NL 1888–1889*, 15(13), where compassion is described as a form of life-negation.

But there is also a close connection between compassion and self-negation. Nietzsche, in this connection, claims that compassion involves self-hatred,[47] even "mortification of self."[48] Behind such hyperboles lies the soberer view that compassion is part of the program of unselving. Fighting self-concerned instincts and passions and destroying desire, as the Buddhists do, is what turns a person into a meek, discreet, unassuming, and compassionate pushover. Devoid of desire, Buddhist types put up no resistance and avoid all possibilities of conflict; full of compassion, they look out for others, are forever sensitive to the ways in which they may harm them or be in their way, share their worries and their concerns, and so on. It is through the self-negation of unselving that they cultivate compassion.

This ethical program follows from the very same sources which also produce suffering as a problem and its elimination as a desideratum. Commenting on the "physiology of *décadence*," Nietzsche explains:

> *The instinctive exclusion of any antipathy, any hostility, any boundaries or divisions in man's feelings:* the consequence of an extreme capacity for suffering and excitement which experiences any resistance, even any compulsion to resist, as unendurable *displeasure* ... and finds blessedness (pleasure) only in no longer offering any resistance to anybody, neither to evil nor to him who is evil ... The fear of pain, even of infinitely minute pain – that can end in no other way than in a *religion of love*.[49]

It turns out, then, that the rise of compassion, which is a key virtue in any "religion of love,"[50] is not just an unavoidable outcome of unselving. It is instrumental to the *décadents'* goal of reducing the risk of interpersonal conflict to nil. As such, the Buddhist injunction to cultivate compassion is, once more, a mere expression of the "idiosyncrasy of *décadents*."[51]

In a similar vein, Nietzsche also attributes to *décadents* a spontaneous propensity to suffer in the face of the other's suffering. This results from their inability to "resist stimuli."[52] As a result, placing compassion on a pedestal, as the Buddhists do, is little more than "parading [one's weakness] as one's virtue" – a true "masquerade," in Nietzsche's opinion.[53] The idea here is that compassion is actually a very common sentiment, which reflects little more than the irritable *décadent*'s inability not to suffer in the face of another person's suffering.

[47] *JGB* §202. [48] *NL 1888–1889*, 15(13). [49] *A* §30.
[50] Consider, in this connection, *M* §132, *FW* §§338 and 345, and *NL 1884*, 25(178).
[51] *EH* "Warum ich ein Schicksal bin" §7. See, in this connection, *EH* "Warum ich so weise bin" §4, where Nietzsche claims that only *décadents* could praise and promote compassion as a virtue.
[52] *EH* "Warum ich so weise bin" §4. [53] *FW* §377.

Part of Nietzsche's idea, in this connection, is that compassion is intrinsically enfeebling. Compassion implies being hurt, damaged, or injured by the other's suffering. Nietzsche explains:

> Compassion stands in opposition to the tonic emotions which enhance the energy of the feeling of life: it has a depressive effect. One loses force when one pities . . . Compassion is the *practice* of nihilism . . . Compassion persuades to *nothingness*![54]

Here we touch upon Nietzsche's biggest problem with compassion. It is a depressive affect. I am weighed down with the other's suffering. It is not surprising that weak and irritable *décadents* should be so prone to it, just as they are prone to anything that might weigh them down.

There is something quite intuitive about Nietzsche's claim on this point. When physically exhausted, I find that I am far more sensitive and vulnerable to the plight of others. Other people's sadness will trouble me more, a melodramatic score underlining the tragic fate of a character in an otherwise terrible movie will bring tears to my eyes, a baby's squeal on the bus will put me in a state of profound discomfort, etc. I seem, in this regard, to have far less self-control. This is what Nietzsche was pointing to. In his view, the Buddhist celebration of compassion as a great virtue is no different from that found in Christianity and other nihilistic systems – it is born of *décadence* and it champions self-enfeeblement.

Accordingly, it should come as no surprise that Buddhist ethics reserves such a special place for compassion. Buddhism, after all, has non-being as its target. A compassionate, altruistic propensity always to think of others rather than oneself hurries the *décadent* down the road toward the great *nihil* through ever greater enfeeblement and unselving. In so far as compassion weakens and exhausts, it is quite naturally the modus operandi of those on the path to the great sleep of *nirvāṇa*.

There is a dense and intricate web of interconnections between Nietzsche's critique of Buddhism as a fundamentally unhealthy response to the nihilist crisis and his stance toward Schopenhauer's philosophy. In assuming the role of Anti-Buddha, Nietzsche is also assuming that of Anti-Schopenhauer.[55] This is in large part because Schopenhauer's understanding of Buddhism, of its relation to Christianity, and of its relation to his own philosophy had a considerable impact on Nietzsche's own understanding of

[54] *A* §7.

[55] As Purushottama writes, Nietzsche's "evaluation of Buddhism as 'nihilistic' and 'spiritually enervating' grew in proportion to his rejection of Schopenhauer's pessimism" ("Nietzsche as 'Europe's Buddha'," p. 361).

Buddhism. As a result, it had a considerable impact on the way he positioned himself vis-à-vis his Indian counterpart. Throwing light on Nietzsche as Anti-Buddha thus requires a close examination of Schopenhauer's thought.

To Nietzsche's eyes, Schopenhauer's thinking is a clear and unmistakable case of history repeating itself. In Schopenhauer's thought, the European nihilist crisis delivers a laying bare of the life-negation at the heart of the nihilist mentality and of the metaphysics it had spawned over the course of Europe's history since Roman times. The result, as in India more than two millennia earlier, is an ethics at the heart of which lies an undisguised will to nothingness. Schopenhauer, in short, is to Europe what the Buddha had been to India. His ethics is the result of a passive nihilism which cannot but aim for non-being once Being is revealed to be a fiction.[56]

But is Schopenhauer's Will (essentially a spiced-up version of Kant's thing-in-itself) not a version of the myth of Being? Is it not a form of *wahre Welt* standing opposed to the merely "apparent world" of representations (*Vorstellung*)? If so, then Schopenhauer, unlike the Buddha, has *not* moved beyond the nihilist mentality's most potent myth. How, then, can his ethics be the result of passive nihilism? Is it not the case that passive nihilism can only take hold once the inebriating fictions of the nihilist mentality have begun subsiding, leading to a value withdrawal of sorts? How could this withdrawal have affected Schopenhauer, if his Will is a version of the fiction of Being? More generally, it seems surprising to see Nietzsche establishing a parallel between the Buddha – who had, as he knew quite well, rejected metaphysical thinking – and Schopenhauer – a metaphysician if ever there was one.

Nietzsche's view, however, concerns Schopenhauer's system as an *event* in the history of ideas, not just as a set of ideas. If his focus and interest were on Schopenhauer's ideas in and of themselves, the problems raised above would be fatal to the Buddhism–Schopenhauer rapprochement so central to Nietzsche's positive thinking. However, in so far as Nietzsche is interested in the larger trends at work in what may be called the history of nihilism, this rapprochement is not affected by the form – metaphysical vs. "positivist" – transparently life-negating thinking takes in the midst of nihilist crises.

Though Schopenhauer is a metaphysician, to Nietzsche's eyes he is also one of the seminal European figures responsible for killing God, and with him much of the fanciful nihilistic thinking that had held sway over Europe for so long. Certainly, the doctrine of the world as Will is a traditional

[56] See, in this connection, *NL 1885–1887*, 9(35).

metaphysical doctrine which pits a real realm of Being against a merely apparent realm of becoming, but to see only this would be to miss the significance of Schopenhauer's philosophy as an event in the history of philosophy and religion. Schopenhauer's version of Being is not God, but a blind Satan of sorts. His thing-in-itself is not Good, but Evil. The fact that there is something residually metaphysical about Schopenhauer's doctrine is barely relevant; what really matters is the undisguised life-negation that stands at its core. The world is evil, life is no good – that is what really matters about Schopenhauer's thought. And that, far more than the contingent metaphysical cloak it wears, is what delivers Schopenhauer's ethics of uncompromising life-destruction.

Fleshing out these rather abstract considerations requires a succinct outline of Schopenhauer's philosophy from a robustly Nietzschean perspective. First, it should be noted that apart from retaining the Kantian naivety of the thing-in-itself,[57] Schopenhauer had seen many things right. Schopenhauer argued that speaking of a self-caused or uncaused creator God is entirely incoherent.[58] What is more, he believed that the world is so obviously full of senseless suffering and sorrow that to posit an omnipotent, benevolent creator God makes no sense at all.[59] To Schopenhauer's eyes, the notion that this pain-ridden world was created by a benevolent God is at best a tasteless joke.

Schopenhauer also forcefully argued that nothing fundamental distinguishes humans from other entities in nature. In fact, he placed all types of events in the world – from the natural phenomena that take place among inanimate bodies to human behavior – on a single continuum.[60] There is only a difference of degree between a rock falling to the ground by virtue of the Earth's gravitational pull and my moving my arm toward an apple because I am hungry and I have just seen something that could nourish me.[61] When it comes to sentient beings, we humans are not so different from other animals, longing and striving as we do after futile pleasures and

Schopenhauer's thought

possibility / rejects idea of God

all events on a single continuum

[57] In the preface to *WWV 1*, Schopenhauer describes the work of Kant as "the most important phenomenon to have appeared in philosophy for two thousand years" (p. xv), though it transpires in the appendix of this work that the only thing Schopenhauer is really impressed with in Kant's philosophy is his doctrine of transcendental idealism. Schopenhauer, in this connection, refers to the transcendental ideality of time and space as "a proved and incontestable truth" (*WWV* 1, "Anhang: Kritik der kantischen Philosophie," pp. 496–7; see also *FM* §22).

[58] See the introduction to the 1847 edition of *WSG*, especially §8. Schopenhauer's argument is analytical. Since (1) everything happens for a reason and (2) even if something uncaused were to exist, it in turn could not cause anything, the very notion of a *causa sui* acting as "prime mover" is incoherent.

[59] On this point, see *FW* §357. [60] See *WWV 1* §29.

[61] This is a point Schopenhauer forcefully makes throughout *FmW*.

ephemeral goals with the same compulsion as that with which a plate is pulled to the ground after being knocked off a table.

This is underscored by what I call Schopenhauer's *empirical materialism*,[62] which led him to adopt a strict naturalist physicalism when it comes to the mind–body problem. As phenomenon, everything in the world is matter through and through.[63] As in Buddhism and Nietzsche's thought, there is no immaterial soul, no I.[64] Consciousness, for its part, is a purely physical phenomenon; it is the result of the brain's activity.[65] Atheism, determinism, naturalism, and physicalism – these are all positions Nietzsche also endorsed.

Nietzsche never ceased admiring Schopenhauer for these views. In some late passages, we find him praising Schopenhauer's "honesty": Schopenhauer, he writes, is the first to have reminded us that we are little more than beasts and that, fundamentally, we are "something stupid."[66] He taught, "long before Darwin ... the doctrine of *milieu* and adaptation," going so far – perhaps even too far for Nietzsche – as to reduce human will to reflexes which operate with the harsh "rigidity of the mechanistic process."[67] Nietzsche, in this context, rightly speaks of Schopenhauer's "*naturalisme*."[68] In short, he considered Schopenhauer to be one of those formidable characters who

[62] Schopenhauer's claim is that, as spatiotemporal phenomena, all things are material. This is because matter is the objective correlate of what he calls the "subjective form of the understanding," namely causality (*WWV I*, §4). The forms of sensibility *(Sinnlichkeit)* in Schopenhauer's epistemology are space and time, as they are for Kant. But Schopenhauer dispenses with Kant's complex analysis of the understanding (*Verstand*), leaving only causality as its "form." What understanding does, when perception occurs, is that it brings space and time together in the form of the "material object," which is thereby inferred as the "cause" of perception (see *WWV I* §4 and his early treatise on vision, *SF*, especially §1). Perceptibility and materiality thus imply each other: "Every object," Schopenhauer declares, "is matter as phenomenon" (*WWV II* XXIV, p. 349). It is appropriate, then, to speak of Schopenhauer's empirical materialism in the same way as Kant spoke of his empirical realism in contrast to his transcendental idealism. In Schopenhauer's case, of course, empirical materialism is tempered by a robust transcendental immaterialism (*à la* Berkeley), namely the world as Will.

[63] *WWV II* XXIV, p. 349.

[64] Schopenhauer forcefully rejects "the I, or ... its transcendent hypostasis called 'soul'" as "an extremely old and universal fundamental error" (*WWV II* XVIII, p. 222).

[65] For Schopenhauer's naturalist epistemology, based exclusively on the subject's brain and nervous system, see *WWV II* I.

[66] *NL 1887–1888*, 9(178). [67] *Ibid.*

[68] *Ibid.* Nietzsche's "naturalist" interpretation of Schopenhauer runs against the grain of the interpretation favored by a number of contemporary Schopenhauer scholars, namely, D. Hamlyn, *Schopenhauer* (London: Routledge and Kegan Paul, 1980), Berman, "Schopenhauer and Nietzsche," J. Young, *Schopenhauer* (London: Routledge, 2005), and R. Wicks, *Schopenhauer* (Oxford: Blackwell, 2008). All of these scholars defend some version or another of what I call the *animist interpretation*, which holds that Schopenhauer's doctrine is that a singular, immaterial World Soul stands behind all phenomena. Nietzsche's view is far closer to that of Janaway, who notes that "in attempting to subsume human action within a wider account of 'striving and active' forces, [Schopenhauer's] aspiration is as much to naturalize humanity as it is to humanize nature."

actively contributed to the death of God by rejecting the metaphysical errors on which more traditional *wahre Welten* are built – theology, mind–body dualism, the attendant superstition of the immortal personal soul, the fiction of libertarian free will, etc.

In accordance with these negative views, Schopenhauer also insisted that the world is nothing but a fluctuating torrent of senseless fear, pain, and striving. There is no Good *wahre Welt* world behind it all, for Schopenhauer. What there is instead is an Evil *wahre Welt*. This, on a Nietzschean analysis, is where Schopenhauer allowed his underlying *ressentiment* to get the better of him.

Consider, in this connection, Schopenhauer's metaphysics of Will. Schopenhauer's contribution to metaphysics consisted in qualifying the Kantian thing-in-itself both quantitatively and qualitatively:[69] the thing-in-itself (1) is singular[70] and (2) may best be described as a blind, unconscious, and purposeless striving, which Schopenhauer calls Will.[71] The essence of all things is thus a singular, groundless, and purposeless Will. As such, this ever-striving Will does not strive "to satisfy" any desire or need in particular – like all forms of causality, that of motivation, after all, applies only to the world as representation.[72] So, unlike in the case of volition as we normally understand it, the Will strives with no particular goal "in mind," so to speak.[73] As a result, satisfaction is fundamentally foreign to the Will's groundless and therefore unquenchable thirst.[74] The Will, then, is not only spontaneous, blind, and aimless, it is also continually unsatisfied. The implication is that because all of us are, in our essence, nothing other than Will, our lives cannot but be endlessly and unavoidably painful.

C. Janaway, *Self and World in Schopenhauer's Philosophy* (Oxford: Clarendon Press, 1989), p. 203; see also B. O'Shaughnessy, *The Will: A Double Aspect Theory* (Cambridge University Press, 1980), p. xxv. Nietzsche would perhaps go even further than this and claim that in making all of nature the expression of the same basic dynamic principle, Schopenhauer was more than anything naturalizing humans.

69 Of course, this overtly contradicts Kant, who wrote: "Never may the smallest thing be asserted of the thing-in-itself which underlies these phenomena" (*KrV* A49/B66). But Schopenhauer was happy to bite this bullet (see the Appendix to *WWV 1*).

70 *WWV 1* §23. 71 *Ibid.* §§19f.

72 Indeed, like any metaphysician (on Nietzsche's model), Schopenhauer infers the properties of his *wahre Welt* through a contradiction of the properties of this world. If everything in this world happens for a reason (on this key point, see Schopenhauer's *WSG*), the Will is on the contrary entirely groundless (*WWV 1* §29).

73 At *WWV 1* §23, Schopenhauer explains that the sentient subject's will is but a species of the metaphysical Will qua genus. Unlike the former, the latter presupposes neither consciousness, intention, nor goal-directedness. It should be noted that on Schopenhauer's account, unconscious activities such as digestion or the beating of the heart are instances of "willing." Even as it relates to the subject and her body, then, Schopenhauer's understanding of willing is markedly different from what is normally understood by the term.

74 *WWV 1* §57.

This is where Schopenhauer's metaphysics veers into psychology. The Will continuously and pointlessly strives just for the sake of striving. Other things, all of them pointlessly striving in their own ways, get in the way. Suffering, which corresponds to unsatisfied desire, to meeting obstacles, etc., thus pervades all of sentient existence.[75] When a desire happens to be satisfied, moreover, the metaphysical nature of the world – the groundlessness of the Will – ensures that another desire takes its place, whereby more suffering is occasioned, ad infinitum. If perchance all of one's desires are satisfied (which can only be a temporary state of affairs), then boredom and restlessness ensue. These are just other forms of suffering, or lack.[76] The forever fluctuating and changing nature of the world of phenomena, moreover, ensures that whatever may in theory makes us happy for longer periods of time eventually fades away before it stops making us happy (e.g. a loved partner who passes away). Such experiences are also eminently painful.[77]

This is the theoretical, metaphysical basis of what Schopenhauer calls pessimism. To Gottfried F. Leibniz's optimistic credo – "this is best of all possible worlds"[78] – Schopenhauer opposes his own pessimistic motto – this is the worst of all possible worlds. A world even slightly worse than the one we live in would be unsustainably chaotic, violent, and self-destructive, claims Schopenhauer.[79] As such, this world is nothing more than an endless torrent of pain and dissatisfaction with no redeeming features. And if it lacks any redeeming feature, it is because its painful character is not accidental. On the contrary, it follows from the world's deepest metaphysical nature. As a result, a lucid appraisal of the human condition leads to the conclusion that non-existence would be preferable to existence. Hence the life-negation at the heart of Schopenhauer's pessimism.

Schopenhauer's ethics, accordingly, is expressly geared toward self- and world annihilation. More precisely, his *summum bonum* involves "seeing through" the illusion by virtue of which life is affirmed and perpetuated. Indeed, a central concept of Schopenhauer's meta-ethics is the *principium individuationis*, which, after Śaṅkara, he also calls the "veil of *māyā* [literally "illusion"]."[80] The *principium* is what stands behind naive common-sense

Schopenhauer ↓ never free of suffering

[75] This argument is found at *WWV I* §56. [76] *WWV I* §57. [77] *Ibid.* §56.

[78] Leibniz's theodicy is presented in his 1710 *Essai de théodicée sur la bonté de dieu, la liberté de l'homme et l'origine du mal*, ed. J. Jalabert (Paris: Aubier, 1962).

[79] *WWV II* XLVI, pp. 669–70.

[80] Schopenhauer saw in the idea of the *principium* a clear area of overlap between transcendental idealism and Indian Brahmanical philosophy (*WWV I* §1). Though Schopenhauer showered merit on himself for seeing this, it turns out he was not that original. One of the most important texts Schopenhauer read (and reread until the end of his life) is Anquetil-Duperron's *Oupnek'hat*, given to him by Friedrich Majer in 1813 (the year Schopenhauer began writing *WWV*). In an appendix to his

realism.[81] The common person thinks of the world as a set of objects and of his own person as a real, independent entity distinct from other things. It is on the basis of this pre-reflective standpoint that all creatures in the world exhibit a fundamental egoism[82] and that the unitary Will appears to express itself in manifold desires and goals.

However, in so far as the illusion of the *principium individuationis* dissipates, individuals become less and less self-centered and increasingly concerned with others. In this connection, Schopenhauer argues that the two pillars of morality – justice (not harming) and benevolence (actually helping) – are grounded in a deeply metaphysical phenomenon, namely compassion.[83] Compassion involves seeing through the illusory veil of plurality and recognizing that we are all just one. Justice and non-harming form the first stage in this process – one refrains from committing injustice because the difference between self and other is starting to fade. Active benevolence is the next – one desires to help others and relieve them of their sorrow as one moves closer to the realization that self and other are really one. The "conception that abolishes the difference between ego and non-ego . . . described by the Hindus as *māyā*, i.e. illusion, deception, phantasm, mirage," Schopenhauer writes, is directly related to the "metaphysical basis of ethics," which "consists in *one* individual once more recognizing in *another* his own self."[84] Compassion, then, is the practical correlate of metaphysical monism.

Virtuous behavior, however, is only the first stage. Indeed, the compassion of the person who has pierced the veil of *māyā* actually gives way to complete self-abnegation.[85] This happens when the compassionate person becomes so utterly disillusioned with the Will and its groundless cruelty that he finally decides to chastise it in and through his own person.[86] If ethical behavior is already counter-natural – egoism and the *principium*, after all, comprise the sole "natural standpoint" – it is only a weak shadow of what happens to the compassionate sage who fully appreciates the illusory nature of individuation and fully turns against his own nature. Full world destruction then becomes his goal.

Latin (re)translation of a Sanskrit–Persian translation of some Upaniṣadic texts, Anquetil-Duperron suggests that the Upaniṣads are essentially saying the same thing as Kant does in the "Transcendental Aesthetic" section of his *KrV* and encourages philosophers and fellow Jesuits to explore this connection. See "De Kantismo," in H. B. Anquetil-Duperron, *Oupnek'hat* (Paris: Argentorati, 1801–2), vol. II, pp. 711–24. Schopenhauer visibly heeded Anquetil-Duperron's call.

[81] *WWV I* §53.

[82] At *FM* §14, Schopenhauer claims that egoism is the "natural standpoint" and explains: "The principal and fundamental incentive in men, as in the animal, is egoism . . . Therefore, as a rule, all of his actions spring from egoism." See also *WWV I* §61.

[83] See *FM* §17. [84] *Ibid.* §22. [85] *WWV I* §70. [86] *Ibid.* §68.

The truly radical nature of Schopenhauer's vision now comes to the fore. Sexuality, as the most essential feature of the will of sentient beings,[87] is the first target of asceticism. Indeed, the ascetic looks beyond his own limited existence and sees that the eradication of the Will and the destruction of nature requires putting an end to the regeneration of the species.[88] Schopenhauer's suggestion, in a passage such as *WWV* I §68, that animals would stop reproducing if humans did, is far from convincing – as is his reliance on idealism to show that nothing would survive the death of the last subject – but at least it has the virtue of making his view very clear. The ascetic saint, through celibacy, embarks on a mission to destroy the entire world.

But this is only the first step. Celibacy and desirelessness are quickly followed by the quest for shame and injury, closely followed by active self-destruction.[89] In this way, the ascetic eventually attains a level of complete willlessness. Everything natural about him has been destroyed. His will is entirely quieted. He attains "complete sanctification and salvation, whose phenomena are the state of resignation previously described, the unshakable peace accompanying this, and the highest joy and delight in death."[90] This is the result of the most advanced denial of the will.

In sum, Schopenhauer's ethics is based on an attendant mystical ability to "see through" the web of appearance and on a mystical motive, namely compassion. Such compassion leads the virtuous man from justice to asceticism. Ultimately, Schopenhauer's salvation (*Erlösung*) consists in the complete inverse of "natural health." If nature and world are Will to life, then Schopenhauer's salvation, precisely, is the complete negation of self and world. Schopenhauer's ethical ideal, in short, is a counter-health, a saintly sickness.

Most fundamentally, the metaphysics behind Schopenhauer's ethics is of relative indifference to Nietzsche. The real problem, for him, is Schopenhauer's jump from the merely descriptive claims that humans are animals, that the world is full of suffering, that struggle is an essential feature of existence, etc., to the normative claim that non-existence is preferable to existence and therefore ought to be aimed at through active self- and life-negation. It is in doing this – in shifting directly from God to *nihil* as the goal of the "good life" – that Schopenhauer's

[87] See, in this connection, Schopenhauer's comments on the primacy of the sexual impulse at *WWV* II XLIV.
[88] *WWV* I §68. [89] *Ibid.* [90] *Ibid.*

thought consists in a repetition of what had happened in India with the Buddha.

In fact, Schopenhauer is Nietzsche's primary source for this idea. From 1840 onward Schopenhauer became an avid reader of all things Buddhological and an ardent proponent of this robust Indian "pessimism."[91] Schopenhauer was particularly struck by what he saw as the many similarities between his thought and the Buddha's. In the second volume of *WWV* (1844), he writes: "Should I wish to take the results of my own philosophy as the standard of the truth, I would have to accord to Buddhism preference over the other [religions]."[92]

Schopenhauer's endorsement of Buddhist views is most obvious in his use of the terms *saṃsāra* and *nirvāṇa* in his later works. He explicitly equates his description of the world as an ocean of suffering with the Buddhist doctrine of *saṃsāra*: "This is *saṃsāra* and everything therein denounces it and, more than everything else, the human world, where moral depravity and baseness and intellectual incapacity and stupidity prevail to a fearful extent."[93] More importantly yet, Schopenhauer equates his vision of salvation with Buddhist *nirvāṇa*. Describing the self- and life-negating ascetic, he writes: "He willingly gives up the existence that we know; what becomes of him instead is in our eyes *nothing*, because our existence in reference to that is *nothing*. The Buddhist faith calls this *nirvāṇa*, i.e. extinction."[94] For the late Schopenhauer, the Buddha's *nirvāṇa* and his own concept of salvation consist in the same ideal.

Schopenhauer's discovery of Buddhism is also what led him to declare that pessimism is the ethical core of all true religion. Not only did his monism and his doctrine of "seeing through the *principium individuationis*" have antecedents in the primeval religion of India (Brahmanism), but his assessment of the world as an ocean of sorrow also found corroboration in Buddhism. Rejecting Judaism, Islam, and Ancient Greek religion as crude optimistic creeds, Schopenhauer groups Christianity, Brahmanism, and Buddhism together as genuine, i.e.

91 As Droit writes, Schopenhauer "transfers unto Buddhism a form of fascinated enthrallment born with the century with regard to Brahmanism" (*L'oubli de l'Inde*, p. 182). For a full list of Schopenhauer's Indological and Buddhological sources, see the appendix to M. Nicholls, "The Influence of Eastern Thought on Schopenhauer's Doctrine of the Thing-in-Itself," in C. Janaway (ed.), *The Cambridge Companion to Schopenhauer* (Cambridge University Press, 1999).

92 *WWV II* XVII, p.186. 93 *PP* II §114.

94 *WW II* XLIV, p. 640. Schopenhauer also attempts to clarify his definition of the Will in terms of the relation between denial of the will and *nirvāṇa*: "We can only describe it [i.e. the Will] as that which has the freedom to be the Will to live, or not to be it. For the latter case, Buddhism describes it with the word *nirvāṇa*" (*ibid.*).

pessimistic, religions.[95] True to the Romantic "Indomania" that informed his understanding of Indian religions,[96] he believed Christianity had Indian roots. "The teachings of Christianity," he claimed, "are to be derived in some way from those first and original religions."[97] This is because "the spirit of Christian morality is identical with that of Brahmanism and Buddhism."[98] The ethical essence of these genuine pessimistic religions, moreover, is precisely what Nietzsche would later call life-negation: "The great fundamental truth contained in Christianity as well as in Brahmanism and Buddhism" is "the need of salvation from an existence given up to suffering and death."[99]

Schopenhauer, moreover, considered Buddhism to be superior to Christianity and Brahmanism because it did not clothe its ethical goal in a superfluous theological coating. For instance, he contrasts the Brahmins and their desire for "*mokṣa*, i.e. reunification with *brahman*," with the Buddhists, who "with complete straightforwardness describe the matter only negatively through the term *nirvāṇa*, which is the negation of this world, or of *saṃsāra*."[100] Nevertheless, in Schopenhauer's mind, all of these spiritual visions had the same hidden sense. Be it *unio mystica*, reunification with Brahman, or attaining Heaven, what the pessimistic creeds really aim for is the negation of the Will to life, or *nirvāṇa*/extinction. Buddhism is simply the most honest and straightforward expression of pessimism among world religions.

In light of this, it is patently obvious that Schopenhauer is the principal source for Nietzsche's philosophy of religion and, by extension, for his views concerning the nihilist mentality, the construction of the *wahre Welt*, Buddhism, etc. Nietzsche's idea that a tacit spirit of life-negation hides behind any ethical or religious quest for Being is a Schopenhauerian idea. When he claims that the desire for *unio mystica* has always been "the desire of the Buddhist for nothingness, *nirvāṇa*,"[101] or that "all pessimistic religions call nothingness God,"[102] Nietzsche is essentially presenting a

[95] *WWV* II XLIV, p. 623: "In truth it is not Judaism with its 'all is good,' but Brahmanism and Buddhism that . . . are akin to Christianity . . . By virtue of its origins, Christianity belongs to the ancient, true, and sublime faiths of mankind. This stands in contrast to the false, shallow, and pernicious *optimism* that manifest itself in Greek paganism, Judaism and Islam."

[96] The phrase "Indomania" was coined by R. Gérard in his *L'Orient et la pensée romantique allemande* (Nancy: Thomas, 1963). On the German Romantic enthrallment with India which provides the background for Schopenhauer's engagement with Indian religions, see also Halbfass, *India and Europe*, A. L. Willson, *A Mythical Image: The Ideal of India in German Romanticism* (Durham, NC: Duke University Press, 1964), and Schwab, *La Renaissance orientale*.

[97] *WWV* II XLIV, p. 623. [98] *Ibid.*, p. 633. [99] *Ibid.*, p. 628. [100] *WWV* II L, p. 698.

[101] *GM* I §6. [102] *Ibid.* III §17.

rehashed version of Schopenhauer's philosophy of religion. More importantly, Nietzsche's idea that something like Buddhism (in this case Schopenhauer's thought itself) is what takes the place of Christianity once its theistic optimistic garb as been cast away is precisely Schopenhauer's position.

Of course, Nietzsche turns the tables on Schopenhauer. If Schopenhauer showered merit on himself for seeing eye to eye with the Buddha when it comes to the denial of the will,[103] Nietzsche accuses Schopenhauer of remaining caught in moralistic, life-negating thinking even after he has seen through so many of Christianity's fictions. For Nietzsche, being to Europe what the Buddha had been to India is no ground for praise – on the contrary. And of course Nietzsche also innovates. He attributes life-negation to *décadence* and *ressentiment* and records its impact far beyond the realm of religion, into the far wider domain of metaphysics of Being in general. Nevertheless, the fact remains that the source for the Schopenhauer–Buddhism rapprochement so central to Nietzsche's assessment of Buddhism is Schopenhauer's philosophy itself. It is on the basis of Schopenhauer's own self-understanding that Nietzsche interprets Christianity, Brahmanism, Buddhism, and Schopenhauer's philosophy as expressions of the same will to nothingness.[104] And it is on this basis that he sees the Buddha's and Schopenhauer's ethics as two cases of the same passive nihilism.

More specifically, Nietzsche sees Buddhist philosophy and Schopenhauer's thought as two forms of the same type of pessimism, namely the pessimism of the weak.[105] This is the pessimism that goes beyond the merely descriptive claim that living implies suffering and draws the normative implications that it is undesirable to live and desirable to die. Nietzsche certainly believed that the Buddhist form of such pessimism is far more mature that Schopenhauer's European variety.[106] Not only is Buddhism beyond metaphysics, it is also more dignified and sober when it comes to concrete ethics. It does not recommend such extreme self-mortification as Schopenhauer's ethics does.[107] It does not give in to explicit self-hatred and active guilt.

Nietzsche views Buddhism through Schopenhauer

[103] Halbfass reports Schopenhauer's pride at expressing timeless, universal truths. Schopenhauer, he writes, "presented his own teachings as the standard and fulfillment of the Indian teachings" and therefore "saw himself as standing at the pinnacle of knowledge" (*India and Europe*, p. 114). This makes sense only in the context of the early Romantic obsession with India as the primeval source of all culture, philosophy, and religion. In this sense at least, Schopenhauer remained an Indomaniac well after the German intelligentsia had moved beyond Romantic Indomania.

[104] This is most obvious at *GM* III §17. [105] *NL 1888–1889* 14(25). [106] *NL 1884*, 25(16).

[107] See, on this point, R.-P. Droit, "Schopenhauer et le Bouddhisme: une 'admirable concordance'?," in E. von der Luft (ed.), *Schopenhauer* (Lewiston: Edwin Mellen Press, 1988), pp. 123–38.

The unselving it prescribes is far more moderate and less sentimental, unrestrained, and plebeian. Buddhism, in short, is less Christian than Schopenhauer's doctrine.[108] Nevertheless, these superficial differences change nothing in the fundamental affinity between these two forms of life-negating ethics. Both fail to see any value in a world of endless struggle bereft of its Peaceful Other-worldly counterpart and therefore condemn this world. Both respond to the death of God by elevating non-existence into a goal. Both lay bare the life-negation at the heart of nihilistic religions and philosophy. And both reveal the underlying pessimism of the weak which has always stood behind apparently optimistic systems like Christianity or Platonism.[109]

As such, the Buddha and Schopenhauer reveal themselves to be *décadents* whose thinking and teaching are fueled by a profound *ressentiment* against reality. Their only virtue is their honesty – unlike in prior philosophies and religions, non-being is the explicit destination of their ethical program.

It is with exasperation that Nietzsche contemplated the possibility that history might repeat itself, not just at the level of ideas, but of entire cultures. Knowing very well that Buddhism had quickly spread across India and Asia and thus had become the dominant Asian ideology for over a millennium, Nietzsche was concerned that the nihilist crisis Europe was now facing could

[108] At *JGB* §56, Nietzsche derides Schopenhauer's pessimism as "half-Christian."

[109] This is why presenting Nietzsche's positive philosophy as a response to Buddhism is *not* to overestimate the role Indian religions played in Nietzsche's intellectual development. Admittedly, Nietzsche is a profoundly Eurocentric thinker primarily concerned with Europe and its predicament. Accordingly, it might be argued that his concern with Buddhism is secondary and somewhat superficial. After all, did Nietzsche not depict himself primarily as Antichrist, and only secondarily and elusively as Anti-Buddha (in an obscure unpublished fragment)? Is it not the case that the late Nietzsche's real bête noire is Christianity, not Buddhism? Is life-affirmation not presented as an antidote to Christian *décadence*, rather than to Buddhism? But careful analyses of Nietzsche's texts – especially against the backdrop of Schopenhauer's thought – reveal that these are not either/or questions. Nietzsche agrees with Schopenhauer that Christianity and Buddhism share a common core. Unlike Schopenhauer, however, he thinks this core is rotten. Buddhist pessimism is the life-negation at the heart of the nihilist mentality *laid bare*. Its *nihil*ism is what is always already there, lying latent behind Christian optimism, Platonism, Idealism, and any system based on the fiction of Being. Buddhism is just more realistic, clearer, and less ensconced in the rabble's hatred of the elite. In its essence, however, it does not differ from Christianity. In fact, it is what Christianity could turn into after the death of God, under the guise of Schopenhauerian pessimism, as Schopenhauer himself had proclaimed. Seen in this light, countering Buddhist life-negation with a diametrically opposed philosophy of life-affirmation is part of Nietzsche's wider project of battling Christianity. In fact, Nietzsche's real target is neither Christianity nor Buddhism as such, but the *décadence*, *ressentiment*, and life-negation that stands at their root. And in so far as it is only in Buddhism that such life-negation becomes entirely transparent and self-aware, it is against the model of this post-metaphysical offshoot of the nihilist mentality that Nietzsche formulates his antipodal vision of a life-affirming great health. There is no contradiction, then, between Nietzsche as Antichrist and Nietzsche as Anti-Buddha. If anything, his role as Anti-Buddha is far more fundamental.

lead to the rapid expansion of Schopenhauerian pessimism over the entire European continent. In view of Schopenhauer's immense popularity in late nineteenth-century Europe,[110] Nietzsche's fears seemed vindicated.

Nietzsche, in this connection, spoke of the silent rise of a new European Buddhism "slowly gaining ground everywhere in Europe."[111] Buddhism's second incarnation as Schopenhauerian pessimism, to Nietzsche's eyes, was "the greatest danger."[112] The pessimistic credo – "Sleep is good, death is better – really / The best would be never to have been born"[113] – threatened to engulf all of Europe now that Christian optimism had been undone. In short, Nietzsche feared that the nihilist crisis might give way to a deeper *décadence*, to a will to *decline* itself. This, for Nietzsche, was the greatest risk the nihilist crisis could involve – a *décadent* ideology envisioning a state of great health which really stands for death. Pessimism of the weak had prevailed over India after its nihilist crisis. The same could happen once more in Europe. This, for Nietzsche, was the most fundamental threat presented by the nihilist crisis.

Like all crises, however, the nihilist crisis also involves a great opportunity. Nietzsche, accordingly, does not only see danger in the nihilist crisis, but also promise. Indeed, passive nihilism is not the only possible response to the nihilist crisis, nor explicit pessimism of the weak its only possible outcome. On the contrary, Nietzsche envisions an "inverse ideal" – an ideal which, unlike the Buddha's or Schopenhauer's, moves resolutely "beyond good and evil."[114] Indeed, Nietzsche is not only an Anti-Buddha in that he condemns Buddhist life-negation. More than anything, he is an Anti-Buddha in that he sketches a new, inverse ideal of great health – an ideal of life-affirmation.

The first point to make in this connection is that Nietzsche does not see in the (European) death of God and the nihilist crisis that ensues something inherently or necessarily nihilistic (in the sense of the nihilist mentality). Admittedly, there are passages in which Nietzsche claims that pessimism (of the weak) precedes and prepares the terrain for the nihilist crisis.[115]

110 Droit's "La fin d'une éclipse?" in R. P. Droit (ed.) *Présences de Schopenhauer* (Paris: Grasset et Fasquelle, 1989), pp. 7–23, provides an excellent account of the wide diffusion of Schopenhauer's ideas between the 1870s and the 1930s. Schopenhauer is arguably the modern philosopher who had the widest and most lasting influence on both popular and erudite culture.

111 *NL 1885–1887*, 2(144). See also *JGB* §202 and *GM* "Vorrede" §5.

112 *NL 1885–1887*, 2(131).

113 This is an excerpt from H. Heine's "Morphine," in *Sämtliche Werke* (Hamburg: Hoffman und Sampe, 1863), vol. XVIII, p. 169. See, in this connection, Nietzsche's praise of Heine at *EH* "Warum ich solche gute Bücher schreibe," *GT* §4.

114 *JGB* §56.

115 *NL 1885–1887*, 2(131).

Nevertheless, it is clear that in these passages Nietzsche can only be telling half the story. Yes, Nietzsche does say that God dies at the hands of Christian morality – namely of Christian, turned scientific, truthfulness.[116] And yes, he does describe modern science with its puritan lie-denouncing atheism as a new embodiment of the nihilist "ascetic ideal."[117] But God's death is not only the work of the *décadent* pessimism of the weak. More specifically, those involved in the process of Christianity's self-overcoming are not weak *décadents* alone, there are also strong, healthy "free spirits" (*freie Geister*) – like Nietzsche – who are heirs to Christian truthfulness as well, yet turn around and wield what they have inherited from Christianity to actively and joyfully destroy *décadent* nihilist myths.[118] This is why Nietzsche vocally celebrated the demise of theism.[119]

Indeed, while the death of God does create a value vacuum, which risks being filled by the weak pessimism of a New Buddhism, this is not the only possible outcome. This is obvious in *FW*, where Nietzsche highlights the ambiguous nature of the death of God. While "some kind of sun seems to have set, some old deep trust turned into doubt" so that "our old world must appear somewhat more autumnal, more distrustful, stranger, 'older,'" it is also true that:

> at hearing the news "the old god is dead," we philosophers and free spirits feel illuminated by a new dawn; our heart overflows with gratitude, amazement, foreboding, expectation – finally, the horizon seems clear again, even if it is not bright; finally we may set out in our ships again; set out to face any danger; every daring of lovers of knowledge is allowed again; the sea, *our* sea, lies open again; there perhaps has never been such an "open sea."[120]

Another text to consider in this connection is the following passage from *GD*:

History of an error

1. The true world, attainable to the wise, the pious, the virtuous – he dwells in it, *he is it*.

   (Oldest form of the idea, relatively sound, simple, convincing. Transcription of the statement "I, Plato, *am* the truth.")

[116] *FW* §357 and *GM* III §25. This point was also discussed in Chapter 1. [117] See *GM* III §§24–5.

[118] It is Nietzsche who coined the now common phrase "free spirit." On the figure of the free spirit as an anti-Christian visionary, see *MM* II §186, *M* §201, *FW* §343, and *GD* IV. The great honesty (*Redlichkeit*) and pitiless truthfulness of the free spirit is highlighted at *JGB* §230, in particular.

[119] The idea that nihilism qua crisis might present an opportunity is very explicitly stated in certain passages – e.g. *FW* §346 and *FN, 1885–1887*, 2(45) – where it is viewed as an opportunity to seek new values and to come to the realization that this world, and human existence more generally, might be far more valuable than formerly thought.

[120] *FW* §343.

2. The true world, unattainable for the moment, but promised to the wise, the pious, the virtuous ("to the sinner who repents").
   (Progress of the idea: it becomes subtler, more enticing, more incomprehensible – *it becomes a lady*, it becomes Christian . . .)
3. The true world, unattainable, improvable, cannot be promised, but still just thought of as a consolation, a duty, an imperative.
   (The same old sun, fundamentally, but shining through mist and skepticism; the idea grown sublime, pale, northerly, Königsbergian.)
4. The true world – unattainable? Unattained in any case. And since unattained also *unknown*. Therefore also not consoling, not redeeming, not binding: how could something unknown provide us with a duty?
   (Grey morning. First yawns of reason. Cockcrow of positivism.)
5. The "true world" – an idea no longer of any use, not even a duty any more – an idea which has become useless, superfluous, *therefore* a refuted idea: let us destroy it!
   (Bright day; breakfast; return of *bon sens* and cheerfulness; Plato blushes out of shame; all free spirits run riot.)
6. We have abolished the true world: what world remains? Maybe the apparent world? . . . But no! *with the true world we have also destroyed the apparent world!*
   (Midday; moment of the shortest shadow; end of the longest error; zenith of mankind . . .)[121]

Here, Nietzsche takes us through the various stages of the *wahre Welt*'s history in the West – from the Platonic notion of Being, or the Good, via Christian theology and Kantian metaphysics, to the nihilism of godlessness. What is notable about this passage is the cheerfulness involved in the "end of the longest error." Here, the nihilism associated with the end of the error of the *wahre Welt* is not a dark cloud that casts the shadow of meaninglessness over the world, but the bright sun that washes away the haze of theistic lies and opens up new horizons. Nihilism as the lack of any absolute values after the death of God is barely even a crisis here. It is a merry, sun-lit breakfast after a long night of confusion.

By paying attention only to passages suggesting that an underlying, arch-*décadent* pessimism of the weak is responsible for the death of God, one fails to distinguish between nihilism as mentality, nihilism as event, and nihilism as response to the nihilist crisis.[122] In reality, the death of God that provokes

[121] *GD* IV.
[122] This seems to be a problem for both Deleuze and Williams (see Deleuze, *Nietzsche*, p. 170, and Williams, "Introduction," p. xiii). Heidegger gets it wrong the other way around, as it were. He reads Nietzsche's texts on the European nihilist crisis (*WM* §§2f.) – the crisis of meaninglessness attendant upon God's death – as texts about nihilism in general, and thus about the entire "history" of human thought (Heidegger, *Nietzsche*, vol. II, pp. 63–71). As a result, he finds himself making the awkward claim that nihilist *wahre Welt* metaphysics was somehow born of a sense of aimlessness, valuelessness,

the nihilist crisis is not only the work of reactive weak pessimists in too advanced a state of decline to continue to uphold higher values, it is also the work of healthy free spirits who actively wield Christian truthfulness for creative purposes.

It is important, in this connection, to highlight the intimate connection between the arch-Christian lie-denouncing truthfulness that kills God and *décadence*. Indeed, the death of God consists in the self-overcoming of *décadence*. This opens up two major possible scenarios:[123] the death of God may be an instance of *décadence* overcoming one of its embodiments to make way for a yet more pernicious form of *décadence* (i.e. European Buddhism), *or* it may give rise to a full overcoming of *décadence*. The first scenario is what had taken place in India. Nietzsche's wish was that things would happen differently this time around in Europe.

Herein lies the hope, the promise, the opportunity in the nihilist crisis. On Nietzsche's horizon is a process of healing which attacks the illness of *décadence* at its root. In the clarity of full daylight, he begins to envision a state of great health fundamentally opposed to the Buddha's, free of any residual attachment to the fictions of Good and evil. Nietzsche writes:

> Anyone who for a long time has struggled, as I have, with a mysterious desire to think down to the depths of pessimism and redeem it from the half-Christian, half-German narrowness and plainness with which it has most recently been expressed, namely in the form of Schopenhauerian philosophy; anyone who has truly looked with an Asiatic and trans-Asiatic eye into – and underneath – the most world-denying of all possible ways of thinking (beyond good and evil and no longer helplessly under the spell and delusion of morality, like the Buddha and Schopenhauer) – this person may, without really intending it, have opened his eyes to the inverse ideal: to the ideal of the most daring, lively, and world-affirming human being.[124]

This passage outlines Nietzsche's Anti-Buddhist, anti-*décadent* project. What he seeks to develop is the "inverse ideal" of the Buddha's. Against the backdrop of the danger of life-negation, Nietzsche sees the antipodal promise of life-affirmation.

and meaninglessness similar to that which Europe faces after the death of God. As such, Heidegger entirely misses Nietzsche's fundamental insight that the *wahre Welt* is first and foremost a product of *ressentiment* against existence. It is not just that the *décadent nihilists* failed to find meaning and purpose in the world, but that their weaknesses prevented them from doing so and that, as a result, they could not but feel anger, resentment, and rancor against existence. Next to this, it is a relatively minor shortcoming of Heidegger's that he fails to see that the crisis of valuelessness only arises after God dies.

[123] Cf. Chapter 3, where I discuss a third scenario. [124] *JGB* §56.

To "redeem pessimism," Nietzsche will oppose his pessimism of strength to the moralistic pessimism of the weak.[125] Instead of drawing the conclusion that life is an evil to be ended on the grounds that it is full of suffering and struggle, such pessimism affirms that life is good and desirable not just in spite of, but because, it is ever turbulent and painful.[126] Indeed, Nietzsche articulates an ethical ideal which involves saying yes to life and therefore yes to suffering in direct opposition to the Buddhist ideal of ending/negating suffering. Buddhism is to Nietzsche's eyes the purest, most transparent, and most mature expression of life-negation. This is why Nietzsche sees it as the ideal counter-model to develop his ethics of life-affirmation. Both Buddhist life-negation and Nietzsche's life-affirmation are founded on pessimism – both begin with a full acknowledgment of the inherently painful nature of existence – but the former belongs to the lamenting and lamentable weak, while the latter belongs to the joyful strong.

Indeed, the Buddha and Nietzsche are harbingers of nihilism – destroyers of the same nihilist myths – yet their responses to the nihilist crisis are diametrically opposed. Nietzsche does not respond to the nihilist crisis by espousing a passive nihilism which meekly settles for non-being as a "second best" once Being is no longer an option. Instead, he endorses the very opposite of such nihilism; he endorses "active nihilism," a nihilism that destroys previous values in order to clear the way for new, positive, and healthy life-affirming values.[127] This is why he is the "antipode" *(Gegenstück)* of his Indian counterpart.[128]

Nietzsche's use of Buddhism as a counter-model for his ethics of life-affirmation becomes all the more obvious when one looks at the details of his positive vision. Recall how Buddhist ethics involves two central components: a specific stance toward one's own suffering – namely the desire to end it by attaining the state of *nirvāṇa* – and a specific stance toward the other's suffering – compassion as prime virtue. Not to suffer and to be fully compassionate – this is what Buddhism understands by "great health." Nietzsche is a perfect Anti-Buddha in this regard. The stances toward one's own and the other's suffering that are constitutive of his antipodal vision of great health are mirror images of those that form the core of

[125] *NL 1888–1889*, 14(25). See also *GT* "Versuch einer Selbstkritik" §1 and *NL 1885–1887*, 10(21).

[126] Pessimism of strength, Nietzsche even tells us, "finds senseless suffering the most interesting" (*NL 1885–1887*, 10(21)).

[127] *NL 1887–1888*, 9(35). On this point, see also Morrison, *Nietzsche and Buddhism*, pp. 22f.

[128] *NL 1882–1884*, 4(2).

nirvana vs. amor fati

Buddhist ethics.[129] To the desire to end suffering in *nirvāṇa*, he opposes the will to suffer in *amor fati*. To the Buddhist injunction to cultivate compassion, he opposes the overcoming of compassion. These are the two axes along which Nietzsche draws the opposition between life-negation and life-affirmation. Both these features of Nietzsche's inverse ideal need to be examined in greater detail.

As a sickly *décadent*, the Buddha constitutes suffering as the greatest problem in life. Its cessation is thus the supreme desideratum. In direct opposition, Nietzsche thus claims that the healthy attitude to suffering involves not even constituting it as a problem to be solved.[130] In fact, Nietzsche's great health involves the very opposite of ending suffering; it involves embracing and celebrating it. This celebration of suffering is what Nietzsche, after the Stoics, calls *amor fati* (literally "love of fate").

Nietzsche's *amor fati* is an anti-*nirvāṇa* in two regards. To begin with, it replaces the quietude of the Buddhist "cessation of suffering" with the turbulent exertion of one's full strength in the heroic affirmation and celebration of the entire world's suffering. Nietzsche's healthy type does not desire contentment, but growth. There is no "hedonism of the weary"[131] here. Instead Nietzsche's healthy types look for struggles. The endless sufferings of life do not discourage them, but urge them on. As obstacles that must be surmounted – resistances that must be overcome – painful events are the rungs of the strong type's ladder toward ever greater vitality, power, and energy.[132] Suffering will not stop such healthy types, or lead them to condemn life as a feeble weakling would. On the contrary, they will ever more suffering, ever more resistance, ever more life.

While the quest for *nirvāṇa* is motivated by the life-negating desire to end suffering which naturally follows from the weakness of *décadence*, the quest

[129] It is no surprise, then, to find Russell pitting Nietzsche against the Buddha in connection to ethics (*History of Western Philosophy*, pp. 737–9). In fact, Russell puts his finger on precisely the two topics I will discuss here, namely Nietzsche's and the Buddha's antithetical attitudes toward suffering and toward compassion.

[130] On the contrary, from a healthy perspective, suffering is not a problem, but an opportunity (*GD* I §8). This is a point I will explore in far greater detail in the next chapter. More generally, everything that will follow on the topic of *amor fati* is only background. Chapter 3 consists in a detailed discussion of the affirmation of suffering in *amor fati*. Likewise, the cursory discussion on the overcoming of compassion below is only a preamble for the more detailed analyses of Chapter 5. The goal, for now, is to show how Nietzsche's ethics of life-affirmation is the mirror image of (alleged) Buddhist life-negation.

[131] *NL 1887–1888*, 10(190). For further comments on the relation between *décadence* and hedonism, see *A* §30.

[132] See *NL 1887–1888*, 11(76) and (77).

for *amor fati* is motivated by a life-affirming will to suffer naturally expressive of the strength of ascendance.[133] This finds its clearest articulation in the test of eternal recurrence:

> *The heaviest weight* – What if some day or night a demon were to slip into your loneliest loneliness and said to you: "This life as you now live it and have lived it, you will have to live once again and innumerable times again; and there will be nothing new in it, but every pain and every joy and every thought and sigh and everything unspeakably small or great in your life must return to you, all in the same succession and sequence, even this spider and this moonlight between the trees, and even this moment and I myself. The eternal hourglass of existence is turned over again and again – and you with it, you speck of dust!" Would you not throw yourself down and gnash your teeth and curse the demon who spoke thus? Or have you once experienced a terrific moment when you would have answered him: "You are a god, and never have I heard anything more divine." If this thought gained power over you, it would, as you are, transform and perhaps crush you; the question on everything, "Do you want this once more and innumerable times again?" would lie on your behavior as the heaviest weight! Or how well disposed would you have to become to yourself and to life to *desire* nothing *more fervently* than this ultimate eternal confirmation and seal?[134]

Nietzschean healthy types are those who would be strong enough to bear this "heaviest of weights." Their life-affirmation is such that they would desire all of existence with all of its suffering to repeat infinitely. *Amor fati* thus consists in embracing the eternal recurrence of the world's limitless suffering. It is the very opposite of the Buddhist's painless state of *nirvāṇa*.[135] *Amor fati*'s role as an anti-*nirvāṇa* is even more obvious from the cosmological perspective. While *nirvāṇa* implies final liberation from the cycle of birth and death (*saṃsāra*), *amor fati* involves the will to repeat the full "circle" of one's pain-ridden life over and over again indefinitely.[136]

[133] On the contrast between Nietzsche's and the Buddha's attitudes to suffering, see also S. M. Amadea, "Nietzsche's Thirst for India: Schopenhauerian, Brahmanist, and Buddhist Accents in Reflections on Truth, the Ascetic Ideal, and the Eternal Return," *Idealistic Studies* 34(3), 2004: 239–62, at pp. 240 and 256–7.

[134] *FW* §341. The connection between the test of eternal recurrence and *amor fati* is made obvious in such passages as *EH* "Warum ich so klug bin" §10: "My formula for human greatness is *amor fati*: that one wants nothing different, not forward, backward, not in all eternity; not merely bear what is necessary, still less conceal it . . . but *love* it."

[135] Indeed, when Nietzsche first speaks of his "inverse" Anti-Buddhist ideal at *JGB* §56, he speaks of "the ideal of the most daring, lively, and world-affirming human being, one who has learned not only to accept and bear what has been and is, but who also wants to have it over again, *just as it was and as it is*, throughout all eternity, calling out insatiably *da capo* ['from the beginning']." It is obvious that Nietzsche is alluding to *amor fati* and its embracing of eternal recurrence here.

[136] Whether eternal recurrence in Nietzsche's thought is actually supposed to be cosmological is not a question I need to answer in the present context. In my opinion, Nietzsche has no cosmological view.

In short, by articulating his view of great health in terms of the Stoics' *amor fati*, Nietzsche selects an Ancient doctrine which perfectly suits his purposes for propounding a counter-Buddhism. Nietzsche's healthy types long for the endless cycle of *saṃsāra*, rather than its end in *nirvāṇa*. In a sense, *amor fati* is a will to *saṃsāra*.[137]

Turning, in light of this, to the psychology of Nietzsche's healthy type, it becomes obvious that he[138] is free of precisely that sickness which plagues the Buddhist type, and therefore also of the symptoms and behavior that accompany this sickness. Nietzsche's healthy type, in short, has overcome *décadence*. In direct opposition to the *décadent* Buddhist type, he is neither so weak and exhausted that he cannot bravely take upon himself the countless struggles of existence, nor so irritable that he cannot but constitute life's limitless suffering as a problem. On the contrary, he wants struggles and embraces suffering. He is a figure of *ascendance*, not *décadence*. Accordingly, Nietzsche's healthy type is entirely free of the principal symptom of *décadence*, namely *ressentiment*. Not only is he free of $ressentiment_1$, but, unlike the Buddhist type, the poison of $ressentiment_2$ – *ressentiment* against reality – has also entirely subsided in him. To take revenge on life does not even pass through his mind, since, healed of *décadence*, he does not feel harmed by life. This entirely rules out the ground for life-negation. Instead, he affirms life. And with life-affirmation comes the very opposite of Buddhist ethics' unselving, namely self-affirmation – a healthy self-love, a celebration of one's passions, instincts, and desires. If *nirvāṇa* is attendant upon the unselving involved in the "destruction of desire," *amor fati*, on the contrary, involves embracing and nurturing the desires and passions which make one alive and healthy.

This closely connects to the second axis of the diametric opposition between the Buddha's and Nietzsche's ethics. Nietzsche inverts the role of compassion in his counter-Buddhist therapy. While the Buddha prescribes the cultivation of compassion as an essential feature of the path toward great health, Nietzsche prescribes the complete overcoming of compassion as a necessary condition for attaining the paroxysm of life-affirmation.[139] The

But this is of no relevance for my immediate purposes. In the present context, what really matters is (1) eternal recurrence as a test of strength and (2) the embracing of eternal recurrence in *amor fati* as an anti-*nirvāṇa*.

[137] As Halbfass writes: "[Nietzsche's] own doctrine of 'eternal recurrence' affirms what the Buddha denies" (*India and Europe*, p. 128).

[138] Because Nietzsche seems committed to the deeply problematic view that only men can attain great health – an opinion he does not share with the Buddha – I will use masculine forms alone when discussing his ethics.

[139] *EH* "Warum ich so weise bin" §4.

cultivation of compassion, for Nietzsche, requires unselving. Continual concern with the other's weal and woe, a consistent sense of responsibility for others, etc., all of these things imply a diminution of self-concern, self-belittling, and self-effacement. Life- and self-affirmation, on the contrary, require a cold overcoming of all compassionate feelings.

What is more, Nietzsche sees compassion as a vulgar and inherently depressive emotion that only the irritable *décadent* with no emotional self-control could describe as a virtue. The real problem with it, however, is that it enfeebles and leads to a thirst for nothingness. From the healthy standpoint of life-affirmation, compassion is thus "more dangerous than any vice."[140] In so far as Nietzsche's therapeutic ethics aims for a great health of ascendance, not for the Buddhist great health of total *décadence*, it is only natural that, contra the Buddha, he should prescribe the overcoming of compassion, not its cultivation.

Nietzsche as Anti-Buddha. This phrase is the key to understanding Nietzsche's positive philosophy. It is the key to understanding his ethics of life-affirmation.[141] Nietzsche is an Anti-Buddha in that he stands resolutely

[140] *NL 1888–1889*, 15(13).

[141] It may be objected that I must be misrepresenting Nietzsche's thought because, at bottom, Nietzsche was in no way interested in upholding an ethical ideal. Indeed, is it not the case that there is something *décadent* in the very gesture of envisaging a state of great health? Is there not an implicit "saying no" to the world as it is in saying that anything "ought to be" different? Should a coherent active nihilism not be purely negative and critical? Should it not *only* destroy myths and fictitious values, and abstain from putting any new ones forward? Should it not involve overcoming the very need to overcome anything? The worry, in short, is that there is still a latent *ressentiment* against reality in pitting an "ought" (great health) against an "is" (quasi-universal *décadence*). Is there not something moralistic and *décadent* in diagnosing the illness of *décadence* itself? It seems inevitable, after all, that in any "yes" – "yes" to eternal recurrence, to *amor fati*, to this world of turmoil and contradiction – there is an implicit "no" – "no" to life-negation, to *décadence*, to *ressentiment*. It is important, however, to see that Nietzsche's no is not pronounced from the standpoint of the Transcendent, of Being, of pure Goodness, or of anything like this. It is a no pronounced from within this world; a no which in and of itself posits no world transcendence, no overcoming of the world, no negation of the world. Yet more importantly, it is a no that follows from a yes – yes to life and health, no to *décadence* and death – rather than a yes that follows from a no – no to life, yes to God. This is why active nihilism must go beyond the negative and still reactive domain of destroying myths, idols, and false "higher" values. It must also embark upon the truly active, creative project of forging new values and new ideals that are entirely immanent. It is for this reason that even the active nihilism Nietzsche opposes to Buddhism's passive nihilism is only an "intermediate pathological state" (*NL 1885–1887*, 9(35)). Nietzsche might reject all previous morals, but his thought is not devoid of a distinctive ethics. Though he may believe very few people can actually heal themselves, he is perfectly serious when he claims that "treatment of the sick" is one of the things that "actually deserves to be taken seriously in life" (*EH* "Warum ich ein Schicksal bin" §8). Indeed, beyond nihilism lies a new, life-affirming ethics geared toward a state in which one recovers from the malady of *décadence*. Such an ethics will invest this world of becoming, struggle, and pure immanence with value, worth, and purpose. Unlike previous morals, this is not an ethics of absolute values and categorical imperatives, but a path to great health.

beyond good and evil; unlike in the Buddha's (or Schopenhauer's) case, no underlying *ressentiment* against reality remains in his thinking. He is an Anti-Buddha in that his ethics of life-affirmation stands diametrically opposed to the Buddha's life-negating ethics; in that his vision of great health is the mirror image of the Buddha's. To the Buddha's *nirvāṇa*, Nietzsche opposes his *amor fati* – a perfect anti-*nirvāṇa*. To the Buddhist's cultivation of compassion, Nietzsche opposes the overcoming of compassion. As Anti-Buddha, in short, Nietzsche combats everything the Buddha stands for – the fight against desire, instinct, and passion, unselving, self- effacement and negation, etc. – by presenting an opposed ethics of unconditional life- and self-affirmation. His (active) nihilism, his (strong) pessimism, and his ideal are all the "inverse" of the Buddha's nihilism, pessimism, and ideal. Nietzsche and the Buddha begin from the same nihilist ground, but head in opposite directions from there. Nietzsche, in this way, is both the Buddha of Europe and the "antipode" of his Indian counterpart.

Nietzsche as anti-Buddha

↓

life-affirmation

N + B = Shared principles,

differ in virtues, response to principles (practice)

PART II

Suffering

CHAPTER 3

Amor fati *and the affirmation of suffering*

As the highest expression of great health, *amor fati* is the heart of Nietzsche's ethics of life-affirmation. And while there is much to gain from understanding it as a deliberate anti-*nirvāṇa*, this is by no means an exhaustive description of Nietzsche's ethical ideal. Certainly, *amor fati* is the vision Nietzsche qua Anti-Buddha propounds as the "inverse ideal" of the Buddha's, but there is more to this ideal than just being an inverse. In broader terms, there is more to life-affirmation than simply being the opposite of life-negation. What is called for, then, is an examination of *amor fati* in its own right, which sets it within the broader context of Nietzsche's philosophy.

This is the task at hand in the present chapter. In the next, Buddhist moral psychology will likewise be examined in its own right, which will then make it possible to assess Nietzsche's *amor fati* vs. *nirvāṇa* opposition from an external, exegetically informed standpoint. In this way, we will move beyond the historical dimension of Nietzsche's relation to Buddhist philosophy – in terms of the influence of, engagement with, and responses to Buddhism in Nietzsche's thought – and move into the comparative, philosophical domain of the relations between Nietzsche's positive, ethical thought and Buddhist moral psychology.[1] To begin, however, we must look at Nietzsche's ethics of life-affirmation in and of itself.

Amor fati is the pinnacle of life-affirmation. Given Nietzsche's views on the character of life, the implication is that *amor fati* involves an unconditional affirmation of suffering. To embrace and celebrate life is to embrace and celebrate suffering.[2] To *will* life is to *will* suffering. This is because life

[1] I will proceed in the same way in Part III. Accordingly, Chapter 5 will be devoted to Nietzsche's ideas on compassion and its overcoming, while Chapter 6 will examine Buddhist views on compassion before plunging into the comparative domain.

[2] Janaway is thinking along the same lines when he writes that, in the context of Nietzsche's philosophy, to give suffering a meaning is to give life a meaning. C. Janaway, *Beyond Selflessness: Reading Nietzsche's Genealogy* (Oxford University Press, 2007), p. 239.

implies struggle, conflict, disorder, unpredictability, destruction, impermanence, and decay, and that all these things are painful. Consequently, to get to the bottom of life-affirmation – let alone of its supreme expression in *amor fati* – it is necessary to get a firm grasp on what exactly it is Nietzsche understands by "suffering" (other than "that which characterizes life" and "that which should be affirmed"). By taking us to the heart of his philosophy, examining Nietzsche's thoughts on suffering is the surest way to comprehend *amor fati* in all of its dimensions.

Unfortunately, suffering is one of the hardest things in Nietzsche's philosophy to get a firm grasp on. In terms of slipperiness, it comes second only to nihilism. Indeed, an attempt at reconstructing a "theory of suffering" on the basis of Nietzsche's writing delivers a frustratingly contradictory model. Indeed, when suffering is treated as an affect – as one would assume it should be – what is arrived at is not a story with a few inconsistencies, but two accounts, which are internally consistent, yet diametrically opposed. What is most disquieting is that these two models happen to be opposed precisely in relation to the most central concept of Nietzsche's ethics, namely that of health. I will provide a quick outline of each of these two models.

On the first of Nietzsche's two accounts, the affect of suffering promotes health. A good point of entry into this model is the (now proverbial) aphorism which Nietzsche coins in *GD*: "*From life's school of war* – What does not kill me makes me stronger."[3] Here we find the general idea that strength, or health, grows by facing adversity. In biology, this is the principle behind vaccination, for instance. To begin with, however, we ought to set the big idea aside for a moment and dwell on Nietzsche's use of the first-person pronoun. This is no mere stylistic trick. On the contrary, it is positively enlightening.

Nietzsche, it is important to remember, credits the excruciatingly painful illness that afflicted him throughout his writing career with making him decisively stronger and healthier.[4] More specifically, it is what "brought [him] back to reason" by allowing him to see through the follies of Schopenhauerian pessimism[5] and, more importantly yet, providing the

[3] *GD* I §8.

[4] *NW* "Epilog" §1: "I owe a *higher* health to it [my illness], a health that becomes stronger from everything that does not kill it!" In reading passages such as this one, it is important to keep in mind the distinction I drew in Chapter 1 between health as conventionally understood in the medical sciences and the *ethical* concept of health on which Nietzsche's positive philosophy hinges.

[5] *EH* "Warum ich so klug bin" §2. See also *MM* II "Vorrede" §5: "It is a fundamental cure against all pessimism . . . to become sick in the manner of these free spirits, to remain sick for quite a while, and

impetus for him to "turn [his] will to health, to life, into philosophy."[6] More generally, Nietzsche explains that it is his agonizing illness and the deep suffering it caused him that afforded him some of the key psychological insights that form the background of his oeuvre.[7] It is by experiencing states of decline (*décadence*) first-hand and observing the effect of illness on his mind and his behavior that Nietzsche became aware of the psychological effects of *décadence* and of the affects of *ressentiment* that follow from it – in short, of how the weak feel and think.[8] This is what allowed him to gain insight into what lies at the core of life-negation, to abandon this unhealthy attitude to life, and to gain the higher health of life-affirmation. On Nietzsche's autobiography,[9] then, suffering was a necessary condition for becoming truly health – instead of killing him, his illness made him stronger.

Of course, the idea that suffering is an agent of health is by no means limited to Nietzsche's autobiographical comments. In fact, the oft-ignored first half of the *GD* aphorism – "*from life's school of war*" – provides a good clue as to where this theory of suffering originated. The phrase "life's school of war" is an unambiguous reference to Heraclitus. One of the few philosophers with whom Nietzsche felt any true affinity,[10] Heraclitus was the first to teach that all things emerge from struggle, grow by facing adversity, and

then, slowly, slowly, to become healthy, by which I mean 'healthier,' again." It goes without saying that the pessimism he refers to here is pessimism of weakness (namely, Schopenhauer's or the Buddha's pessimism).

[6] *EH* "Warum ich so weise bin" §2.

[7] This is obvious from several passages in *EH*, though the idea is by no means expressed in Nietzsche's "autobiography" alone. For instance, there is a distinctly self-referential air to passages like *FW* "Vorrede" §3, *M* §114, and *JGB* §270, where Nietzsche extols the heightened insight and sensibility of the sufferer.

[8] Nietzsche might be criticized for using the rather unreliable method of introspection to formulate broad generalizations about human psychology. This is a valid point, though I think Nietzsche should be judged on the basis of his results, so to speak, not of his method. In my opinion, there is much to gain from positing *décadence* as a widespread human condition and *ressentiment* as a fundamental psychological mechanism, though the theory, like any other, also has its limitations.

[9] Nietzsche denounces past philosophies as unconscious autobiographies which owe more to their author's predispositions, physiologies, and (primarily moral) biases than to any genuine "impersonal" insight (*JGB* §6). What is supposed to distinguish his own philosophy from that of his forebears is not that it is not autobiographical, but that it is a "conscious autobiography" (Berman, "Schopenhauer and Nietzsche," p. 180). Even Nietzsche's concern with the allure of Buddhism for a *décadent* Europe faced with the nihilist crisis is rooted in the attraction Buddhism exerted on him in the early years of his illness, as his 1875 letter to Carl von Gersdorff attests (*NB 1875–1879*, 495) – on this point, see also Morrison, *Nietzsche and Buddhism*, p. 15, and Amadea, "Nietzsche's Thirst for India," pp. 239–41.

[10] *EH* "Warum ich so gute Bücher schreibe" *GT* §3; see also *GD* III §2. Heraclitus first impressed Nietzsche when he was a young philologist in Basle. This is clear from Nietzsche's lectures from the late 1860s and early 1870s (collected in *VP*), as well as from *PtZG*. In his lectures on "pre-Platonic" philosophers, many important strands of Nietzsche's later thought are anticipated in his treatment of Heraclitus, especially his rejection of substance metaphysics.

eventually fade away in the great fiery torrent of becoming – in short, that "war is the father of all things."[11] Heraclitus describes the cosmos as a "fire ever-living, kindled in measures and in measures going out."[12] The idea, as Nietzsche understood it, is that everything arises and passes away; that the universe is a dynamic process analogous to combustion rather than a static, unmoving Whole. Permanence, Endurance, and Being, Heraclitus recognized, are little more than "empty fiction[s]."[13] This is the worldview that underpins the *GD* aphorism. The world as Heraclitus understands it is a torrent of struggle governed, as it were, by the law "what does not kill you makes you stronger."

However, what is most significant about Heraclitus' role in Nietzsche's development is not his thought, but his example. Heraclitus served as a model for Nietzsche. And he serves as a model for him precisely in so far as his case confirms Nietzsche's "law." Heraclitus suffered greatly, yet only grew stronger from this ordeal. More specifically, Heraclitus had the honesty and courage to recognize this world of brutality, sorrow, and contradiction for what it is, but he also had the strength not to condemn it as unjust all the while.[14] Like Anaximander before him, Heraclitus came to the shocking realization that this world is one of turbulent becoming alone, and yet, unlike Anaximander, he refused to condemn the world as "guilty" and proclaimed its "innocence" instead.[15] Going further yet, Heraclitus rises to the occasion by translating his dread and horror before becoming into "brave joy."[16] Anaximander condemned the passing away of all things as unjust and this world of struggle and suffering as evil. He thus condemned the world of becoming as a whole. Heraclitus, in contrast, not only accepts it as it is, he even celebrates it as a "beautiful, innocent play of the aeon."[17] Instead of succumbing to life-negation in the face of the horrors of a senseless world of becoming, Heraclitus emerges stronger from the ordeal – he adopts the fundamentally healthy attitude of life-affirmation.

In short, Heraclitus' response to the existential vertigo caused by the realization that pain, contradiction, and struggle are of the nature of life provided Nietzsche with the very paradigm through which he came to

[11] Fragment LXXXIII.a, in C. H. Khan (ed.), *The Art and Thought of Heraclitus* (Cambridge University Press, 1981). It is of no relevance to the present discussion that Classicists are now calling into question whether any of Heraclitus' aphorisms can be attributed to Heraclitus himself, rather than to the Stoics in whose texts these fragments have been preserved. What matters is that Nietzsche attributed these aphorisms to Heraclitus.

[12] Fragment XXXVII.c–d, in Khan, *The Art and Thought of Heraclitus*. [13] *GD* III §2.

[14] On this point, see D. N. Lambrellis, "Beyond the Moral Interpretation of the World: The World as Play: Nietzsche and Heraclitus," *Philosophical Inquiry* 27(2), 2005: 211–21.

[15] *PtZG* §7. [16] *Ibid.* §5. [17] *Ibid.* See also *VP* §10.

understand great health. Heraclitus could not have attained the great health of rejecting his predecessor's life-condemnation in favor of life-celebration without being subjected to the tremendous suffering caused by seeing the world for what it is.[18] What did not kill Heraclitus made him stronger. Similarly, what did not kill Nietzsche also made him stronger.[19] Heraclitus' case, in short, is the model for Nietzsche's conception of a healthy attitude to suffering, and thus to life.

It is precisely this Heraclitean feat of not just accepting, but affirming and celebrating a horrible, unfair, and painful world, which is instantiated in Attic tragedy. According to Nietzsche's analysis of tragedy in *GT*, Dionysus qua pain-ridden, tumultuous torrent of destruction and becoming – Heraclitus' vision, in short[20] – is given an individuated, Apollonian form so that he may be worshiped.[21] In this way, this entire world of endless suffering can be deified and affirmed. The sense of the tragic which is the hallmark of Classical Greek culture is thus a Heraclitean trait. It takes the world and all its senseless horrors at face value, but it steers away from an unhealthy, Anaximanderian moral evaluation of it, and celebrates it instead as an aesthetic phenomenon. Moreover, it is precisely in suffering the truth that the world is a torrent of becoming and suffering – in being courageously open to the profound sorrows and turmoil of existence – that the Greeks were given the opportunity to transform their profound pain and dread into the great health of Dionysus worship. The story is the same as Heraclitus' or Nietzsche's – what did not kill the Greeks made them stronger.

In sum, it is from Nietzsche's early Classical studies that his Heraclitean rule "*from life's school of war*" emerged. What is more, his entire vision of

[18] Consider, in this connection, Nietzsche's description of Heraclitus' worldview at *PtZG* §5: "The eternal and exclusive becoming, the complete impermanence of everything real, which continuously acts and becomes and is not, as Heraclitus teaches, is a terrifying and appalling idea, and in its effect it is closest to the sensation with which one loses one's trust in the solid earth during an earthquake."

[19] Indeed, one gets the distinct impression in reading texts like *PtZG* or *VP* that Nietzsche identifies Anaximander with Schopenhauer and Heraclitus with himself, thus anticipating the development of German pessimism from a philosophy of life-negation to a philosophy of life-affirmation. While Anaximander/Schopenhauer is the life-negating pessimist who interprets the world as a moral phenomenon, Heraclitus/Nietzsche interprets the world as an aesthetic phenomenon and faces this pain-ridden torrent of becoming without flinching.

[20] Looking back upon the days of *GT* in *EH*, Nietzsche makes it very clear that Heraclitus' vision is "something essential for a Dionysian philosophy" ("Warum ich so gute Bücher schreibe" *GT* §3).

[21] Hence Nietzsche's notion of tragedy as an "Apollonian theodicy" (see *GT* §4, especially). This is no place to go into any detail concerning the Dionysus–Apollo opposition in *GT*. Suffice it to say that while Dionysus is the god of the undifferentiated and terrible whole of existence – so that, inexpressible and unfathomable as he is, he escapes any representation – Apollo is the dream-god of individuation and representation. Attic tragedy is the synthesis of the two – the representation, in Apollonian form, of Dionysus.

life-affirmation has its roots in this soil. The philosophy of life-affirmation is a Heraclitean "tragic wisdom."[22] The pinnacle of great health in *amor fati* is a tragic stance toward life/suffering. If Buddhist *nirvāṇa* provides the negative counter-model for this ideal, then, it is the tragic Greek's celebration of life through the worship of Dionysus that provides the positive model for *amor fati*. And in so far as this is the case, a central feature of Nietzsche's ethical doctrine is that attaining the great health of *amor fati* is not possible without suffering greatly.

Indeed, the cases of Heraclitus, of the tragic Greeks, and of Nietzsche all suggest that the *GD* aphorism really only tells half the story. It is not only that what does not kill you makes you stronger, but, more importantly, that in order to become strong, you must be under threat. Health, in Nietzsche's Heraclitean worldview, is not a state, but a dynamic process of overcoming;[23] as Nietzsche proclaims, "in order to become strong, you must need to."[24] Had the tragic Greeks been self-deluded optimists or weak theists putting their hopes in a Transcendent realm of Peace and Stable Being, they could never have attained the summit of cultural health that Attic tragedy represents.[25] Similarly, had Nietzsche been a relatively comfortable, (medically) healthy, self-contended, well-loved bourgeois, he would not have unmasked the *décadent*, *ressentiment*-fueled life-negation lurking behind Christianity, Buddhism, and German pessimism. More importantly yet, he would not have envisioned the tragic great health of life-affirmation.

Suffering, as a consequence, is not just *an* agent of health – it is *the* agent of health. Nietzsche describes it, in this connection, as a "lure to life" (*Reiz des Lebens*),[26] where life stands for any growth, be it intellectual, aesthetic, or physical. This model applies at both the macrocosmic level of cultures, peoples, and epochs and at the microcosmic level of particular individuals.

a health as overcoming process of

[22] Consider Nietzsche's words at *EH* "Warum ich so gute Bücher schreibe" *GT* §3:

> Nobody had ever turned the Dionysian into a philosophical pathos before: *tragic wisdom* was lacking . . . I had some doubts in the case of *Heraclitus*; I generally feel warmer and in better spirits in his company than anywhere else. The affirmation of passing away *and destruction* that is crucial for a Dionysian philosophy, saying yes to opposition and war, *becoming* along with a radical destruction of the very concept of "being"– all these are more closely related to me than anything else people have thought so far. The doctrine of "eternal return" . . . is nothing Heraclitus could not also have said.

[23] As Kaufmann writes, "Nietzsche – though he does not use exactly these expressions – defines health not as an accidental lack of infection but as the ability to overcome disease." Kaufmann, *Nietzsche*, p. 131.

[24] *GD* IX §38.

[25] Brogan observes: "Suffering, here, is the very force which underlies and makes possible the creative act." W. A. Brogan, "The Central Significance of Suffering in Nietzsche's Thought," *International Studies in Philosophy* 20(1), 1988: 53–62, at p. 57.

[26] *NL 1887–1888*, 11(77).

"The discipline of suffering, of *great* suffering," Nietzsche tells us, "has given rise to every enhancement in humanity so far,"[27] to wit: "Every important growth is accompanied by a terrible *crumbling* and *passing away*: Suffering ... belong[s] in the times of tremendous advances."[28] The idea is the same at the level of individuals. Danger, risk, and suffering are essential for happiness and growth – "the path to one's own heaven leads through the voluptuousness of one's own hell."[29] Nietzsche presents a poetic expression of the general principle that suffering qua resistance is a necessary condition for any increase in life and health in *Z*: "Where do the highest mountains come from? I once asked," confides Zarathustra, "then I learnt that they come from the sea."[30]

Ultimately, Nietzsche's conviction that health and life thrive on suffering, or are lured on by suffering, is grounded in an even more abstract principle. The idea is that resistance is an essential ingredient for any action. For Nietzsche, any genuine activity (as opposed to mere reactivity) requires some form of resistance, or some obstacle to overcome.[31] He illustrates the idea with a few examples: "The normal *dissatisfaction* of our drives, e.g. of hunger, of the sexual drive, of the drive to motion ... works as an agitation of the feeling of life ... This dissatisfaction ... is the greatest *stimulus* of life."[32] Nietzsche, in this connection, is careful not to make pleasure and pain plain opposites, claiming instead that they are "false opposites."[33] While pleasure indicates that an obstacle has successfully been overcome, pain does not merely signal the presence of an obstacle, but corresponds instead to the stimulation provided by the presence of an obstacle, of a resistance to be overcome.[34] Suffering, seen in this light, is enticing. It lures

27 *JGB* §225. See also *ibid.* §44.

28 *NL 1887–1888*, 10(22). In this fragment, this rule is applied to the nihilist crisis, which Nietzsche thus interprets as an opportunity for great advances.

29 *FW* §338. In this same passage, Nietzsche explains that "happiness and misfortune grow and ... *remain small* together" (*ibid.* §338; see, in this connection, Nietzsche's earlier thoughts on the "rational man" at *WL* §2). Consider, also, *MM II* §591, where Nietzsche tells us that happiness can only ever grow on the volcanic soil of the world's woes. The more dangerous the volcano of suffering, the greater the fertility of its soil.

30 *Z* III "Der Wanderer".

31 See *NL 1887–1888*, 11(77): "In so far as any force can expend itself only on what resists it, there is necessarily in any action an *ingredient of displeasure.*"

32 *NL 1887–1888*, 11(76). 33 *Ibid. 1888–1889*, 14(173).

34 See, especially, *NL 1888–1889*, 14(173). This distinguishes Nietzsche's account from Spinoza's otherwise very similar account, according to which "joy" and "sadness" are likewise mere symptoms that supervene on something more essential. For Spinoza, "joy" corresponds to "a man's passage from a lesser to a greater perfection" (*E* III Def. II) and "sadness" to "a man's passage from a greater to a lesser perfection" (*E* III Def. III). For Nietzsche however, pleasure and pain are false opposites in so far as suffering is actually a necessary condition for what Spinoza called "passing to greater perfection" – and thus for experiencing pleasure.

the person on and acts as a necessary condition for the joy of overcoming an obstacle. The great health of *amor fati* is itself an overcoming – an overcoming of the limitless suffering involved in the very realization that this world is full of suffering. As such, the joy it involves is also unparalleled.

It is precisely with the tragic feat of total life-affirmation in mind that Nietzsche describes suffering not only as valuable, but as desirable.[35] It is in facing the supreme threat of complete despair before the dreadful nature of existence and in being thus burdened with the greatest pains, turmoil, and anguish that one can overcome the greatest of obstacles. The result is the great health of *amor fati* – the highest demonstration of strength there can be. Suffering, seen in this light, is necessary and desirable.

A surprising corollary of this theory of suffering is that the healthiest and strongest are precisely those who are most prone to suffering. The tragic Greeks, Nietzsche tells us, were such extraordinary artists and dramatists precisely because they were "uniquely capable of the most exquisite and heaviest suffering."[36] Nietzsche would later present the idea more generally with his claim that "order of rank is almost determined by just *how* deeply a person can suffer."[37]

Nietzsche's healthy type, then, is by definition highly sensitive to suffering. This sensitivity might even bring him to the brink of despair and as such it is potentially dangerous – Nietzsche could have remained a pessimist, Heraclitus might have gone down Anaximander's path, the Greeks could have embraced the life-negating wisdom of Silenus, etc.[38] But without this great danger, without this tremendous obstacle, higher health will not be attained.

The healthiest are thus not only those who suffer the most deeply, but those whose will to suffer is the greatest. What does not kill them makes them stronger and healthier, and so they want to be exposed to what could

[35] See *Z* IV "Vom höheren Menschen" §6, *FW* §338, *NL 1887–1888*, 10(118), and (103). On this point, see also Janaway, *Beyond Selflessness*, pp. 68 and 243.

[36] *GT* §7. See also *DW* §2, where Nietzsche explains in connection to the Greeks that "talent for suffering, wisdom of suffering" is the "correlative of artistic talent." On this point, see A. Danto, *Nietzsche as Philosopher* (New York: Macmillan, 2005), pp. 34–5.

[37] *JGB* §270. See also *NL 1887–1888*, 10(118). It is interesting to note that in an early text Nietzsche presented Schopenhauer in a similar light, claiming that it was the philosopher's great capacity for suffering and his ability courageously to accept the truth of the world's horrors that made him the great thinker he was (*UB* III §3).

[38] According to Aeschylus, Silenus was a wise demon, a companion of Dionysus. When forced to share his wisdom with King Midas, he reveals himself to be a true prophet of life-negation: "Miserable, ephemeral race, children of chance and of hardship," he roars, "why are you forcing me to tell you that which it would be most profitable for you not to hear? The best thing of all is entirely unreachable: not to have been born, not to *be*, to be *nothing*. However, the second best thing for you is – to die soon" (*GT* §3; see also *DW* §2).

very well "kill" them. It is in this sense that the great health of *amor fati* involves not only accepting and embracing suffering, but also willing it. For without great suffering, there is no great health.

What are we to do, then, with the second of Nietzsche's two theories of suffering, which states that suffering is an agent of sickness, or *décadence*, and that it is the weak type, precisely, who is most prone to suffering? There is indeed a wealth of passages in Nietzsche's work that unequivocally describe life-negation in general and the Christian variety in particular as a product of the suffering masses, and the Christian as the quintessential sufferer type.[39] More specifically, it is the *décadents*' extreme weakness and "irritability" (*Reizbarkeit*)[40] that cause them to despise the world and to cook up the fiction of a realm of Peace, Bliss, and Stability to take their revenge on it. It is the suffering of the nihilist *décadent*, in short, that is responsible for the emergence of the metaphysics of Being. The great suffering of the masses, in short, accounts for some of the unhealthiest ideological developments in the history of mankind.

Suffering, on this model, is what breeds the illness of *nihil*ism qua longing for the great *nothing*. Accordingly, Nietzsche accuses the *décadent* of paying too much attention to trivial pains and discomforts[41] and of placing too much emphasis on the pleasure–displeasure dichotomy.[42] What the *décadent* desires is a realm of "coziness."[43] But this vision of pleasure is really negative; the heavenly *wahre Welt* is just an absence of

[39] See, for instance, *GM* III §15 as well as *NL 1887–1888*, 9(18) and (159), 11(112), 14(125) and (142), 15(110), and 16(476).

[40] *JGB* §293. [41] See *NL 1887–1888*, 11(228) and 17(6).

[42] *JGB* §225. In this passage, Nietzsche derides modern philosophers' obsession with pleasure and suffering, claiming that "any philosophy that would confine itself only to these is naive" on the grounds that "there are more important problems than pleasure and suffering." But is it not the case that Nietzsche's philosophy likewise accords tremendous importance to suffering? Is Nietzsche being somewhat hypocritical, then, in criticizing others for what he himself does? The solution to this problem is to read *JGB* §225 in relation to the broader framework of Nietzsche's discussion of suffering. What Nietzsche is actually critical of are philosophies that posit pleasure and suffering as plain opposites and aim for a pleasure that in its essence is really nothing more than the absence of suffering. As seen above, suffering and pleasure are actually "false opposites" for Nietzsche, in so far as resistance – which implies a certain degree of pain – is necessary for any genuine experience of joy (*NL 1888–1889*, 14(173)). It is precisely in assuming that they really are opposites that most philosophies reveal themselves to be "naive." Moreover, as we will soon see, the negative notion of pleasure that these types of philosophies (implicitly or explicitly) aim for – i.e. pleasure as absence of pain – can be a goal only for weary *décadents* who want to end suffering. For now, suffice it to say that a change in perspective on suffering and thus a change in approach to suffering is precisely one of the "more important matters" Nietzsche thinks philosophy should deal with. Nietzsche's thinking on the problem of suffering, in short, has nothing in common with the fundamentally life-negating, reactive philosophies he condemns at *JGB* §225.

[43] *FW* §338.

adversity, an absence of suffering – a complete "unreality," in short.[44] This reactive mechanism transpires in the Christian goal of reaching Heaven, in the Buddhist quest for *nirvāṇa*, etc. Extreme irritability and oversensitivity to pain is what lies at the root of this.

In *GM*, Nietzsche explains that what the ascetic priest does when he presides over the reactive, *ressentiment*-fueled cooking up of the *wahre Welt* is that he gives a meaning to the suffering of the masses. On Nietzsche's view, what humanity suffers from most is not so much suffering itself as senselessness.[45] This is precisely what nihilistic religions and philosophies seek to remedy. They develop a framework in which to interpret suffering, and thus to make it more bearable: "The *wahre Welt* is Good, Pure and Still. We who inhabit this false, evil world of conflict and becoming are impure. This is because of sin/ignorance/lack of faith, etc. (depending on the nihilist ideology in question)." With such fictions, the senselessness of suffering can be given a meaning, or at the very least an explanation and a justification.

But the ascetic priests' explanation is already expressive of a deep antipathy to life. This affect of *ressentiment* manifests itself as a condemnation of everything this world involves. Hence the *religieux*'s or philosopher's moral judgment on existence. We in this world suffer because nature itself is evil. We are guilty just by virtue of existing in this filthy, corrupt world. The upshot, of course, is that we ought to feel guilty about everything this-worldly about us – the body, emotions, desires, volitions, etc. The ascetic's explanation of suffering is a guilt-mongering explanation.[46] If we suffer, it is because of what is really most natural about us – our "sinful" behavior, our "ignorance" of the Real and Good, or our "doubt." Hating life means hating oneself for being part of nature. Such guilt is the fuel for the battle against the instincts, which is also the battle against life.

Nietzsche explains the institutionalization of guilt in terms of his theory on slave vs. master morals.[47] Nihilistic, moralistic interpretations of suffering, according to Nietzsche, lead to morals that pour scorn over everything self- or life-affirming. These are slave morals. On Nietzsche's (quite consciously non-historical) account, the *ressentiment*$_1$ of the suffering masses is

[44] See *NL 1885–1887*, 37(8) and *ibid. 1887–1888*, 9(107) and 10(57).

[45] *GM* II §7 and III §28. This is a feature of Nietzsche's views on suffering which has received much attention from commentators, including, most notably, an excellent essay by Williams, *The Sense of the Past*, pp. 331–7. See, also, Nehamas, *Nietzsche*, pp. 121–2, Danto, *Nietzsche as Philosopher*, pp. 159f., and Janaway, *Beyond Selflessness*, pp. 106f.

[46] *GM* III §16.

[47] This theory first appears in *JGB* (§§195 and 260–1) and gets worked out more fully in *GM*.

directed first against the naturally strong ruling classes. It thereby leads to a fundamentally reactive inversion of the ruling classes' moral code.[48] The rulers' "good" becomes the slaves' "evil" (*böse*), and the rulers' "bad" (*schlecht*) becomes the slaves' negative "good" (e.g. not-proud, not-strong, not-rich, not-powerful, and so on).[49] But this is only the first step. The ascetic priest then turns such morals against the very subject of *ressentiment.* Turned inward, *ressentiment* militates against everything lively, natural, and healthy that remains in the weak type. These are characterized as "sinful." This results in guilt and bad conscience. The self-loathing of guilt becomes the leitmotif of morality.[50] It is in this type of ideological context that suffering, enfeeblement, and illness qua diminution of life are looked upon as valuable in themselves. Hence asceticism in all of its forms.

Ressentiment and guilt ultimately make suffering much worse, however.[51] By further weakening and suffocating the little life force of the weak, the self- and life-negating ethics of the ascetic ideal makes them even more vulnerable and prone to suffering. The nihilist *décadent* response to suffering, in short, increases *décadence*, which increases suffering by "*infecting the wound*,"[52] as it were. Nihilistic ideologies are supposed to be soothing, but they actually create conditions in which more pain is experienced.

Accordingly, Nietzsche suggests that it is in fact because of Christian morals that Europeans have become the suffering-prone creatures that they are.[53] Nietzsche's idea is that had it not been for the morality of guilt and *ressentiment* spawned by the nihilist mentality, Westerners would not be as effete, sensitive, and prone to suffering as they are today.

Nowhere is the contrast between this theory of suffering and Nietzsche's Heraclitean model greater than when it comes to who suffers, then. While the latter tells us that greatness is a function of how much one suffers, the former says exactly the opposite – those who suffer from existence are the weak, the ill, the feeble. This second theory, in short, underscores the irritability of the *décadent* and its disastrous cultural and "physiological" effects. Nietzsche, in certain passages, even attacks *décadents* for their extreme sensitivity to pain and contrasts them to the strong masters who

48 *GM* I §10.
49 *GM*'s first essay "Gut und Böse, Gut und schlecht" is entirely devoted to this theme.
50 *GM* III §15.
51 I say "ultimately" because the ascetic priests' morals do also, in the short term, relieve some of the *décadents'* suffering by giving them an outlet for their frustration (hatred of life, of the masters, of existence in this world, etc.) and by distracting them through a profusion of affects (rancor, guilt, moralizing condemnation, etc.). On this point, see *GM* III §15.
52 *GM* III §15. This idea is further developed at *ibid.* §§16–17.
53 *M* §§52 and 476.

are possessed of "skepticism concerning suffering."[54] The strong are here described simply as the "happy."[55] The contradiction with the theory of suffering I presented first could not be greater.

Is the affect of suffering an agent of health and growth, or an agent of sickness and *décadence*? Is the healthy type the primary suffering type, or is it the over-sensitive sick type who suffers most, in contrast to the happy and careless strong type? Looking for a unified theory of suffering in Nietzsche leads to fundamentally contradictory answers to both these key questions. Looking at the Heraclitean model in which health is conditional upon suffering, it seemed as though progress was being made toward a fuller understanding of *amor fati* not only as an affirmation of suffering, but as conditional upon the greatest suffering possible. In light of the second model, however, Nietzsche's views on suffering seem so contradictory that the very cogency of this ideal is compromised. Unless, of course, Nietzsche's two contradictory models can somehow be reconciled.

What is required to unify Nietzsche's two contradictory theories of suffering is a shift of focus away from suffering itself and toward the way in which suffering is experienced. This, in turn, means a typology of sufferers is needed if we are to make sense of what Nietzsche says about the relationship between suffering and health/sickness. Nietzsche gestures toward such a typology in the following fragment:

> We have confused suffering with one kind of suffering, with exhaustion; the latter, indeed, does represent ... a measurable loss of force. That is to say: there is displeasure as a means of stimulation for the increase of power, and displeasure following the exhaustion of power; in the first case it is a stimulus, in the second it is the result of excessive stimulation ... Inability to resist belongs to the latter: challenge of that which resists belongs to the former ... The only pleasure which anyone will still feel in the condition of exhaustion is falling asleep; victory is the pleasure in the other case ... The exhausted want rest, relaxation, peace, calm – this is the happiness of the nihilistic religions and philosophies. The rich and lively people want victory, opponents overcome, the overflow of the feeling of power across broader regions than before.[56]

Here Nietzsche begins with two distinct types of suffering – suffering qua decrease of strength vs. suffering qua resistance to be overcome – and two correlative types of pleasure – a purely negative pleasure qua absence of suffering and a positive pleasure qua overcoming of resistance. Toward the end of the passage, however, it becomes abundantly clear that the real

[54] *JGB* §46. See also *GM* III §16. [55] *GM* III §14. [56] *NL 1888–1889*, 14(174).

typology is not between types of suffering, but between two "ideal" types of sufferers who experience suffering in very different ways.

Healthy, strong types experience suffering as an enticing challenge. Because they are sturdier and more resilient, suffering does not diminish them, but, on the contrary, summons them to ever greater heights. Sick, weak types experience suffering as something enfeebling. Because they are already so weary, they cannot respond to suffering, but only passively react to it by suffering its impact, so to speak. In light of this typology, there is nothing contradictory about the idea that suffering is an agent of health/ascendance and an agent of sickness/*décadence*. Really, it all depends on who is suffering.

This points to the crucial distinction between extensional and intensional suffering.[57] Extensional suffering is the actual physical or psychological harm that a person undergoes. Intensional suffering involves the interpretation of extensional suffering. The real difference between the healthy and sick types' experience of suffering plays out at the level of intensional suffering. In short, it is all about how suffering is interpreted.

Take the most glaring contradiction between Nietzsche's two models, namely the contradiction over who, the strong or the weak, suffers most. What Nietzsche focuses on in texts where he attacks *décadents* for being over-sensitive to suffering is closely linked to their interpretation of suffering. The idea is that the *décadent*'s interpretation opens an entire domain of extensional suffering to which the strong, indeed, are not susceptible. This is the moral domain of guilt.[58] Of course, it is not just that we suffer more from guilt, but also that systematically interpreting suffering in moral terms – for example: "an accident has occurred, how atrocious, how unfair, something/somebody must be to blame" – makes us overall more sensitive to suffering and less capable of enduring and accepting it. In this sense, slave morals have made wide swathes of humanity more prone to moral suffering, thereby considerably widening the scope of extensional suffering through a specific mode of intensional focus. This is what Nietzsche means when he says *décadents* "suffer more" and that we in the modern age are more susceptible to suffering, more irritable, than our forebears.

But this is only half the story. By inventing theological and metaphysical fictions to make life bearable and by distracting themselves with the affects of moral outrage – inwardly and outwardly directed – sick types also shelter themselves from the profound existential suffering which the healthy type alone can dare to withstand. By giving suffering a meaning, moreover,

[57] See Danto, *Nietzsche as Philosopher*, pp. 259–60. [58] *GM* III §8.

they take much of the sting out of it. Finally, through the unselving morals of self-belittlement, *décadents* avoid expending their energy by entering conflict or putting up resistance. In this way, they meet as few obstacles as possible, and thus suffer less. *Décadents* thus close down an entire domain of extensional suffering to which healthy types remain fully open. In remaining open to all suffering and willing it – even the greatest suffering of all, namely the very realization that this world is senselessly and perpetually satiated with suffering – healthy types really are the ones capable of the greatest suffering. In intending suffering not as a moral, but an aesthetic phenomenon, and thus in accepting its senselessness, they are in fact far more open to it than those who wrap it up in a cloak of moral significance.

This typology of sufferers points in turn to a fundamental typology of pessimisms. Here we leave the domain of individual people experiencing and interpreting suffering in different ways and we enter the domain of broader, often unarticulated approaches to the greatest problem of life. There is in pessimism a descriptive element which is common to both unhealthy ideological developments – namely, Buddhist and Schopenhauerian pessimism, but also Christianity and any form of metaphysics of Being, delusional optimism, millennialism, etc. – and healthy ones – namely, tragic Greek culture and Nietzsche's philosophy of life-affirmation. Be it Anaximander or Heraclitus, the Buddha/Schopenhauer or Nietzsche, the ascetic priest or the free spirit, the Christian or the Dionysian, all at least implicitly agree that to live is to suffer. Whether or not they believe there is a realm of Being where suffering is absent – Christians, for instance, do, Buddhists do not – there is clear agreement on the fact that this world of becoming is a world of perpetual struggle and limitless suffering. Where the discrepancy arises is in responding to this fact.

This points to a central distinction between pessimisms. On the one hand, there is the healthy type's "pessimism of strength,"[59] which Nietzsche also refers to as the "artist's pessimism,"[60] or "Classical pessimism."[61] This is the tragic pessimism that stands behind Heraclitus' celebration of life, Attic tragedy, and Nietzsche's Dionysian wisdom. On the other hand, there is the sick type's "pessimism of the weak,"[62] also dubbed "moral-religious [as opposed to the artist's] pessimism,"[63] or "Romantic [as opposed to Classical] pessimism."[64] This is the pessimism "of all great nihilistic religions (of Brahmanism, of Buddhism, of Christianity)" – religions, Nietzsche

[59] *GT* "Versuch einer Selbstkritik" §1. See also *NL 1885–1887* 10(21), and *ibid. 1888–1889*, 14(25).
[60] *NL 1887–1888*, 10(168). [61] *Ibid. 1888–1889*, 14(25). [62] *Ibid. 1887–1888*, 11(294).
[63] *Ibid.* 10(168). [64] *Ibid. 1888–1889*, 14(25).

explains, which "can be called nihilistic because all three have elevated the opposite of life, nothingness, to a goal, to the highest good, or to 'God.'"[65] These two pessimisms correspond to the two fundamental types of response a person may have to the reality of limitless suffering. Pessimism of strength corresponds to the healthy type's experience of suffering as something enticing, as a lure to life. Pessimism of weakness, in contrast, is exactly what one would expect of the *décadent* type for whom suffering implies enfeeblement.

Accordingly, these two pessimisms are diametrically opposed on every point. Pessimism of weakness poses a negative moral judgment on existence: this world is evil. Pessimism of strength refuses to cast a moral judgment on life and casts instead a positive aesthetic judgment: this world is beautiful.[66] Pessimism of weakness is fundamentally reactive: it steps back from the great obstacle suffering represents. Pessimism of strength is fundamentally active: it steps forward and seeks to engage with suffering. Pessimism of weakness sees the senselessness of suffering as a problem and needs to explain it. Pessimism of strength finds nothing more interesting than senseless suffering and has no need of an explanation, let alone a justification, for suffering.[67] Pessimism of weakness looks upon life itself as guilty on the grounds that suffering is unfair and arbitrary, which leads to weak types' sense of personal guilt and self-loathing when they exhibit signs of vitality. Pessimism of strength has no place for guilt: neither life nor the strong pessimist is "guilty" of anything. Pessimism of weakness leads one to take measures to limit suffering, to numb oneself, etc. Pessimism of strength rejects anything that would have a numbing effect, for it wills suffering as a condition for the joy of overcoming obstacles. Pessimism of weakness, finally, leads to life-negation. Pessimism of strength, in contrast, paves the way to life-affirmation.[68]

The opposition between the pessimism of the weak and of the strong is the paradigm in which Nietzsche thinks health and sickness. The sick type of Nietzsche's ethics – the *décadent* – is a weak pessimist. The healthy type of Nietzsche's ethics is a strong pessimist. The inescapable reality of suffering is the same for both; what is different is how these two "ideal

[65] *Ibid.* See also *GM* III §27. [66] *NL 1887–1888*, 10(168).
[67] *Ibid. 1885–1887*, 10(21). See also *ibid. 1887–1888*, 10(168).
[68] There are of course several interconnections between all the oppositions just listed. For instance, the concept of guilt is central to weak pessimists' explanation of apparently senseless suffering and to their moral take on the world. The reactivity of pessimism of weakness is also closely connected to the quest for a meaning to suffering and to the weak pessimists' flight from suffering through anesthetic measures. Similarly, the strong pessimists' aesthetic judgement is a sign of their being active, as opposed to reactive, and is intimately linked to their will to suffer, etc. These are but a few connections. The idea is that each of these two pessimisms presents an internally coherent attitude toward suffering.

active / engaged
avoidance of guilt = confidence + power fre

types" interpret suffering. Consider, in this connection, Nietzsche's notes on the martyrdom of Dionysus and Jesus Christ:

> Dionysus versus the "Crucified": there you have the opposition. It is *not* a difference with regard to martyrdom – it is just that this same [martyrdom] has a different meaning. Life itself, its eternal fruitfulness and recurrence, creates torment, destruction, the will to annihilation ... In the other case, suffering, the "Crucified as the innocent one," is an objection to this life, a formula for its condemnation. One will guess that the problem is that of the meaning of suffering: either a Christian meaning or a tragic meaning.[69]

Here Dionysus and Christ are presented as the ultimate symbols of life-affirmation and life-negation: of the pessimism of the strong and of the weak. They both suffer horrendous deaths and come back to life, and to this extent they are similar, but it is in the meaning of this great suffering that they diverge so strongly. The suffering and resuscitation of Dionysus stands for the destructive–creative torrent of becoming. It incites us to celebrate life joyfully. The martyrdom of Christ, in contrast, denounces life as unfair and brutal, and his resurrection points to the deathless realm of Being. The aesthetic celebration of pessimism of strength is thus opposed to the moralizing spite of pessimism of weakness. The opposite of pessimism of weakness, then, is not optimism – all delusional optimisms are in fact predicated on an underlying pessimism of weakness – but pessimism of strength. These consist in opposite interpretations of suffering – a fundamentally healthy, i.e. life-affirming, interpretation vs. a fundamentally unhealthy, i.e. life-negating, interpretation.

It is now clear that the distinction between life-negation and life-affirmation hinges on how suffering – and especially the limitlessness and senselessness of suffering – is interpreted. If suffering can breed both health and sickness, it is because its effects are a function of how the particular sufferer construes suffering. The affirmation of suffering constitutive of life-affirmation, then, is a matter of interpreting suffering in a certain way. What is thus required to complete our reconstruction of Nietzsche's positive philosophy is an examination of Nietzsche's theory of interpretation.

Understanding the role and nature of interpretation in Nietzsche's philosophy involves a close examination of his infamous theory of the will to power.[70] It is indeed in terms of the will to power doctrine that

[69] *NL 1888–1889*, 14(89).

[70] I do not capitalize the phrase "will to power" because, as I will explain below, the will to power is *not*, strictly speaking, a metaphysical doctrine. Nietzsche's theory of the will to power has received considerable attention in commentarial literature and many of the debates surrounding this doctrine

joyful in sense of accepting suffering

Nietzsche's theory of interpretation is articulated. Conversely, Nietzsche's theory of the will to power is, most fundamentally, a theory of interpretation.[71] Nevertheless, the relation between interpretation and the will to power is not immediately obvious. The only way to disclose it is through a careful exploration of the will to power doctrine. Doing so will also afford us a fuller understanding of all of the phenomena discussed in this chapter, in so far as, ultimately, they are all a matter of interpretation and, as such, are all expressions of the will to power.[72]

The doctrine of the will to power can be bifurcated into two fundamental claims: (1) a claim about the fundamental drive that animates all living creatures, and (2) a broader claim about how the nature of everything in the universe may best be characterized.[73] As a "psychology" of the living organism, the will to power doctrine is pitted against three principal features of biological theory as it stood in Nietzsche's day. The first is the view that self-preservation is the primary motive behind all living creatures' behavior.[74] The second is the assumption that humans, along with other higher animals, are fundamentally pleasure-seeking and pain-averse.[75] The third is a broad theoretical commitment to an explanatory model founded on the concept of adaptation.[76] To espouse these principles, for Nietzsche, is fundamentally to misconstrue what it means to be alive.

More than anything, claims Nietzsche, being alive involves expanding one's sphere of control as much as possible. To posit self-preservation as "the cardinal drive of an organic being," accordingly, is to mistake an effect for the cause; the drive to self-preservation "is only one of the indirect and most frequent *consequences* of" the truly fundamental drive governing animal and human behavior: namely, the will to power.[77] This is the will

are technical and highly confusing, if not simply confused. M. Clark's *Nietzsche on Truth and Philosophy* (Cambridge University Press, 1990) provides an excellent survey of the principal interpretations of the doctrine of the will to power up to the late 1980s. More recent notable works which discuss the will to power include G. Abel, *Nietzsche: Die Dynamik der Willen zur Macht und die ewige Wiederkehr* (Berlin: W. de Gruyter, 1998), V. Gerhardt, *Vom Willen zur Macht: Anthropology und Metaphysik der Macht am exemplerischen Fall Friedrich Nietzsches* (Berlin: W. de Gruyter, 1996), Reginster, *The Affirmation of Life*, and Janaway, *Beyond Selflessness*.

71 See, on this point, Nehamas, *Nietzsche*, pp. 74–105.

72 Though Richardson misrepresents the doctrine as a genuine metaphysics, there is something to be said for his observation on Nietzsche's "*power ontology*" to the effect that "Nietzsche thinks his other thoughts *in its terms*" (*Nietzsche's System*, p. 16). See, in this connection, Janaway's exhaustive overview of the several arguments in *GM* that explicitly or implicitly rely on the view that "life is the will to power" in *Beyond Selflessness*, pp. 143–7. I take exception to Richardson's use of the term "ontology," however. The will to power doctrine admits of processes alone, and not of a single "thing" (*ontōs*).

73 Horstmann, in this connection, distinguishes between the "psychological" and the "cosmological" doctrine of the will to power. See "Introduction," in R.-P. Horstmann and J. Norman (eds.), *Beyond Good and Evil*, trans. J. Norman (Cambridge University Press), pp. ii–xxviii.

74 *JGB* §13. 75 *NL 1888–1889*, 14(121); *ibid. 1887–1888*, 11(75). 76 *GM* II §12 77 *JGB* §13.

to discharge one's strength, to "grow, spread, grab, win dominance," and so on.[78] Remaining alive is merely instrumental to this more fundamental purpose. This is why there are numerous examples of organisms forfeiting self-preservation in the pursuit of power.[79]

The same can be said of pleasure. This is because pleasure is not what organisms seek. What organisms strive for is power, pleasure being little more than "the symptom of the feeling of power attained."[80] As Kaufmann puts it, on Nietzsche's account, "the feeling of pleasure is an epiphenomenon of the possession of power" and "striving for pleasure is an epiphenomenon of the will to power."[81] Nietzsche's idea is that pleasure simply supervenes on the successful exercise of power and therefore that positing it as a motive for action betrays a superficial sense of psychology. A corollary of this position is that organisms are no more pain-averse than pleasure-seeking. As I mentioned above, Nietzsche considers pain and pleasure to be false opposites in so far as pain simply registers the resistance that is necessary for any action, or exercise of power.[82] In so far as this exercise of power is successful and thereby results in pleasure, the feeling of pain is a necessary condition for the feeling of pleasure, not its opposite.[83] Power is what organisms really strive for, not pleasure (and even less the avoidance of pain).

Evolutionary theory's focus on adaptation, finally, appears quite problematic when it is seen that "life simply is the will to power," or that will to power is "just the will to life."[84] The problem, for Nietzsche, is that standard accounts of evolution focus on a fundamentally reactive phenomenon.[85] Indeed, the adaptation view of evolution is thoroughly mechanistic; it describes organisms continually reacting to their environment in the same way as inert marbles move around in a jar as the result of reactions alone. Reactive forces, however, are only one of the two types of forces that govern an organism on the will to power model.

Here we go beyond the will to power as psychology and enter the domain of will to power as a theory of the fundamental forces that make up living organisms. Bodies – which in the case of higher organisms include brains and thus the so-called mind – are will to power through and through. That

78 *Ibid.* §259. 79 On this point, see *FW* §349 and *JGB* §13. 80 *NL 1888–1889*, 14(121).
81 Kaufmann, *Nietzsche*, p. 262. See, in this connection, *NL 1888–1889*, 14(174).
82 *NL 1887–1888*, 11(77).
83 *Ibid. 1888–1889*, 14(173). Consider, in this connection, Brogan, "The Central Role of Suffering," p. 55: "Power does not avoid suffering. It grows out of suffering. Suffering is not to be avoided; it is normal and necessary as an aspect of growth. Intrinsic to the feeling of pleasure, which is a response to an increase in power, is displeasure or the experience of an obstacle to this power."
84 *JGB* §13. 85 *GM* II §12.

is to say, they are made up of forces, each of which is systemically geared toward the full discharge and expansion of its strength. (There is obviously no volition here – the "will" to power is here a mere turn of phrase.) Now, among the forces that make up the body, there are on the one hand reactive forces, which are dominated and exercise their power through mechanical means designed to secure final ends (e.g. digestion, which is performed by a cluster of reactive forces), and on the other hand active forces, which dominate and exercise their power through the domination, steering and coordination of reactive forces.[86] Reactive forces always merely adapt, or react. Active forces give form, or spontaneously create. What is more, active forces are responsible for assigning reactive forces their function. To account for evolution in terms of adaptation alone is thus to miss out on what is really most fundamental to life. In the theories of the early Darwinians of Nietzsche's day "the essence of life, *its will to power*, is ignored; one overlooks the essential priority of the spontaneous, aggressive, expansive, form-giving forces that give new interpretations and directions, although 'adaptation' follows only after this."[87]

Nietzsche's general idea is that, with its focus on the reactive, biological thinking is fundamentally mistaken on the character of life. If human, animal, and plant behavior is to be accounted for in terms of one primary drive, it is not self-preservation that should be posited but the will to expand the sphere of one's control maximally. In fact the reactive will to self-preservation (through adaptation, among other things) is merely "in the service" of the active drive for power. Similarly, most often suffering is not so much reactively avoided as actively sought, being an occasion for beings to "test their strength," so to speak. Success in overcoming this resistance is what positive joy corresponds to. When pain is avoided and the negative joy of "absence-of-pain" is sought, it is because the being in question is not strong enough to withstand the affront of resistance and will therefore suffer a setback – a diminution of its sphere of control – by encountering it. With the theory of the will to power, then, Nietzsche claims to be offering a more accurate and comprehensive account of life – an account which focuses not only on mechanistic, reactive functions like adaptation, but also on spontaneous, active forces like creation, direction, and steering.

There are three things to note about Nietzsche's theory as it has been presented so far. The first is that while the will to power is the fundamental

[86] On this point, see Deleuze, *Nietzsche*, pp. 46–8.

[87] *GM* II §12. For a systematic study of Nietzsche's anti-Darwinism, see D. R. Johnson's *Nietzsche's Anti-Darwinism* (Cambridge University Press, 2010).

drive of the entire organic realm, not all organisms will always look, on the face of it, as though they were blindly striving to extend their dominance at all costs and in all circumstances. The will to power is a drive, not necessarily a conscious desire. Just as, according to contemporary social biologists, gene-transference is not necessarily the conscious goal of all our actions though it is the primary drive that guides them,[88] will to power drives us without our necessarily realizing it. It is no more of a "mental cause" than the drive to pass one's genes on in Dawkins's theory: will to power characterizes the body just as much as the mind. Moreover, as the primary affect of sentient beings' psychology,[89] the will to power is best understood as the overarching genus of which various affects are species. There is no "pure" will to power affect. The will to power, in short, does not necessarily produce itself as a desire for power (let alone as a conscious volition), nor does it necessarily lead to manifestly power-enhancing behavior. In fact, there are important cases in which the will to power will give rise to a will to powerlessness and to behavior which seems to reduce power, strength, and liveliness. This will be the case among primarily reactive types.

Second, if the "will" in "will to power" is very much unlike standard volition, the "power" at issue in this doctrine is equally distinctive. When it comes to the sub-individual forces that make up organisms, it is clear that in "willing power" these forces are really just exhibiting their systemic propensity to expend themselves. This is true of both reactive and active forces, which are not different in kind, only in degree – and as a consequence of the role they play within the organism.[90] Moreover, when it comes to human behavior, Deleuze aptly makes the point that, even if Nietzsche occasionally (and polemically) uses such language, "power" in the phrase "will to power" should not be understood in terms of common representations of power – physical superiority, political control, wealth, honors, reputation, etc.[91] This is what sets Nietzsche's theory apart from Thomas Hobbes's, for instance. The idea is that such a conception of power corresponds to the ways in which weak, dominated people – the slaves of *GM* I – reactively represent it.[92] Moreover, it is a kind of conformist desire for "power" which slaves harbor;

[88] This theory was first set out in R. Dawkins, *The Selfish Gene* (Oxford University Press, 1976).

[89] *NL 1888–1889*, 14(121).

[90] As Deleuze explains very clearly (*Nietzsche*, pp. 48–50), there is no qualitative difference between reactive and active forces in so far as the seemingly qualitative difference between "reactive" and "active" is reducible to a quantitative difference in the relative strength of various forces. It is to relations between forces of different strengths that the reactive/active dichotomy pertains.

[91] Deleuze, *Nietzsche*, pp. 90–4. [92] *Ibid.*, p. 91.

they want the "goods" society has already agreed on for them.[93] However, from the standpoint of the spontaneous exercise of power – from the standpoint of activity – power is creation, vision, invention. In many cases it might have very little to do with actual political domination.[94] At the most exalted level, moreover, it is in fact the very opposite of conformism – it is the creation, envisioning, and invention of new values, new "goods." This will be the case among primarily active types.

The third thing to note is that, according to Nietzsche, organisms are by no means unitary entities that "will power." Each sentient being's psyche is composed of a plurality of clusters of active and reactive forces – impersonal sub-individuals, as it were – which pull and tug in different directions.[95] This generally occurs at subconscious levels, though the internal conflicts occasionally bubble up to the surface of consciousness. Of course, all of these sub-individuals are driven by a will to power and may thus be "at war" with one another. Ultimately, however, some will come out stronger than others and will thus establish themselves as dominant and active, in opposition to their dominated, reactive counterparts. Will to power does not just give rise to conflicts between people, then, but also, and perhaps more importantly, to conflicts *within* people. Having said this, in the case of most organisms, a number of "peace treaties" hold so that the organism acts in a relatively coherent fashion and with an apparent unity of purpose.[96] In fact, however, "willing" is never something simply and unitary.[97] Consciousness, which ultimately offers only a very superficial view of what is happening within, represents willing as something unitary, but in fact there is no unitary "will" that wills, only various instances of "willing" produced by a formidable effervescence of plural, often conflicting "wills" whose battles are played out beneath the purview of consciousness.

The will to power, then, is not so much about "what we all actually want," as "how best to account for the whole range of human, animal, and

[93] *Ibid.*, p. 92.

[94] Consider, in this connection, the following fragment from one of Nietzsche's early notebooks:

> I have found strength where one does not look for it: in simple, mild, and pleasant people, without the least desire to rule – and, conversely, the desire to rule has often appeared to me a sign of inward weakness: they fear their own slave soul and shroud it in a royal cloak . . . The powerful natures dominate, it is a necessity, they need not lift one finger. Even if, during their lifetime, they bury themselves in a garden house! (*NL 1880–1881*, 6(209))

[95] See, on this point, *JGB* §19. [96] *Ibid.*

[97] *Ibid.*: "In every act of willing there is a plurality of feelings." See also *FW* §127. Nietzsche, in this connection, berates Schopenhauer for building his metaphysics on the "folk-prejudice" that willing is something unitary (*JGB* §19).

plant behavior." For Nietzsche, this involves positing a fundamental drive that does not simply pertain to individual psyches, but to the plurality of forces that make up both these psyches and, for that matter, the bodies from which they are ultimately inseparable.

And this is where the shift to Nietzsche's broader claim about how the nature of everything in the universe may best be characterized becomes inevitable. Since there is no qualitative difference between what the organic and the inorganic realms are made out of, it follows that both must be reducible to the same type of forces. The entire world, accordingly, consists in quanta of force which exhibit will to power.[98]

It is already obvious from my outline of the psychology of the will to power that the doctrine goes beyond merely stating what drives organisms and makes a statement about what drives all of the forces that make up an organism's body and mind. This non-dualist reductionism of mind *and* body to the units of will to power of which they are constituted also extends to the non-organic realm. Nietzsche's argument for this position is laid out in *JGB* §36. Here Nietzsche evokes the perennial problem of the causality between matter – objects which are given to perception, the nerves that receive stimuli, and so on – and a presumably immaterial "mind." A coherent account of the very possibility of perception requires that mind, on the one hand, and objects, together with the nerves that are affected by them, on the other hand, should not be thought of as qualitatively different. In short mind–body non-dualism is methodologically required. Finally, Nietzsche argues that in so far as the body (which includes the mind) is recognized to be made up of units of will to power, we are compelled to suppose that positing such forces is also "*sufficient* to understand the so-called mechanistic (or 'material') world."[99] Non-dualism is the key idea here. The mind–body apparatus and the objects that make up the world are really constituted of the same "stuff"; the "material world" belongs "to the same plane of reality as our affects themselves" and vice versa.[100] From the most complex psychological states to the most basic chemical reaction, what is at work in the entire universe are various forces, all of which are of the

[98] *NL 1888–1889*, 14(81–2). In *Nietzsche on Truth and Philosophy*, Clark tries to distinguish firmly between Nietzsche's psychological views and his presumed cosmological pretensions. Given Nietzsche's mind–body non-dualism, however, it seems very difficult to see why and how what he says of the sub-personal and impersonal forces that make up the subject's body (and thus also psyche) could fail to apply equally to what makes up the inorganic realm.

[99] *JGB* §36. [100] *Ibid.*

same essential type. It is by virtue of this that perception is possible.[101] Conversely, this is also what entitles Nietzsche to say that the nature of everything in the world, like that of the mind-body that perceives and thinks, is will to power.

According to Nietzsche, describing, understanding, and explaining the various physical, chemical, and biological phenomena that make up the world in terms of the will to power constitutes a marked improvement on mechanistic atomism, or materialism more generally. Like biology's focus on adaptation, materialist-atomist mechanistic thinking is intent on reaction alone and entirely ignores action and creation. Mechanistic accounts point to reactive processes alone. This is why, for Nietzsche, the mechanistic theory can only describe events, but never really explain them.[102] The will to power theory, in this sense, is more comprehensive in so far as it takes into account both reactive and active forces. It can thus go beyond the mere description of events in terms of reaction and explain them in terms of the struggles among various forces continually testing each other's strength.

There is a second reason, in this connection, for favoring the will to power as a philosophy of nature.[103] Nietzsche describes the atom and matter more generally as God's shadows.[104] Thinking in terms of matter is thinking in terms of an inert, static, and enduring Substance. Thinking in terms of atoms, accordingly, is thinking in terms of what still "stands still."[105] As a philosophy of nature, the will to power recognizes no substantial "thing," no "entity," no "being" whatsoever. It recognizes only processes and events, understood in terms of forces. Its questions are not of the form "what is this?," but rather "what is happening here?" and more specifically "how is this happening?" In itself, moreover, the doctrine of the will to power does not answer the question "what is the world?" (for Nietzsche everything only ever "becomes," nothing "is") but the question "how does arising and passing away – i.e. becoming – take place?" In this sense, it stands beyond any

[101] At *NL 1888–1889*, 14(81–2), Nietzsche points out that his theory solves the problem of causality. In truth, any non-dualist doctrine which argues for the "co-substantiality" of matter and mind does away with the perennial problem of physical objects affecting a presumably immaterial mind/soul.

[102] *NL 1885–1887*, 2(76).

[103] On Nietzsche's scientific sources for the doctrine of the will to power as an alternative to atomism and materialism, see Janaway, *Beyond Selflessness*, pp. 159–60, and G. Moore, *Nietzsche, Biology and Metaphor* (Cambridge University Press, 2002).

[104] *FW* §109. [105] *JGB* §12. See also *FW* §§109–10.

metaphysics of Being. It is a *philosophy of becoming* which, unlike standard naturalism,[106] has truly moved beyond the myth of Substance.

One major problem with the will to power doctrine is that it does not seem to cohere with the main thrust of Nietzsche's negative views. As R.-P. Horstmann puts it, it seems difficult to "avoid the unsettling conclusion that the doctrine of a 'Will to power' shares all the vices which Nietzsche attributes to metaphysical thinking in general."[107] The dilemma, as it seems, is as follows: either Nietzsche is unwittingly presenting yet another metaphysics of Being, or the will to power theory is not a sincere philosophy of nature, but a mere demonstration of life-affirming intellectual gymnastics. As my analysis will reveal, this is a false dilemma.

The main problem with the will to power is that it appears to be a form of reductionism. With regard to human behavior, it claims that all forms of behavior and the motives with which we justify them can actually be redescribed in a certain way. Everything we do is actually expressive of will to power; everything we do is "motivated," so to speak, by an underlying striving for power, even when this is far from obvious and certainly not experienced as such. In and of itself, this is not a problem. Standard scientific accounts, after all, also hold that all actions and motives can be reduced to a primary drive, be it the quest for evolutionary advantage, the maximization of reproductive chances, or gene-transference. But for a thinker such as Nietzsche, reductionism is not an option. Saying that love, or charity, is "actually" will to power implies a "real vs. apparent" distinction. Since Nietzsche rejects this distinction, it seems as though he cannot reduce all actions and motives to a primary drive.

The scope of this objection can then be extended to the will to power theory qua philosophy of nature. By telling us that the "stuff of the world" is will to power – that all things are reducible to the will to power – Nietzsche seems to be presenting a *wahre Welt* of sorts. Things appear to be what they are (chairs, tables, organisms, rocks, etc.), but really in their essence they are Will to Power. The idea, in short, is that reductionism implies metaphysical realism; it implies that there is a "way things really are" in and of themselves and a neutral, "mind-independent" description of the world that provides an accurate picture of this "Reality." How can a thinker who rejects the

[106] Janaway, *Beyond Selflessness*, pp. 34–9, is right to point to some difficulties with Leiter's discussion of Nietzsche's naturalism. See B. Leiter, *Nietzsche on Morality* (London: Routledge, 2002). Indeed, it is hard to accept the idea that there is much continuity between Nietzsche's philosophy and the results of the empirical sciences (*ibid.*, p. 3) when, with the will to power, Nietzsche so radically departs from the scientific establishment's view of the world.

[107] Horstmann, "Introduction," p. xxvi.

true-world/apparent-world divide be a reductionist and thus a realist? How can Nietzsche ever tell us about the "way things really are though they appear otherwise." Indeed, there seems to be a fundamental inconsistency between the will to power doctrine and Nietzsche's critique of Truth. Does he not himself argue that such a critique implies abandoning the quest for knowledge of the Truth in favor of perspectivism?[108] Why, then, does the will to power look like something more than a mere perspective?

One response to this challenge is to present the will to power as just one perspective among many.[109] Nietzsche, on this reading, did not actually think that all things are reducible to quanta of force. He simply felt that such a perspective on the world's nature was most expressive of a healthy attitude to life – that describing the world as will to power is a gesture of self-affirmation.[110] On this view, describing the world and human psychology in this way is neither more nor less true that describing it in mechanistic terms; it is just healthier. The will to power, then, is just a life-affirming fiction.

This interpretation of Nietzsche suffers from three weaknesses. First, it makes Nietzsche's entire philosophy seem completely idiosyncratic and "private." The will to power made sense to Nietzsche, it made him feel good, but that is about as far as we can go. We can thus study Nietzsche as a psychological case, but not as a philosopher.

Second, Nietzsche's very notions of health and life-affirmation are intimately tied to the will to power doctrine. Indeed, as I will soon argue, it provides the conceptual framework in which Nietzsche thinks of health/sickness and life-affirmation/negation. There is something circular, then, in saying that this doctrine is no less deluded than any other, just healthier and more life-affirming. Now, if Nietzsche's philosophy were a closed system of idiosyncratic, circular definitions, then there would be no problem per se in saying that the "world as will to power" is a healthier and more life-affirming perspective while defining health and life-affirmation in terms of will to power. The principle of charitable interpretation, however, demands that an attempt at least be made to read Nietzsche's thought as something more than a closed system of circular signification, which really says nothing about the world or the human predicament.

Third, what this interpretation starts with, namely the doctrine of perspectivism, is itself intimately tied to the will to power. Indeed, if all of knowledge is interpretation – if there are only perspectives and no definitive

108 *NL 1885–1887*, 7(60).

109 The best version of this interpretation can be found in Clark's *Nietzsche on Philosophy and Truth*.

110 *Ibid.*, p. 32.

objective statements of fact – it is precisely because the subject of knowledge qua nexus of forces always brings his/her interests, feelings, and wills to bear in every instance of "knowing."[111] This is precisely why there is no knowledge – in the sense of correspondence to truth[112] – only interpretation.[113] In short, perspectivism itself is a corollary of will to power reductionism, which reduces both the subject and the object of knowledge to quanta of forces. If there is no "view from nowhere," it is because there is no detached subject of consciousness standing "outside the world"; it is because everything is will to power and every perspective, or interpretation, is the result of struggles among forces.

This seems to push us in the direction of a Heideggerian interpretation of Nietzsche. According to Heidegger, Nietzsche ought to have bitten the metaphysical bullet. The Will to Power is a metaphysics of Being. It is Nietzsche's answer to the perennial question of philosophy, namely "what is being?"[114] On this reading, it is Nietzsche's views on what beings actually are – will to power – that leads him to his perspectivism.[115] This is a pragmatic, instrumentalist theory of knowledge founded on a conception of a subject of knowledge who, as will to power, continually interprets the world in terms of his interests and will.[116]

This reading comes at a heavy cost, however. It implies that Nietzsche was actually mistaken in critiquing the distinction between the "true world" and "the apparent world" – that he was a metaphysician of Being without realizing it. Independent of the fact that this makes Nietzsche look as though he was not really aware of what he was doing, this interpretation also makes it difficult to take Nietzsche seriously when he describes the metaphysical need as an expression of the *décadents*' weakness.

Fortunately, this is not the only way to interpret the will to power doctrine in a way that coheres with Nietzsche's critique of Truth. It is of utmost importance, in this connection, to distinguish carefully between the metaphysical dichotomy between the "True/transcendent world" and the "apparent/immanent world," on the one hand, and the more practical epistemic distinction between "truth" (with a small t) and "untruth," on

111 *NL 1888–1889*, 14(186).
112 Clark rightly argues that Nietzsche's critique of Truth is really a critique of the correspondence theory of truth (*Nietzsche on Truth and Philosophy*, pp. 29–61). What she fails to see is that the reason there can be no neutral correspondence and only involved interpretation is precisely because everything is will to power.
113 *NL 1885–1887*, 7(60). 114 Heidegger, *Nietzsche*, vol. 1, p. 12.
115 See, especially, *ibid.*, vol. 11, pp. 473–516.
116 On this point, see R. H. Grimm's detailed monograph, *Nietzsche's Theory of Knowledge* (Berlin: W. de Gruyter, 1977).

the other. Nietzsche certainly does away with the first, but there is no reason to think he does away with the second.[117] To say that there is no transcendent realm of Being – of "what is but does not become" – and therefore no Truth (with a capital T), does not imply that all statements concerning the world we are left with are equally untrue. To draw this inference would be a sign of nihilistic withdrawal. Certainly all statements about this mundane world used to be looked upon as statements about an "illusory" world and were thus regarded as 'untrue' relative to the Truth of the True/ Real World. After the collapse of the True vs. the illusory world distinction, however, statements that describe the world (now neither "true" nor "merely apparent") may be looked upon as far truer than they were formerly assumed to be. To go from "there is no Truth" (about Being, about the Real, etc.) to "there is no relative truth, relative accuracy, etc. about this world of becoming" is the epistemic equivalent of the passive nihilist's ethical jump from "there is no Good" to "the world has no value whatsoever." Neither is warranted.

The critique of *wahre Welt* metaphysics, then, does not imply that it is impossible to present better or worse interpretations of how this world of becoming should be understood. Such descriptions will not have the robust, determinate character of claims about Being. There will be no absolute, final "fact of the matter." But there can still be more or less accurate perspectives.[118] Knowledge of definite Truths will be replaced with interpretative models that seek to explain various processes with varying degrees of success. The world as will to power is the model Nietzsche proposes. Presenting such a description of the world of becoming is an option for Nietzsche.

Indeed, the will to power is not a metaphysics of Being, but an account of becoming, or a "process metaphysics" in today's parlance. It does not claim that, beneath appearances, things are actually will to power. It simply claims that the processes that make up the entire world are constituted of forces – that this is what best explains phenomena as we experience them.

[117] This is evinced with particular clarity in Nietzsche's comments on religion and morality, where he exhibits a clear commitment to a distinction between truth and figments of the imagination. See, for instance, *GD* VII §1:

> Moral judgments have this in common with religious judgments, that they believe in realities which are not realities. Morality is only an interpretation of certain phenomena – a *mis*interpretation. Like the religious judgment, the moral judgment belongs to a stage of ignorance at which the very concept of the real and the distinction between what is real and what is imaginary are still lacking: so that "truth," at this stage, designates a number of things which today we call "figments of the imagination."

[118] As Nehamas writes, "perspectivism does not result in the relativism that holds that any view is as good as any other" (*Nietzsche*, p. 72).

This "neither true nor apparent" realm of becoming is an ocean of conflicting forces in perpetual struggle, and this is what accounts for the perpetual arising and passing away of all things. There is no qualitative difference between what makes up non-organic entities and organic beings, and this is what accounts for the so-called mind's perception of objects, for the so-called will's effects on the body, etc. The fundamental drive governing an organism's behavior is not self-preservation or a desire for wellbeing, but the will to power, which accounts, among other things, for why people are restless and dissatisfied even when all their needs are met and thus continue tormenting themselves and one another. The subject of knowledge is an actively interpreting nexus of forces in contact with other such nexuses, which accounts for why all knowledge is really interpretation and all provisional "truths" are really perspectives. In short, Nietzsche's doctrine of the will to power is a non-dualist process metaphysics which does without the twin fictions of metaphysics of Being, namely Being itself – the domain of Truth and the Good – and the soul – this "divine breath" which alone has access to Truth and the Good. It might not be the definitive Truth about the world, but there is every reason to think Nietzsche thought it was a far superior interpretation than most. What is more, he was perfectly entitled to hold this belief.

The will to power doctrine is the conceptual framework in which Nietzsche elaborates his views on suffering and, yet more importantly, on how suffering is interpreted. As such, it constitutes the background for his understanding of pessimism and thus also of health and sickness.

To begin, it should be noted that Nietzsche's doctrine is, in its essence, a (strong pessimistic) Heraclitean worldview. The world as will to power is essentially a vision of the world as Dionysus – an endless, shifting struggle where war is quite literally the father of all things.[119] In itself, this directly implies descriptive pessimism. A world of perpetual struggle is a world of limitless suffering. At the psychological level, moreover, the insatiability of the fundamental drive at the heart of our being ensures that satisfaction never lasts. Will to power does not will any particular thing other than its exercise of power; acquiring an object, establishing one's control, or giving rise to a

[119] That the will to power qua philosophy of nature owes much to Heraclitus is intimated in one of Nietzsche's 1869 lectures. Here Nietzsche discusses Heraclitus' "scientific" view of the world. Everything is in perpetual motion and struggle, nothing is permanent, and all of "reality" consists of shifting exchanges of forces, which, each in their own way, strive for power: "Nowhere is there firm persistence, because in the end we always come to forces, whose effects simultaneously comport a desire for power" (*VP* §10).

particular state of affairs will never quench it. Dissatisfaction, restlessness, and discontent are thus the norm.[120] Hence descriptive pessimism.

In so far as the will to power directly implies a theory of interpretation, however, its main import concerns not suffering itself, but the way suffering is construed. Interpretation consists in giving something a meaning. It is the result of a particular nexus of forces constituting a particular fact, object, or state of affairs[121] in terms of a perspective that reflects its fundamental character qua nexus of force.[122] Pessimism of weakness, then, is expressive of the way in which weak, fundamentally reactive types interpret the reality of limitless, senseless suffering. It reflects the meaning reactive types give to the boundlessness of suffering.

Indeed, Nietzsche's typology of forces within a body – active vs. reactive – extends to a typology of fundamental types of people. *Décadents* are people constituted by endlessly conflicting clusters of forces – this is why they are in decline.[123] As a result of endless inner struggles, they do not have the required strength to engage actively and creatively with the outer world. In the overall economy of forces in the world, they are thus reactive parties. Their response to the endless suffering they meet in the world is to react to it by saying no to it, by declaring it evil, and to denounce it by inventing an antithetical True/Real World entirely bereft of struggle and suffering. The moral element in pessimism of the weak is the gesture of reaction par excellence.

120 Cf. Schopenhauer's observation on his Will's groundlessness at *WWV I* §57. Nietzsche can agree with Schopenhauer on this point, while disagreeing with him on the notion of Will as thing-in-itself and with the idea of willing as unitary.

121 Nietzsche claims that there is no "thing" *prior* to this constituting and that the object, "thing," or "fact" is entirely constructed by the process of interpretation (*GM* II §12). But this position should not be construed as radical subjectivism, let alone idealism. Two key ideas are actually at play here. First, the implication of Nietzsche's views is that the definition, meaning, and function of a particular "thing" never reflect its presumed "mind-independent" properties, but rather grow out of the dynamic relation between the "thing" in question and the interpreter. As Nehemas explains, perspectivism is not so much "a traditional theory of knowledge as the view that all efforts to know are also efforts of particular people to live particular kinds of lives for particular reasons" (*Nietzsche*, p. 73). Second, Nietzsche's idea is that the world is not made up of things, precisely, but of processes and events. Engaging with the world, however, requires us to organize and categorize an ever-fluctuating reality of ceaselessly dynamic becoming along the lines of more or less strict, static categories. Various groups of processes and events, which commonly appear in specific sequences, are thus given particular names and definitions and construed as static "things" in specific causal relations, e.g. the seed, the sapling, the tree. The idea is that, because there are really only processes and events, the boundaries between so-called things are always somewhat arbitrary, or conventional. More specifically, the way a set of events is constituted as a "thing" reflects the needs and the character of the subject doing the constituting. What is at play here is the "will to untruth" at the heart of all interpretation. I discuss this essential feature of the will to power in greater detail below.

122 *NL 1885–1887*, 7(60), *ibid. 1888–1889*, 14(186), and *GM* II §12.

123 *GD* II §11. See also *A* §17.

As such, it remains very much an expression of the will to power. Commenting on the nihilist *décadent* who longs for the great Nothing, Nietzsche explains that "the human will . . . *requires a goal*; it would sooner will *the void* than *not* will at all."[124] Since the *décadents* are too weak to produce any purpose for themselves in this world – since they find it too exhausting, difficult, and painful to truly engage with the world as it is – the only possible object of their striving is a non-world, i.e., God, Being, or the Real. Of course, the very object of their striving exhibits their entirely reactive attitude to the world. The desire to end suffering (and thus to end life itself), to attain a state of painlessness (their version of pleasure), their worship of Nothing as the *summum bonum* – in short, their pessimism of weakness – all of this is to be explained in terms of their will to power and its radical reactivity.

But Nietzsche's analysis goes further than this. It would be an error to think that everything that grows out of the *décadents*' pessimism of weakness actually wages war on life.[125] In reality, the rise of *décadent* nihilism and its life-negating ideologies constitutes a gigantic attempt, on the part of reactive forces, to gain the upper hand over active forces. This is true of reactive forces both within and among individuals. Recall how *ressentiment* is the potent, pregnant force whereby reactive *décadents* become creative in their own way. More specifically, it is what allows them to create values and to impose them on the world, and onto those unruly parts of themselves that still will life. This is how reactive forces go from being dominated to being dominating. This is a matter of one type of life trying to gain dominion over other types of life.

At the level of groups, the spread of nihilistic ideologies allows weak types to create spiritual, social, political, and cultural conditions in which they may not only survive and proliferate, but also dominate.[126] This dual function is served by all the outgrowths of the nihilist mentality – the cooking up of the *wahre Welt* of Being and saying no to the allegedly "immanent" world of becoming, the cultivation and institutionalization of guilt and self-loathing, the spread of slave morals to all strata of society, etc. These impoverish life and thereby create conditions in which a particular sort of life – the life of the *décadent* – is more bearable and widespread.[127] Fueled by *ressentiment* and its rancor, they allow the *décadent* to become a dominant type, not just numerically, but also qualitatively, through his/her moral tyranny over strong, affirmative, creative types. As

[124] *GM* II §1. [125] *Ibid.* §13. [126] *Ibid.* §14.
[127] This is the unfolding drama Nietzsche describes in *GM* III.

such, these ideological developments manifest the reactive weak types' will to power. They are pro-life (pro-*décadent*-life) in being anti-life.

Perhaps more importantly yet, at the level of the person's "inner life," the nihilist *décadent* morals of unselving allow unhealthy reactive forces within a person to combat and dominate the active, pro-life forces that are also at work within. It is in this sense that Nietzsche describes *décadence* as the need "to fight the instincts" (by which he means active, life-promoting instincts).[128] This is how reactive forces go from being dominated to being dominating within the individual. Through guilt, shame, and remorse, along with the self-belittling and self-enfeebling prescriptions of unselving morals, whatever is left inside the *décadent* of active, creative forces willing to engage genuinely with life is undone. This again is the work of the will to power of reactive forces seeking to expand their control over the very active forces which are meant to coordinate and direct them.

Décadence, *ressentiment*, the invention of the *wahre Welt*, and unselving morals are all accounted for in terms of the will to power in Nietzsche's thought. And at the basis of it all is pessimism of the weak, this fundamentally reactive response to or interpretation of the reality of limitless suffering. This is what, as a result of the *décadents*' fundamental weakness, construes suffering as a problem, as an argument against life, and as something to be removed.

Pessimism of strength, of course, is also an expression of the will to power. But it is an interpretation of suffering that indicates a predominance of active forces in an individual. Nietzsche's healthy type is a person in whom creative, active, form-giving forces are in control of reactive forces. It is in this sense that he is a fundamentally healthy, well-turned-out type. In facing suffering, the healthy strong pessimist does not spare himself the most profound of troubles. He keeps himself open to the greatest dread by rejecting any appeal to a world of Being behind becoming and with it to all false optimisms. He embraces suffering wholeheartedly. In doing so, he is creating conditions in which he will grow stronger and healthier, for, unlike in the *décadent*'s case, "what does not kill him, makes him stronger." Indeed, in exposing himself to the highest suffering through an open and unconditional recognition of the world's senseless suffering, the strong pessimist qua healthy/active type stands before the greatest stimulant, the most challenging "lure to life." This is what he needs to attain the pinnacle of great health, to grow as strong as can be. Finally, the strong pessimist's life-affirming declaration that "life is beautiful" in the face of all of its horrors and turmoil is his active will to power overcoming the resistance

[128] *GD* II §11.

involved in pessimism's harsh openness to suffering and gaining victory over what would otherwise lead to the defeat of life-negation, as it does in the weak/reactive type's case.

It is of crucial importance to see that the rise of the pessimism of both weakness and strength are processes of the same fundamental type. Indeed, on Nietzsche's theory of the will to power, the very dynamics at play in both the reactive *décadent*'s and the active, healthy type's behavior is governed by a fundamental law that regulates all of becoming qua will to power. This is the law of self-overcoming.

The verb to "to become," Nietzsche explains, is to be understood as "to overcome one's very self."[129] Self-overcoming is what accounts for the fundamentally dynamic nature of all things (or processes, strictly speaking). Everything either grows and develops or fades away, depending on the context, through an overcoming and destruction of its own previous form. To grasp this idea, one need only think of the destruction involved in the transition from seed to sapling, from star to supernova, or from child to adolescent – the latter being a destruction and loss particularly painful to parents, who sometimes even grieve the "dead" child. In short, it is the principle according to which everything comes into existence and eventually disintegrates. As such, self-overcoming is the fundamental character of the will to power. It is the operation through which forces extend the scope of their control and thus achieve the "power" which by nature they "will."

Though illustrative, the simple examples I have provided above are slightly misleading. This is because Nietzsche is above all interested in self-overcoming in the domain of ideology and psychology, not in the physical realm. As I mentioned in Chapter 1, at the macro level of ideology, self-overcoming is illustrated by the demise of Christian dogma at the hands of Christian morals.[130] The death of God is the result of Christian truthfulness turned scientific probity.

There are three possible outcomes of Christianity's self-overcoming according to Nietzsche. The first outcome is Christianity's survival in the form of superficially anti-Christian and atheist, but actually ultra-Christian, faith in science and in various secular ideologies. Science continues to exhibit its reactive Christian roots through its obsession with Truth, its perpetuation of the myth of Substance – the atom, or particle, matter, etc., all of them shadows of God – and its faith in Reason. Secular ideologies (right and left) exhibit their Christian roots through their rationalism and

[129] *NL 1885–1887*, 7(54). [130] *GM* III §27. See also *FW* §357.

optimism, or millennialism (the end of history). Under this scenario, Christianity's deluded, *décadent* optimism survives Christianity's self-overcoming. Christian nihilism, moreover, will not be overcome, let alone even apprehended. Ultimately, what is at the heart of Christianity emerges strengthened by its self-overcoming.

The second possible outcome is a laying bare of the life-negation at the heart of Christianity (and of its optimistic, atheist offspring) in the form of a New Buddhism. Here, delusional metaphysics and optimism truly perish and the *décadent* is faced with the bare fact of the world's hopelessly senseless and boundless suffering, and its lack of intrinsic worth, meaning, and purpose, etc. The result will be an ethics geared toward the great health of non-being, i.e. *nirvāṇa*. Unselving morals will remain in a soberer, more moderate, and less offensive form. *Décadence* will continue to wear away at Europe's health. Here, the life-negation at the heart of Christianity will, again, survive its self-overcoming. What is more, it will adopt an even stronger, more convincing form.

The third outcome is a complete overcoming of the life-negation and *ressentiment* at the root of Christianity and other nihilistic religions and movements. Here, the self-overcoming of Christianity through its truthfulness will be an opportunity for healthy types and free spirits to tear away at the cloak of world condemnation in which life has been wrapped and suffocated. Hence Nietzsche's ethics of life-affirmation as an inversion of what all morals so far have been predicated on,[131] namely the judgment "life is evil." This consists in the "self-overcoming of nihilism" itself, which Nietzsche defines as a "saying yes to everything that was previously denied."[132] The same dreadful sense of valuelessness and worthlessness that throws the *décadents* into the bleak despair of a New Buddhism is here interpreted by the healthy free spirit as an opportunity to rehabilitate the world and create new values based on life-affirmation. Here, Christianity fully destroys itself in the process of self-overcoming.

At the micro level of the individual's psychology, self-overcoming is exhibited with particular clarity in the battle reactive forces wage on what is left of active forces within the *décadent* through the morals of unselving.[133] By leading them to overcome themselves in this way, the *décadents'* values and behavior are instrumental in the increase in power of the reactive forces

[131] In this connection, Nietzsche speaks of the "self-overcoming of the moralist into his opposite – into *me*" (*EH* "Warum ich ein Schicksal bin" §3).

[132] *NL 1885–1887*, 9(164).

[133] Hence Nietzsche's frequent use of the term "self-overcoming" with reference to life-negating, self-negating morals, namely, at *M* §183, *GM* III §16, and *NL 1885–1887*, 1(129).

within them. Self-overcoming is also instantiated in the battle reactive types wage on all active forces through the ethics of life-negation and the defamation of everything in the world that is healthy, creative, active, and life-promoting. In fact, what we witness here, according to Nietzsche, is life overcoming itself through the proliferation and domination of everything anti-life.[134]

Most fundamentally, however, the pessimism of weakness that stands at the root of all these nihilistic developments is itself the work of self-overcoming. The reactive, weak type experiences suffering in general as a setback, as a diminution in strength. In the face of the dreadful fact that suffering is senseless and limitless – the most tormenting type of suffering of all – his despair is beyond measure. But all is not lost. Indeed, the will to power of reactive types manifests itself as this potent, creative albeit sick affect, namely *ressentiment*. Animated by *ressentiment*, they overcome their paralyzing dread. From the fact that the world is full of suffering, they draw the resentful moral implication that the world should not be. They attack and condemn life, invent *wahre Welt* fictions, institutionalize guilt and unselving morals, worship the great Nothing of No-Pain as God, etc., even to the point of openly embracing a life-negating ethics transparently geared toward extinction when their metaphysical fancies come crashing down under their own weight (Buddhism). In short, the *ressentiment*-fueled moral character of pessimism of weakness is a manifestation of *décadents*' attempt to overcome their dread before the boundless suffering of the world. This is the work of will to power qua will to self-overcoming.

However, self-overcoming is not limited to reactive forces alone. To remain healthy, the healthy type must continually overcome the reactive forces – the sub-personal sick types, as it were – which are no less part of his being than the predominant active forces.[135] This is also a form of self-overcoming.

In this connection, the healthy active type's pessimism of strength is particularly telling. Indeed, facing suffering in all of its senselessness and limitlessness constitutes the ultimate opportunity for the healthy type to overcome himself most thoroughly. Undergoing this supreme suffering – dread and horror before the reality of limitless suffering itself – is indeed the ultimate test of strength. This is because there are *décadent* forces within

[134] See, in this connection, *GM* III §13. At *GD* V §5 Nietzsche explains, in a similar vein, that "even that anti-natural morality which conceives of God as the counter-concept of life is only a value judgment of life," albeit of "declining, weakened, weary, condemned life."

[135] See, in this connection, Kaufmann, *Nietzsche*, p. 131.

even the healthiest type. The possibility of developing *ressentiment* against existence is a real one for any person. Reactive forces are at work, always ready for rebellion in every organism, even the best constituted one. By confronting becoming and its senseless horrors face-to-face, with an unswerving gaze, the healthy type creates the ideal conditions for the reactive forces within him to become dominant. He is in a sense flirting with the risk of developing *ressentiment* against reality – hatred of reality. He is exposing himself to the danger of descending into pessimism of the weak, *décadence*, world condemnation, etc. But if the active forces within him then succeed in overcoming this reactivity, in celebrating life not only in spite of, but because of suffering's limitlessness and senselessness, he will have effectively overcome the greatest of all obstacles. This is the highest show of strength, the most supreme health, the greatest victory. It is the blossoming flower that crowns the pessimism of the strong. This complete affirmation of suffering, this complete affirmation of life, is what Nietzsche refers to as *amor fati*. It corresponds to the healthy type's complete overcoming of *ressentiment*, guilt, and no-saying. As such, it is the most profound self-overcoming – the work of the most active and dominant will to power, which wills life and wills suffering.

It should be noted, finally, that in both cases – that of the nihilist crisis and that of responding to descriptive pessimism – the *décadent* and the healthy type are faced with exactly the same situation. In one case it is the crisis of valuelessness; in the other it is dread and horror before a world of ceaseless struggle and suffering. This is why these situations represent the ultimate challenge for the healthy type – they are exactly the type of situations in which *décadents* despair and embrace life-negation most forcefully. The healthy type wants to get as close to *décadence* as possible, perhaps even to taste *décadence* and *ressentiment*.[136] This is how he can then overcome himself most fully.

There remains one more important thing to note concerning the parallel macro/micro cases of the nihilist crisis and dread before descriptive pessimism. The markedly different forms of self-overcoming that take place among healthy vs. sick types is, again, a matter of how valuelessness/suffering are interpreted. The "situation" is the same. What leads to different outcomes is the way this situation is construed. There is thus an intimate link between types of interpretation and modes of self-overcoming.

[136] See, in this connection, Nietzsche's comments on being both a *décadent* and the opposite of a *décadent* and on how flirting with illness is essential to attaining great health (*EH* "Warum ich so weise bin" §2).

Any interpretation, any attribution of meaning, for Nietzsche, involves falsification. As a theory of interpretation, the will to power may thus also be characterized as the "will to untruth,"[137] or the "will to illusion."[138] As such, there is in both pessimism of the weak and in pessimism of strength a great lie about the world. These lies are what give both life-negation and life-affirmation their ethical force and their character as modes of self-overcoming.

Falsification through simplification is part of what makes life in a world of becoming possible. "Untruth," Nietzsche explains, is a "condition of life."[139] This is because knowledge is not possible with regard to becoming; knowledge is knowledge of static things.[140] The manifold interpretations that make up knowledge of a world of fixed objects is thus a manifold of falsifications. But the falsification Nietzsche refers to is not the production of an "appearance" that is false in contrast to a "true" reality "in itself." The idea, rather, is that the inherent dynamism and instability of the world of becoming is glossed over and simplified in the production of knowledge.[141] Through reification and hypostasis, we form around us a world of identities, equivalences, and enduring objects.[142] This is what makes the world graspable, understandable; it is what makes it possible to engage with the world by giving us power over it. Faced with dynamic becoming, we intend static beings. One may thus speak of an Apollonian drive at the heart of sentient beings – a drive to differentiate and individuate, to reify and hypostatize. This is the work of will to power qua will to interpretation; it is an active and creative work. Indeed, Nietzsche speaks of the eminently practical falsification presupposed by the notions of "knowledge" and "experience" as an artistic activity[143] – an Apollonian activity.

Reactive types, in this connection, are deluded when it comes to the element of fabrication in all knowledge. Just as they are oblivious to the

137 *JGB* §59. See also *NL 1885–1887*, 38(20), *ibid. 1882–1884*, 20(63) and (295).

138 *NL 1885–1887*, 7(54).

139 *JGB* §4. See also *NL 1882–1884*, 27(48) and *ibid. 1885–1887*, 34(352).

140 *NL 1885–1887*, 7(54).

141 Nietzsche first articulates his views on the "falsification" involved in knowledge in *WL* §1. Williams's critique of this text attributes to Nietzsche the view "that 'in itself' the world does not contain ... anything ... you might mention." See B. Williams, *Truth and Truthfulness* (Princeton University Press, 2002), p. 17. Given Nietzsche's critique of the appearance/reality divide in his later work, this is certainly not what he has in mind in *JGB* and his late notes. Here, the falsification at work in the production of graspable "things" does not falsify the determinate, unconstructed "Truth" of things as they are in and of themselves. Rather, falsification involves reifying what is really a flux of becoming into a property-bearing "being," or "thing." What is "false" is the form of the concept (a static as opposed to a dynamic, property-bearing substance/substratum, etc.) rather than its content.

142 See, in this connection, *JGB* §§4 and 17, *GM* II §12, and *NL 1885–1887* 40(13).

143 *NL 1885–1887* 38(2). Consider, in this connection, Lévi-Strauss's comments on the continuity between mythical or magical thought and scientific knowledge and the aesthetic activities of taxonomic categorizations and modelization which both involve. C. Lévi-Strauss, *La pensée sauvage* (Paris: Plon, 1962), pp. 37f.

hypostasis that delivers the "self," they ignore the falsifying reification that delivers a world of apparently stable, fixed objects, which "corresponds" to the knowledge they have of them. They grasp both "self" and "things" because these fictions are consoling; they make it look like the world is a more or less predictable universe of Being and beings. It is through this same process of falsification, on a grand scale, that reactive types invent a *wahre Welt* of pure Being entirely devoid of becoming.

When it comes to life-negation in all its forms, including that which has moved beyond the metaphysics of self and Being, the interpretation that forms the crux of pessimism of weakness is that becoming as a whole – i.e. the entire world – is to be understood and dealt with as "that which is evil, deceptive and corrupt." The meaning given to this world is arrived at through the invention of the counter-concept of the Good, or God for theists. This, of course, is result of the *ressentiment*-harboring *décadent*'s will to untruth and its invention of Being. As such, it is creative and artistic in its own life-negating way. It is, like all art, a will to untruth, a will to power. The "*homines religiosi*," Nietzsche muses, might be counted "among the artists, as their *highest* class."[144] If they form the highest class of artist, it is because they have swayed the most people, and in the deepest way, with their art. And this in spite of the fact that they are deluded artists who believe their own fictions are the Truth.

The *summum bonum* at the heart of Nietzsche's ethics of life-affirmation also involves a grand falsification, albeit a deliberate and conscious one. Recall how Nietzsche's positive model for the ideal of life-affirming great health is the tragic Greek,[145] the supreme pessimistic artist. Nietzsche's Anti-Buddhist healthy type is a tragic, Heraclitean *esthète*. *Amor fati* – his great *anti-nirvāṇa* – is the worship and celebration of the terrible God Dionysus himself. Indeed, the positive aesthetic judgment that forms the heart of the pessimism of the strong and leads to the worship of Dionysus instantiated in Attic tragedy is also what embracing eternal recurrence in *amor fati* ultimately involves. This is why Nietzsche claims that art is "the only superior counterforce to all will to life-negation, the anti-Christian, anti-Buddhist, anti-nihilist *par excellence*."[146]

Genuine, spontaneous, and *self-conscious* art (as opposed to mere delusion) is the fruit of the pessimism of strength. The aesthetic is the essence of

144 *JGB* §59.
145 Nietzsche opposes the "Buddhistic" to the "Hellenic" in relation to the meaning of suffering as early as 1872, at *GT* §§7 and 18.
146 *NL 1888–1889*, 17(3).

true health and strength. As Nietzsche explains, the judgment "this is beautiful" is the form of life-affirmation par excellence.[147] The healthy type of Nietzsche's positive philosophy, accordingly, is the supreme artist who enacts tragedy in *amor fati*. For this he must look upon the whole of becoming as the God Dionysus; he must stamp the Apollonian falsification "Dionysus" unto the world.[148]

Indeed, what is genuinely artistic about the affirmation of life and suffering in *amor fati* is not just the aesthetic judgment "this is beautiful," but, yet more importantly, the creation and embracing of a new, grand fiction. This fiction is the tragedy of eternal recurrence. Nietzsche's healthy type is not just an *esthète*, he is also a tragic artist who invents and embraces the supreme fiction that his life will recur eternally.[149] To "love fate," to worship Dionysus, he must first give a meaning, a specific life-affirming interpretation, to the object of his worship. And this is where his will to power as will to untruth comes into play. As Nietzsche explains:

> To *stamp* becoming with the character of Being – that is the supreme *will to power* . . .
>
> That *everything recurs* is the closest *approximation of a world of becoming to one of Being.*[150]

With the fiction of eternal recurrence, Nietzsche's healthy type gives to the world of becoming the character of Being, which, after all, is what the will to power qua will to interpretation/meaning always does on a smaller scale. In embracing Dionysus in this way the healthy type pronounces his resounding yes not only to life, but also to himself. Indeed, the healthy type makes himself into a "being" through the tragic myth of eternal recurrence – he becomes enduring and "fixed" through eternal recurrence.[151] In this way, this great artist reinstates the twin Apollonian fictions of self and Being, but

147 *NL 1887–1888*, 10(168).

148 From the point of view of the Apollonian–Dionysian dichotomy, it is true that the Dionysus of *GT* and the Dionysus of the later works is not exactly the same character. Kaufmann, in this connection, argues that the Dionysian, which was initially "conceived as a flood of passion to which the Apollonian principle of individuation might give form," later gave way to a post-Zarathustrian "union of Dionysus and Apollo: a creative striving that gives form to itself" (*Nietzsche*, pp. 281–2). Indeed, with the will to untruth, the Apollonian in Nietzsche's late works becomes an essential feature of the Dionysian.

149 For a detailed discussion of why there is no conclusive reason to believe Nietzsche actually held the theory of eternal recurrence as a cosmological doctrine, see Nehamas, *Nietzsche*, pp. 143–50.

150 *NL 1885–1887*, 7(54).

151 This is what prompts Nehamas to describe eternal recurrence as, more than anything else, "a view of the self" (*Nietzsche*, p. 150). Nehamas's discussion of eternal recurrence in relation to the construction of one's identity and one's "eternal life" is particularly enlightening in this regard (*ibid.*, pp. 150–69).

from a specifically life-affirming perspective. Life is affirmed as the Being "Dionysus" and he also affirms himself as an eternally recurring Self.[152]

After all, this is what the healthy type needs to do. First, considering the possibility of eternal recurrence, and with it the perpetual repetition of all of one's sorrows and troubles, is the greatest challenge there can be. It is the most difficult obstacle – that which presents the highest risk of faltering into despair and nay-saying. As such, it is what the healthy type must confront if he is to attain full self-overcoming. Second, at a psychological level, the will perpetually to relive one's life exactly as it has unfolded and as it will unfold allows the healthy type to entirely subvert any and all forms of guilt, shame, or remorse. In this sense, to want it all over and over again is essential to move beyond acceptance and resignation to guiltless celebration and affirmation.[153] By recasting becoming as a form of Being and his own contingent and unnecessary self as an eternal recurring Self, the healthy, artistic type invents the object of his love and worship, of his life- and self-affirming *amor fati*.

There is, however, a fundamental difference between the artistic falsification of Nietzsche's healthy type and the nihilist theist's. The twin fictions of *amor fati* – the falsification of becoming into Dionysus qua Being and the fiction of the eternally recurrent Self – are performed by an artist who is perfectly aware of the falsification he is engaged in. Irony thus has a key role in the healthy type's *summum bonum*.[154] In *amor fati*, both Dionysus – the "eternally recurring" – and the fixed, necessary Self are embraced and celebrated, but the healthy type never forgets these are fictions. He

[152] Nietzsche's ideal vis-à-vis the self finds an early expression in the following fragment: "Let us imprint the emblem of eternity on our life! This thought contains more than all religions, which have condemned this life as ephemeral and have taught us to place our hopes in an indeterminate other life" (*NL 1881–1882*, 11(159)).

[153] It is in this sense that Nietzsche's *amor fati* is not the Stoics' ideal. The Stoic sage is no artist. He accepts suffering and its necessity with dignity, but he does not engage with the world aesthetically and dynamically. In his wish to "live in accordance" with Nature, he is, on the contrary, aiming for staticity and firmness (*JGB* §12). There is a latent nihilism here, which is absent in Nietzsche's ideal. See, in this connection, Deleuze's discussion of the distinction between the ass's affirmation, which is just a "putting up" and "pure" Dionysian affirmation, which involves an element of *creation* (*Nietzsche*, pp. 174–5). On my reading, the Stoic is an ass.

[154] Heidegger completely misses out on the irony of the healthy type who embraces eternal recurrence in *amor fati* (*Nietzsche*, vol. 1, pp. 465f.). As an artist, the healthy type, who gives the meaning "Dionysus" to the mass of becoming that constitutes the world, knows he is falsifying becoming by stamping it with the character of Being. There is thus no reason to believe Nietzsche sincerely wants to reinstitute Being with the idea of eternal recurrence, even less that his so-called "fundamental metaphysical position" is "at bottom the very opposite [of 'atheism']" (*ibid.*, vol. 1, p. 471). Though *amor fati* is effectively the worship of Dionysus, Nietzsche is by no means proposing a new theism. Contra Heidegger, embracing eternal recurrence in *amor fati* is an ironic gesture. Like any non-delusional artist, the healthy type knows his creation is not real.

embraces them with irony, in full knowledge of the fact that they are his creations, his inventions. This is how he becomes, quite literally, the artist of his destiny (*fatum*). This is the conscious lie through which "one becomes what one *is*."[155]

In sum, Nietzsche's ideal of *amor fati* is modeled on the example of the tragic, Heraclitean Greek, who steps toward suffering and wills suffering as a condition for growth. This is the supreme expression of great health, defined in terms of the predominance of the active, creative, form-giving forces in man. Through a robust pessimism of the strong, Nietzsche's healthy type wills the greatest suffering of all – that which made Heraclitus such a hero and the tragic Greeks such artistic geniuses – namely dread and horror before the boundlessness and senselessness of suffering and struggle in a world of perpetual, unfathomable becoming. This is the ultimate test of strength, for such dread invites reactive, life-negating forces to come to the fore and creates ideal conditions for the poison of *ressentiment* to proliferate. By overcoming the great challenge of looking at this monstrous world with an unswerving gaze, and yet to declare it "beautiful" rather than "evil," the healthy type secures the greatest victory over everything reactive and *décadent* inside him. This is the highest self-overcoming, the most exalted manifestation of the will to power.

The healthy type's affirmation of suffering takes the form of embracing eternal recurrence in *amor fati*. At the prospect of a perpetual replay of one's entire existence, with all its sorrows and mistakes, eternal recurrence is the most brutal vision of the pessimism of strength. By embracing it, the healthy type overcomes the greatest of horrors and wipes away all traces of guilt. He says yes to all of life, and to all he was, is, and ever will be. In the form of eternal recurrence, becoming assumes the character of Being, or the God Dionysus, and the tragic healthy type "becomes what he is" as an enduring, fixed Self. It is through an ironical embrace of these deliberate and conscious fictions that the healthy type, qua artist, attains the highest health of *amor fati*. It is in this way that he goes beyond enduring and resigning himself to suffering, but embraces, affirms, celebrates, and wills it.

Nietzsche's ethics of life-affirmation form a coherent whole. His vision of *amor fati* as the absolute affirmation of suffering through the embrace of eternal recurrence seems, on the face of it, to provide a true life-affirming

155 This is the subtitle of Nietzsche's pseudo-autobiography, *EH*. I emphasize "is" because the healthy type knows he never "is," but only "becomes." This, of course, is part of the essential ingredient of irony in *amor fati*.

alternative to Buddhism's weak pessimistic flight from suffering. Nevertheless, there are two enigmatic passages from Nietzsche's late *EH* that seem to contradict Nietzsche's vision. Discussing *GT*, Nietzsche declares that tragedy will be reborn when humanity learns to undergo the greatest ordeals "*without suffering from them.*"[156] Echoing this claim a few pages further on, Nietzsche alludes to *amor fati* and describes it as not suffering from "what is necessary."[157] This second passage is particularly surprising. *Amor fati* consists precisely in embracing everything as interconnected and necessary. Everything, after all, is included in the eternal recurrence of the same.[158] So if the healthy type's *amor fati*, which consists in embracing everything as necessary, also involves not suffering from what is necessary, it follows that it consists in not suffering at all. But is the healthy type not animated by a will to suffer? Is suffering not a condition for his great health and strength? Is it not the Buddhist who is supposed to long for the cessation of suffering? How can *amor fati* involve the cessation of suffering when *amor fati* and *nirvāṇa* are supposed to be diametrically opposed? Or could it be that *amor fati* and *nirvāṇa* are not as opposed as Nietzsche believed them to be? To answer all these questions, it will be necessary to turn to the Indian Buddha's vision of great health.

[156] *EH* "Warum ich so gute Bücher schreibe" *GT* §4. [157] *Ibid. FW* §4.

[158] *FW* §341. See also *NW* "Epilog" §1: "What my innermost nature tells me is that everything necessary, seen from above and in the sense of a *great* economy, is also useful in itself – it should not just be tolerated, it should be loved . . . *amor fati.*"

CHAPTER 4

Nirvāṇa *and the cessation of suffering*

It is against the counter-model of the Buddha's ideal of *nirvāṇa* that Nietzsche articulates his life-affirming ideal of *amor fati*. To the life-negating goal of achieving great health characterized by the negation of suffering, he opposes the life-affirming goal of great health characterized by the affirmation of suffering. In Chapter 3, the ideal of *amor fati* was examined independently, on its own terms. The same must now be done for *nirvāṇa*.

Once this ground is covered, it will be possible to begin assessing Nietzsche's life-negation vs. life-affirmation dichotomy with clarity, and in the process to refine our understanding of the role of suffering in the post-theistic great health ethics of the Indian Buddha and the European (Anti-)Buddha. Indeed, before proper comparative work can be done, it is necessary to examine both terms of the comparison in isolation and in its own terms. This chapter, then, begins with an in-depth exploration of Buddhist moral psychology based on Buddhist texts alone, rather than through the lens of Nietzsche's interpretation, as was done in Chapter 2.

According to Buddhist philosophy, *nirvāṇa* stands for a state of supreme health in which suffering comes to complete cessation. Literally, *nirvāṇa* means "going out," or "extinction," as might be said of a flame or a fire. It would be reasonable to ask, then, what the going out of a flame could have to do with health. The first two 1925 Pāli Text Society definitions for *nirvāṇa* as a colloquial, non-technical term provide the missing link. The definitions read: "1. the going out of a lamp or fire (popular meaning). – 2. health, the sense of bodily wellbeing (probably, at first, the *passing away of feverishness* ...)."[1] The combustive and medical connotations of the term *nirvāṇa* can thus be seen to overlap very neatly if we regard fever as a "fire" of sorts, and feverishness as a form of burning.[2] *Nirvāṇa*, on this

[1] T. W. Rhys Davids and W. Stede (eds.), Pāli Text Society's Pāli–English Dictionary (Chipstead: Pāli Text Society, 1925), p. 198 (my emphasis).

[2] Cf. the Greek *pyrum* (fire), from which English derives "pyretic" ("relating to fever").

interpretation, is a state of health in the sense that it corresponds to the "going out" of a burning fever.[3]

What, we may first ask, is the nature of this fever? The Buddha's discourses provide a clear answer to this question. In the strictest sense possible, *nirvāṇa* simply corresponds to the "destruction of thirsting (*tṛṣṇā*)."[4] The Buddhist *summum bonum*, in short, is a state of wellbeing reached when the fiery fever of thirsting has "gone out."

What, we may then ask, is the relation between such a conception of great health and the complete cessation of suffering? The second noble truth of the Buddha's foundational teaching has it that suffering originates from thirsting. The third, accordingly, claims that the complete cessation of thirsting entails the cessation of suffering.[5] It follows that in so far as *nirvāṇa* stands for the cessation of thirsting, it also implies the cessation of suffering. Recovering from an illness always brings about a form of well-being characterized by the cessation of the symptoms of the illness. *Nirvāṇa* is no different. As a recovery from the malady of thirsting, it involves the cessation of suffering.

The relation between the health of *nirvāṇa* qua "going out" of the fever of thirsting and the cessation of suffering qua consequence of the "going out" of this fever suggests that there is something slightly mistaken about most presentations of noble truth teaching as a medical discourse. Thirsting, not suffering, is the illness Buddha actually diagnoses in the noble truth teaching.[6] Indeed, the fiery fever of thirsting is the pathological condition that is overcome in *nirvāṇa*: suffering is merely the symptom. The diagnosis of the debilitating condition Buddhism combats, then, is not contained in the first truth – which merely states the universality of the symptom. Rather, it is contained in the second truth – which tells us about the origin of the symptom, i.e. about the illness itself.

[3] By no means does this imply that other, more common, fire metaphors in Buddhist moral psychology should be discounted: namely, the canonical idea that *nirvāṇa* corresponds to the "going out" of the three fires, or "afflictions," of attraction, aversion, and delusion (*SN* IV.28f.). Having said this, as this chapter will show, there is much more to gain, philosophically, from building on the fire–fever analogy that colloquial uses of the word *nirvāṇa* in Ancient India apparently presupposed.

[4] *SN* III.190. See also *AN* I.133, *SN* I.136, and a host of other passages. In Chapter 2, I spoke of "desire" rather than "thirsting" because I was presenting Nietzsche's perspective. Henceforth, I will use the term "thirsting" to render the technical Buddhist term *tṛṣṇā*, which really has a far more specific meaning that the generic English "desire." Though *tṛṣṇā* can simply be rendered as "thirst" (the two forms are actually cognates), the verbal noun "thirsting" better conveys its dynamic nature.

[5] *V* I.10–11.

[6] This claim admittedly flies in the face not only of the vast majority of contemporary commentaries on Buddhist doctrine, but also the traditional accounts on which they are based. Philosophical rigor, however, demands that tradition not be followed on this point.

This shift in perspective with respect to Buddhist moral psychology makes it possible to offer a compelling response to a standard objection to the Buddha's foundational teaching. The objection goes like this:

> The Buddha claims that suffering is caused by desire, so that absence of desire leads to absence of suffering. But this is clearly contradicted by experience. The pain I feel when I burn my hand has nothing to do with desire. Similarly, even if I had no desires whatsoever – not even the desire to live by escaping the fire – flames *would* hurt me. The Buddha's account of suffering, then, is unsatisfactory.

The standard, traditional reply to this objection has it that desire, or thirsting, is what keeps us bound up in the world of cyclical transmigration. As a result, thirsting is responsible even for the suffering to which it is not directly related, and the cessation of thirsting effectively brings suffering to an end by virtue of bringing rebirth to an end.[7] This response does not have much purchase, however, in that it presupposes metempsychosis. What is more, it suggests the Buddhist goal is indeed to attain non-existence, as Nietzsche surmised.

However, if thirsting is seen as the illness and suffering as the symptom, it becomes possible to present a promising alternative response. The second noble truth should not be read as a blunt causal claim about the origin of suffering. Instead, it becomes evident that the suffering the Buddhist seeks to bring to cessation is something slightly more specific than what falls under the scope of the generic notion of pain, or suffering. Indeed, if thirsting is the illness and *duḥkha* the symptom, then we are entitled to consider under the heading "*duḥkha*" all of the dissatisfaction, frustration, exasperation, and pain that may arise from thirsting, but we are not entitled to draw the conclusion that all and any form of suffering must at bottom result from thirsting. On this interpretation, the semantic scope of "*duḥkha*" is not as wide as that of the generic English "suffering."[8] Rather, it specifically stands for the vast family of torments – big and small – that afflict people when they suffer from the fever of thirsting. As such, the second noble truth is not designed to explain why the flame hurts my finger, or the splinter my foot.[9]

7 This response, admittedly, coheres with the word of the second noble truth, which states that thirsting is "related to rebirth" (*punarbhāvika*) (*V* I.10). Later in this chapter, I will explain why it would be a mistake to read too much into the Buddha's use of pan-Indian idioms relating to the cycle of rebirth and its cessation in *nirvāṇa*.

8 This is why I will henceforth use the Sanskrit form *duḥkha* rather than the far less specific "suffering" to discuss Buddhist ideas.

9 I use the splinter example because my account of how *duḥkha* should be understood actually makes it possible for Buddhists to explain away the apparent contradiction in a famous story about the historical Buddha. The story tells of how Devadatta, the Buddha's jealous cousin, attempts to murder the Buddha

Nevertheless, the second noble truth does claim to explain a particularly salient feature of existence, namely its overall unsatisfactory, if not painful, character. A preliminary account of the Buddhist etiology of *duḥkha* goes something like this, then. The fever of thirsting designates a specific mode of affective engagement with the world. In the noble truths discourse, the Buddha identifies its three basic forms: (1) thirsting for objects of desire, (2) thirsting for things to come into existence, or arise, and (3) thirsting for things not to be, or to disappear.[10] Another frequently evoked idea is that the fiery fever of thirsting manifests itself as the "three fires" of attraction, aversion, and apathy/somnolence. This highlights the egotistic ("I" as center) and egoistic ("I" as measure of all things) structure of the affective mode of engagement characterized by thirsting. Indeed, under the influence of the three fires, I (1) develop desire and attachment for what serves my interests (attraction), (2) develop anger and hatred toward things that oppose my interests (aversion), and (3) remain ignorant of, or indifferent to, what has no bearing on my interests (apathy/somnolence).[11]

In sum, thirsting designates a mode of experiencing and engaging with the world on the basis of self-centered needs. The general idea is that I continually "thirst" for particular objects, persons, positions, states of mind, situations, feelings, outcomes, etc. It is this mode of affective engagement with the world, Buddhists claim, that gives rise to a large family of sentiments – e.g. discontent, dissatisfaction, disillusion, disappointment, frustration, fear, anxiety, etc. – which are commonly designated as "painful" (*duḥkha*). *Duḥkhatā* ("painfulness") therefore characterizes the life of whoever is afflicted by thirsting. This is why the Buddha, as a therapist of mankind, propounds the destruction of thirsting and with it the great health of *nirvāṇa*.

Though there is also evidence for this in the Buddha's discourses, later developments in Buddhist philosophy during the Classical period make it clear that the Buddhist etiology of *duḥkha* goes far deeper than the fever of thirsting. Fever, after all, remains a symptom. What, we may ask, is the underlying illness of which the fever of thirsting is only a consequence?

by hurling an enormous rock at him. Devadatta only succeeds in injuring the Buddha's foot, which is pierced by a splinter from the boulder. At *SN* I.27, we are told that though this caused him excruciating pain, the Buddha endured his suffering unperturbed. Since the Buddha has attained *nirvāṇa*, he has entirely recovered from thirsting, which in theory makes it impossible for him to experience *duḥkha*. And yet the Buddha suffers from his injury. How is this possible? The story coheres with Buddhist moral psychology, of course, if we keep in mind that the *duḥkha* that ceases in *nirvāṇa* is specifically the suffering caused by thirsting, not all forms of suffering and physical harm.

10 *V* I.10. 11 On this point, see MacKenzie, "Enacting the Self," p. 269.

The Buddha gives us a good hint in the widely overlooked *Paṭipadāsutta* ("Path Discourse"). He begins by rehearsing the twenty standard ways of conceptualizing the self's relation to the person's constituent parts. For each of the five constituents, one may believe either that it is the self, that it is an attribute of the self, that it is contained by the self, or that it contains the self.[12] The Buddha then explains that positing a self in any of these ways is what is responsible for our sorry condition. "Self," he concludes, is the "conception leading to the origin of *duḥkha*."[13] Conversely, he explains that the elimination of the self construct in all of its forms is the path leading to the cessation of our unhappy condition. "Not-self," accordingly, is "the conception leading to the cessation of *duḥkha*."[14] With two straightforward synonym substitutions, we arrive at the following result: "Self" is the conception leading to thirsting (i.e. the "origin of *duḥkha*," as defined by the second noble truth) and "not-self" is the conception leading to the cessation of thirsting (i.e. the "cessation of *duḥkha*," as defined by the third noble truth). The Buddha, then, seems to be saying that there exists some sort of relation between the fiction of the "self" and the fever of thirsting. More specifically, in so far as the conception "self" is said to lead to thirsting, it would appear that it is in fact the underlying psychological ground for, or cause of, thirsting.[15]

This view finds a clear echo in the works of Classical Buddhist philosophers.[16] The idea, here, is that what is ultimately responsible for the arising of *duḥkha* is our pre-reflective commitment to the existence of the self. As a consequence, *nirvāṇa* involves uprooting the deeply entrenched habit of looking upon oneself as, precisely, a robust, unitary "self." On the face of it, this account of moral psychology openly contradicts the second noble truth, which states that it is thirsting, and not the idea "self," which is responsible for suffering. But if thirsting is a consequence of the "self"-delusion, as the *Paṭipadāsutta* suggests, then the contradiction is quickly resolved. Thirsting, it turns out, is the proximate cause of *duḥkha*, while the ego-principle is its

[12] *SN* III.44. This certainly does not exhaust all the possible ways of conceptualizing the self, but that does not alter the point being made here. It seems that in the recension of this discourse, a shorthand version of self-views was used. Other discourses make it obvious there were other theories of self around (see *DN* I.12f., for instance).

[13] *SN* III.44. [14] *Ibid.*

[15] Cf. Albahari, *Analytical Buddhism*, pp. 61–3. Alhabari reads this text in a very similar light, yet draws only the more modest, allegedly "empirical" conclusion that thirsting and the sense of self "co-arise." Contra Alhabari, it is obvious that the *Paṭipadāsutta*'s claims is that thirsting is conditional upon a "self"-delusion of sorts.

[16] These include Vasubandhu (*AKBh*, p. 478), Candrakīrti (*MV*, p. 349 and *MA* VI.120), Śāntideva (*BA* IX.78), and Prajñākaramati (*BAP*, p. 492), among many others.

root cause.[17] Translating this back into the medical discourse, we can say that the ego-principle is the underlying infection of which the fever of thirsting is a symptom.

To tell the full story of the arising of thirsting qua fever on the basis of the ego-principle qua infection, it is necessary to bring another pathogenic character into play. Indeed, the Buddha's discourses indicate that there is in fact an intermediate link between the notion and sense of "self," on the one hand, and thirsting, on the other. Explaining what happens to an accomplished Buddhist, the Buddha states that a person who has relinquished all modes of conceptualizing the self "does not grasp anything in the world, on account of not grasping, thirsts no longer, and on account of not thirsting, attains complete *nirvāṇa*."[18] What this suggests is that between the "self" view and thirsting stands a form of "grasping" (*upādāna*).[19] This last concept needs to be examined closely.

The Sanskrit form "*upādāna*" is confusing. Not only does it refer to "grasping" or "clinging," but it also means "fuel" as an object noun and something like "combustion" as an action noun. In the latter sense, it stands for what a flame "does" to the fuel it consumes. The flame, in Ancient and Classical Indian languages, "clings" to the fuel it consumes. In Buddhist texts, the ambiguity surrounding the term *upādāna* is deliberately played upon. For instance, *upādāna* as the psychological activity of "grasping" is clearly alluded to when the five psycho-physical constituents are described as the "fuel" that one clings to.[20] *Nirvāṇa*, in a similar vein, is spoken of as the going out of a fire resulting from the exhaustion of fuel.[21]

17 On this point, see A. Panaïoti, "Anātmatā, Moral Psychology and Soteriology in Indian Buddhism," in N. Mirning (ed.), *Puṣpikā: Tracing Ancient India through Text and Traditions. Contributions to Current Research in Indology*, vol. 1 (Oxford: Oxbow Books Press, forthcoming). The idea that the ego-principle (*ahaṃkāra*) is the root cause of *duḥkha* is borrowed from Śāntideva (*BA* IX.78.a). Cf. Candrakīrti on the "view of the real self" as the root of all afflictions and of *saṃsāra* itself (*MV*, p. 349; see also *MA* VI.120 (in *MV*, p. 340)), or Vasubandhu on "grasping at the self" as the source of all afflictions (*AKBh*, p. 461).

18 *DN* II.68.

19 In the central canonical teaching of dependent co-arising, the Buddha states that grasping arises dependent upon feelings (*vedanā*), which in turn requires a sensory apparatus, and so on (see *V* I.1). But this doctrine only tells us about the necessary condition for grasping to arise, not about its psychological ground. What concerns us here, in contrast, is the underlying ground of grasping – namely the ego-principle – not the conditions required for it to arise.

20 *V* I.11. The term used is *upādānaskandha*, which may be rendered as "fuel-constituent," i.e. "constituent that is fuel." See Ganeri, *The Concealed Art of the Soul*, p. 200.

21 Hence the following simile for the accomplished Buddhist: "[He 'goes out'] just as a fire without fuel would go out because it is not fed more fuel" (*SN* II.85). Consider, in this connection, the Buddha's deliberately ambiguous claim – *nibbuto 'ham asmi anupādāno 'ham asmi* (*MN* II.237) – which can be rendered as "I am 'put out,' I am without fuel" *or* "I am 'put out,' I am without attachment."

It should be noted that the appearance of "grasping" in the Buddhist psychological story gives rise to something of a conflict in explanatory frameworks. In a number of passages in the canon, *nirvāṇa* is described not as the "going out" of the burning fever of thirsting – or, more precisely, as the destruction of thirsting – but more literally as the "extinction" of the fire that feeds off the fuel which is the mind-body apparatus. This leads to a number of questions. What is the relation between these two images? What is grasping and how does it relate to thirsting? What does it mean to say that the psycho-physical elements are "fuel"? If they are fuel, what kind of "fire" are they fuel for? And what, finally, does this have to do with the infection of the ego-principle?

All of these questions can be answered by turning to the writings of Nāgārjuna and his Mādhyamika followers. Here, it is claimed that the relation between the self qua mental construction and the psycho-physical constituents that make up the so-called person is analogous to the relation between a flame and the fuel that feeds it.[22] The idea finds its first articulation in Nāgārjuna's *MMK*. Nāgārjuna begins by showing that "fire" and "fuel" are so thoroughly interconnected, both logically (as concepts) and empirically (as events), that a series of insoluble paradoxes arises if the two are thought of as "things" bearing some form or another of fixed relation.[23] The upshot is that "fire" and "fuel" are not substantial entities, but mere abstractions developed to describe a single process – namely combustion – which is then bifurcated between agent (fire) and patient (fuel). Nāgārjuna concludes with the key claim that the relation between fire and fuel is analogous to the relation between the self and the psycho-physical constituents that make up a person.[24] Neither the self (qua agent of combustion) nor the constituents (qua fuel, or patient of combustion) have an independent existence – there is really only an impersonal process of grasping, or, more precisely, of appropriation. As Candrakīrti explains: "What is appropriated is the fuel, i.e. the five [types of] elements that are appropriated. What is constructed in their appropriation is called the appropriator, the thinker, the performing self."[25]

The Mādhyamika idea, then, is that the "self" – more precisely the sense of self – feeds off the psycho-physical elements in the same way as a flame feeds off fuel. The relation is one of appropriation (i.e. inward-directed grasping); the flame-like "self" is the appropriat*or* (*upādātṛ*) and the psycho-physical constituents are the fuel that is

[22] See Nāgārjuna's *MMK* x.15 and *Pp*, p. 212. [23] MMK x.1–14. [24] *Ibid.* 15.a–b. [25] *Pp*, p. 212.

appropriated.[26] On the Buddhist account, then, my sense of self as an enduring unitary entity is generated and maintained through a perpetual pre-reflective activity of appropriation whereby the psycho-physical apparatus is laid claim to and constituted as "mine." Ganeri rightly describes this as a "performativist view" of the self.[27] Self-identification, on this account, is generated through the spontaneous activity of appropriation. It is through the performance of appropriation that the performing "self" constitutes itself as the "owner" and "controller" of physical and mental events. The ego-principle (*ahaṃkāra* – literally "I-maker") "makes" the "I" through this activity of appropriation.

It is now possible to see how the infection of the ego-principle, the appropriation of the constituents by the performing self, and the fever of thirsting are related. The process of "I"-making at the heart of the ego-principle is analogous to a process of combustion. The sense of being a unitary enduring self is generated and maintained in the same way as a flame is: namely, by feeding off the psycho-physical "fuel" which it "appropriates" in the process of combustion/identification. If the fire analogy is translated back into the medical discourse, it becomes possible to describe "appropriation" as a vast inflammation of the entire psycho-physical apparatus. It is by virtue of this inflammation that mental and physical events are "fuel" for the fire of identification via appropriation. The sense of "self," in turn, arises in so far as the mind and body are thus inflamed. As for the burning fever of thirsting, it is consequent upon the inflammation of appropriation. The mind and body are "inflamed" as a result of the infection of the ego-principle, and by virtue of this inflammation there arises the fiery fever of thirsting.

The relation between grasping and thirsting, however, is really far more complex than that between an "inflammation" and a "fever." To see how this is so, it is necessary to put the pyretic analogy aside and to enter head first into the domain of Buddhist moral psychology. Thirsting, seen in this light, is conditional not only upon the construction of the self through inward-directed grasping (appropriation), but also through the construction of the ego's self-referential horizon through the outward-directed component of grasping.

[26] On this point, see also Ganeri, *The Concealed Art of the Soul*, pp. 200f. and D. S. Ruegg, The Literature of the Madhyamaka School of Philosophy in India (Wiesbaden: O. Harrassowitz, 1981), p. 40. I will henceforth render inward-directed grasping, or *upādāna*, as "appropriation."

[27] Ganeri, *The Concealed Art of the Soul*, p. 203. See also J. Ganeri, "Subjectivity, Selfhood and the Use of the Word 'I'," in Siderits, Thompson, and Zahavi, *Self, No Self?*, pp. 176–92, at p. 190; MacKenzie, "Enacting the Self," pp. 264–5; and M. Siderits, "Buddhas as Zombies: A Buddhist Reduction of Subjectivity," in Siderits, Thompson, and Zahavi, *Self, No Self?*, pp. 308–31, at p. 311.

Indeed, if the egotistic mode of engagement with the world that characterizes thirsting presupposes and depends upon the robust sense of "self" that the ego-principle generates via appropriation, it also co-arises with specific forms of cognitive behavior which are closely related to outward-directed grasping. More specifically, outward-directed grasping co-arises with the conceptual proliferation (*prapañca*) of hypostatized constructs (*vikalpa*) and reifying views (*dṛṣṭi*).[28] The idea is that to constitute something as an object of attraction or aversion is de facto to constitute it as a stable "entity" bearing specific properties. Thirsting is thus conditional upon the mental operations of hypostasis and reification that constitute this world of evanescent becoming – i.e. of instable processes – as a world of fixed substances and fleeting attributes. Our unhealthy affective take on the world, in short, goes hand in hand with an unhealthy cognitive take on the world.

The Buddhist claim is that thirsting-based attraction or aversion for *x* implies thinking of *x* as a static thing with specific qualities, rather than as a dynamic, ever-changing process. Indeed, it is to reified "things" alone that attraction and aversion can pertain. Nothing, for instance, tests love or enmity so much as changes in "who" the loved/hated person "is." Such affective responses imply being able to "grasp" a given *x* in the sense of "comprehending" *x* in a particular way, namely as an entity that is either desirable/useful/good or undesirable/harmful/bad for me. Through the discursive proliferation of conceptual constructs and reifying views, we thus create an all-encompassing justificatory scheme for our desires and aversions.[29] If this were not unconscious and pre-reflective, this activity of self-referential horizon construction might be described as large-scale rationalization. Since it is unconscious and pre-reflective, we must look upon it as the spontaneous expansion of beliefs that corroborate our desires or aversions and co-arise with these. Most fundamentally, the idea is that the occurrence of thirsting implies that the ego has situated itself in the center of a world populated by stable entities to which it bears determinate relations. Since the world as I experience it is already structured in reference to myself, all of the desires, hopes, expectations, aversions, etc. that make up

[28] Though this idea has firm roots in canonical texts – namely, *DN* II.276f., *MN* I.108f., *Sn* 780–7, 796–803, 824–34, and 862–77, to list but a few sources – it is in Madhyamaka texts that it is most thoroughly worked out, especially in commentaries to *MMK* XVIII.5. Nāgārjuna's root verse describes the intimate connection between the conceptual proliferation of hypostatized constructs and forms of behavior conditioned by the three "afflictions." The account which follows is a philosophical reconstruction of the Madhyamaka position.

[29] On this point, see Gethin's comments on the ethical impetus behind Nāgārjuna's critique of substance metaphysics in *The Foundations of Buddhism*, pp. 240–2.

thirsting seem perfectly legitimate. My thirsting-based affective responses, as a result, seem to be a matter of common sense.

The relation between the grasping that delivers a world of stable entities and the ego-principle is threefold. There is, to begin with, a *genetic relation* between the "self" and its "horizon." Grasping involves the performance of the self not only through its laying claim to the physical and mental events that "belong to me" – e.g. my body, my feelings, my desires, my thoughts, my convictions, etc. – but also through the construction of a horizon comprising entities whose very constitution as "grasped by me," or "part of my horizon," reflect my interests, concerns, fears, desires, etc. Constructing the self thus also involves constructing the world as it is for the self. It involves, in other words, the construction of a thoroughly self-referential horizon with the self at its center and as the "measure" of all things in its horizon. This is the work of conceptual proliferation which produces myriad hypostatized constructs and reifying views which the subject "grasps" as part of its identity. So what I attribute to myself is only part of my identity. In reality, my identity is related to the entire world around me, which I grasp in a particular way.

The second relation is a *structural relation*. Indeed, though the content of this horizon and the value attributed to the things it comprises vary from person to person (though there is much overlap in the horizons of most humans at least, given a large number of shared needs, fears, interests, etc.), the form of this horizon construction is common to all mentally healthy humans. I organize the world around me as a world of stable "entities." I am pre-reflectively committed to substance metaphysics. And it is in this activity of reification and hypostasis that the second relation between the ego-principle and outward-directed grasping – i.e. grasping views and "entities" that constitute the object of these views – becomes manifest. Indeed, in so far as it is an integral part of my fixed identity, my horizon must be maximally stable and optimally intelligible. It is this twin demand for stability and intelligibility that thrusts us in the direction of substantialist and thus anthropomorphic thinking. Indeed, in so far as the primary "stable thing," or substance, is precisely the "I," it is on analogy with the self and its relation to "its" constituents (i.e. the agent–patient, substance–attribute, substratum–quality relation) that we construct the world of "objects" that "possess" qualities. As intelligibility and familiarity go hand in hand, moreover, it is only natural that we take that with which we are most familiar – the "I" – as the model for self-standing things.

Simply stated, the ego-principle results not only in a pre-reflective commitment to a substance view of the self, but also to a pre-reflective commitment to substance metaphysics. The self as substance is constructed through the appropriation of what "belongs to me." Entities as substances, for their part, are constructed through the outward-directed grasping of hypostatized constructs and reifying views that deliver "my horizon." In this way, the self-delusion gives rise to a substance delusion which far exceeds the delusion that the self is a substance. Substance metaphysics turns out to be primal anthropomorphism. At work is a systemic mechanism of personification whereby this world of dynamic processes is interpreted as a world of static things – "selves" – bearing certain properties – their "constituents."

The third relation between grasping and the self is an emotional relation. If the world needs to "make sense" and thus to be constituted of fixed "things/selves" relating to one another on the basis of rigid rules in a regular and predictable fashion, it is because this is required if the integrity of the self is to be maintained. Identity, after all, is closely related to the horizon the self constitutes. But the integrity of the self is perpetually threatened by change, both external and internal. Faced with the intractable reality of change and impermanence that perpetually endangers the self and its horizon, the subject needs, in order to preserve its own uniformity and stability, to generate various explanatory frameworks which can at least account for change while consolingly preserving the underlying order and stability of "things." In this way, self and world can remain impervious to the "merely contingent" changes which, it is presumed, do not alter their essence.

And with this idea we come full circle, back to thirsting. My identity is intimately tied to my concerns, desires, interests, beliefs, etc. In short, it is tied to the entire domain of thirsting-based affective behavior and responses. The grasping through which the mental construction of my horizon is performed presents me with a world that is mapped out in terms of my needs, tastes, fears, and concerns. As such, the self-centered, need-based mode of engaging with the world which follows from the ego-principle and manifests itself as thirsting implies the conceptual organization of my world in terms of static entities, which speak to me, as it were.[30] This, in turn, not only justifies my thirsting-based behaviors, but also preserves, protects, and reinforces my identity, which is itself so closely tied to my tastes, interests, concerns, etc. In this connection, Nāgārjuna presents a telling analogy: "Just as a fool falls in love with his reflection in a mirror because he conceives it be true, people here in the

[30] This idea finds its first articulation in an early Buddhist verse, which states that "the thought 'I am' is the root of [all] labeling (*sāṃkhyā*) and conceptual proliferation (*prapañca*)" (*Sn* 916.a–b).

world, by virtue of delusion, are locked into a cage of objects."[31] Here, Nāgārjuna underscores the robust narcissism involved in the development of the conceptual structure that delivers a world of static things. Indeed, the cognitive habit of constituting the world as a self-referential world of stable beings only reinforces the self-centered mode of our engagement with the world. In producing a world of robust "things" which can be grasped, be it physically or intellectually, it produces a world that reflects (and justifies) our concerns and thus perpetuates our egotistic attitude to self and world.[32]

There is, finally, one more key relation between thirsting, the "self," and the grasping-fueled conceptual proliferation of hypostatized constructs and reifying views. This concerns a specific type of reifying view designed to quench a specific form of thirsting. Every "thing" – including many things "inside me," e.g. my body, my emotional states, even my desires – continually escapes my grasp, in the sense both of control and of understanding. This is because there really are no "things" with endurance or even momentary stability, but only intertwined processes in continual flux. This is as true of my "self" as it is of its attributes, of the "entities" around me, and of their attributes. Among other things, the frustration and insecurity ensuing from the disjunction between the world "as it really is" (*yathābhūtaṃ*) – i.e. impermanent, in constant flux, and radically indeterminate – and the way we delude ourselves into believing it is (or should be) gives rise to a thirst for an Abiding Beyond and/or for "systems." When it comes to devising these consciously elaborated fictions, the "self" is again the only model I use. Hence *brahman* as the Supreme Self, say, or substances as discrete selves. The thirst for regularity and predictability is at the source of all "realism" in ontology among more erudite types. The more popular thirst for Unperturbed Being, for its part, gives rise to all forms of theism and speculative metaphysics. Thirsting, in short, is at the root of the metaphysical need, to use Schopenhauer's and Nietzsche's phrase. The self-delusion at its source does not only provide the model for the substance/Being delusion, then: it is also the psychological source of the very need for these fictions.

31 *YṢK* 53.

32 Ganeri is not quite right, then, to claim that *prapañca*, which he translates as "thesis-thinking," is "the primary source of attachment" (*The Concealed Art of the Soul*, p. 104). The idea, rather, is that attachment and discursive proliferation are two sides of the same coin – the affective side and the cognitive side. In so far as one is attached to things, one thinks of them in a certain reifying way. Conversely, in so far as one thinks of things in a certain reifying way, one experiences attachment (either to the "thing" or to one's beliefs concerning the thing).

Now that the rudiments of Buddhist psychology have been examined, it will be possible to provide a clearer picture of what the ideal that stands at the helm of Buddhist ethics actually involves. Because this ideal is first and foremost that of a recovery from illness, it is important to begin by bringing together everything we have covered so far to examine the nature of the sickness Buddhism targets.

The first thing to point out is that according to Buddhist philosophy the "self" is not merely an illusion, but first and foremost a delusion. The idea that I have an unchanging core at the heart of my being is far more than "mismatch between reality and appearance."[33] Rather, it is the result of active (though pre-reflective) self-deceit. The distinction between illusion and delusion is the key to gaining a proper understanding of Buddhist moral psychology.

The first thing that distinguishes illusions from delusions is that the latter involve active distortion. On the Buddhist account, the illusion of an enduring, unitary self does not just "happen"; it does not simply arise as a result of perceptual or cognitive flaws. There is no doubt that autonomous, unconscious mechanisms – such as "blindness to change"[34] and the "illusion of stability"[35] – have a role to play in the arising of the self-fiction. But these mechanisms alone do not exhaustively explain the arising and maintenance of the sense of self. The self, indeed, is constructed through the activity of appropriation. Having the illusion of "self" is not a mere state or condition, which I passively undergo. Rather, it is something that is actively sustained. This is in keeping with Buddhist philosophy's view of the world as a play of dynamic processes and events. The illusion of self is not "just there." It is the result of a specific activity of "selving," or I-making, effected through laying claim to mental and physical events and the construction of a self-referential horizon. This implies that the "self"-delusion, in so far as it is "done," can also be undone.

The second thing that distinguishes illusions from delusions is that delusions, unlike illusions, are pathological. The self is not a harmless illusion like the false impression that the straight stick that is half-submerged in clear water is crooked. Rather it is a debilitating delusion by virtue of which people are rendered dysfunctional and maladapted. Illusions can be dangerous in so far as they misrepresent states of affairs. But

[33] Alhabari, "Nirvana and Ownerless Consciousness," p. 88. Like practically all scholars of Buddhism, Alhabari thinks the self is a mere illusion according to Buddhist philosophy. As far as I know, I am the first to make the point that it is more than an illusion, but a pathological delusion.

[34] Dreyfus, "Self and Subjectivity," p. 131. [35] *Ibid.*, p. 124.

delusions are far worse. They can distort the way in which the subject constitutes a great number of states of affairs, thereby warping a vast range of the subject's behavior. As we have just seen, Buddhist philosophy makes the bold claim that the self-delusion actually affects the full scope of the subject's affective and cognitive behavior.

Under the spell of the self-delusion, I am convinced that I am a fixed, enduring self at the center of a world of fixed, enduring things, and that I see and evaluate the entire world through the sieve of a foundationless self-interest. As such, I am prey to a large family of debilitating mental states, which include fear, frustration, apprehension, disappointment, despair, anxiety, identity crises, etc. This is domain of *duḥkha*. Buddhist philosophy adds that the self-delusion and the thirsting it gives rise to also cause me to act in (often unwittingly) manipulative, contriving, disingenuous, and opportunistic ways. In short, the operative mode of thirsting-based behavior is best characterized as one of systemic egotism, (often counter-productive) egoism, and enmity toward all that is adverse and "other." Such an attitude only broadens the scope of *duḥkha*.

The idea that the self-delusion is pathological and debilitating can be fleshed out with two analogies. Consider the case of a person suffering from a paranoid personality disorder.[36] This condition is characterized by a profound narcissism. When paranoid subjects hear someone laughing across the street, they assume they are being laughed at. Hearing something tangentially related to their life on the radio, they will assume that someone, somehow, is trying to "tell them something." If a child accidently steps on their foot in a crowded shop, they will believe this is an intentional attack. In extreme cases, those suffering from paranoia will interpret practically all events as evidence that "the system" or "society" is plotting against them, that they are under surveillance, that everyone around them is play-acting, etc. More generally, when presented with the threat of harm or disappointment, people who suffer from paranoia do not see that practically everything that happens "to them" has nothing to do with them, but is, on the contrary, purely accidental, contingent, and arbitrary. As a result of such delusional egotism, they will constitute the harm as somehow intended, the narcissistic-paranoid implication being that they matter quite a bit more than they really do. Now, the *structure* of narcissistic self-referentiality so characteristic of paranoia is essentially what Buddhist philosophy attributes to standard human behavior. Such

[36] On this devastating disorder, see R. J. Waldinger, *Psychiatry for Medical Students* (Washington, DC: American Psychiatric Press, 1997), pp. 147–51.

delusional self-importance, it is claimed, goes hand in hand with the self-delusion and gives rise to an attitude of systemic enmity.

Another dimension of the Buddhist idea is brought out by the (slightly clichéd) example of a developer who visits a farm with his animal-loving children. Initially reluctant to take his children to the country for lack of time, our developer has finally found a way of conciliating business interests and parental duties by taking his children to visit an educational farm whose owners also happen to be looking to sell their property. While his children are busy enjoying country activities such as grooming and feeding animals, the developer walks around the farm and proceeds to evaluate the property. He notes everything that increases the value of the property with excitement (attraction), and everything that decreases its value with disappointment, or frustration (aversion). Of course, his cost-benefit analyses leave him blind to everything that does not affect the property's value (apathy). The entire evaluation, of course, is done in relation to the capital he has at his disposal and the profit or loss he stands to make. On the Buddhist view, the self-delusion implies that one's emotional world operates in a way that closely resembles the developer's attitude toward the farm. The evaluative claim is that such an experience of the world is particularly impoverishing, and ultimately disabling.

Overall, Buddhist philosophy regards the effects of the self-delusion on the human psyche at the emotional, conative, and cognitive level as deeply debilitating. The idea, in its most basic form, is that we set ourselves up for disappointment. This is because this world of flux, disorder, and impermanence cannot satisfy a person looking for stability, order, and permanence. Our bodies and minds change in ways that are contrary to our desire – especially, though not exclusively, through aging and death. The people we love all eventually behave in ways that disappoint or frustrate us, and ultimately die during our lifetime if we do not precede them in exiting this world. Moreover, we have very limited control over the fate of our material possessions or over the behavior of all the potentially harmful agents around us. At the conceptual level, moreover, reality continually seems to evade our capacity to conceptualize it and render it predictable. As for the Supra-Natural realm of Being – be it Heaven, God, Pure Forms, *brahman*, and so on – which we may hope to attain after death, this is probably the vainest and most delusional hope we have. It is in all of these ways that thirsting constitutes the condition for our experience of the world as painful and unsatisfactory. This, most fundamentally, is what it means to be "in *saṃsāra*."

How, then, does one gain liberation from *saṃsāra* and attain *nirvāṇa*? What is required is an antibiotic which can remove the infection of the ego-principle and thereby bring the inflammation of grasping and the fever of thirsting to an end. In short, what is required is an antidote, which undercuts the cognitive and affective effects of the self-delusion. This antidote is the teaching of "selflessness" (in a metaphysical, not an ethical sense), which in Madhyamaka circles is extended to all things under the guise of the teaching of universal "emptiness of own-being/substance." In positive terms, this is the teaching that all things are dependently co-arisen – that the world is made up of dynamic processes and entirely devoid of stability and permanence.

The Buddhist strategy, in short, is to focus on the cognitive expressions of the self-delusion. Presumably this is because average people have more control over their beliefs than their feelings. Now the doctrine of emptiness, Nāgārjuna tells us, "brings conceptual proliferation to cessation."[37] The Buddha, he also claims, gave his teaching "so that all reifying views may be abandoned."[38] On Nāgārjuna's view, learning to see that the very notions of "self" and "thing" are delusional is supposed to lead the Buddhist eventually to bring to an end the mechanisms of reification and hypostasis that deliver rigid views.

Consider, in this connection, the passage in which the Buddha insists that instead of metaphysical knowledge concerning abstruse speculative subjects, the only thing he has knowledge of are the five constituents, their arising, and their passing away. He concludes by stating that this phenomenalistic knowledge of processes, as opposed to metaphysical knowledge of reified, hypostasized entities, is what leads him to a state where the ego- and mine-principles are dismantled and grasping has ceased.[39] The underlying idea is that bringing grasping and thirsting to an end requires specifically undermining those ways in which I implicitly think about self and world when grasping and thirsting hold sway.

I love myself. I am constantly concerned with myself. I filter all of reality, organize the entire world, in terms of myself. I am the measure of all things. I have strong desires and aversions, which are debilitating in so far as they render me perpetually fretful, tense, anxious, dissatisfied, if not positively distraught, disappointed, frustrated, angry, or depressed. All of this is the result of the self-delusion. The Buddhist therapy consists in learning to see and eventually to feel that there is no permanent, enduring "I": that the sense of

[37] *MMK* xviii.5.c–d. See also the propitiating verses at the opening of the *MMK*, which claim that the doctrine of dependent co-arising, the positive formulation of emptiness, brings conceptual proliferation to an end.

[38] *Ibid.* xxvii.30.c–d. [39] *MN* i.486.

"self" is something that is performed through the active appropriation of physical and mental events. With the knowledge of lack of self, I learn to accept that my body and my mind are made up of transient events and that there is nothing to hold on to or to fear to lose. Likewise, I am taught that to look upon the world as a world of static entities is a form of large-scale anthropomorphism or personification, and, what is more, that it is a corollary of my self-centered, need-based approach to the world. The hypostatized conceptual constructs and reifying views generated by conceptual proliferation, I learn to see, are just a vast, delusional justificatory framework that provides the attractions and aversions which form the core of my worldview with a false legitimacy.

When I learn to see, in accordance with the principle of emptiness, that there are only dependently co-arisen processes and events, and no things, these debilitating attractions and aversions are undercut. There are no longer "things" to desire and to hate; there are only interlocking processes, all of which are subject to arising and passing away. Selflessness, substancelessness, and dependent co-arising, indeed, all imply universal impermanence. When this impermanence is truly and fully accepted – with regard to both "self" and "things" – grasping, both inward- and outward-directed, ceases. This is because there is no point in "grasping" what cannot be grasped – e.g. a gush of water coming from a tap. Indeed, one seeks to grasp in this way only in so far as one is deluded with regard to the transient nature of what is grasped. With the inflammation of grasping, the fever of thirsting ceases. I no longer encounter *duḥkha*. I am "liberated from *saṃsāra*" and attain the great health of *nirvāṇa*.

There are three important things to note about the Buddhist therapy. The first is that the teaching it presents to undo the self-delusion is not itself a reifying view. In *VV*, we find Nāgārjuna's Brahmanical adversaries attempting to undermine his philosophical project by claiming that in so far as the claim "all things lack substance" is itself empty of substance, it cannot effectively deny self and substance.[40] Alternatively, if the claim is substantive, then it contradicts itself, for it is then not the case that all things are empty of substance and merely contingent, or dependently co-arisen.[41]

Nāgārjuna, in reply, begins by clarifying his position. "Empty of substance" does not mean non-existent, null, or causally inefficient. He writes:

And, just as such things as chariots, cloths, and pots, although they are empty of substance by virtue of being dependently co-arisen, function in their respective

[40] *VV* 1. [41] *Ibid.* 11.

tasks – i.e. transporting wood, hay or soil, containing honey, water or milk, protecting from the cold, the wind, or heat, etc. – just so, this statement of mine, although it lacks substance on account of being dependently co-arisen, functions in establishing the inexistence of substance.[42]

At the same time, Nāgārjuna does concede that, strictly speaking, he is not putting forward a thesis per se. Emptiness is unlike any other philosophical position because it does not posit reified, hypostatized entities. Nāgārjuna explains: "I have no thesis whatsoever . . . How could there be a thesis when all things are empty, completely appeased and devoid of [inherent] nature?"[43] It is obvious that this reply turns on a very specific understanding of "thesis," namely that "theses" and more generally "views" make claims about real, self-standing entities. In so far as emptiness denies that there are any such things, the doctrine of emptiness is not a thesis or a view.

Instead, the doctrine of lack of self and substance is nothing more than a therapeutic doctrine. And it is an antidote precisely in so far as it "halts all constructed reifying views."[44] To look upon it as a positive view – "all things are empty of substance" – is a mark of the greatest foolishness there can be. Emptiness, Nāgārjuna explains, is taught as a "remedy to get rid of all reifying views. Those who look upon it as a view are declared to be incurable."[45] Nāgārjuna justifies this claim with great clarity: "If something [in the world] were non-empty [of substance], then there might also be something empty [of substance]. And yet there is nothing non-empty [of substance] [in the world], so how could there ever be something empty [of substance]?"[46] Similarly, claims Candrakīrti, the Buddha's teaching that there is no self is only a provisional teaching, a conventional truth. In so far as the very notion of an enduring, unitary "self" is incoherent – in so far as it is a pure fiction that does not correspond to anything in the world at all – the real fact of the matter, or ultimate truth, is that "it is neither the case that there is a self, nor that there is not a self."[47]

In this way, the real point of the Buddhist teaching is not so much to negate a thesis (the existence of self and substance) and to replace it with another thesis (lack of self and substance), but to undermine the very delusion that gives rise to this dichotomy.[48] Ganeri describes this move as a sort of "Trojan Horse" strategy.[49] The doctrine of lack of self looks like a

42 *Ibid.* xxii, Commentary. 43 *Ibid.* xxix, Commentary. 44 *Pp*, pp. 248–9.
45 *MMK* xiii.8.
46 *Ibid.*10. Hence the infamous Madhyamaka doctrine of the "emptiness of emptiness."
47 *Pp*, p. 358. See also *MMK* xviii.6.
48 On this point, see Ganeri, *The Concealed Art of the Soul*, pp. 103–4. 49 *Ibid.*, p. 105.

substantive position which makes a clear assertion. In this way it can be admitted into the mind, so to speak, which is habituated only to consider substantive views about "how things are." Once inside, however, it discharges its antibiotics and works away at those very conceptual proclivities which bind us into thinking in terms of reifying views and theses.

Considering the case of God's existence might help bring the Buddhist point into relief. The standard atheist claim is that God does not exist. Pressed to defend this view, atheists might explain that there is no evidence for the existence of God. The "Buddhist strategy," so to speak, would be to explain that the very concepts of an uncaused cause, of an immaterial consciousness, or of an omnipotent agent, are incoherent. Alternatively, the strategy might be to say that, like "self" or "substance," "God," by virtue of his attributes, is either non-existent or explanatorily redundant. In this light, even the claim "there is no God" is nothing more than an argumentative position designed to counter the theist's claim. The truly enlightened position is that "God neither exists nor does not exist," in so far as the concept "God" makes no sense.[50] This is what happens to the concepts of "self" and "substance" in Buddhist philosophy. The claim that everything lacks self and substance is a therapeutic maneuver, and nothing more.

There is a useful analogy in the discourses which might help illustrate this point. The idea is that the Buddhist teaching is like a raft. The raft is useful to reach the "far shore" (i.e. *nirvāṇa*) and leave the near shore (i.e. *ātman*) behind, but once *nirvāṇa* is reached, the sage should let the raft go.[51] This has problematic implications, in that it makes it sound like Buddhism is not interested in truth, but only in devising instruments that have no value other than securing the ends they are designed to deliver.[52] On the one hand, there is no doubt that dependent co-arising is meant to "describe the world" adequately (though it also makes any determinate description of

[50] Cf. Rorty's comments on pragmatism:

> When [pragmatists] suggest that we not ask questions about the nature of Truth and Goodness, they do not invoke a theory about the nature of reality or knowledge or man which says "there is no such thing" as Truth or Goodness. Nor do they have a "relativistic" or "subjectivist" theory of Truth or Goodness. They would simply like to change the subject. They are in a position analogous to that of secularists who urge that research concerning the Nature, or the Will, of God does not get us anywhere. Such secularists are not saying God does not exist, exactly; they feel unclear about what it would mean to affirm His existence, and thus about the point of denying it. Nor do they have some special, funny, heretical view about God. They just doubt that the vocabulary of theology is one we ought to be using. (*The Consequences of Pragmatism*, p. xiv)

[51] *SN* IV.174–5. [52] On this point, see Ganeri, *The Concealed Art of the Soul*, pp. 46f.

the world in terms of entities impossible). At the same time, it seems as though even the principle of lack of self is a conventional truth, which the sage eventually discards. Buddhist philosophy's relation to truth, indeed, seems unclear. But this fuzziness can be dispelled if the raft analogy is replaced with the analogy of swimming. To learn how to swim, one must follow a series of instructions about how to position and move various parts of the body to keep afloat, go forward in a relatively straight line, breathe adequately, etc. Once one has mastered the art of swimming, however, it is no longer necessary to remember all of these instructions – keeping them in mind might even impede the now spontaneous exercise of swimming. At this stage, one will only give the instructions to teach others how to swim, but for one's own purposes one will have cast them aside, like the raft. Indeed, the art of undoing the self-delusion and living without it is a skill. Once it is overcome, the scaffolding required to undo the self-delusion can be cast away.

Of course, to reach the level where one can step beyond "self" *and* "no-self" one needs to be far advanced on the Buddhist path. This brings me to my second point about the Buddhist therapy. When Nāgārjuna explains that *nirvāṇa* is "simply the proper understanding of becoming"[53] – i.e. of dependent co-arising – we should not be mistaken into believing that a merely intellectual grasp of lack of self, emptiness, and dependent co-arising is sufficient to recover from the self-delusion. Indeed, merely subscribing to the doctrine of emptiness or recognizing that there is no "self" qua bearer of physical and mental properties will not do. It is not very difficult to assent, intellectually, to the view that self and world are made up of dynamic processes. But to gain an experiential understanding of this is something altogether different.[54] Returning to the swimming analogy, the idea is that one can know by heart all the appropriate instructions to swim impeccably, and yet be unable to keep afloat once one jumps in the water. This is also true of the self-delusion. The substance view of self and world is so profound and so fundamental to the way in which we think of and engage in the world,[55] that to overcome it requires a sustained effort and formidable discipline. Indeed, bringing the grasping that delivers the sense of a robust "I" and of static "things" to cessation, and with it all of its pernicious effects, requires a radical overhaul of one's entire psychology. This is why it can take a lifetime of practice before one can progress from the therapeutic Buddhist

[53] *YṢK* 6.c–d. [54] See, on this point, Westerhoff, *Nāgārjuna's Madhyamaka*, p. 13.

[55] The discourses speak of latent, unconscious dispositions (*anuśaya*) which take tremendous work to remove. On the effects of these dispositions, see *MN* III.285f. At *SN* III.126–32, it is revealed that the most pernicious of these, unsurprisingly, is precisely the thought "I am."

motto "there is no self" to the accomplished sage's "there is neither self nor no-self."[56]

The third thing to emphasize, in this connection, is that the Buddhist therapeutic program is not purely cognitivist.[57] Certainly, emptiness and lack of self target the cognitive outgrowths of the self-delusion, but it would be a mistake to assume that Buddhist philosophy simply understands *duḥkha* to be the result of erroneous beliefs and of the desires that follow from them. Buddhist therapy is only partially cognitivist. It is not simply concerned with rectifying a false belief. This, again, is because the self is not a mere illusion, but a delusion. Belief in the "self" – which, admittedly, is belief in an "illusion" – is a mere surface phenomenon for Buddhist philosophy. What is of far greater significance is the pre-reflective construction of the self and its horizon through grasping and its effects on our affective and cognitive behavior. The problem, then, is far more serious than a mere misalignment between the way I think things are and the way they really are. At issue is a deeply delusional mind-set. "Knowing" that there is no self and that all supposed "things" are really impermanent fleeting groupings of intertwined processes is not enough. To undermine grasping (both inward- and outward-directed) and with it thirsting in all of its forms, it is not enough to merely realize that all things are changing, unstable, and impermanent and to align one's desires and expectations accordingly. What is required is something far more radical. What is required is a complete transformation of the way in which we not only think self and world, but also feel and experience them.

Beyond the mere cessation of *duḥkha*, what is the outcome of the great transformation that leads to *nirvāṇa*? How does the Buddhist healthy type live and experience the world? One concern is that the cessation of the activity of grasping – whereby body and mind are constituted as "mine" and my world horizon is organized around "me" – would lead to a state which contemporary psychiatrists call "depersonalization." This state is linked with specific pathologies which render people entirely dysfunctional: namely, epileptic automatism, akinetic mutism, and advanced Alzheimer's disease.[58] Is this what the Buddha's vision of great health involves?[59]

[56] Similarly, secular societies remain far from the stage at which talk of God – "there is a God" vs. "there is no God" – can be abandoned altogether.

[57] But cf. Burton's cognitivist (and therefore deeply unsatisfactory) account of Buddhist moral psychology at "Curing Diseases of Belief and Desire," pp. 190f.

[58] A. Damasio, *The Feeling of What Happens: Body and Emotion in the Makings of Consciousness* (London: William Heinemann, 1999), p. 98.

[59] Other attempts to answer this question can be found at Albahari, "Nirvana and Ownerless Consciousness," pp. 111–12, and Dreyfus, "Self and Subjectivity," pp. 139–40.

Other, related concerns may arise. Rid of the sense of self and with it the desires and aversions born of thirsting, how can the Buddhist healthy type be motivated to act to bring about or avert a certain state of affairs? Free of all reifying views and hypostatized conceptual constructs, will healthy types hold no beliefs whatsoever? Are they global skeptics or dismal relativists who admit only of unfathomable universal becoming, or indeterminate dependent co-arising? Can they still use language, when language so clearly seems to presuppose the existence of subjects and predicates, or substances and attributes?[60]

Looking at the figure of the Buddha and of other advanced Buddhists believed to have attained (or come close to attaining) the great health of *nirvāṇa*, it is questionable whether these concerns are justified. The Buddha was manifestly functional physically and psychologically. He acted, deliberated, expressed a wide range of ideas, and carried out projects with a clear sense of purpose. The skeptic will say that this merely proves that he had not attained the "goal" he propounded, or he would have been rendered entirely dysfunctional, non-engaged, and globally non-committal with regard to his views and doctrines.

There is, however, one way to account for the apparent normality of Buddhist healthy types without denying that they have actually overcome the self-delusion. Buddhist healthy types, I suggest, are masters of irony.[61] This is true at the level of their identity, of their engagement in the world through various projects, and of the views they propound.

Consider, to begin, the problem of post-*nirvāṇa* identity. The real problem with the activity of inward-directed grasping, or appropriation, is that the identity it delivers is not recognized to be a fabrication. If the self-delusion has all the pernicious effects on human psychology that Buddhist philosophy claims it has, it is because of the delusion that the fabricated, performed self is somehow real. The delusion lies not in constructing the self, but in taking it to be real, or unconstructed. The difference between the common person and Buddhist healthy types, then, is not that the latter have no sense of personal identity whatsoever, but that they are no longer deluded as regards this identity's fabricated status. A Buddhist healthy type who has recovered from the self-delusion could thus continue to perform a

[60] On this point, consider Dennett's neuroscientific research, which has led him to the conclusion that the conceptual construction of the self is intimately tied to our linguistic capacities, and vice versa. D. Dennett, *Consciousness Explained* (London: Little, Brown and Co., 1991).

[61] I am indebted to Siderits for first suggesting that ironic engagement plays a key role in the accomplished Buddhist's functioning in the world – see Siderits, *Buddhist Philosophy*, pp. 106–9, 184–5, and 202–3.

"self" for the sake of the functional integration of body and mind, but with full knowledge that this "self" is a construction.

A foray into contemporary discussions of personal identity might be useful at this juncture. The metaphysical focus of philosophical discussions on personal identity has recently been criticized on the grounds that what really matters is how we characterize ourselves, not whether we think of ourselves as "selves" with robust numerical identity over time.[62] Siderits, Thompson, and Zahavi aptly describe the main thrust of this so-called narrativity approach:

> The basic idea is that as agents in the world in time, we require some scheme for fitting individual affordances into an overall hierarchy that facilitates prioritizing our responses. This is provided when we view our lives as narratives that we are simultaneously living out and making up. By viewing ourselves as both the author and the central character in the story of our lives, we achieve the ability to formulate long-term plans and projects, work out subordinate goals, and thus avoid paralysis each time we are presented with a new opportunity for action.[63]

Proponents of this approach tend to criticize views that reject the existence of an enduring self on the grounds that the metaphysical considerations that underlie them are simply beside the point.

Things are not so simple, however. The no-self theorist can happily reply that the vast majority of narrative constructions in fact already presuppose (often pre-reflectively) the metaphysical view that there is, in effect, "an entity that is both the author and the central character of one's life-story."[64] The Buddhist position in this debate would be that the self is indeed a narrative construct – hence the horizon construction which is an essential component of the construction of a fixed identity – but that most of us mistake the fictional character we construct for a real, robust self. On the Buddhist view, this form of performance of the narrative self is unhealthy. It is rather like the case of the delusional actor who becomes convinced that he is his character – e.g. Val Kilmer who spent months convinced he was Jim Morrison after shooting *The Doors*.

Buddhist healthy types, in contrast, will carry on with their performance – they will continue to generate a narrative self through conscious,

[62] See, in particular, M. Schechtman, *The Constitution of Selves* (Ithaca, NY: Cornell University Press, 1996).

[63] Siderits, Thompson, and Zahavi, "Introduction," p. 6. Proponents of this approach find support in Dennett's neuroscientific views about the construction of a narrative identity that is essential to survival in the world. On Dennett's view of narrative selfhood see, especially, *Consciousness*, p. 418.

[64] Siderits, Thompson, and Zahavi, "Introduction," p. 7. Siderits, Thompson, and Zahavi say this of narrativity approaches, but the claim applies *mutatis mutandis* to narrative constructions.

deliberate, skillful appropriation – but will do so in a healthy, non-delusional way.[65] In short, they will assume and construct an identity, they will lay claim to the psycho-physical constituents that "make them up" and construct a world horizon around themselves, but they will do so with irony and thus also with detachment. Indeed, ironic distance will make it possible to preserve all the advantages of being functionally integrated as a unitary person without falling prey to the pernicious effects of taking the fiction of the "self" for something real. In fact, the Buddhist claim is that such an ironic performance of self is supremely enabling and empowering.[66]

The reason for this is that Buddhist healthy types' mode of action in the world is likewise one of ironic engagement.[67] In so far as they construct and maintain their consciously fabricated identity with irony, the healthy types' projects, plans, and desires are also characterized by a certain detachment. Having attained the highest wellbeing of *nirvāṇa* and undone the self-delusion, Buddhist healthy types are in no way wanting, dissatisfied, or fretful. This makes it possible for them to engage in the world with specific intentions and projects all the more freely and lightly. Moreover, it is precisely in terms of their specific projects that healthy types will construct and maintain their functional narrative identity. The Buddha, indeed, is described as changing and adapting with incredible skill to the situation he is presented with. Different roles and characters, different masks, or personae, are called for, depending on the situation. All of this, of course, is done with irony – with a full awareness of the performance at play.

Accordingly, Buddhist healthy types' fundamentally ironic attitude reaches all the way down to the views they propound. As a therapist, the Buddha is known to have given different cures for different conditions. To some he taught that there is a self, to others that there is no self, and to others, finally, that there is neither self nor no self.[68] This is but one example. The basic idea is that, for a healthy type, purely pragmatic, contextualist concerns dictate what should be taught and, more importantly, how the interlocking web of processes that make up this world of dependent co-arising should be splintered into particular

65 In reply to the accusation that this flies in the face of the ideal of authenticity, the Buddhist will point out that the very idea of "authenticity" presupposes a delusional view of the self.

66 For a similar point on Buddhist enlightenment, see Dreyfus, "Self and Subjectivity," p. 139.

67 Cf. Siderits, *Buddhist Philosophy*, pp. 106–9 and 202–3. Note that Siderits places the emphasis on the irony involved in treating people as "persons" when it is known that they are but bundles of psycho-physical events. Here, instead, the emphasis is placed on the irony involved in a healthy type's fabrication of a self-consciously fictional identity and on the forms of engagement in the world that follow from this.

68 See, on this point, Ganeri, *The Concealed Art of the Soul*, pp. 108f.

"things."[69] This is the art of describing the world in terms of conventions that are appropriately fitted to the context. There can be no absolute realist ontology in a world comprising only dependently co-arisen processes. Any entity one might wish to describe will, under analysis, turn out to be empty of own-being, or substance. As such, ultimate truth will never consist in truths, let alone the Truth, about the Reality behind appearances; at best it will involve negative statements about the constructed status of conventional truth.

In this way, even the analysis of the "person" into the five psycho-physical constituents is somewhat arbitrary. It makes sense to teach the doctrine of lack of self in this way because everyone can understand what physical events, feelings, conceptualizations, volitions, and cognitions refer to.[70] But are these really the ultimate building blocks out of which the person is made? Was the Buddha ever really reductionist? The answer is no.[71] No absolute, real reduction base is recognized. This would be a roundabout commitment to substance metaphysics.[72] The teachings of Buddhism are always only skillful teachings – skillful in so far as they advance the Buddha's therapeutic ends. They are conventions, which serve the purpose of exposing the ultimate truth of dependent co-arising and with it radical ontological indeterminacy.[73] Conventions (*saṃvṛti*) might generally conceal (*saṃ-√vṛ*) the empty status of all things, but in the case of the advanced Buddhist's teachings, they also disclose this empty status. As such, Buddhist healthy types will maintain their ironic stance even in their teachings and utterances.[74] Just as they perform their "self" and the construction of their horizon with irony, all of the descriptions of the world and doctrines they set forth are developed with ironic detachment. This is why, once the far shore of *nirvāṇa* has been reached, the accomplished Buddhist abandons even the raft of the Buddha's teaching.

This interpretation of the Buddhist healthy type's engagement with self and world as a form of ironic engagement is intimately tied to the central

[69] See Siderits, *Buddhist Philosophy*, pp. 184–5.

[70] See Dreyfus, "Self and Subjectivity," pp. 118–19.

[71] This is why Nāgārjuna had to step in and check the ontologizing tendencies of some of his Ābhidharmika contemporaries.

[72] On this point, see also MacKenzie, "Enacting the Self," pp. 250–1, though McKenzie wrongly attributes realist reductionism to all Abhidharma, as do many scholars in the field of Buddhist studies: namely, Siderits in *Buddhist Philosophy* and Burton in *Emptiness Appraised.*

[73] As Nāgārjuna highlights, "the ultimate truth cannot be taught without relying on conventions" (*MMK* XXIV.10).

[74] As Candrakīrti explains, "the sage does not resist the conventional world, but recognizes it for what it is" (*Pp*, p. 495).

distinction between illusion and delusion. As Jonardon Ganeri notes, "many illusions exhibit a kind of independence from belief, the illusion persisting even when one knows that it is an illusion."[75] If self and substance were illusions, then, it would follow that the best Buddhists could do is gain an awareness of the fact that the sense of self that inhabits them, and the world of substantial entities that surrounds them, are illusory, and little more. Such an "*internal exile of the mind*," as Ganeri calls it, would involve an attitude of perpetual "circumspection and cognitive distance."[76]

But self and substance are not mere illusions, they are delusions. They are not merely passively undergone, but actively constructed. Once their fictional and constructed status is fully, experientially understood, however, the delusion itself ends. And from that point on, Buddhist healthy types can engage in skillful play with the fictions of self and "things." They will not simply continue to be prey to these illusions, yet know they are illusions. Buddhist ethics is more ambitious than this. Far beyond systemic, ataraxic circumspection, it reaches for a goal of supreme empowerment in a state of perfected great health. Buddhist healthy types can forge the "self" they want and use the play of ideas and beliefs about how "things" are and what "things" there are to achieve their purposes. Self and beings, of course, will no longer be delusions, let alone illusions. They will merely be useful fictions produced in a spirit of detached irony.

The first step toward appraising the presumed opposition between Nietzsche's *amor fati* and the Buddha's *nirvāṇa* is to examine the relation between *nirvāṇa* and Schopenhauer's salvation (*Erlösung*). This is because Nietzsche's understanding of Buddhist ethics as life-negating is intimately related to the parallels he sees between Schopenhauer's theory of salvation and the Buddha's doctrine of *nirvāṇa*. As was seen in Chapter 2, these parallels find their source in Schopenhauer's works, in which he repeatedly claims that he and the Buddha see eye to eye. But Schopenhauer was mistaken on this point. Superficial similarities between his thought and Buddhist philosophy only hide a yawning gap between their ethical visions. This, in turn, has important implications for Nietzsche's life-affirmation/negation dichotomy.

First, Buddhist so-called "pessimism" is in need of some qualification. Buddhism does not teach, as Schopenhauer does, that we live in "the worst possible world." More specifically, it is not accurate to claim that Buddhist philosophy portrays all of life as necessarily unpleasant and painful at every

[75] Ganeri, *The Concealed Art of the Soul*, p. 120. [76] *Ibid.*, p. 123.

twist and turn, as Schopenhauer does. On the contrary, Buddhist texts speak of several forms of existence that are almost entirely pleasant and in which one barely meets with suffering.[77] Admittedly, the Buddha pointed out that none of this pleasure lasts. As a result, frustration, nostalgia, and sorrow are never far ahead.[78] However, this is far from being as radical as Schopenhauer's claim that pleasure is nothing other than the absence of suffering.

What are we to make of the first noble truth, then? Does it not claim that *saṃsāra* is replete with *duḥkha*? Is this not a clear statement of pessimism *à la* Schopenhauer? One promising way of gaining a better understanding of the Buddhist attitude to suffering is to analyze the compound *āryasatya* ("noble truth").[79] Using the tools of Sanskrit syntactical analysis, this compound may be analyzed in either of two ways. It can be analyzed as what Sanskrit grammarians called a *karmadhāraya* compound where *ārya* has the role of an adjective that qualifies *satya*. An *āryasatya*, on this analysis, is a truth that is noble. Alternatively, the compound can be analyzed as a so-called *ṣaṣṭhi-tatpuruṣa* compound, which implies a genitive relation between *satya* and *ārya* as a substantive ("noble *person*"). An *āryasatya*, on this analysis, is a truth *of* the noble one(s). However, the sixth case (*ṣaṣṭhī*) in Indian languages does not only indicate possession, but also a looser relation which overlaps with the dative case. As a *ṣaṣṭhitatpuruṣa* compound, *āryasatya* can thus mean a truth *for* the noble one(s), i.e. for an enlightened being, such as the Buddha.[80] This, I suggest, is how the first noble truth ought to be understood.

The upshot of this analysis is that the view that *duḥkha* pervades the world is a matter of perspective.[81] Many of us might be relatively satisfied with our lives. From the perspective of an enlightened person who has attained the supreme health of *nirvāṇa*, however, everyone seems to be suffering. Such considerations significantly soften Buddhist pessimism. It makes it clear why the Buddha would not have shared Schopenhauer's view that the world is objectively saturated with pain and sorrow. From the standpoint of great health, the Buddha sees that all states involve *duḥkha* to some degree or another, but this does not make him as radically pessimistic as Schopenhauer.

77 See, on this point, Morrison, *Nietzsche and Buddhism*, p. 34.

78 Hence *vipariṇāmaduḥkhatā*, or "suffering due to change" (*SN* IV.259).

79 I borrow this grammatical approach to a philosophical problem from Indian philosophical literature, in which this strategy is very commonly used.

80 Grammatically speaking, this is not so far from one of Buddhaghosa's analyses: "Because noble ones such as the Buddha penetrate them, they are called noble truths ... The noble penetrate them; therefore they are called 'noble-truths'" (*Vsm*, p. 395). My point, however, is slightly different. The idea is that the first truth is a truth *for* the noble person. The view that life is permeated by *duḥkha* is how things look from a healthy type's perspective.

81 On this point, see also Morrison, *Nietzsche and Buddhism*, pp. 34–5.

The whole point is that things could be significantly better for me, not that everything in my life is terrible. Underlying the Buddhist view that life is full of suffering is a message of hope, not existential despair. The Buddhist quest for *nirvāṇa* and the Schopenhauerian thirst for salvation, then, are based on very different assessments of the human predicament. The Buddha's assessment is perspectival, relative, and geared toward a state of wellbeing. Schopenhauer's assessment, in contrast, is absolute, dogmatic, and hopelessly negative. Nietzsche was manifestly not aware of this nuance.

Another point of apparent overlap between Schopenhauer's ethics and Buddhist moral psychology concerns the role of the individuation principle. In both Schopenhauer's thought and Buddhist philosophy, the source of ordinary human beings' problems is that they take the "personal self" much too seriously. Accordingly, both Buddhist philosophy and Schopenhauer's thought claim that progress toward the *summum bonum* is a function of one's emancipation from the primordial delusion of the "I."

The overlap stops here, however. Indeed, there is an enormous difference between saying, as the Buddha did, that there is no abiding self, ego, or soul, and saying, as Schopenhauer did, that we are all the same great "one." There might be a "self"-delusion for the Buddha, but there is no "I am different from you" illusion.[82]

Nirvāṇa does not involve the realization that all differences in this world, including that between self and other, are illusory and, as a result, that we all partake in a mystical, non-spatiotemporal oneness.[83] Strictly speaking, I attain *nirvāṇa* when I recover from the self-delusion which conditions my entire affective and cognitive approach to the world. There were in Ancient as well as in Classical India several schools which taught, as Schopenhauer does, that the key to ending *duḥkha* is to reject the illusory personal self in favor of the Real Self, i.e. the abiding One beneath all illusory, transient things.[84] On the Buddhist view, however, this in no way constitutes a true recovery

[82] On this point, see also Panaïoti, "Wrong View, Wrong Action," pp. 15–16.

[83] Certainly, Nāgārjuna's deconstruction of any possible realist ontology, or taxonomy of real, irreducible entities, does deny that any *substantial* differences between things can be established. But this is because the world we experience is a world of processes and dynamic relations, and not of discrete, concrete things amenable to analyses in terms of substance and attribute. It is not because we are really a unified One.

[84] This is the position of the Advaita Vedānta and of several Śaivite schools, among others. It should be noted, admittedly, that the Advaita Vedāntin also employs the Nāgārjunian strategy of showing "that our discursive knowledge of the phenomenal world is beset with contradictions, antinomies and sublation." D. Chattopadhyaya, "Skepticism Revisited: Nāgārjuna and Nyāya via Matilal," in P. Bilimoria and J. Mohanty (eds.), *Relativism, Suffering and Beyond: Essays in Memory of Bimal K. Matilal* (Delhi: Oxford University Press), pp. 50–68, at p. 58. The Advaita Vedāntin does so, however, for a very different end: namely, to show that behind the "veil of *māyā*" lies a Unitary Absolute.

from self-delusion. Rejecting the "personal self" is a move in the right direction, but seeking refuge in a cosmic "Me" indicates that one is still under the sway of the self-delusion. Such ethics remains conditioned by thirsting and attachment to Being. One who follows such a path remains susceptible to *duḥkha*. The kind of metaphysics that underpins Schopenhauer's salvation, in short, has no appeal to a proponent of Buddhist philosophy. In fact, it only betrays large-scale Ego-ism.

Indeed, below the surface of superficial similarity between Buddhist moral psychology and Schopenhauer's meta-ethics lie opposite attitudes to the problem of the self. Schopenhauer's ethics are based on a metaphysical monism, which bloats the self into a universal One. Buddhist moral psychology, in contrast, consists in a global critique of the ego that ultimately denounces traditional metaphysical thinking itself as an outgrowth of the self-delusion and thus as something that stands in the way of *nirvāṇa*.

Nietzsche, of course, was well aware of the fundamental difference between Schopenhauer's philosophy and Buddhism with regard to metaphysics. Nevertheless, he seems to have been blind to the important implication this difference has at the level of ethics. Consider, in this connection, the misleading similarity between Schopenhauer's Will and the fever of thirsting. The Will and thirsting are alike in that they are closely related to the mechanisms of individuation and, as such, represent the source of suffering. Schopenhauer's and the Buddha's *summum bonum*, accordingly, corresponds to their cessation and destruction. But Nietzsche seems to have read too much into this parallel.

Indeed, the Will and thirsting otherwise play markedly different roles in Schopenhauer's thought and Buddhist philosophy. For Schopenhauer, the Will is the very stuff of the world – it is the metaphysical correlate of empirical matter, or the essence of life. There is no parallel for such an extravagant metaphysical claim in Buddhism. Thirsting, indeed, is nothing like the essence of life. It is not a substance, let alone something metaphysical, nor is it even a "thing." Rather, it stands for specific forms of affective behaviors which, like everything else in the Buddhist worldview, are the result of a process: namely, identification through appropriation. Thirsting might be characteristic of most people's psychic life, but it is never suggested that thirsting is life, or that existing consists in thirsting.[85]

[85] But cf. Morrison's misguided attempt to show that thirsting has a cosmological role in Buddhism as "the most 'primitive form of affect'," a role which he (wrongly) sees as being identical to that of the will to power in Nietzsche's philosophy. Morrison, *Nietzsche and Buddhism*, pp. 132–54, especially pp. 137–8.

The upshot is that Schopenhauer's self-negation qua Will-negation has no parallel whatsoever in Buddhist thought. Schopenhauerian salvation consists in destroying what one is. It consists in denying and killing off that which "I" really am. According to Buddhist philosophy, in contrast, "I" am not really anything in particular. Like everything else, "I" am a series of continually changing and shifting processes. Thirsting is grounded in the delusion that "I" am something over and above these processes, that there is a body and a mind that is "mine," that this and that belongs to "me," etc. Becoming aware that this is delusional and eventually gaining a full experiential realization of selflessness is what puts out the fever of thirsting, thus leading to the cessation of suffering. The Buddhist *summum bonum*, then, is certainly not a matter of denying and destroying what "I" really am, but of abandoning any delusions about what, in fact, "I" am not. There is no self-denial or self-destruction in Buddhism, as there is in Schopenhauer's ethics. There is only freedom from the pathological delusion of the self. Accordingly, there is nothing "anti-life" per se about the Buddha's ethical ideal. There is only recovery from wrong-headedness. Thirsting is not life. In fact it is an impediment to living healthily. Contra Schopenhauer and Nietzsche, then, destroying thirsting is not destroying life, but putting an end to unhealthy living.

Admittedly, it is not altogether surprising that Schopenhauer and Nietzsche got the impression that Buddhism is life-negating and that its goal is simply to end life. Buddhist texts, it is true, often describe *nirvāṇa* as bringing cyclical rebirth to cessation.[86] Enlightened ones are said to have finally gained release from cyclical existence when they attain *nirvāṇa*[87] and the Buddha is repeatedly quoted as saying that, after his enlightenment, he knew that there would be "no more of this [life]" for him.[88] In short, it does sometimes seem as though the physician Siddhārtha Gautama was trying to cure people of life. Is Nietzsche correct, then, in describing Buddhism as life-negating in spite of the differences between Schopenhauer's and the Buddha's thought?

There are good reasons to doubt that he is. First, it should be noted that many of the idioms and phrases on escaping *saṃsāra* and bringing rebirth to cessation are common to practically all discussions of ethics in Indian religious and philosophical literature. As such, they are not particularly reliable sources for distinctly Buddhist ideas.

86 *MMK* xviii.4.

87 More specifically, *nirvāṇa* is sometimes described as the cessation of becoming (at *SN* ii.117, for instance) and thus of death and rebirth in *saṃsāra*.

88 *SN* iii.12.

Considered against the backdrop of Buddhist moral psychology, moreover, it is not clear that these formulations are negative in content, even though they are certainly negative in form. Indeed, let us assume for a moment that we can interpret the terms "life," "*saṃsāra*," or "rebirth" in these idioms as simply standing for "existence permeated with *duḥkha*." It is then possible to see how "gaining liberation from life/*saṃsāra*/rebirth" does not necessarily imply self-extermination, but simply entering a mode of life in which *duḥkha* has been removed. *Nirvāṇa*, in this light, does not imply final death or permanent sleep. On the contrary, it is a state of fulfillment, wellbeing, and strength. In saying that enlightened people will "know no more of this life," then, the point is not so much that they will finally attain lasting death, but that they have got rid of that which is characteristic of normal, sickly existence, or *saṃsāra*. They have, in other words, recovered from the infection of the ego-principle which, via the inflammation of grasping and the fever of thirsting, leads us to experience the world as *duḥkha* and thus to be "in *saṃsāra*."

Moreover, the pan-Indian paradigm of reincarnation which such idioms presuppose, strictly speaking, is not relevant to the Buddhist notion of *nirvāṇa* qua great health. The account of *nirvāṇa* I have outlined is logically independent of any account of reincarnation. This is not because anything essential was left out. The fact of the matter is that, as philosophy, Buddhism presents a model of moral psychology which in no way depends on the doctrine of reincarnation. If we were to understand *nirvāṇa* simply as the "end of rebirth," then a relatively unimportant factor owing principally to inessential cultural and historical contingencies would be preventing us from seeing something of far greater philosophical and psychological significance.

Consider, in this connection, Nāgārjuna's surprising statement to the effect that "nothing distinguishes *saṃsāra* from *nirvāṇa*."[89] Nāgārjuna's point is that there is no ontological or metaphysical difference between the "realm" of *nirvāṇa* and that of *saṃsāra*[90] – *nirvāṇa* is not some sort of Heaven. Nor is the difference between the two a matter of being reborn or no longer being reborn. The real difference lies in one's experience of the world. They who are infected with the ego-principle, and as a result are

[89] *MMK* XXV.19.

[90] This is because what distinguishes *saṃsāra* from *nirvāṇa* is the subject's perspective (or, more precisely, its attitude toward the world), not because there is an actual ontological identity between the two, as is too often assumed – see Rupp's simplistic claim that the Mahāyāna's "insistence that *nirvāṇa* and *saṃsāra* are ultimately one constitutes an at least potentially positive valuation of the whole of being." D. Rupp, "The Relationship between *Nirvāṇa* and *Saṃsāra*: An Essay on the Evolution of Buddhist Ethics," *Philosophy East and West* 21(1), 1971: 55–67, at p. 65.

feverishly thirsting, experience this world as a world of *duḥkha*. They are "in *saṃsāra*." They who have recovered from the infection of the ego-principle, and for whom the fever of thirsting has gone out, know no *duḥkha*. They are "in *nirvāṇa*." Metempsychosis is not relevant. All that is relevant is the self-delusion.

As such, the goal of Buddhist ethics is no more to stop living than it is to suffocate what is most natural about us. The goal, rather, is to recover from a debilitating illness and to attain great health. This state of wellbeing, moreover, is supposed to be supremely enabling, not disabling. All things considered, then, there is no true affinity between the great sickness of Schopenhauer's salvation and the great health of Buddhist *nirvāṇa*.

Contrary to what Nietzsche believed, the ethical ideal of *nirvāṇa* is not expressive of life-negation. As a result, it cannot be the opposite of the life-affirming ideal of *amor fati* that Nietzsche understood it to be. If *amor fati* is not an *anti-nirvāṇa*, then what is its relation to *nirvāṇa*? It turns out that this relation is far more interesting and complex than one of mere antagonism. In fact, under close examination, these two visions of great health are seen to share a number of interesting features and even to complement each other in certain regards.

Consider, to begin with, what Nietzsche says about Buddhists' relation to *ressentiment*. His claim is that Buddhists effectively shield themselves from suffering and attain a state of profound serenity and contentment by virtue of combating *ressentiment*.[91] The idea is that *ressentiment* is the *décadents*' most natural urge, but that by giving in to it they expend much of the little energy they have at their disposal. In this way, the affects of *ressentiment* further enfeeble the *décadents*, which in turn makes them even more irritable and susceptible to suffering.[92] The Buddha, as befits a "profound physiologist," thus advises his followers to resist *ressentiment*. Buddhists will thus freeze all their instincts, especially those that urge them to exact revenge, so that they enter into as little conflict with the world as possible. They thereby attain the negative happiness of painlessness, the epitome of which is the deep sleep of *nirvāṇa*. Just as they ward off the conscious affects of *ressentiment* – *ressentiment*$_1$ – however, Buddhists also harbor the underlying, pre-reflective "*ressentiment* against reality"[93] – *ressentiment*$_2$ – characteristic of *décadence* and its life-negating interpretation of suffering as an objection to life.

[91] *A* §20, *EH* "Warum ich so weise bin" §6, *NL 1887–1888*, 11(240) and 10(57).
[92] *EH* "Warum ich so weise bin" §6. [93] *A* §15. See also *NL 1885–1887*, 8(2).

The first thing to note is that, from the standpoint of Buddhist moral psychology, Nietzsche's explanation of how Buddhists bring suffering to an end seems rather superficial. There is no doubt that the Buddha urges his followers to stamp out the "fire" of aversion.[94] All forms of animosity, resentment, and desire for revenge are manifestations of thirsting and result from the self-centered attitudes that the self-delusion gives rise to. What Buddhists regard as proper conduct accordingly includes relinquishing not only harmful acts and slanderous speech, but also any angry thoughts. But this alone is not what leads to the cessation of suffering. Rather, such physical, verbal, and mental actions are condemned because they reinforce the deeper self-centered biases and proclivities that "bind" us to *saṃsāra*. The real target of Buddhist therapy is the self-delusion; the "affects of thirsting" – among which we may count Nietzsche's *ressentiment*$_1$ – are combated precisely in so far as they reinforce the egocentrism in which they find their source. Fundamentally, the Buddha's therapy focuses on what is at the root of resentment, anger, and aversion; tackling these surface phenomena alone is not sufficient to attain *nirvāṇa*. Nietzsche's description of Buddhist therapy is not entirely inaccurate, then, but it is slightly off the mark.

What Nietzsche entirely fails to see, however, is that in undermining the self-delusion, the Buddhist does not only destroy the root of *ressentiment*$_1$, but also that of *ressentiment*$_2$. On Nietzsche's analysis, *ressentiment*$_2$ is the product of the *décadents*' great irritability and weakness. Life for the exhausted *décadents* is studded with perpetual pains and sorrows. As a result, they feel "targeted" by life and decide that life is evil. This is what leads them to take revenge on life through various forms of life-negating ideologies. Nietzsche writes:

> The instinct of revenge has gained domination over mankind in the course of millennia, so that all of metaphysics, of psychology, of the idea of history, but above all of morality bears its mark. And so far as man has simply thought, he has introduced the bacillus of revenge into things.[95]

The very idea of Buddhist great health, however, is to recover from the debilitating, enfeebling fever that causes one to experience life as *duḥkha*, or painful. Thirsting, on the Buddhist analyses, is that by virtue of which unpleasant experiences hurt me, harm me, discourage me, cause me to despair from life, etc. Free of thirsting, I no longer feel targeted by life. I am no longer fearful, fretful, and defensive, let alone aggressive. This is not because I have "frozen my instincts," or "fallen asleep," but because I have

[94] See, for instance, *SN* IV.28. [95] *NL 1888–1889* 15(30).

overcome the delusional form of thinking and feeling that made me so irritable to begin with. As such, I am in fact more "awake" (*buddha*) and stronger than I have ever been – I am a "victor."[96] In Nietzschean terms, we could say that the Buddhist healthy type has overcome that very illness by virtue of which life is "interpreted" as painful. As such, Buddhist healthy types have removed the very condition for experiencing *ressentiment*$_2$. They cannot subliminally desire revenge against reality, because they do not even experience reality as harmful.

Recall, in this connection, the two enigmatic passages on *amor fati* discussed at the end of Chapter 3. In these passages, Nietzsche makes the surprising claim that *amor fati*, which is supposed to involve an unconditional will to suffer, also involves not suffering.[97] Recall, also, that Nietzsche does not have a unitary theory of suffering, but holds very different views about suffering as weak, reactive types experience it and suffering as strong, active types experience it. It is the reactive sick type's experience of suffering as an enfeebling setback that stands behind life-negation, the invention of Being, unselving morals, and so on. In short, *ressentiment*$_2$ – the mother of life-negation – has its source in the *décadent*, reactive sick type's suffering. Accordingly, in that it involves the complete overcoming of all reactive forces, the life-affirming ideal of *amor fati* will also involve not suffering in the way reactive types suffer, i.e. in a way that leads to *ressentiment*$_2$ and its instinct of life-negation. This is what Nietzsche means when he says *amor fati* involves "not suffering."

But "not suffering" in precisely this way is exactly what happens to the Buddhist healthy type for whom the fever of thirsting has gone out. The Buddhist "cessation of suffering" means no longer "interpreting" life as discouragingly unsatisfactory. *Amor fati* and *nirvāṇa* thus involve "not suffering" in exactly the same way. Both involve overcoming the enfeebling sickness by virtue of which life is experienced as depressingly, despairingly painful. Seen in this light, something like the Buddhists' "destruction of thirsting" would in fact be conducive to attaining the great health envisioned by Nietzsche. In this way, attaining the psychological state characteristic of Buddhist *nirvāṇa*, far from being a life-negating goal, might actually be necessary if one is to overcome internal reactive forces and reach the height of life-affirmation.

96 *MMK* xiii.8. This is but one of several epithets that suggest that the Buddhist healthy type is strong and powerful. For other such epithets, see *Sn* 29, 213, and 646.

97 See *EH* "Warum ich so gute Bücher schreibe" *GT* §4 and *ibid. FW* §4.

This might explain why reaching *nirvāṇa* seems to involve everything but the unselving that Nietzsche attacks. *Amor fati* is an anti-unselving ideal. It is an ideal of self-love and self-affirmation. As paradoxical as this may seem, the Buddha's overcoming of the self-delusion apparently leads to a similar result.[98] In both their self-praise and in third-person descriptions of them, Buddhist healthy types seem to radiate a healthy self-love, an exuberant confidence, and an unconditional affirmation of their superiority.[99] It would seem, then, that on the Buddhist account, the self-affirmation and self-love Nietzsche extols is conditional upon victory over the debilitating sickness of the self-delusion. Beyond the absence of all forms of *ressentiment* and the cessation of depressing suffering, then, *nirvāṇa*, like *amor fati*, also involves genuine self-affirmation and self-love.

Turning to the self-delusion opens the terrain for further rapprochement between the psychology of the Buddhist healthy type and of Nietzsche's healthy type. Recall how Nietzsche traces the concepts of reality, existence, Substance, Being, etc., back to the primitive "subject"-feeling.[100] On Nietzsche's analysis, the entire history of metaphysics and religion reduces to the history of the "soul superstition."[101] This claim finds an echo in Buddhist philosophy, which likewise regards the notions of Being, existence, substance, and even "entity" to be modeled on the primitive first-person notion of the self as the person's enduring, unitary core. The same is true of Nietzsche's claim that all of metaphysics and religion – which, precisely, are based on the fiction of Being – have their source in the deep suffering which gives rise to both a need for the Peace and Stillness of Being and a rancorous desire to depreciate the realm of becoming by contrasting it to the realm of Being. Buddhist philosophy does not discuss the sick type's desire for revenge against the world, but it does claim, like Nietzsche, that the countless frustrations and disappointments experienced by the common person give rise to a need for Being and Permanence. This can manifest itself as a longing for an attribute-less Absolute (*brahman*) or a Lord/God (Īśvara, Śiva, Viṣṇu, etc.), or as a need for the comforting order and regularity of a realist taxonomic grid that identifies the irreducible, substantial particulars of which the world is made up. In short, Buddhist philosophy and

98 The paradox quickly dissolves when it is seen that "self" in idioms such as self-love, self-affirmation, etc., only designates a reflexive grammatical relation devoid of any ontological implications concerning a robust "self" that would act as the "object" of love or affirmation.

99 A few canonical passages in which this is obvious include *V* I.7, *MN* I.68, *SN* I.278, and *Sn* 213 and 646.

100 *GD* III §§2 and 5, *NL 1885–1887*, 7(63), *ibid. 1887–1888*, 9(98), and *ibid.* 10(19).

101 *NL 1885–1887*, 7(63).

Nietzsche agree not only that the "model" for Being is the "I" but also that the psychological source for the fiction of Being modeled on the "I" is some form of deep dissatisfaction with life.

Nietzsche does not make the relation between the subject-feeling and the existential despair that fuels the invention of Being (on the "I" model) explicit. It is possible, however, to merge Nietzsche's account with the Buddhist story. A Buddhist version of Nietzsche's theory would trace the heightened irritability characteristic of *décadence* back to the self-delusion. On this view, if Nietzsche's sick, reactive type is so prone to suffering, sorrow, and despair, it is precisely because of the fundamental delusion that stands behind the "subject-feeling." The Self-delusion would therefore be at the basis of the *décadents*' longing for a realm of Bliss and Stillness. It would also be at the basis of their *ressentiment*$_2$, which, in Buddhist terms, might be described as a form of thirsting-based anger vis-à-vis a world of becoming that continually frustrates sick types' needs. Nietzsche's explanation that it is on account of fear and a desire for comfort and relief that we explain the world to ourselves by slipping "a doer ("subject") . . . behind everything that happen[s]," posit stable, discrete "things" as causes in analogy with the ego, etc.,[102] could then be taken one explanatory step further. At the root of the suffering and fear that fuels such large-scale personification lies the very delusion that there is a unitary, enduring "core" at the heart of one's being. On this Buddho-Nietzschean hybrid account, the debilitating self-delusion is what stands behind the sickly reactivity of interpreting the world in terms of stable things and enduring substances – and then of inventing the fictions of a *wahre Welt*, a Heaven, or a God. The predominance of reactive forces, on this account, is a function of the self-delusion.

Ultimately, the question of whether or not Nietzsche would have assented to a Buddhist explanation of reactivity, or *décadence*, is moot.[103] What is worth noting is that the Buddhist psychological account can, in theory at least, complement Nietzsche's. What is more, if what Nietzsche calls reactive behavior relating to the self and individuation lines up so neatly with what is regarded as unhealthy behavior in Buddhist philosophy – so neatly that the Buddhist explanation for this behavior also fits Nietzsche's

[102] *GD* VI §§3 and 5.

[103] It should be noted, however, that a specific passage in *GM* suggests Nietzsche might in fact have recognized a genetic relation between the self-delusion and reactivity. The passage speaks of the slave's reactive *ressentiment* against his masters in the following terms: "Slave morality from the outset says no to what is 'external,' 'what is other,' what is 'not self'; and this no is the creative act" (*GM* I §10). This fits with the Buddhist analysis, which has it that the constitution of the "inimical other" is dependent on a robust sense of self.

model – it should not be entirely surprising to find that there is also a parallel when it comes to what, in Nietzsche's thought and Buddhism, is looked upon as active/healthy behavior with regard to self and world.

First, there is no doubt that the Heraclitean healthy type of Nietzsche's philosophy has overcome both the delusion that he has a robust "self" and the delusion of "thinghood." He knows Being is a fiction. This means he knows there is only a torrent of dynamic becoming in which nothing endures and in which every "thing" – himself included – is really the product of the interplay between plural, ever-changing forces. He also knows that any representation on his cognitive horizon of a stable "thing" with specific attributes is the product of a reifying interpretation which, through hypostasis, imputes to "things" meanings and values reflective of his preferences, projects, and goals. More generally, he knows that there is an element of art and thus also of artifice in any representation that abstracts, simplifies, overlooks details, etc., in order to forge "things" out of evanescent processes, to group these things into categories, and thus to make the world intelligible. This knowledge is something the healthy type of Nietzsche's philosophy has in common with the Buddhist healthy type.

But what is of far greater significance has less to do with what these two healthy types know and more to do with the spirit with which they then engage in the world. Unlike the Schopenhauerian saint who relinquishes the *principium individuationis* which produces "self" and "thing" to bask in the mystical Oneness of the universe, the healthy types of Buddhist and Nietzsche's thought continue to fabricate self and thing with full knowledge of the fabrication involved. Both Nietzsche's active type and the Buddhists' healthy type are masters of irony.

Like actors who know they are playing out a role, both of them perform their personae, or mask-like selves, and in the process also perform the artful individuation of things and beings in the world. The only difference between their performance and that of ordinary people, in this regard, is that they know they are creating themselves and their horizon. In their relation to self and Being, both are ironic figures. In short, the contrast between the relationship of the reactive, sick type and the active, healthy type to the fictions of self and Being in Nietzsche's thought essentially runs parallel to the contrast we find in Buddhist philosophy between the sick and the healthy types' relation to these same fictions. In both cases, what is at stake is the contrast between deluded naive realism and irony.

There is of course an important difference in terms of the idioms used in both philosophies. Buddhist philosophy does not articulate its ethical ideal with reference to the figure of the artist. More importantly, nothing in

Buddhist philosophy comes close to the ideal of embracing the grand fiction of eternal recurrence in *amor fati*. Self-love and a certain form of self-affirmation are obviously part of Buddhist great health, but there is no parallel in Buddhism for the ironic fictions of an eternal Self and a Cosmic Being (Dionysus) that play a central role in Nietzsche's ideal of life-affirmation.

And this, in turn, points to the distinct role irony plays in Nietzsche's and the Buddha's ethical ideals. The irony of the Buddhist healthy type has a purely functional role. It is something pragmatic that allows healthy types to carry out their projects in the world. The ironic fictions of Self and Being in Nietzsche's great health, in contrast, are part and parcel of *amor fati*. Nietzsche's healthy type says yes to a tragic Life in a tragic World, and it is in order to do so that he ironically embraces the fictions of Self and Being. The fictions of self and being, for the Buddhist healthy type, are merely useful constructs which the healthy type can freely play with, but they play no direct role in the attainment of the great health of *nirvāṇa*. Even if there is much overlap in our two healthy types' relation to self and being and in the irony with which they perpetuate these fictions, there is thus also an important difference in the role this irony plays in our two ethical visions.

This difference in the role of irony in Buddhist philosophy and Nietzsche's ideal of great health points to a far more significant discrepancy between *nirvāṇa* and *amor fati*. Certainly, both might involve the same kind of "cessation of suffering." Both, that is to say, involve no longer suffering as the reactive, sick type of Nietzsche's thought suffers. But what about the active type's interpretation of suffering as a resistance or obstacle to overcome? This, after all, is how Nietzsche's healthy type looks upon the dread and horror experienced in the face of eternal recurrence. And it is for the sake of thus looking upon existence that he invents the ironic fictions of an eternally recurring Self and World. To have this healthy stance toward great suffering is the whole point of *amor fati*. Indeed, the cessation of the weak type's suffering in *amor fati* is only meant to prepare the terrain for the heroic will to suffer. *Nirvāṇa*, in contrast, might imply no longer interpreting experiences and states as "painful" in the way Nietzsche's reactive type interprets things as painful, but it does not seem to leave any place for suffering qua stimulation.

Of course, in so far as the Buddhist concept of *duḥkha* stands for something that presupposes thirsting, prima facie there can be no discussion of such suffering in Buddhist philosophy, let alone of a will to *duḥkha*. Without thirsting, there is no *duḥkha*. Whatever obstacles an enlightened person may meet will not be experienced as *duḥkha*. On the face of it, then, it looks as though nothing in Buddhism could play the role of suffering qua stimulating resistance to overcome.

Having said this, there is a sense in which the Buddhist healthy type is stimulated by suffering and seeks out challenges, adventures, and obstacles to overcome. According to Buddhist texts, this is the result of the healthy type's boundless compassion, which, it would appear, is a positively painful affect.[104] At this point, however, any rapprochement between Buddhist ethics and Nietzsche's positive philosophy seems to fall apart. Nietzsche, on the face of it, is an unflinching enemy of compassion. Suffering born of compassion cannot be the healthy type's lure to life and action. On the contrary, Nietzsche has it that compassion itself is to be overcome if one is to attain great health.

It may be, however, that the compassion of Buddhist healthy types and the compassion Nietzsche has in mind are significantly different affects. It is thus to compassion that we must turn in order to bring greater focus to the relation between Nietzsche's and the Buddha's visions of great health. This will be our task in the next two chapters.

[104] See, for instance, Vasubandhu's *TV*, p. 28, and *AKBh*, p. 182.

PART III

Compassion

CHAPTER 5

Overcoming compassion

Nietzsche's life-affirming crusade against life-negation concerns not only the fundamental healthy/unhealthy attitude toward one's own suffering, but also toward the suffering of the other. The (Anti-)Buddha of Europe thus pits the "noble virtue" of "overcoming compassion"[1] against the Buddhist "cultivation of compassion." He thereby combats one of the core elements of life- and self-negating nihilist morals. A central component of the path to Nietzsche's life-affirming great health, then, is the inhibition of compassion. Nietzsche, however, does not directly tell us what "overcoming compassion" involves. Thankfully, he has a lot to say on compassion. Ultimately, the content and sense of the ethical ideal of "overcoming compassion" in Nietzsche's positive thought can only be brought out through a careful examination of the full range of Nietzsche's views on compassion.

Nietzsche's critique of compassion represents a consistent strand in his published works from 1878 onward.[2] Nietzsche's critical views on

[1] *EH* "Warum ich so weise bin" §4. I translate *Mitleid/Mitleiden* as "compassion" rather than "pity" for two reasons. First, "com-passion" (literally "suffering-with," or "shared suffering;" cf. "commiseration") is morphologically and semantically closer to the German (*Mit-leid*) and, as such, evokes one of the central ideas behind Nietzsche's critique of compassion, namely that feeling compassion involves suffering (*leiden*). Second, it seems clear in view of recent terminological discussions that compassion, not pity, is what Nietzsche is concerned with. Contra earlier attempts to distinguish pity from compassion in terms of the potential for contempt which pity would supposedly involve and compassion be immune from, Tappolet argues that the real difference is that a person who is not aware of a misfortune (e.g. of having recently lost a loved one) or who feels no suffering (e.g. an apathetic alcoholic) can be pitied, whereas one must be actively and consciously suffering to be the object of compassion. C. Tappolet, "Compassion et altruisme," *Studia Philosophica* 59, 2000: 175–93, at pp. 177–8. For reasons that will soon be obvious, the emotion Nietzsche is concerned with clearly has its origin in the other's suffering, not in one's assessment of the other's state or condition. It is compassion, not pity.

[2] This strand has been under-examined. A few exceptions aside, Nietzsche's views on compassion have received very little attention in commentarial literature, though this has begun to change in the last two decades. Nevertheless, this is the first study in which an attempt is made to present a systematic exposition of Nietzsche's critique(s) of compassion.

compassion can be subsumed under two broad headings. First, there is what I call Nietzsche's *psychological critique* of compassion. Second, there is what I call Nietzsche's *cultural critique* of compassion. Though both these critiques imply each other and ultimately form a whole, each of them needs to be examined independently, for the sake of clarity and precision. Together, they serve as the background for practically everything Nietzsche has to say about compassion.

The psychological phenomenon of compassion as Nietzsche understands it has four fundamental features. The first is that compassion is little more than immature sentimentality. This is one of Nietzsche's earliest critical views on compassion. The first formulations of this view, in *MM I*, are founded on the opposition between reason and emotion, head and heart, mind and gut. Here, Nietzsche echoes La Rochefoucauld's claim to the effect that compassion is a mere passion useful only to those who lack reason and therefore need an emotion to be prompted to help others.[3] Nietzsche also enlists the Ancients to back his case against compassion. In contrast with the modern moralists' obsession with compassion and altruism, the Ancient Greeks allegedly saw the propensity to feel compassion as a common flaw of character among feeble souls.[4] This is because they had the maturity and good sense to recognize compassion as a vulgar and sentimental reaction that owes everything to the heart and nothing to the head. Nietzsche concurs. Conversely, he speaks of the people who do not feel compassion as rational, level-headed, and self-controlled individuals who are embarrassed by the "faint-heartedness" which lies at the root of compassion.[5]

[3] *MM I* §50. Nietzsche concludes: "One should certainly *manifest* compassion [to please weak and ailing people], but guard oneself against *having* it." This seems to be directly drawn from La Rochefoucauld's 1659 self-portrait: "Autoportrait," in *Maximes et réflexions diverses*, ed. P. Kuetz (Paris: Bordas, 1966), p. 20. La Rochefoucauld's cynical views on human psychology are laid out there (1678, 3rd edn). This text had an enormous influence on Nietzsche, especially in the late 1870s and early 1880s. For a systematic study of Nietzsche's engagement with La Rochefoucauld, see R. Abbey, "Descent and Dissent: Nietzsche's Reading of Two French Moralists" (unpublished doctoral dissertation, McGill University, 1994), especially pp. 142–66. See also R. Abbey, *Nietzsche's Middle Period* (Oxford University Press, 2000), pp. 58–63.

[4] *MM I* §50. See also *M* §134 and especially §131, where Nietzsche explains that the ethics of the Ancients prescribed sustained, self-controlled egoism and strove precisely against "feeling with others." Of course, Nietzsche is ignoring an important number of Greek authors who did not see compassion in this light, foremost among them Aristotle (*Eudemian Ethics* III.7). In fact, Nietzsche seems to be specifically thinking of the Stoics when he speaks of "the Ancients" and their attitude toward compassion. On this point, see M. Nussbaum, "Pity and Mercy: Nietzsche's Stoicism," in R. Schacht (ed.), *Nietzsche, Genealogy, Morality: Essays on Nietzsche's* On the Genealogy of Morals (University of California Press, 1994), pp. 139–47.

[5] *M* §133.

It is of no small significance that Nietzsche continues to regard compassion as sentimental and immature even after distancing himself from *MM I*'s and *M*'s praise of cold, hard reason in contrast to fickle affects and instincts.[6] In *MM II* (1886), he describes the prevalent morality of sentimental compassion and bleeding-heart benevolence as "an instinctive morality which has no head and seems to consist only of heart and helping hands."[7] In a fragment from the same year, he complains that "compassion does not depend upon maxims, but upon affects."[8] Nietzsche, at this stage in his thinking, has nothing against instincts and affects, so why does he continue to blame compassion for being an emotional, rather than a rational, response to the other's suffering?

It turns out that Nietzsche's problem with compassion is not in itself that it is an affect, but that it is an affect born of weakness. In *EH*, Nietzsche explains that compassion is "a particular case of being unable to withstand stimuli – compassion is called a virtue only among *décadents*."[9] Nietzsche's main idea from *MM I* to *EH*, then, is that compassion results from a lack of self-control. It is a sentimental response to which are prone weak and irritable people bereft of emotional and physical resilience – i.e. those Nietzsche eventually called *décadents*. As such, compassion is a reactive response to the other's suffering.[10] It is undergone purely for lack of control and resilience.

The second fundamental feature of compassion on Nietzsche's psychological critique is that it is a painful affect. Nietzsche takes the term *Mitleid* in a very literal, etymological sense. Compassion is suffering; it involves suffering (*leiden*) with (*mit*) the other, or, more precisely, because of the other. The idea is that compassion is a weakening affect: "Compassion, in so far as it creates suffering . . . is a weakness, like all self-loss through a damaging affect."[11] Nietzsche thus blames compassion for "increas[ing] the suffering of the world."[12] It is, in short, a depressive,

6 The rehabilitation of "instincts" in contrast to the more rationalist tone of *MM I*, *M*, and some sections of *FW* (first edition) are generally regarded as characteristic of Nietzsche's "late period" (as opposed to his "middle period").

7 *MM II* "Der Wanderer und sein Schatten" §45.

8 *NL 1885–1887*, 7(4). Consider, in this connection, Nietzsche's claim that no "man of knowledge" could ever take compassion seriously (*JGB* §172). "Man of knowledge," here, is not a pejorative term (as it is elsewhere in Nietzsche's writing). On the contrary, it seems to designate higher men. The sentimentality of compassion, Nietzsche also tells us in *JGB*, is made evident by the fact that it exhibits "an almost feminine inability to be a witness, to let suffering happen" (§202).

9 *EH* "Warum ich so weise bin" §4.

10 On reactivity (as opposed to activity) and the *décadent* as the fundamental reactive type, see Chapter 3.

11 *M* §134. 12 *Ibid.* See also *JGB* §30.

"harmful" affect – whoever actually tries to contemplate all the suffering in the world, claims Nietzsche, will "inevitably grow sick and melancholic."[13] And, of course, Nietzsche does not hesitate to use medical analogies to describe this feature of compassion. "Compassion is a waste of feeling," he writes, "a parasite that is harmful to moral health . . . It is pathological; the other's suffering infects us, compassion is an infection."[14] Consider, in this connection, the following passage from *A*:

> Compassion stands in opposition to the tonic emotions which enhance the energy of the feeling of life: it has a depressive effect. One loses force when one pities. Through compassion, the loss of force which suffering has already brought upon life is increased and multiplied. Suffering itself is made contagious through compassion.[15]

The more people are compassionate and lack the self-control not to feel pain when faced with the other's suffering, the more contagious suffering becomes. Compassion, in this sense, is a fundamentally enfeebling, infectious affect.[16]

This feature of compassion stands behind Nietzsche's view that compassion is little more than immature sentimentality. The irritable, oversentimental *décadent* cannot but undergo harm as a result of feeling compassion. The *décadent*, after all, is a reactive type for whom all forms of suffering involve a setback and loss of force. And indeed, if compassion is so common among *décadents*, it is precisely because it is symptomatic of a propensity to be easily hurt and an inability to resist psychological damage. Feeling pain in the face of the other's suffering is something utterly banal for Nietzsche. It is the default mode of the *décadents*' rapport with the other, precisely in so far as it is a fundamentally reactive affect. Far from being a virtue, then, compassion is a manifestation of sentimentality and excessive psychological susceptibility.

The third feature of the psychology of compassion outlined by Nietzsche is that the actions to which it leads are in fact indirectly self-regarding. In so far as *mitleiden* ("having compassion for") reduces to *leiden* ("suffering"), claims Nietzsche, to call actions born of compassion selfless or altruistic betrays a superficial grasp of psychology. Nietzsche, in this connection, argues that *Mitleid* is a misleading form because the suffering experienced in

[13] *M* §134. [14] *NL 1885–1888*, 7(4). [15] *A* §7.

[16] Nietzsche thus finds himself in perfect agreement with Spinoza. In *E*, Spinoza describes pity as "*sadness which arises from injury to another*" (III, P22, Schol.; see also *ibid.* Def. XVIII). "Sadness," of course, is nothing but the "passage from greater to lesser perfection" (*E* III, Def. III), i.e. loss of power (see, on this point, *E* III, P11). It is quite likely that Spinoza was one of Nietzsche's sources on this point. See, in this connection, *GM* "Vorrede" §5.

the face of the other's woe is really very much one's own suffering.[17] What we call compassionate action, Nietzsche contends, is profoundly self-centered.[18] At bottom, to act out of compassion is really to act on one's own behalf.[19] It is my own suffering that I get rid of in performing acts motivated by compassion.[20]

The fourth and final feature of the psychology of compassion is that it motivates the agent to superficial actions alone. Nietzsche explains:

> Compassion has a singular form of impudence as its companion: Because it absolutely desires to help, there is no concern either as to the means of healing, or as to the form or origin of the illness, but instead it happily starts quackdoctoring the health and reputation of its patient.[21]

Compassion does not pierce to the heart of the other's suffering. As such, "it strips the other's suffering of what is actually personal."[22] The result is superficial, even insulting action.[23] To the compassionate person, why or how the other suffers is of no interest. Nor, more importantly, does the compassionate person care whether this suffering might actually be good for the other – i.e. make the other stronger, rather than killing him. The impersonal fact that a person suffers is the problem for me, because this is what causes me to suffer, and thus prompts me to act.

Of course, the deeper root of this phenomenon is the very painfulness of compassion. Because I am really concerned with my own pain and not what has provoked it – i.e. the other's suffering – I make no attempt to understand the nature of the other's sorrows and unreflectively rush to "help."

17 *M* §133. Cf. La Rochefoucauld, *Maximes*, 264.

18 Added to the pain felt by the compassionate person, other relatively selfish and/or self-referential motives might come into play. One might, for instance, feel ashamed in front of onlookers for not being able or willing to prevent the other's misfortune, or this misfortune might be indirectly threatening by virtue of serving as a reminder of one's own frailty and vulnerability (*M* §130).

19 See, also, *MM I* §103 and *NL 1885–1888*, 7(4): "If one does good only out of compassion, one is actually doing oneself good, not the other." Of course, in describing compassionate action as self-regarding Nietzsche is not denying that people actually feel compassion. This is why the type of arguments used to reject psychological egoism would not be effective as objections to Nietzsche's critique of compassion. Indeed, arguing that compassion is real and genuine just by virtue of the very fact that one does in effect suffer in the face of the other's suffering would not carry much weight here. Nietzsche does not question that the other's suffering really does make me suffer. Rather, his point is that there is no reason to call compassion a virtue. For Nietzsche, it is little more than sentimentality and leads to no true other-regarding acts, since what motivates compassionate agents is really their own suffering. Nietzsche, then, does not deny that there is com-passion, but simply that this sentiment is in any way praiseworthy.

20 Again, Nietzsche and Spinoza are in agreement on this point. On Spinoza's view, "benevolence" is the will to alleviate what "injures" those for whom one feels pity and has for its source the loss of power (i.e. "sadness") one feels in the face of the other's injury (*E* III, P27; see also *ibid.* Def. XXXV).

21 *MM II* §68. 22 *FW* §338. 23 *M* §135.

Compassionate people thus have a crude and ultimately self-referential perspective on the other's suffering that does not go beyond the bare fact that the other is suffering. Their support and "help," as a consequence, are of no true service. In fact, they may very well be insulting and useless, if not harmful.

Nietzsche's harsh judgment of compassion is open to a number of criticisms. Most fundamentally, it seems questionable whether the psychological phenomenon he describes is really compassion. Is this what I feel when I watch a televised report on famished African children on the news, or when I see a beggar freezing to death on a street corner? In his *Wesen und Formen der Sympathie* (1923), Scheler famously accuses Nietzsche of mistaking compassion for other forms of emotional response. Toward the beginning of his work, Scheler claims that Nietzsche confused compassion with "emotional infection" (*Gefühlsansteckung*).[24] As Scheler explains, emotional infection is a common phenomenon whereby an emotional state is transferred from one individual or group to another. I will feel sad when I stand in the middle of a mourning crowd, for instance, or I will feel jolly upon entering a boisterous pub. Unlike genuine sympathy (*Mitgefühl*), then, emotional infection is not intentionally directed toward the other. As such, it is passively undergone, with only a faint awareness of the feeling's source; Scheler describes it as unintentional (*unwillkürlich*) and unconscious (*unbewußt*).[25] Compassion, in contrast, is intentionally directed toward the sufferer and thus constitutes the other's suffering as the other's. In this way, claims Scheler contra Nietzsche, compassion even prevents emotional infection.[26]

It seems clear, however, that the compassion Nietzsche criticizes is not mere emotional infection, irrespective of what he says about compassion making suffering contagious. Compassion might be undergone, and compassionate people might thus have little control over the pain they feel, but this does not mean the emotion Nietzsche describes is not intentionally directed toward the sufferer. Nietzsche's compassionate *décadent* is focused on the other and is fully aware that the other's suffering is the other's and the other's alone. In this sense, the compassion of Nietzsche's psychological critique has nothing to do with Scheler's emotional infection or its more recent incarnations, such as Darwall's "emotional contagion."[27] Scheler's

[24] M. Scheler, *Gesammelte Werke* (Bern: Francke), vol. VII, pp. 28–9. [25] *Ibid.*, p. 27.
[26] *Ibid.*, p. 28.
[27] On Darwall's account, "emotional contagion is only a primitive form of empathy, involving no projection into the other's standpoint nor even, necessarily, any awareness of the other as a distinct self." S. Darwall, "Empathy, Sympathy, Care," *Philosophical Studies* 89(3), 1998: 261–82, at p. 266.

claim that feeling compassion prevents emotional infection, in so far as it involves recognizing the other's suffering as the other's, seems unconvincing and question-begging. I do cringe and suffer when I direct my attention to a television screen depicting famished children crying, even though I constitute the children's suffering as their own. I may have a full stomach and feel no hunger whatsoever, but I will nonetheless suffer on account of the hunger that they alone are undergoing. This is something Nietzsche's account of compassion as a reactive affect astutely captures. In contrast, Scheler's claim that "compassion would only be a 'multiplier of suffering' if it were identical to emotional infection"[28] seems utterly naive.

Scheler seems to offer a more promising critique when he accuses Nietzsche, several pages later, of confusing sympathy with "*apparent* sympathy" (Schein*mitgefühl*).[29] Commenting on this distinction in her discussion of compassion, Christine Tappolet carefully distinguishes between the "object of attention" and the "intentional object."[30] True vs. apparent/false compassion, she suggests, are alike in having the other's suffering for their intentional object. But whereas true compassion also has the other's suffering for its object of attention, merely apparent compassion has one's own suffering for its object of attention.[31] In light of this distinction, it seems reasonable to suspect that Nietzsche, as Scheler claims, confused real and apparent compassion.

The whole point of Nietzsche's psychological critique, however, is that there is only "apparent compassion." It follows from this that such compassion is neither "merely apparent," nor in any way "false." What we commonly call compassion, according to Nietzsche, is a form of suffering that I undergo in the face of the other's woe and which leads to indirectly self-regarding acts which only superficially seem to be on the other's behalf.[32] Because Nietzsche also recognizes that we only have a very limited grasp of the workings of our mind, moreover, he can happily acknowledge that most of us believe that the "object of attention" of our compassion is actually the other's suffering rather than our own. In reality, however, what really motivates us when we act out of compassion is the desire to ward off our own suffering.

There are three principal implications to Nietzsche's psychological critique of compassion. The first is that compassion is little more than "bad

[28] Scheler, *Gesammlte Werke*, vol. VII, p. 29. [29] *Ibid.*, p. 52.
[30] Tappolet, "Compassion et altruisme," p. 188. [31] *Ibid.*
[32] Note that in the conclusion to her discussion, Tappolet herself wonders whether "true compassion" ever really takes place and expresses doubts as to whether it could ever be established to occur, from a third person perspective at least. "Compassion et altruisme," p. 191.

taste"[33] and "bad manners."[34] Compassion is "bad taste" in the sense that it exhibits the weakness, emotional fickleness, and lack of self-control of the lowly *décadent*. It is, in short, characteristic of over-sensitive, whiny individuals who cannot but feel pain and sorrow when faced with someone else's suffering. Moreover, *décadents*' compassion-born lament is really only about their own woe. To exhibit compassion, in view of this, is shameful. Actions motivated by compassion, accordingly, are "bad manners" in so far as they are ultimately self-regarding, and as such superficial and misdirected, if not outright hypocritical. Imagine a person who suffers from hunger and yet cannot eat for several hours so as to avoid undermining the effectiveness of the medication she has been prescribed to cure a disease. An idiotic compassionate agent, afflicted by the signs of hunger-induced suffering, will urge this person to eat. Seen in this light, "bad manners" is something of an understatement.

The second implication concerns Nietzsche's views on the enigmatic figure of the physician of mankind. Whoever "wants to serve as a physician for humanity *in any sense at all*," Nietzsche writes, "will have to be very careful to guard against such a sensation [compassion]."[35] Given Nietzsche's characterization of compassion, it is not surprising to find him making the claim that compassion is unfit for a true physician. Nietzsche's physician will not be concerned with his own suffering, but with his patient's – in fact, it is not clear that he will suffer in the face of his patient's suffering. The idea Nietzsche gestures toward here is that only when one does not feel compassion can one be of any help to the other. Moreover, Nietzsche's reference to the figure of the physician in this regard is no coincidence. With his vision of great health, after all, Nietzsche himself is something of a physician of humanity. As such Nietzsche strives to overcome compassion. This is a point I will return to shortly.

The third implication of Nietzsche's psychological critique of compassion is that compassion constitutes "the greatest danger"[36] for healthy types on their path to great health. What could this mean? Nietzsche's broader claims on nihilist morals and their impact on higher types provides us with an answer. Every morality of altruism and compassion, Nietzsche warns, is "a seduction and an injury to the higher men."[37] The "greatest danger" idea is twofold, then: (1) being the object of compassion can "injure" the healthy type, and (2) being the subject of compassion can "seduce" him away from fulfilling his destiny.

§293. [34] *EH* "Warum ich so weise bin" §4. [35] *M* §133.
271. See also *NL 1888–1889*, 15(13). [37] *JGB* §221.

With regard to the risk of injury through compassion, Nietzsche contends that so-called "benefactors" may hurt the healthy type more than his enemies do.[38] He explains: "In some circumstances, compassionate hands can interfere most destructively in a great destiny, in the isolation under wounds, in the privilege of a heavy burden."[39] Such a claim presupposes that great suffering is a necessary condition for achieving higher health. The idea is that being the object of compassion – being continually helped, assisted, and supported by bleeding hearts – prevents the healthy type from growing stronger from what does not kill him.

As far as the seduction of compassion is concerned, Nietzsche's idea is that even superior types may lapse back into sentimental fickleness and, on account of compassion, squander their energy on some unworthy cause.[40] Compassion, Nietzsche thus claims, is the easiest way to "lose one's way."[41] It is in this context that he speaks of the "seduction" inherent to anything "compassion-eliciting" (*Mitleid-erweckend*).[42] For Nietzsche, compassion is such a natural, intuitive reaction to the other's woe that there is always a risk that even the highest type may be prey to such enfeebling, distracting sentimentality. This is why the overcoming of compassion is a "noble virtue."[43] The overcoming of compassion, after all, is a true "victory over ourselves."[44] It is a victory over a fundamentally reactive affect which represents a threat to everything affirmative and creative in man.

We can now turn to Nietzsche's cultural critique of compassion. The target of this critique is the collective glorification of compassion which Nietzsche witnessed in late nineteenth-century Europe. Though it originates from the soil of Christianity, this "religion of compassion"[45] is the creed standing behind even the most secular ethical systems of modern Europe. Fundamentally, all of these morals and ideologies exhibit an obsession with disinterestedness, altruism, selflessness, etc.[46] As such, the religion of compassion represents the supreme ideological victory of unselving morals, the *décadents*' most potent instrument of life- and

[38] *FW* §338. [39] *EH* "Warum ich so weise bin" §4.

[40] On this point, see P. Berkowitz, *Nietzsche: The Ethics of an Immoralist* (Cambridge, MA: Harvard University Press, 1995), pp. 105 and 204, as well as Taylor's comments on the dangers of benevolence for higher types according to Nietzsche. C. Taylor, *Sources of the Self* (Cambridge, MA: Harvard University Press, 1989), pp. 343, 423, 455, 499, 516, and 518.

[41] *FW* §338. [42] *Ibid.* [43] *EH* "Warum ich so weise bin" §4. [44] *M* §146. [45] *FW* §338.

[46] See *M* §132, *FW* §345, *NL 1884*, 25(178), and *ibid. 1885–1888*, 2(188). Staten neatly summarizes Nietzsche's view: "*Mitleid*, derived from Christianity, is the foundation of or fountainhead of humane liberalism." H. Staten, *Nietzsche's Voice* (Ithaca, NY: Cornell University Press, 1990), p. 81. The idea that Christianity is responsible for making "moral" synonymous with "disinterested," "selfless," etc., is a point Taylor convincingly argues for in *Sources of the Self*, albeit with a very different intention from Nietzsche's, namely that of rehabilitating Christianity.

self-negation.[47] Nietzsche's cultural critique of compassion, accordingly, is a critique of the jewel in the crown of European *décadence*'s great program of unselving.

The religion of compassion, indeed, is far more than a "parading" of the *décadents*' weakness as their virtue – the "masquerade . . . of a deep weakening, of weariness, of old age, of declining force."[48] It is not merely a matter of weak, compassion-prone *décadents* making virtue of necessity. As the ripest fruit of the ideology of unselving, it also serves the dual purpose of allowing *décadents* to (1) become dominant, and (2) take revenge on life. Each of these two points requires elucidation.

Unselving morals in general and the glorification of compassion in particular are essential to the *décadents*' growing domination. As such, they are expressions of what Nietzsche calls herd instincts. Nietzsche's idea is that the ailing, weak, and reactive masses – the "slaves" of *JGB* and *GM* – think as a group, or a herd. They do so for the simple reason that this is the only way they can survive. The herd thus glorifies group mentality. This goes beyond mass conformism and an aversion to individualism. Indeed, it involves the self-righteous celebration of herd-animal qualities, such as goodness, benevolence, cooperativeness, meekness, altruism, etc.[49] Nietzsche explains that the cardinal virtues of modern morals – compassion, goodwill, consideration, industry, moderation, and the like – are precisely those virtues that happen to be useful to the herd. As such, they are little more than the expression of herd instincts.[50] Nietzsche's idea, then, is that the *décadent* herd as a whole makes a virtue of necessity. It is in this light that Nietzsche assesses the cultural situation of late nineteenth-century Europe and its compassion-based moral absolutism.[51] That which Europeans claim is objectively good, he tells us, is just an expression of the instinct of man as "herd animal."[52]

According to Nietzsche, then, the herd's unselving morals of compassion and selfless altruism are far from being grounded in genuine altruism. On

[47] See, on this point, *GD* VIII §37. On unselving morals and its relation to *décadence*, see Chapter 2.

[48] *FW* §377. See also *NL 1888–1889*, 17(6).

[49] At *NL 1885–1887*, 9(85), Nietzsche points out that unegoistic behavior is "the result of an actual herd instinct in the individual." On this point, see R. Havas, *Nietzsche's Genealogy: Nihilism and the Will to Knowledge* (Ithaca, NY: Cornell University Press, 1995), pp. 211f. Nietzsche's account, it should be noted, is compatible with recent developments in evolutionary psychology, though evolutionary psychologists, unlike Nietzsche, tend to look upon the prevalence of "herd instincts" as a positive development. See E. Sober and D. S. Wilson, *Unto Others: The Evolution and Psychology of Unselfish Behaviour* (Cambridge, MA: Harvard University Press, 1998). This only confirms Nietzsche's suspicion concerning the scientist as the modern incarnation of the ascetic priest (*GM* III §§24f.).

[50] *JGB* §199. [51] See, in particular, *GD* VIII §37. [52] *JGB* §202.

the contrary, it is just what happens to be convenient to the herd. In reality, the tyrannically egalitarian herd seethes with hatred and aversion for those who by nature are anything but tame herd animals – for those who "stand out."[53] Irrespective of its moral harangues against egoistical drives, to its enemies the herd is "*hostile, selfish, unmerciful*, full of lust for control, distrustful, etc."[54] The altruistic drives, Nietzsche concludes, are "in the service of an instinct which is *fundamentally foreign* to these *conditions of virtue*."[55] The "cult of altruism,"[56] in short, is grounded in something that is fundamentally inconsistent with the explicit tenets of such a morality. It is really an expression of the herd's mass egoism.

This underscores the profound *ressentiment* and instinct of revenge that animates the herd and pushes it to embrace the cult of unselving which is the religion of compassion. Commenting, in this connection, on the Christian hatred of all egoism at the core of this secular religion, Nietzsche explains that it is:

> a value judgment under the influence of revenge . . . This discharge of *ressentiment* in the judging, rejecting, punishment of egoism is . . . still an instinct of self-preservation among the underprivileged. *In summa:* the cult of altruism is a specific form of egoism which regularly appears under specific physiological conditions.[57]

The morality of compassion and altruism, then, is not only instrumental to the predominance of *décadent*, reactive life, it is also the result of the slaves' vindictive reaction to their master's spontaneous egoism. Here the "instinct of self-preservation" does not manifest itself through the selection of a valuation system that is optimal for herd animals, but in a violent, reactive instinct of revenge against the master. As such, the religion of compassion is yet another expression of *ressentiment*.

This is where the *décadents*' will to negate life through the cultural and ethical prevalence of the unselving of compassion comes to the fore. Indeed, the folly of turning such a self-enfeebling, debilitating impulse as compassion into a cardinal virtue does not only betray the calculated self-interest of the *décadent* herd,[58] it also exhibits its fundamentally life-negating, world-loathing disposition. It is precisely on the basis of "the value of the 'unegoistic,' the instincts of compassion, of self-denial,

53 *NL 1885–1887*, 9(85). The figure of the "free spirit" is the prototypical non-conformist whom the herd despises. See, in this connection, the figure of the "inquirer, the seeker, the overcomer" who lives in the wilderness, in contrast to the "famous sages" who feed the masses the wisdom they wish to be fed (*Z* II "Von den berühmten Weisen").

54 *NL 1885–1887*, 9(85). 55 *Ibid.* 56 *Ibid. 1888–1889*, 14(29). 57 *Ibid.*

58 I should mention that though I use the term "calculated self-interest," there is actually no deliberate and conscious "calculation" here. Instincts do all the work.

and self-sacrifice," Nietzsche reminds us, that "[Schopenhauer] *said no* to life and to himself also."[59] The ethical primacy of compassion, accordingly, is a matter of mankind "turning its will *against* life."[60] This idea is forcefully expressed in *A*:

> We have made compassion into *the* virtue, into the ground and origin of all virtues – certainly ... but from the point of view of a philosophy which was nihilist, which inscribed the *negation of life* on its shield. Schopenhauer was right about this: life is negated through compassion, it is made *worthy of negation* – compassion is the *practice* of nihilism.[61]

Even as he blames Schopenhauer for misunderstanding the psychology of compassion,[62] then, Nietzsche also agrees with the father of German pessimism that compassion and radical self- and life-negation lie on a continuum. The idea is that the cultivation of compassion is part of the process of unselving – a process which is already expressive of self-negation and, as such, eventually leads to active self-abnegation.[63] What is more, in so far as compassion is a painful affect – in so far as compassion "doubles the amount of suffering in the world"[64] – it makes life all the more unbearable and despicable. This only adds grist to the *décadent*'s life-negating mill.

Nietzsche's view that compassion is the practice of nihilism comports another, slightly more worrying, feature. Adopting a particularly abrasive tone, Nietzsche describes Christianity and its secular heir, the religion of compassion, as "the counter principle of selection."[65] "What is 'virtue,' what is 'love of man' in Christianity," Nietzsche asks, "if it is not just the mutuality of preservation, the solidarity with the weak, the impeding of selection?"[66] The life-negating tendencies of the *décadent*, Nietzsche claims, translates into an ethics that protects, shelters, and cares for the sickest and weakest. This is one of the ways in which *décadents* actively harm life.

This radical, polemical claim must be placed in its appropriate context, lest Nietzsche should be misinterpreted. Nietzsche, here, is giving expression to a particularly screeching voice. His goal is to shock, provoke, and unsettle his readers. This is why it would be a mistake to read a political

[59] *GM* "Vorrede" §5. [60] *Ibid.* [61] *A* §7.

[62] *M* §133. On this point, see Kiowski, "Nietzsches Kritik an Schopenhauers Mitleidsbegriff," *Prima Philosophia* 12(1), 1999: 47–61.

[63] In a key fragment, Nietzsche explicitly groups "mortification of the self, compassion," and "the negation of life" together (*NL 1888–1889*, 15(13)). See also *JGB* §225: "There are moments, when we look upon *your* compassion with indescribable fear, when we fight against this compassion ... Wellbeing as you understand it – that is certainly no goal, it looks to us like an *end*! A condition that makes decline something *desirable*."

[64] *JGB* §30. [65] *NL 1888–1889*, 15(110). [66] *Ibid.* See also *A* §7.

program into his claim that compassion acts against evolution. Indeed, there are good reasons to think that Nietzsche would never support the mass murder or quarantining of the physically weak and unhealthy. To wit: Nietzsche's concepts of health and sickness do not correspond to those of biological medicine or contemporary genetics. Consider Nietzsche's case. Nietzsche was ill for most of his adult life, and yet he believed that his sickness was precisely what allowed him to attain a "higher health." Accordingly, many medically healthy people might count as "sick and weak" for Nietzsche. Likewise, many medically unhealthy people might count as "healthy and strong."[67] In itself, this gives us good reasons to take the passages on compassion as the "counter-principle of selection" with a pinch of salt.

What does Nietzsche mean, then? Nietzsche's comment at *MM II* §45 might prove helpful on this point. This passage ridicules the morality of compassion for implying that others must be hurt so that a person may "become good." Seeing as "suffering is necessary for compassion," what results is a "case for all injury on earth."[68] On the face of it, this argument seems utterly sophistical. The whole point of praising compassion, the critic will object, is that it is good to feel compassion, so there is nothing about the morality of compassion that implies that others ought to be injured. But this objection misses Nietzsche's point. What Nietzsche is concerned with is an ideology in which "compassion with the lowly and the afflicted" is "*the measure* for *the elevation of the soul*."[69] It is not just that feeling compassion is good, but that "goodness" consists in being compassionate. In such a context, it is correct to point out that ethical prowess will require that people be suffering, unwell, downtrodden, etc. In light of this, the religion of compassion will effectively militate against the "evolution," or development, of higher, stronger types who are not so susceptible to sorrow, sadness, and depression.

67 This simple observation is enough to undermine much of Richardson's naive reconstruction of Nietzsche's ethics and "politics" in *Nietzsche's System*, pp. 142–219; see also Richardson's more recent reconstruction of Nietzsche's ethics as a form of radical social Darwinism in *Nietzsche's New Darwinism* (Oxford University Press, 2004). More generally, it seems to me that many of the commentators who read Nietzsche as a political philosopher committed to a crude (and cruel) aristocraticism – namely, Berkowitz, *Nietzsche*, B. Detwiler, *Nietzsche and the Politics of Aristocratic Radicalism* (Chicago University Press, 1990), F. Appel, *Nietzsche contra Democracy* (Ithaca, NY: Cornell University Press, 1999), and D. Losurdo, *Nietzsche, il ribelle aristocratico: biografia intellettuale e bilancio critico* (Turin: Bollati Boringhieri, 2002) – overemphasize and fail to place Nietzsche's polemical and often ironic claims in their appropriate context.

68 *MM II* "Der Wanderer und sein Schatten" §45.

69 *NL 1887–1888*, 9(44).

The religion of compassion, in this sense, requires the perpetuation and spread of *décadence*. Moreover, it might even tyrannize those who, by virtue of growing stronger and healthier – in Nietzsche's sense – make themselves unsuitable objects for compassion precisely in so far as they suffer less – or differently, at least (which is to say in a way that does not look like suffering to the *décadent*).

Adopting such a perspective makes it possible to gain a better understanding of the dual function of compassion as the "practice of nihilism." Consider the following passage from *A*:

> This depressing and contagious instinct thwarts those instincts, which work for the preservation and enhancement of life: as both a *multiplicator* of misery and a *conservator* of the miserable, it is the principal agent in the rise of *décadence* – compassion persuades to *nothingness*![70]

Compassion is a "multiplicator" of suffering in that it is itself a painful affect. It is also a "conservator" of those who suffer, precisely in so far as "suffering is necessary for compassion."[71] The idea is that a morality of compassion has every interest in preserving as many people as possible in a state of weakness and sickness – i.e. *décadence* – and in spreading this illness so that compassion itself may always have ever more objects.

In sum, the thrust of Nietzsche's cultural critique of compassion is that the rise and victory of unselving morals in and through the ethical prevalence of compassion in religious and secular ideologies is an unambiguous symptom of *décadence*. Europe's nihilist predicament, moreover, only becomes graver as the religion of compassion takes its toll on the health of Europe. What Nietzsche describes, in short, is a positive feedback loop. The religion of compassion, Nietzsche tells us, is both a consequence of the spread of *décadent* nihilists' herd mentality and a cause of further and deeper life-negating nihilism. The ethical primacy of compassion is both a "symptom of life in decline" and a great "calamity" which leads to an explicit will to nothingness.[72] On a medical analogy, the cultural predominance of compassion is something like a violent cough which, though it is only the symptom of a virus, consolidates the virus's grip on the body by harming the throat, thereby making it more vulnerable to further, deeper infection by this same virus. The religion of compassion, in short, is what allows the malady of *décadent* nihilism to maintain and consolidate its grip on Europe after the death of God.

[70] *A* §7. [71] *MM II* "Der Wanderer und sein Schatten" §45. [72] *GM* III §14.

Nietzsche's cultural critique of compassion, accordingly, culminates with a vision of a nihilist Europe engulfed in a new form of Buddhism. Nietzsche, in this connection, speaks of an "involuntary rise in gloom and sensitivity, under whose sway Europe seems to be threatened with a New Buddhism."[73] In the preface to *GM*, Nietzsche is more explicit yet:

> I understood the morality of compassion which attracts always more to itself, which even grasps philosophers and makes them sick, as the uncanniest symptom of our European culture which has itself grown uncanny, as its detour to a New Buddhism perhaps? To a new European Buddhism? To ... *nihilism*?[74]

The cultural critique of compassion, then, finds its epitome in Nietzsche's warning against the danger of a pure, self-conscious *nihil*ism born of the sickness of compassion – a life-negating "New Buddhism" hooked to the unselving of compassion and geared toward the final unselving of *nirvāṇa.*

It would be an unfortunate mistake to assume, on the basis of his vociferously critical views, that Nietzsche assumes a purely negative stance vis-à-vis compassion. A more careful reading of his oeuvre reveals, on the contrary, that there is room in Nietzsche's philosophy for a healthy form of compassion.[75] Examining this counterweight to Nietzsche's critique of compassion is the key to gaining a proper understanding of what is really involved in "overcoming compassion."

In a few highly significant passages, Nietzsche accuses the nihilist prophet of unselving of misconstruing compassion by illegitimately tracing it back to false roots. Consider the following fragment:

> Under the pressure of the ascetic unselving morals precisely the affects of love, goodness, compassion, even fairness, generosity, heroism had to be *misunderstood* ... It is *richness in personality*, fullness in oneself, overflowing and giving out, instinctive wellbeing and yea-saying to oneself which produces great sacrifice and great love: it is out of this strong and divine selfhood that these affects grow.[76]

Nietzsche's claim here is fundamentally different from that found in his psychological and cultural critiques. What we have here is not a frontal attack on compassion, but a critique of the *décadent* nihilist's understanding

[73] *JGB* §202. [74] *GM* "Vorrede" §5.

[75] On this point, see also L. P. Thiele, "The Agony of Politics: The Nietzschean Roots of Foucault's Thought," *American Political Science Review* 84(3), 1990: 907–25, Abbey, *Nietzsche's Middle Period*, and M. L. Frazer, "The Compassion of Zarathustra: Nietzsche on Sympathy and Strength," *Review of Politics* 68(1), 2006: 49–78, who likewise challenge the simplistic view that Nietzsche is opposed to compassion and benevolence in all its forms (a view uncritically accepted by most Nietzsche commentators).

[76] *NL 1887–1888*, 10(128). On the misunderstanding of compassion, love, and justice in the framework of ascetic unselving morals, see also *NL 1888–1889* 12(1).

of compassion. Really, affects such as genuine compassion, love, generosity, etc. are not rooted in the self-belittlement of unselving and its idealization of impersonal, impartial concern. Rather, they grow out of health and ebullient self-affirmation.

For Nietzsche, then, genuine compassion involves a thought of a radically different nature to that of the self- and life-negating nihilist – "I am strong, well and powerful. *Unlike* others, I *can* help, I *will* help ... in *my* way." In a similar vein, Nietzsche explains that love of mankind, compassion, and self-sacrifice are all, most fundamentally, healthy manifestations of the strong type's active, creative will to power.[77] Such behavior is expressive and characteristic of active forces, not reactive ones. This is to be contrasted to the *décadent*'s glorification of compassion in terms of "*lack* of self and self-assurance."[78] The *décadent's* enfeebling compassion born of unselving, it turns out, is something of a counterfeit.

How, in light of this, is Nietzsche's psychological critique of compassion to be understood? Is the entire psychological critique concerned with a chimera invented by the *décadent*? If compassion is really an active affect born of strength rather than reactive affect born of weakness, then what exactly is it that Nietzsche spends so much energy critiquing?

As is often the case when our polyphonic Nietzsche appears to be mired in an inexorable net of contradictions, what is called for is a shift in perspective. As with suffering and pessimism, the question to ask is not so much "what is compassion?" but "who feels compassion?" and thus also "how and why is compassion felt?"

In a passage from *JGB*, Nietzsche explains that "the noble man also helps the unfortunate, though not, or not entirely out of compassion, but rather out of an impulse produced by the overflow of power."[79] In spite of Nietzsche's hesitation, this makes it sound as though the term "compassion" only stands for the compassion of his critiques. Another passage from the same text suggests quite the contrary, however. After hyperbolically eulogizing the "man who is by nature a *master*," Nietzsche becomes somewhat more serious and writes: "If a man like this has compassion, now, *this* compassion is worth something. But what is worth the compassion of those who suffer?"[80] Here, Nietzsche suggests that it is in fact the strong type's compassion alone that is worthy of the name "com-passion" in so far as the weak type's compassion is just another type of "*Leid*" devoid of a genuine "*mit*."

[77] *NL 1887–1888*, 9(145). A parallel could be drawn between Nietzsche's description of compassion in passages such as these and J.-J. Rousseau's in *Émile* (Paris: Garnier Frères, 1967 [1762]) in particular.
[78] *GD* VIII §37 (my emphasis). [79] *JGB* §260. [80] *Ibid.* §293.

Nietzsche's view of genuine compassion

The general idea behind Nietzsche's comparison between the strong and weak types' relation to compassion is that there are really two forms of compassion, as it were. One is born of weakness and is symptomatic of an inability to resist psychological damage; the other is born of strength and is expressive of an active, expansive propensity to extend one's care, to shelter others under one's wings, etc. Just as there is both a pessimism of weakness and a pessimism of strength for Nietzsche, there is also a compassion of the weak and a compassion of the strong. In both cases, the "given" is the same – "boundless, senseless suffering" in the case of pessimism, "the other's woe" in the case of compassion – but the psychological effect is quite the opposite.

Admittedly, Nietzsche does not tell us very much about compassion of strength. His discussion of "his compassion," however, provides an interesting hint. Indeed, it would appear that the compassion of the weak and the compassion of the strong have very different intentional objects. To explain what distinguishes "his compassion" from that of his contemporaries, Nietzsche points to the bipartite nature of human beings: a so-called individual is part creat*ure* – or "matter, fragment, excess, clay, filth, nonsense, chaos" – and part creat*or* – or "sculptor, hammer-hardness."[81] Recall the distinction between reactive and active forces in the individual. The difference between Nietzsche's compassion of strength and the herd's compassion is that the former is concerned with the active creat*or* side of the individual, while the latter focuses on the reactive creat*ure* in the individual – what should be broken, molded, and overcome.[82] From the prevalent standpoint of the herd, the compassion of the strong is thus inverted (*umgekehrt*) compassion. This is the form of compassion Nietzsche alludes to when, in his notebooks, he likewise defines "my compassion" as the emotion he feels when a superior type wastes his potential and finds himself halted on his path to greatness or diverted away from attaining this goal, or when he looks at modern Europe and the deep nihilism in which it wallows.[83] In short, while the compassion of the strong looks out for what is active in human beings and will seek to assist these active forces against the onslaught of reactive forces, the compassion of the weak is concerned with what is reactive in the human being. As such, the compassion of the weak will even combat active forces in so far as these are a threat to the dominance of reactive forces.

The key to gaining a fuller understanding of what compassion of the strong involves is to build on the idea of the compassion of strength as

[81] *Ibid.* §225. [82] *Ibid.* [83] *NL 1884–1885*, 36(7).

"inverted" compassion of weakness. The first thing to note is that the opposition between compassion of strength and compassion of weakness neatly lines up with the weak vs. strong types' more general responses to suffering. The compassion of the strong involves responding to the suffering of the other as a challenge to meet, as an opportunity actively to engage in the world. This, after all, is how the strong type constitutes suffering in general. The compassion of the weak, in contrast, involves suffering from the other's suffering passively and thus responding to it reactively, as a source of enfeeblement rather than stimulation. This, likewise, is how the weak type always constitutes suffering.

What this suggests is that compassion of strength also involves suffering on account of the other's woe, but that this suffering is experienced as stimulating and invigorating rather than enfeebling and depressing. All compassion thus involves a certain measure of pain, but not all compassion can be described as fickle sentimentality. An important difference lies in how this pain is constituted and thus also in how it is responded to. More specifically, because the strong type is not distraught (but on the contrary stimulated) by the suffering he witnesses, it follows that the "object of his attention" will genuinely be the other and his/her woe. It turns out, then, that while the sick type experiences what Scheler describes as "apparent sympathy," the healthy type actually experiences something closer to Scheler's "real" sympathy. Indeed, it would appear that, on Nietzsche's account, higher health and confident self-affirmation is a condition for breaking out of the confines of the egocentrism in which the reactive, weak type remains mired. This implies that actions carried out on the basis of the compassion of the strong will not be superficial, foolish, and insulting, unlike actions carried out on the basis of the compassion of the weak. This is because they are not indirectly self-regarding, but genuinely concerned with the other's woe.

What Nietzsche says about "his compassion" also suggests that compassion of the strong involves a mechanism whereby the suffering that would actually be good for a person – the suffering that will "make him stronger instead of killing him" – will not be constituted as grounds for compassion. Rather, compassion of strength will focus on everything that makes suffering enfeebling rather than strengthening – e.g. the prevalence and proliferation of reactive forces, their expression in *ressentiment*, the supremacy of nihilist ideologies, etc. Such compassion of strength, accordingly, is certain never to act in the disservice of higher types, be it as injury or seduction. Moreover, it is presumably what will motivate the genuine "physician of mankind" of *M* §133.

Such a characterization of the compassion of the strong gives rise to a worrying set of questions, however. Does compassion of the strong only focus on the rare higher types made for great health? Will it ignore not only the suffering that will prove useful to fellow strong types, but also the "useless" suffering of the great masses of reactive types who will never overcome their *décadence*? Accordingly, though his concern will be genuinely other-regarding, is it not the case that the strong type will engage in far fewer acts of benevolence? Will his compassion of the strong not have a far narrower scope than the *décadent*'s compassion of weakness?

Prima facie, it seems that all these questions have to be answered in the affirmative. Nevertheless, a significant passage on Nietzsche's wider project with regard to morals urges us to at least give him the benefit of the doubt with regard to just how cruelly indifferent to "useless" suffering his healthy type will actually turn out to be. Consider the following passage from *M*, the work in which Nietzsche began waging his war on our "moral prejudices":

> I do not deny, as is self-evident – granted I am no fool – that many actions which are called immoral should be discouraged and fought against and similarly that many actions which are called moral should be done and encouraged. But I think the one like the other should be for other reasons than hitherto. We must *learn [to evaluate] differently* in order, finally, perhaps in quite a while, to attain even more: *to feel differently*.[84]

This passage suggests Nietzsche's entire attack on morality is not really concerned with what actions are carried out, but with how and why they are. This seems to imply that the healthy type will be no less helpful, supportive, caring, compassionate, and benevolent than the preachers of herd morals superficially appear to be. A model for the healthy type, in this connection, might be La Rochefoucauld, one of Nietzsche's heroes. In his self-portrait, La Rochefoucauld claims that he always did everything in his power to help and assist others, but never out of the vulgar and stupid sentiment of *pitié*.[85] Similarly, compassion of strength might prompt a great many benevolent actions – actions which will have the advantage of being genuinely helpful and other-regarding.

Following *M* §103's line of thought, what distinguishes the healthy from the sick type is not what he does, but his way of feeling his way around the world. He does not rush to assist the other out of contrived selflessness because he is really too weak to resist suffering psychological damage at the sight of the other's woe. He helps spontaneously, on account of an

[84] *M* §103. [85] La Rochefoucauld, "Autoportrait," p. 20.

overflowing of energy and confident self-affirmation. The suffering he feels in the face of the other's suffering is experienced as stimulating and invigorating. It provides an opportunity for him to act, to expand his strength and power. The act might be very similar to the compassionate weak type's, but the way of feeling, or interpreting, the situation is very different.

This at least suggests that the scope of compassion of strength and of the benevolence it gives rise to is not much narrower than that of compassion of weakness and its self-regarding benevolence. Admittedly, this is far from being a conclusive case. On the face of it, it seems like suffering-prone reactive types who are positively harmed by the other's suffering will do more for the other – irrespective of their underlying motivations – than healthy types exclusively concerned with the "creator in man." Ultimately, it is not clear that this question can be settled by looking at Nietzsche's ideas alone. This is why we will have to return to it at the end of the next chapter.

Our survey of Nietzsche's views on compassion is now complete. It is at last possible to gain a proper understanding of what Nietzsche means when he speaks of "overcoming compassion." To begin with, it is clear that it is the compassion of weakness that Nietzsche thinks healthy types need to overcome. Compassion of weakness, after all, is a depressive, enfeebling affect by virtue of which the compassionate person is damaged by the other's suffering. It is both grounded in *décadence* and itself an agent of further *décadence*. It involves a reactive and thus a paradigmatically unhealthy response to the other's suffering. As such, it reinforces whatever is reactive. In so far as Nietzsche's great health requires of the healthy type that he overcome everything reactive within, it is only natural that he should learn to "overcome compassion (of weakness)."

What is most interesting (and seemingly paradoxical) about Nietzsche's injunction to overcome compassion, however, is that it is actually the fruit of compassion. More specifically, Nietzsche's injunction is articulated from the standpoint of compassion of strength. This is the healthy, active compassion that strives against the enfeeblement and despair characteristic of the reactive, and thus also strives against the reactive compassion of weakness. This explains Nietzsche's confusing war-cry in *JGB*: "Compassion *against* compassion!"[86] As paradoxical as it may seem, then, when the (Anti-)Buddha of Europe presents the overcoming of *décadent* compassion as a cardinal virtue of life-affirmation, this is really the result of a healthy compassion concerned with the strong type's welfare and ascendance.

[86] *JGB* §225.

CHAPTER 6

Cultivating compassion

The cultivation of compassion is essential to attaining the Buddhist great health of *nirvāṇa*. With his typical spirit of contradiction, Nietzsche thus prescribed the overcoming of compassion as a key step in the progress to what he regarded as the Anti-Buddhist great health of *amor fati*. Seeing as *amor fati* is far from being the "inverse ideal"[1] of *nirvāṇa* that Nietzsche meant it to be, however, it is doubtful whether the opposition between the cultivation of compassion and its overcoming will fare any better. What is more, given the underlying affinities between *amor fati* and *nirvāṇa* that emerged in Chapter 4, it is probable that, here again, there will be a significant degree of overlap between the two ideals. Cultivating compassion and overcoming compassion, though nominally contradictory, might have more in common than might first appear. To see how and why this is so, it is necessary to begin by gaining a clear understanding of what cultivating compassion means in Buddhist philosophy.

To comprehend what the Buddhist cultivation of compassion involves, it is important to elucidate compassion's role in Buddhist philosophy. Why cultivate it? What kind of an emotion is it? How does it compare to similar feelings which are perhaps not conducive, not to say detrimental, to attaining the great health of *nirvāṇa*? Does it involve suffering? How does it manifest itself, concretely, in terms of compassionate actions?

There are very few systematic discussions of compassion in Buddhist texts. It is as though the concept was so essential to the tradition that no one bothered to flesh it out in full.[2] To answer our questions, then, Buddhist texts have to be carefully interrogated.

[1] *JGB* §56.
[2] On this point, see also L. Viévard, *Vacuité* (śūnyatā) *et compassion* (karuṇā) *dans le bouddhisme madhyamaka* (Paris: Collège de France, 2002), p. 16.

The first thing to note about compassion in Buddhism is that it is said to be a, if not the, characteristic feature of the Buddha's psychology. The Buddha is the "compassionate" agent par excellence,[3] the only being in this world whose sole purpose is to act for the welfare of all creatures "out of compassion."[4] Accordingly, a central Buddhist idea is that it is out of compassion that the Buddha dispensed his teaching.[5] There is thus a fundamental link between the Buddha's compassion and his therapeutic teaching. The Buddha is a boundlessly compassionate physician, or therapist, and it is out of his boundless compassion that he offers mankind his teaching.

An important component of this therapeutic teaching, moreover, is the prescription to cultivate compassion. In the discourses, this finds its expression in the oft-repeated injunction to develop limitless compassion, along with the three other great virtues characteristic of the Buddha's supremely healthy mind. Cultivating infinite compassion – as well as goodwill, sympathetic joy, and equanimity – is described as the path to the "mental liberation" characteristic of the great health of *nirvāṇa*.[6] The idea, then, is that there is a special connection between developing compassion and attaining great health.

There is one simple way to explain this special relation. Implicit in the Buddhist injunction to cultivate compassion is an underlying theory not unlike that of contemporary cognitive behavioral therapy.[7] The idea is to have the patient combat unhealthy mental behavior by cultivating the psychological traits, thought patterns, and emotive behavior characteristic of a healthy mind.[8] In the case of Buddhism's ambitious therapeutic program, the goal is nothing short of the state of psychological health that

[3] *MN* II.100. See also *SN* I.110, where the Buddha is described as "having compassion for all beings."

[4] *AN* I.22; *DN* II.212.

[5] This view is repeatedly expressed in the discourses (namely, at *MN* I. 23, II.238, and III.302; *SN* I.110 and IV.359; and *AN* I.22, III.6, and IV.139). The idea that the most salient characteristic of the Buddha and other enlightened beings is their compassionate disposition is particularly emphasized in later Sanskrit texts, especially (though not exclusively) those of the Mahāyāna tradition. For a survey of the several Sanskrit passages in which compassion is described as the root of enlightenment and of all of the Buddha's and/or *bodhisattva*'s qualities, see Viévard, *Vacuité*, p. 156.

[6] I am referring to the meditative exercises centered on the four so-called "*brahma*-abodes," in which the trainee is instructed to imagine pervading the entire world with a mind full of goodwill, compassion, sympathetic joy, and finally equanimity (*DN* I.251). This instruction is repeated verbatim several times in the Pāli canon.

[7] This is something Ellis, one of the founders of cognitive behavioral therapy, seems to have been aware of. A. Ellis, *Reason and Emotion in Psychotherapy* (New York: Carol Publishing Group, 1991), p. 35.

[8] Admittedly, most cognitive behavioral therapy, especially that of Beck and his followers, is more cognitivist than Buddhist therapy. See A. T. Beck, *Cognitive Therapy and the Emotional Disorders* (New York: International Universities Press, 1976). Overall, Buddhist psychology focuses more on "states of mind" in which there is no clear line of demarcation between the cognitive, emotive, and conative. If anything, then, Buddhist therapy is more behavioral – in a sense that includes "cognitive behavior" – than cognitive. In reality, this therapeutic model and the psychology that underpins it is not

characterizes the perfected Buddha. In so far as boundless compassion is the most essential feature of the Buddha's supremely healthy mind, a central part of the path to great health is to cultivate just such a mental disposition. As circular as this may seem, then, cultivating boundless compassion is instrumental to attaining the great health of *nirvāṇa* precisely in so far as having boundless compassion is a result of attaining *nirvāṇa*.

Prima facie, Buddhist philosophy's account of the relation between compassion and great health seems to be rather problematic. The great health of *nirvāṇa* is said to be characterized both by the absence of suffering (*duḥkha*) and by the presence of boundless compassion. But is it not the case that feeling compassion involves a certain measure of distress? Is Nietzsche not correct to note that one suffers when undergoing compassion? Does compassion not involve a form of identification with the other that makes me "suffer with" him/her? And if this is the case, then is it not contradictory to say that the Buddha knows no suffering, yet feels limitless compassion?

The first avenue to explore in defense of the very coherence of the Buddhist ideal consists in arguing that the Buddha's compassion, unlike that of the ordinary human being, does not involve suffering. There is some support for this view in Theravāda literature.

Consider the passage in the canon in which the Buddha is explicitly criticized for dispensing his teaching to others. His opponent, Śākya by name, seems to believe that there is something contradictory about a truly liberated one teaching others: "It is not good that you, a liberated wanderer who is free from all ties, should instruct others."[9] "Śākya," answers the Buddha, "he who is endowed with insight is not capable of that mental compassion which originates in attachment. And if, with a clear mind, he instructs others, he bears no ties on account of [teaching others]. *That* is compassion. *That* is caring concern."[10] What the Buddha seems to be saying is that his compassion, unlike that of those who lack insight – i.e. are not enlightened – is not tainted by the common sentimental attachment that compassion normally involves. Such a "detached compassion," the Buddha

specific to Buddhism, but is common to a number of Indian traditions. Fort points out that in Advaita Vedānta the psychological traits of the *jīvanmukta* ('liberated soul') – the Advaitin "healthy type" – are also those the cultivation of which lead to this status. A. Fortin, "Liberation while Living in the *Jīvanmuktiviveka*," in A. Fort and P. Mummes (eds.), *Living Liberation in Hindu Thought* (Albany, NY: State University of New York Press, 1996), pp. 135–55, at p. 144. C. M. Brown observes something similar in the case of the *Mahābhārata*'s ethics in "Modes of Perfected Living in the Mahābhārata and the Purāṇas," also in Fort and Mummes, *Living Liberation in Hindu Thought*, pp. 157–83, at p. 161. In short, it seems to have been a widespread belief in India that to make oneself think and feel more like one would if healthy, or healthier, is effective in warding off harmful symptoms.

9 *SN* 1.206. 10 *Ibid.* (my emphasis).

concludes, is what genuine compassion and care actually involve. Free of ties, this genuine compassion is presumably also free from pain.

This idea finds further support in the fifth-century CE Theravādin commentator Buddhaghosa's discussion of compassion. Buddhaghosa specifies the false manifestation of each of the four great virtues whose cultivation leads to *nirvāṇa*. Just as goodwill should not give rise to attachment, or sympathetic joy to unrestrained excitement, Buddhaghosa points out that genuine compassion should not give rise to sorrow.[11] A few lines further on, he adds that if cruelty, or malice, is compassion's "far enemy" – i.e. its opposite – self-regarding sadness is its "near enemy" – i.e. the affect it may easily be mistaken for.[12] The upshot of Buddhaghosa's commentary, then, is that cultivating compassion involves the cultivation of something quite distinct from the everyday sentimental responses that we commonly refer to as "compassion." Genuine Buddhist compassion, it is implied, does not involve suffering in so far as it involves no attachment.

However, though the view that true compassion involves no suffering finds some indirect support in Theravāda literature, it is openly contradicted in Sanskrit Buddhist texts. A number of Buddhist philosophers of the Classical period, Mahāyānist and Non-Mahāyānist alike, speak with one voice on this point: all forms of compassion involve suffering, even that of the exalted *bodhisattva* (i.e. the Mahāyāna healthy type).[13] Buddhist great health, then, does not preclude suffering, at least not that which is born of compassion. In fact, if the supremely healthy mind has boundless compassion, it seems to follow that it is also boundlessly tormented.

The problematic implications this has for Buddhist ethics are twofold. First, it is no longer clear what distinguishes the Buddhist healthy type's compassion from the sentimental sympathy exhibited by the ordinary people as a result of their attachments. Second, there is something contradictory about a state of great health characterized both by the cessation of *duḥkha* and the manifestation of boundless *duḥkha*-causing compassion. Is there anything in Buddhist texts that suggests that these problems can be solved?

Our first concern seems to be further corroborated by Buddhaghosa's instructions regarding the cultivation of compassion. Buddhaghosa instructs

[11] *Vsm*, p. 318.

[12] *Ibid.*, p. 319. The technical term employed here is "sorrow based on the home life," which, as the canonical citation Buddhaghosa adduces makes clear, stands for the sadness that results from losing possessions and/or loved ones.

[13] As Viévard points out, a great number of Classical Indian Buddhist authors were in agreement on this point. Viévard presents several citations from these authors concerning the personal distress involved in compassion in *Vacuité*, pp. 180–1.

trainees to begin by developing compassion for family and loved ones, then to progressively extend the scope of their compassionate concern to people they are indifferent to, and finally even to enemies.[14] Such training suggests that the healthy type's compassion is not qualitatively different from what everyone naturally feels toward those to whom they are attached. This comes as something of a surprise given that Buddhaghosa then tries to qualify this form of compassion as firmly distinct from sorrow and self-regarding sadness. There is at the very least a palpable tension here. Is the Buddha's compassion qualitatively different from the common person's, or is it only that it has a broader scope?

Fortunately, this is a question to which Vasubandhu and Asaṅga provide two complementary answers. Vasubandhu distinguishes between the compassion that the trainee is preliminarily instructed to develop and the 'great compassion' characteristic of the Buddha's supremely healthy mind. While the former is characterized by the absence of aversion alone, the latter is also characterized by the absence of delusion.[15] What, one might ask, is the delusion of which the Buddha's compassion is supposed to be devoid? This is a question Asaṅga can help us answer. While discussing the love involved in compassion, Asaṅga explains that unlike the father's or mother's love, which "consists in thirsting," a Buddhist healthy type's love "consists in compassion."[16] Though this distinction is somewhat circular, it nevertheless makes it very clear that the Buddha's compassion is different from mundane compassion in that it *does not involve thirsting*. This, in turn, suggests that though compassion might involve suffering, this suffering must be qualitatively different from the thirsting-based *duḥkha* which is brought to cessation in *nirvāṇa*. What is more, we can now infer, on the basis of Asaṅga's claim, that it is from the *self*-delusion that Vasubandhu's great compassion is free. Buddhist philosophy, after all, traces thirsting back to the self-delusion. The Buddha's great compassion, then, is qualitatively different from the ordinary person's attachment-based sympathy in that it is free of the self-delusion (Vasubandhu) and therefore does not involve thirsting (Asaṅga).

There is thus an intimate link between the full realization of selflessness and the arising of boundless compassion in a Buddhist healthy type's perfected mind. Consider, in this connection, Viévard's synopsis of Madhyamaka moral psychology: "The compassion of the profane individual rests on the *ātman* . . . The perfection of compassion is proportional to the disappearance of the idea of *ātman*. Such [perfection] is progressive, and

[14] *Vsm*, p. 314. [15] *AK*, p. 415. [16] *MSA* XVII.43, Commentary.

operates simultaneously with the gradual understanding of emptiness."[17] This idea finds an echo in the writings of Dhammapāla, Buddhaghosa's Theravādin commentator. Dhammapāla speaks of insight and compassion as the twin poles – cognitive and affective – of the Buddha's mind. Insight and compassion, it is suggested, are really two sides of the same coin. The passage concludes as follows: "Just as the master's compassion was devoid of sentimental affectation or sorrow, so his understanding was devoid of the thoughts 'I' and 'mine.'"[18] The implication, of course, is that there is an intimate connection between the liberating insight into lack of self, which is the hallmark of Buddhist philosophy, and the Buddha's compassion, which is the hallmark of Buddhist ethics.

Buddhist moral psychology, then, exceeds the scope of what was discussed in Chapter 4. Recovering from the self-delusion and gaining freedom from all of its pernicious effects at the cognitive and affective level does not only bring *duḥkha* to an end; it is not only a matter of recovering from the debilitating, narcissistic, and delusional egocentrism with which we are all afflicted. Attaining the great health of *nirvāṇa* also involves feeling genuine compassion for all beings. In place of systemic egotism arises systemic altruism. On the Mādhyamika's account, accordingly, the realization of emptiness and the arising of compassion go hand in hand. Such compassion, however, is qualitatively different from that of the ordinary person. Free from the self-delusion, the Buddhist healthy type's compassion has nothing to do with the thirsting that permeates the ordinary person's affective take on the world. This compassion, in turn, manifests itself as a desire to assist others in attaining the great health of *nirvāṇa* and thereby bringing *duḥkha* to cessation. As is explained in the *DBhS*, he whom gains full knowledge of emptiness "has no desires other than to bring beings to ripeness, [a desire] which has for its cause great compassion."[19]

This focus on the other's ethical progress, moreover, provides the key to understanding the nature of the suffering involved in the compassion of the Buddhist healthy type. It is already clear that such suffering will be qualitatively different from the far more standard thirsting-based *duḥkha* that pervades most of our lives. But to provide a positive account of such suffering, it is necessary to look at the relation between compassion and the fate of those for whom it is felt. Asaṅga, in this connection, explains that

[17] Viévard, *Vacuité*, p. 241. See also Siderits, *Buddhist Philosophy*, p. 199.
[18] *Pm*, p. 194, quoted in Bhikkhu Ñāṇamoli, *The Path of Purification* (Kandry: Buddhist Publication Society, 1975), p. 774.
[19] *DBhS*, p. 34.

though *bodhisattvas* first recoil before the suffering they experience out of compassion, this same suffering fills them with joy when it is properly apprehended.[20] He goes on to explain that in compassionately assisting others in their progression toward the great health of *nirvāṇa*, the *bodhisattvas*' "compassion-caused suffering turns into happiness."[21] This is presumably why the *bodhisattvas*' compassion-born suffering fills them with joy to begin with.

Śāntideva evokes a similar idea. He explains that the suffering born of Buddhist healthy types' compassion is far outweighed by the formidable pleasure they feel when the other is helped to get closer to *nirvāṇa*.[22] Though the suffering involved in compassion might take most unreflective people aback, Śāntideva tells us, it is really only a preamble for the happiness of sympathetic joy. Compassion-born suffering, it follows, acts as a stimulant for Buddhist healthy types, propelling them to altruistic action. Moreover, it is described as a necessary condition for the profound pleasure of sympathetic joy, and thus as a preamble for a higher happiness. Far from being a problem for Buddhist ethics, then, the fact that Buddhist compassion is supposed to involve suffering actually brings into relief deeper and subtler aspects of Buddhist moral psychology. It points to a stimulating, healthy form of suffering.

There is perhaps no better way of gaining a correct understanding of the Buddha's compassion than to contemplate him at work. In his commentary on a collection of verses by great figures of early Buddhism, Dhammapāla reports the story of how the female sage and poet Kisagotamī was brought into the Buddhist fold. This illustrative example of the Buddha's compassion says more about its spirit than would ever be possible with a theoretical discussion. Here is the story as Dhammapāla tells it:

> Her name was Gotamī, but on account of her lean body people called her "Skinny Gotamī." After she had gone to her husband's family [i.e. after she had married], people treated her with contempt, [saying:] "She is the daughter of a miserable family." She bore a son. And by obtaining a son, she acquired honor. But her son, after reaching the age where he could run about, died during his play time. Because of that, she was driven mad by sorrow. She [thought:] "Having formerly suffered contempt, I obtained honor from my son's lifetime [onward]. They will try to separate my son from me." Maddened by sorrow, she placed the dead body on her hip and went from one house to the next in the city, [saying:] "Please give me medicine for my son!" People reviled her: "Medicine? Why?" She did not understand them. Now a wise man thought: "She is mentally perturbed by grief for her

[20] *MSA* XVII.46. [21] *Ibid.* 47, Commentary. [22] *BA* VIII.104–8.

son. The one with ten powers [i.e. the Buddha] will know of a medicine for her." He spoke: "My dear, go to the Awakened One and ask him for medicine for your son." Having gone to [his] abode while the master was teaching the doctrine, [Kisagotamī] said: "Exalted one, please give me medicine for my son!" Having seen the promise in her, the master said: "Go! Enter the city and bring me a mustard seed from a house which has never known death." "Very well, sir!" [she said], her mind pleased. She entered the city, went to the first house and said: "The master wishes to be brought a mustard seed for my son's medicine, if this house has never known death, [then] please give me a mustard seed." "Who is able to count the dead here?" [was she answered,] "what, then, is the use of this mustard seed?" She went to a second, a third, a fourth house. [Then,] freed from frenzy thanks to the Buddha, [Kisagotamī] regained normal consciousness. She thought: "Certainly this will hold in the whole city. The lord will have seen this out of compassion and concern for my welfare." She developed *saṃvega*,[23] went away from there, abandoned her son in a charnel grove, and uttered these verses:

> This is no village law, no town law,
> Nor is it a law for a single family.
> For this entire world, including the gods,
> This very law holds: everything is impermanent.[24]

There are a number of things to note about this striking story. The first is the medical discourse in which the entire story is couched. Kisagotamī is repeatedly described as "mad with sorrow" until she is finally freed from her frenzy and restored to "normal consciousness." Kisagotamī is truly ill on account of sorrow. This is something the wise passerby immediately sees. In fact, there is a telling and most probably deliberate ambiguity in the formulation of the wise man's thought – "the Buddha will know of a medicine for her." Will the Buddha's medicine be for her son, or for her? This is not clear. When he addresses her, after all, the passerby explicitly speaks of a medicine for her son. What is very clear, however, is that it is ultimately Kisagotamī, and not her son, who is treated. The Buddha, finally, does not so much cure her as create conditions in which she recovers.

Note, in this connection, that the Buddha sees "promise" in Kisagotamī. This presumably affected the form of treatment he devised. The Buddha seems to foresee that going from grief-stricken house to grief-stricken house will not only lead Kisagotamī to recover from her frenzy, but also lead her to higher pursuits. His compassionate action, then, is not directed at her immediate pain, but at something deeper. Accordingly, the Buddha neither

[23] *Saṃvega* is a technical Buddhist term that designates the kind of agitation caused by the realization of the impermanence of all things, which leads to the taking up of the Buddhist path.
[24] *ThGA* x.1.

consoles nor comforts Kisagotamī. He does not even try to reason with her. Instead, he sends her off with the false hope that her son will be cured from death if she can find the right mustard seed. This cold-hearted, almost unsympathetic intervention is what the great physician's compassion translates into. It is Kisagotamī herself, finally, who arrives at the realization that all is impermanent, that attachment is futile, etc., which eventually leads her to embark upon the path to the great health of *nirvāṇa*. She is the one who will ultimately cure herself of the most fundamental of illnesses.

Many people are disturbed upon first hearing this story. The supposedly compassionate Buddha appears inhuman, unsympathetic, and almost cruel. Even his teaching of impermanence is indirect and takes the form of what may be looked upon as a tasteless practical joke. How, one may ask, can this be the great compassionate physician admired and worshipped for more than two millennia? This impression, of course, derives from the unreflective assumption that the compassion the Buddha feels is identical to what most of us experience when we feel compassion. But this assumption is wrong. In reality, the story of Kisagotamī is one of the most illustrative and telling examples of what active Buddhist compassion consists in. The Buddha sees the potential for great health in Kisagotamī and leads her to arrive, on her own, at the conclusion that will set her on the path to *nirvāṇa*, even if this happens via profound disillusion. His compassion does not manifest itself as commiseration or consolation. Rather, it translates into cool, dispassionate, straightforward, and ultimately effective action. What is more, he does not do anything directly for Kisagotamī. He only orchestrates the conditions in which she will come to help herself. Kisagotamī's suffering is her responsibility alone. No one can put an end to it other than Kisagotamī herself.

Prima facie, there seems to be a certain ethical ambiguity about the practice of compassion^{Buddhist}.[25] In the discourses, we find the Buddha claiming that he would not hesitate to cause harm out of compassion if necessary. Just as most of us would decide to pull a pebble out of a child's throat if it was choking on it "even though blood may be drawn," the Buddha, out of compassion, will occasionally cause suffering and torment with his words.[26] Conversely, Kisagotamī's case makes it evident that suffering can easily be turned to profit, especially at the hands of a skillful

[25] Henceforth I will use the superscripted "compassion^{Buddhist}" to designate the compassion that accompanies the great health of *nirvāṇa* as opposed to other emotions commonly referred to as compassion. Cf. Flanagan's "eudaimonia^{Buddha}," "happiness^{Buddha}," etc., as opposed to "eudaimonia^{Aristotle}," "happiness^{Aristotle}," etc., in *The Bodhisattva's Brain*.

[26] *MN* I.395.

therapist. To the question of how much suffering can be caused for the sake of healing someone can thus be added the question of how much suffering may be allowed to take place. How much harm and laissez-faire does compassion^{Buddhist} really involve?

Most formulations of the Mahāyāna *bodhisattva* vow seem to imply that compassion^{Buddhist} prompts one to help anyone who suffers in every way and in any situation.[27] But if the goal of healthy types is to direct people toward the great health of *nirvāṇa* – which implies the complete cessation of *duḥkha* – not just to fight any and every instance of suffering as it presents itself, then it is far from clear that this is what compassion^{Buddhist} actually prompts them to do.

The Buddha does not offer Kisagotamī a shoulder to cry on. Instead, he sends her off on a futile quest for a mustard seed he knows she will never find, thereby prolonging her suffering and even temporarily feeding her delusional hope that her son can be cured from death. In short, it looks as though Buddhist healthy types will both cause suffering and allow it to occur with an eye to nudging the other in the direction of *nirvāṇa*. The practice of compassion^{Buddhist} might thus involve less benevolence than some Buddhist texts seem to suggest. More worryingly yet, one could wonder whether the Buddha, seeing the "promise" in Kisagotamī, would have even prevented her son from dying had he been able to. This, after all, might have delayed Kisagotamī's recovery from the fever of thirsting.

Consider, in this connection, the Buddhist concept of skillful means (*kuśalopāya*) which comes to the fore in Classical Indian Buddhist philosophy. The idea here is that in assisting others in their progress toward great health, the Buddhist healthy type exhibits perfect "skillfulness in means."[28] This notion is intimately related to the Buddha's formidable versatility as a teacher.[29] According to some Buddhist texts, almost any action is admissible, including murder or sexual intercourse for a nominally abstinent monk, if it will help a fellow creature stuck in *saṃsāra*.[30] This only adds to the worry that compassion^{Buddhist} and its skillful use of means might involve both causing suffering and/or allowing more suffering to happen.

Nevertheless, there are also good reasons to believe that compassion^{Buddhist} involves neither causing nor being indifferent to that much harm. Buddhist

[27] See, for instance, *BA* III.8–10, one of the most famous formulations of this vow.

[28] On this difficult feature of Buddhist ethics, and its role in the Mahāyāna in particular, see M. Pye, *Skilful Means: A Concept in Mahāyāna Buddhism* (New York: Routledge, 2003).

[29] See, on this point, Gethin, *The Foundations of Buddhism*, p. 228.

[30] On this point, see P. Williams, *Mahāyāna Buddhism: The Doctrinal Foundations* (London: Routledge, 1989), pp. 144f.

authors throughout the ages have made it clear that too much suffering is profoundly *distracting* and prevents people from embarking onto the path to the great health of *nirvāṇa*. This is why those in the human realm of traditional Indian cosmology are far better off than those in the three inferior realms.[31] Hell-beings, ghosts, and animals all suffer far too much to have the leisure to think about life or to take up the Buddhist path. If we translate cosmology into psychology, as Buddhist texts invite us to do,[32] we obtain the principle that people who are too miserable cannot even begin helping themselves. If the *bodhisattva* vow seems to involve such broad benevolence, then, it may be because there is an enormous mass of distracting suffering in the world which needs to be removed before people can even begin to heal themselves.

Nevertheless, living in happy (though also impermanent) godly realms is also considered to be less favorable to attaining great health than living in the human realm, in large part because gods suffer too little. If we translate this cosmological claim into psychology, we obtain the principle that some people "have it too easy" for their own good, so to speak. As a result, the practice of compassion^{Buddhist}, which aims to help creatures put an end to suffering by attaining the great health of *nirvāṇa*, might very well involve allowing suffering to occur in the case of someone who may not have encountered enough suffering so far – and perhaps even to cause them harm. After all, with the arch-pragmatic skillfulness in means doctrine, there are no categorical constraints on what the Buddhist healthy type may do out of compassion.

While active compassion^{Buddhist} does involve much free and spontaneous benevolence for the simple sake of relieving suffering, then, things are not as straightforward as they are depicted in some Buddhist texts. The Buddhist healthy type will fight much suffering just because it distracts people from the pursuit of great health. But the ultimate goal of compassion^{Buddhist} is to direct the other toward the complete self-healing that will bring all suffering to an end. And to this end some harm might be caused, and some might be allowed, albeit with sharp discrimination.

The idea, in short, is that always helping someone might not be truly helpful to them. Take, for instance, the case of a parent who rushes into its one-year-old child's room as soon as it cries, only to spend ten minutes consoling it and singing it back to sleep each time. This parent's lack of restraint, though motivated by concern for the child's welfare, is actually

[31] *MN* I.73; *DN* III.234.

[32] On the "principle of the *equivalence of cosmology and psychology*" in interpreting the Buddhist cosmological scheme, see Gethin, *The Foundations of Buddhism*, pp. 119f.

harming the child, who is deprived of the opportunity to develop the capacity to comfort itself, to gain a certain autonomy, etc. Admittedly, things are not so clear-cut in most cases and it thus requires a very fine judgment to evaluate the situation and settle on the optimal course of action. Fortunately, Buddhist healthy types are supposed to be the finest psychologists. This is in large part thanks to their freedom from the self-delusion and the ensuing cessation of the debilitating egotism that clouds the normal person's judgment.

Now that Buddhist compassion^{Buddhist} has been examined in greater detail, it is possible to return to Nietzsche and to see whether the second axis of the life-negation/affirmation dichotomy fares any better than the first. When it comes to the ideal response to one's own suffering, Nietzsche's thought and Buddhist philosophy are far from being as opposed as Nietzsche believed. But are their views effectively opposed when it comes to the other's suffering? Or could it be the case that, here also, the implosion of the life-negation/affirmation dichotomy delivers significant overlap in ethical visions?

Setting Buddhist views and Nietzsche's views on compassion side by side delivers two apparent oppositions: (1) Nietzsche's injunction to overcome compassion vs. the Buddhists' injunction to cultivate compassion; (2) Nietzsche's compassion-free "physician of mankind" vs. the Buddhists' boundlessly compassionate "great physician." Of course, Nietzsche's two apparently Anti-Buddhist positions concern compassion of weakness alone. It is this form of compassion that the healthy type must overcome and from which the genuine physician of mankind must be free. For the oppositions between Nietzsche's thought and Buddhist philosophy to hold up, then, it would have to be the case that the Buddha's compassion^{Buddhist} and Nietzsche's compassion of the weak designate similar phenomena.

This condition, however, is far from being satisfied. Consider the most salient points raised by Nietzsche in his critique of compassion of weakness:

(1) It exhibits weakness, or "inability to resist stimuli," unrestrained sentimentality, and lack of self-control.
(2) It gives rise to a type of suffering that is depressing and debilitating.
(3) Its motivational structure is one of subliminal self-regard – the underlying purpose of the actions it leads to is to assuage one's own suffering.
(4) It is focused on the creature, not on the creator, in man, potentially at the expense of the creator.
(5) In view of (1) and (2), it is a "seduction" for the higher men on their way to great health, i.e. the seduction to relapse into fickle, dissipated, and self-enfeebling sentimentality.
(6) In view of (4), it is an "injury" to the higher men who are its object.

At the level of ideology, moreover, Nietzsche makes the following points concerning the ethical primacy of compassion of weakness:

(1) It operates an ethical reduction to the lowest common denominator – the parading of a banal form of weakness as an outstanding virtue.
(2) It is an expression of the calculated self-interest of the "herd" – it makes a virtue of what is a necessity for the herd.
(3) As a product of the *décadents' ressentiment*, it is a key component in the life- and self-negating program of unselving morals.

Compassion[Buddhist], it should now be obvious, has very little to do with the object of Nietzsche's psychological and cultural critiques.

Compassion[Buddhist], to begin, shares none of the psychological features of compassion of weakness. It is firmly distinguished from the unrestrained sentimentality characteristic of those who remain in the grip of the fever of thirsting. As such, it is an expression of the great strength and self-control the Buddhist healthy type derives from overcoming the self-delusion and bringing its debilitating effects to cessation. As an expression of the great health of *nirvāṇa*, moreover, compassion[Buddhist] is entirely immune from *duḥkha*, the depressing and enfeebling pain the sick type is afflicted with in the midst of this sea of transient becoming. On the contrary, the suffering involved in compassion[Buddhist] is a stimulating suffering, which prompts to action and acts as a preamble to the profound pleasures of sympathetic joy. As such, feeling compassion[Buddhist] will never constitute a "seduction" for a Nietzschean higher type.

What is more, because agents motivated by compassion[Buddhist] are free from the suffering born of systemic egotism, their actions are not self-regarding, or subliminally geared toward averting their own pain. On the contrary, their actions are genuinely concerned with the other's wellbeing. In so far as the supreme wellbeing of *nirvāṇa* is the only thing that can bring suffering to an end, finally, compassion[Buddhist] is concerned not with the Buddhist equivalent of the suffering "creature" in wo/man, but in the "creator" who holds the promise of destroying the very root of debilitating *duḥkha*. This is clearly brought out by the case of Kisagotamī. As such, being the object of compassion[Buddhist] will never "injure" the Nietzschean higher type – especially as it is the same form, or interpretation, of suffering that comes to cessation in *nirvāṇa* and in *amor fati*.[33]

Things do not look very different at the ideological level. To begin with, the primacy of compassion in Buddhist ethics is the very opposite of an ethical reduction to the lowest common denominator. Cultivating compassion[Buddhist]

[33] On this point, see Chapter 4.

consists in cultivating a virtue that is the exclusive province of the highest and healthiest – a virtue of a fundamentally different nature from that of the ordinary person's thirsting-based, self-delusion-fueled "compassion." Though it might be to the herd's advantage to have masters motivated by compassion^{Buddhist}, then, the ethical primacy of compassion is no more the disingenuous glorification of a herd instinct than the expression of the herd's calculated self-interest. Though Buddhism did fight the Brahmins' oppressive hereditary class system, there is in fact something strikingly hierarchical about its ethics. Buddhism is not egalitarian when it comes to ethical worth; the hatred of rank order (*Rangordnung*) characteristic of the herd animal[34] is entirely foreign to it. The Buddha did not have it that there are no Brahmins (in the sense of higher types), only that there are no Brahmins by birth. If anything, from a historical perspective, the rise of Buddhism was not a slave revolt, but on the contrary a master revolt against the priestly class to which the aristocratic class came second in the caste system. The Buddhist healthy type who exhibits compassion^{Buddhist} is thus a superior type if ever there was one. If anything, Buddhist ethics and its focus on compassion are expressive of a ruler mentality, not a herd mentality. As such, cultivating compassion^{Buddhist} has nothing to do with the self-belittlement and self-effacement characteristic of life-negating unselving morals as Nietzsche describes them. Compassion^{Buddhist} is expressive of the exuberant self-love, the potent confidence, and the overflowing strength that attend the overcoming of the debilitating self-delusion. As in the case of attaining *nirvāṇa*, cultivating compassion^{Buddhist} is not a matter of self-mortification and life-negation – i.e. of unselving – but of attaining an empowering state of supreme wellbeing; it is a matter of recovering from everything that might "hold me back."

It is clear, then, that overcoming compassion (of weakness) and cultivating compassion^{Buddhist} are not diametrically opposed ideals. It is likewise clear that Nietzsche's "physician of mankind" has no reason to guard against compassion^{Buddhist}. On the contrary, it seems as though the emotion Nietzsche targets is an emotion advanced Buddhists on their way to great health also need to guard against. While Buddhist philosophy does not harbor the same suspicions as Nietzsche does concerning the ill social effects of more standard forms of attachment-based sympathy,[35] it is clear that, in so far as it "consists in thirsting" (Asaṅga), the Buddhist healthy type

[34] *JGB* §62; *GD* VIII §37.

[35] In fact, the Buddha urged common people not destined to embark on the path to great health to show sympathy and other such feelings, even though they could result from (and reinforce) thirsting. Cf. Nietzsche's comments on the utility of compassion and other nominally other-regarding feelings for the herd.

must also discard everyday compassion. In fact, Nietzsche's warning that compassion of weakness can constitute a "seduction" for higher types finds an echo in Buddhaghosa's claim that the mundane, self-regarding sadness that passes for compassion among ordinary people is the "near enemy" of compassion^{Buddhist}.[36] It turns out, then, that the "cultivation of compassion" advocated by the Buddha actually requires that the emotion Nietzsche critiques be overcome. Far from being opposites, then, the Buddhist cultivation of compassion implies and requires Nietzsche's overcoming of compassion.

If cultivating compassion^{Buddhist} requires overcoming the compassion Nietzsche derides, it should come as no surprise that compassion^{Buddhist} is remarkably close to Nietzsche's compassion of the strong. It is from the standpoint of this healthy compassion, after all, that Nietzsche prescribes the overcoming of the compassion of the weak, a prescription the advanced Buddhist would be advised to follow. And indeed, the compassion the Buddhist cultivates and Nietzsche's compassion of the strong share a surprising *air de famille*.

Consider, in this connection, the principal features of Nietzsche's compassion of strength:

(1) It is expressive of strength and potency, confidence in one's distinctive ability to intervene, masterly self-control, affirmative self-love, etc.
(2) The type of suffering to which it gives rise is stimulating and tonic – unlike the reactive type, the healthy active type always constitutes suffering as an obstacle to be overcome.
(3) The motivational structure of the actions it gives rise to is one of genuine other-regard – the other's suffering is not only the intentional object, but also the object of attention.
(4) It is focused on the creator, not on the creature, in man.

All of these features stand diametrically opposed to the psychological features of Nietzsche's compassion of the weak. Now, not only is compassion^{Buddhist} firmly distinct from the compassion of the weak, but it also turns out that it is endowed with the four essential attributes of Nietzsche's compassion of the strong. This is obvious for (1) and (3). Moreover, though Buddhist moral psychology is not articulated in terms of the reactive/passive vs. active/creative dichotomy, and thus does not employ the artistic creator/creature idiom, it is clear that compassion^{Buddhist} also has characteristics analogous to features (2) and (4) of compassion of strength. Indeed, the suffering it involves is a tonic and a preamble to the victorious happiness of

[36] *Vsm*, p. 319.

sympathetic joy. And its ultimate focus is on the promise of great health a person holds, not on the despondent sufferer as such.

A quick glance at the three other great virtues that complement compassion^{Buddhist} and likewise characterize the Buddhist healthy type's perfected mind only confirms that there is much affinity between Nietzsche's and the Buddha's ideal. When it comes to Buddhism, Nietzsche cannot complain, as he does in *FW*, about an exclusive concern with suffering. Unlike other "preachers of compassion,"[37] the Buddha also reserves an important place for the giving and sharing of happiness. The former is the province of the prime virtue of goodwill, while the Buddhist emphasis on sympathetic joy resoundingly answers Nietzsche's call for "*Mitfreude*" (literally, "shared happiness") as a counterweight to *Mitleid*.[38] The Buddhist psychology of compassion^{Buddhist}, moreover, actually connects the two, with the suffering of compassion^{Buddhist} serving as the prelude for a surge of sympathetic joy.

The fourth great virtue of the discourses, equanimity, also fits quite nicely with what Nietzsche says about rank order in *JGB*. "Value and rank," Nietzsche tells us, may be determined "in terms of how much one can carry and take upon oneself, how *far* one can extend one's responsibility."[39] This extension of responsibility and care is precisely what the Buddhist healthy type's cultivation of the great virtue of equanimity involves. Perfected equanimity implies that one extend one's responsibility and care to all beings. The healthy type's limitless goodwill, compassion, sympathetic joy, and equanimity, in short, are precisely the manifestations of a boundless responsibility arising out of strength and health. The virtues cultivated by Buddhists are the Nietzschean virtues of the strong.

This further rapprochement between Nietzsche's ethics and Buddhist philosophy makes it possible to address two potential difficulties for Nietzsche's views on compassion. The first is that Nietzsche can really only be telling half the story when he says progress toward great health involves overcoming compassion. The reason for this, presumably, is that compassion is a debilitating, painful affect. But Nietzsche's active type is supposed to interpret and thus experience all pain not as depressive and harmful, but as stimulating and ultimately empowering. Why, then, would he wish to avoid the suffering born of compassion?

Unlike Buddhist moral psychology, it seems as though Nietzsche does not establish clearly enough a link between great health – or the prevalence

[37] *FW* §338. [38] *Ibid.* [39] *JGB* §212.

of active over reactive forces – and the arising of compassion of strength. While Buddhist philosophy establishes that being supremely healthy and being boundlessly compassionate imply each other, Nietzsche only tells us that genuine compassion grows out of higher health. A coherent Nietzschean position would align itself with the Buddhist view. Great health, on this model, would necessarily involve a shift away from a compassion that reactively constitutes the suffering born of the other's woe as something diminishing and dejecting and toward a compassion that actively constitutes this suffering as something stimulating and invigorating.[40]

At the end of Chapter 4, I noted that there is a place for the Nietzschean active type's "suffering as stimulant" in Buddhism, namely in the form of compassion itself. And sure enough, the happiness that corresponds to such suffering is very close indeed to the active type's "happiness as victory." This is the sympathetic joy that attends the Buddhist healthy type's success in effectively bringing the other's suffering to cessation. It is telling, in this connection, that Śāntideva admonishes advanced Buddhists never to turn away from difficulty because everything that was once reviled will soon become the necessary condition for their pleasure.[41] A Nietzschean psychology of higher types would have much to gain from replicating the structure of the Buddhist healthy type's rapport with the other's suffering and applying it to the active type's experience and interpretation of compassion. In this way, Nietzsche's healthy type will genuinely be saying yes to all forms of suffering, including that which derives from (healthy) compassion.

The second difficulty with Nietzsche's account, which I alluded to toward the end of Chapter 5, concerns the scope of the compassion of the strong and of the benevolence it gives rise to. A reasonable concern is that its focus on the "creator" rather than the "creature" in wo/man – and thus on the few "tragic artists" actually capable of overcoming the rebellious reactive forces within them – implies cold indifference to the plight and woe of the vast majority of humankind. Earlier in this chapter, a similar concern was raised (and put to rest) concerning compassion^{Buddhist}, relating, more specifically, to how much suffering may be caused and/or allowed to occur in its name. Given the general affinities between compassion^{Buddhist} and Nietzsche's compassion of the strong, it may be possible to look at the psychology of compassion^{Buddhist} to make a few suggestions on the scope and nature of Nietzsche's healthy type's compassion. These come in the form of three independent principles.

[40] Frazer also gestures in this direction in "The Compassion of Zarathustra." [41] *BA* VIII.119.

First, there is what I call the *overflow principle*. Let us assume that Nietzsche's healthy type, like his Buddhist counterpart, necessarily manifests compassion of the strong, as I suggest he should. In so far as both manifest such compassion out of an "overflow" of the confidence and strength born of great health, there will be no clear limit to the scope of their compassion-born care and responsibility. Since this compassion is born of what, in Nietzschean terms, might be described as an overflowing fullness of self, there will be no need for healthy types to be sparing with what they give, and to whom. This is what stands behind the Buddha's and the *bodhisattvas*' limitless benevolence and boundless goodwill. In the case of both Nietzsche's and Buddhists' healthy types, the only real constraint on compassionate action will thus be on misguided "benevolence," which could actually impede a higher type in achieving greatness. Such a constraint, however, would only hold for those made for greatness. Actions designed to alleviate the suffering of those who are hopelessly mediocre will know no such constraint. On such people, the torrent of the healthy type's cheerful compassionate care will be allowed to flow unimpeded.

Second comes what I call the *suffering as distraction principle*. Buddhist philosophy recognizes that many beings are far too deeply ensconced in suffering to even begin helping, and ultimately healing, themselves. Their great suffering distracts them from pursuing higher aims. This is why the Buddhist healthy type's compassion-born benevolence far exceeds the more limited domain of actions that directly assist the other in progressing toward the great health of *nirvāṇa*. Something similar might hold for Nietzsche's healthy type and his exercise of compassion and benevolence. In order to enable a higher type or free spirit to attain the epitome of life-affirmation in *amor fati*, it might be necessary for a kindred soul to alleviate some of his burden. The principle that great suffering is necessary for great health does not imply that all suffering, sorrow, and illness is conducive to *amor fati*. As in Buddhism, Nietzsche's healthy type could, out of compassion, feel impelled to ward off suffering, which, by virtue of its intensity or nature, will prove to be distracting for a higher type who might not yet have it in him to turn this suffering to profit.

Third comes what I call the *uncertainty principle*. Coupled with the "suffering as distraction principle," this principle has the power to support both Buddhist and Nietzsche's ethics in case the overflow principle is rejected. The idea is that it is far from certain who in the midst of this sea of sick types has the potential to attain great health. Several Buddhist stories reminiscent of Christian tales of saintly transfigurations (e.g. the parricide Saint Julian) tell of figures who rapidly go from being profoundly ensconced in illness to attaining great health (e.g. Kisagotamī). Given that the tragic life-affirming health of *amor fati* is conditional upon a heightened tension between reactive and active forces, it likewise comes as no surprise that thoroughly *décadent* figures are among those who hold the highest promise of attaining great health on Nietzsche's account.[42] Nietzsche, after all, even describes himself as both a *décadent* and the "opposite of a *décadent*."[43] The upshot is that even if compassion of strength were exclusively focused on what impedes those "with promise" from attaining great health, uncertainty as to who may ultimately turn out to hold promise would imply a considerable amount of liberality in compassion-born benevolence.

The relation between the ethics of compassion in Buddhist philosophy and in Nietzsche's thought is rich and complex. Contrary to appearances, "cultivating compassion" and "overcoming compassion" are not opposite ideals. In fact, there is a deep sense in which the former presupposes the latter. What is more, compassion^{Buddhist} is very close indeed to the compassion of strength that Nietzsche attributes to healthy types, himself included. As such, Nietzsche's account of the healthy type's attitude to the other's suffering stands to gain from a more careful examination of the Buddhist psychology of compassion. Not only does the opposition between cultivating and overcoming compassion implode, but beneath the rubble lie exciting patterns of complementarity.

[42] Consider, in this connection, Zarathustra's ten higher men in *Z* IV.
[43] *EH* "Warum ich so weise bin" §2.

Conclusion: Toward a new response to the challenge of nihilism

If Nietzsche wished to push his ship resolutely beyond good and evil, the ultimate purpose of the present study is to explore the seas that lie beyond life-affirmation and life-negation. We are now approaching the wide open horizon which has been our destination from the very start. The guiding star which has illuminated our tortuous path is nothing other than a new response to the challenge of nihilism. At stake, ultimately, is the formulation of a human ideal in and for a world of evanescent becoming and pure immanence – an ideal that stands beyond the bankrupt dichotomy that forms the spine of Nietzsche's attempt to respond to the challenge of nihilism. On the horizon lies a new, hybrid vision of great health.

The challenge of nihilism is not a philosophical pseudo-problem cooked up by an over-imaginative Nietzsche. On the contrary, it is a concrete cultural, ethical, and existential challenge, which we have not yet really begun to face up to. The challenge of nihilism is the challenge of finding some grounding for value after the collapse of the fiction on which all values formerly relied. It is, in short, the challenge of developing an ethics entirely divorced from the *wahre weltlich* fiction of Being.

In trying to evade or sidestep the challenge of nihilism (consciously or not), contemporary secular moral philosophers only reveal that they remain under the sway of this inebriating fiction. Consider one of the main strategies contemporary atheists employ to find a way out of the nihilist impasse. A quick glance at the history of ideas suggests that morality has always been intimately tied to notions of the Transcendent and, in particular, to doctrines pertaining to God. Today, the trend is for secular moralists to claim that this is a purely contingent association. Nothing, on their view, should be read into the historical fact that moral systems have relied on metaphysical creeds, and vice versa. Morality is not a branch shooting off from the trunk of religious thought, but a self-standing tree that just happens to have entwined around religion, a contingent proximate neighbor.[1] When the tree of religion is felled, then, morality need not come crashing down with it.

It is obvious that these arguments are put forth so as to diffuse the theists' fear-mongering. The idea is to defang the theists who insist it is important to retain God, lest all morality is washed into the sea. The atheists' morality–theism disjunction appears to be ideologically motivated, then. Some plausible arguments might be adduced in its favor, but it uncannily fits the agenda. This does not in and of itself imply the atheist moralists' thesis is wrong, but it does make it look suspiciously polemical. The fact that religion and morality have been so thoroughly intertwined at the level of institutions and ideas is hard to explain without acknowledging that there is some sort of profound connection between traditional morality and religious/metaphysical thinking. The burden of proof falls upon the atheist moralist. To insist that morality is really a self-standing edifice that owes nothing of substance to religious thought, notions of ritual purity, and various metaphysical conceptions without giving any reasons for things appearing otherwise does not make the atheist's case particularly compelling.[2]

Nietzsche represents an altogether different strand of atheistic thought. According to him, we have no choice but to be honest and bite the theists' bullet. Morality as we have known it is dependent on religion. More precisely, prevalent moral systems have all been dependent on the broader type of which various religion are mere genera, namely the metaphysics of Being. In fact, Nietzsche flips the picture entirely upside down. It is neither the case that morality and metaphysics/religion are two independent currents in human thought, nor that morality derives from the experience of the sublime to which philosophical insight and/or revelation provides access.[3] Rather, it is the metaphysics of Being itself that stems from a

[1] This view is expressed with particular clarity by J. Baggini in *Atheism: A Very Short Introduction* (Oxford University Press, 2003).

[2] The atheist moralists' best argument for their position is that all important 'moral laws' can be derived on the basis of non-religious premises, be they "empirical" or "purely rational." A cogent and compelling Nietzschean reply consists in arguing that a close examination of these premises reveals that, despite appearances, they are not metaphysically non-committal, but on the contrary rely on some form of the *wahre weltlich* fiction of Being, if not on an outright deification of nature. This is the line of thought that will be developed over the next few pages.

[3] Taylor, in *Sources of the Self*, espouses a form of the latter view. Having said this, his arguments to the effect that many of our modern liberal moral intuitions are grounded in their genetic Christian context are otherwise very convincing. On this front, he and Nietzsche work hand in hand.

distinctive pre-reflective "moral prejudice." The metaphysical/religious urge is the result of a frustration and disenchantment with life and raw nature, which as a consequence is denounced as unfair, brutish, contradictory, unpredictable, foul, and loathsome – in one word, as evil. It is with this pre-reflective weak pessimistic moral sentiment, not with some pre-established and fully worked out moral system, that the invention of Being/God begins. The cooking up of a non-contingent, non-impermanent, non-arisen, not-impure, not-unfair – these negative terms are meant to emphasize the reactive nature of this process – realm of the Real, the True, and the Good is thus a gesture of resentful condemnation against this contingent and impermanent world of perpetual struggle and evanescent becoming. Nietzsche's claim, of course, is psychological, not historical; at issue are the psychological roots of metaphysics and morals, not their historical genesis.

Returning to the proponents of secular moral and/or political ideologies, it is not difficult to see how they remain committed, in one way or another, both to the fiction of Being and to the implicit pessimism (of weakness) that underlies their deluded optimism. Nietzsche denounced the neo-Hegelians, Marxists, and anarchists of his day – however atheistic they may have been – for thinking of history as having a purpose, of humanity (and with it the cosmos) as geared toward a determinate goal, of society as progressing toward a final stage of Peace, Justice, and Virtue. These nihilists believe that behind the maze of apparently arbitrary natural and man-made horrors, behind the plurality of apparently contradictory social and cultural movements and forces, lies a true purpose – a *telos* which will ultimately justify everything that has come to pass. "*Tout est pour le mieux dans le meilleur des mondes*," can we hear them sing in unison. The End of History will mark the end of becoming – it marks the attainment of Static Being, the Kingdom of God.

A Nietzschean assessment of the capitalist ethics derived from Adam Smith's work or of the utilitarianism of John Stuart Mill and his followers delivers a very similar verdict. This is underscored by the distinctly eschatological flavor of capitalist–utilitarian systems, according to which the principles of rational self-interest in conditions of optimal liberty will eventually lead to a collapse of the egoism–altruism dichotomy, to wealth and well-being for all, to free and just societies, etc. Again, behind the maze of apparently senseless and arbitrary exploitation and treachery, behind the flurry of apparently plural self-interests and their contradictory tugging and pushing in every direction, there is actually a true, unitary direction to human progress and development, and a concealed common interest. A *wahre Welt* of sorts lurks behind this ethics as well. Faith in liberal democracy is also faith in the End of History (Fukuyama's fantasy[4]) or the Kingdom of God.

Had Nietzsche had the pleasure of reading the atheist scientists and humanists of today, he would not have failed to notice that inebriating *wahre Welt* myths continue to suffuse the soberest of scientific circles. Dawkins's defense of Einstein's God – i.e. Nature *à la* Spinoza – in the opening chapter of his infamous *The God Delusion* (2006) is an enlightening case in point.[5] The Cosmos, for Dawkins, is Awe-inspiring and Sublime. The Regularity of natural and physical laws, the underlying Coherence of all of the universe's parts and the mathematical Neatness of natural selection, accordingly, make Nature an appropriate object of worship. Nature becomes the new God. This goes hand in hand with a form of rule-utilitarianism centered on "enlightened selfishness" and relying on a distinctive form of meta-ethical realist naturalism. This is supposed to be "atheistic," scientific morality – truth-telling, loyalty, patience, sexual faithfulness, benevolence, self-sacrifice, etc. are all explained away as naturally selected strategies for maximizing the chances of gene transference. But the opening chapter of *The God Delusion* makes it obvious that such a morality remains predicated on an implicit deification of nature, on wrapping a senseless world of accidents and chaos in a fictive, self-deluding veil of *telos*-infested functionalism on the basis of which are enounced immutable laws. Symptomatic of the *wahre Welt* basis of these morals is, again, the distinctive eschatological flavor of such discourses – of which transhumanism is only the most explicitly eschatological, and deluded.

Those who wish to divorce morality and religion, then, remain caught in the web of *wahre Welt* fictions. The author of *The God Delusion*, Nietzsche would aver, has not really fully recovered from the "God delusion" in its more sublimated, "scientific" form. Evolution was a violent and completely arbitrary process in which random environmental and ecological contingencies had far more of an impact on which species were "selected" than the adaptive qualities of their members, but let us focus on the discreet magnificence of the human hand's skeletal structure or the flamboyant beauty of the butterfly's wings; are they not just magical? The attempts at unifying the incompatible theories of general relativity and quantum mechanics have so far proved fruitless, and every potential basic ontological unit is turning out

4 F. Fukuyama, *The End of History and the Last Man* (New York: Free Press, 1996).

5 See R. Dawkins, *The God Delusion* (Boston: Houghton Mifflin, 2006), pp. 11–27. See also the opening chapters of Genesis in A. C. Grayling's *The Good Book: A Humanist Bible* (New York: Walker and Co., 2011).

to be further analyzable, but let us forget all that and celebrate with awe and adoration the immutable laws of Nature discerned through the marvelous work of Reason. More than 20 percent of humanity suffers from malnutrition and/or famine (and the numbers are rising) while we produce ever more food; in the twentieth century technology and scientific organization contributed to the industrialization of murder and unparalleled military horrors; chauvinistic totalitarianism is doing quite alright, and seems to be perfectly compatible with the market economy, as "communist" China's example indicates; we are set for ecological meltdown – but didn't the Beatles write great songs, didn't Philip Roth write great novels, didn't Steve Jobs make all of our lives so much easier, and aren't we all heading for great things if we just get our act together, follow the strictures of enlightened self-interest, and continue to innovate? Deluded optimism, indeed, remains the norm.

The point Nietzsche helps us appreciate is that secular optimistic Enlightenment eschatology in all its forms (socialist, communist, anarchist, liberal, libertarian, utilitarian, scientific, etc.) remains predicated on one form or another of the naive, *wahre Welt* fiction. All these ideologies postulate a True, Static Being behind the treacherous appearances of dynamic, unstable becoming. As such, they also remain essentially nihilist. The psychological grounds for all optimism, after all, is a judgmental form of pessimism. It is fear and repulsion before this world of senseless becoming, painful change, and bewildering contradictions that create a need for the Security and Stability of Being – for a Meaning, a Purpose, a Good behind the apparent evil. Accepting what I called descriptive pessimism – accepting that the world has no inherent meaning, purpose, or unity, that history will have no end, that life is and always will be replete with pain and sorrow, that a "theory of everything" will always escape us – is the first step in facing up to the challenge of nihilism with dignity and clear-headedness. It is a step the world has not yet shown the courage to take.

Abandoning the optimistic fiction of Being is only the first step in facing up to the challenge of nihilism, however. In fact, this is only where the difficulties begin. As in the case of intoxication, when the inebriating fiction of Being comes to an end, the result is a harsh hangover. More specifically, humankind must then deal with a value withdrawal from which it may be difficult to recover. All ethics formulated so far, after all, has been predicated on the metaphysics of Being. It may seem impossible, then, to develop an ethics in and for a world of pure becoming. Nihilistic despair is a real and tangible risk. Schopenhauer decided to declare nature evil. Many today unwittingly follow his example and espouse a cowardly, cynical attitude to the human condition – "such is human nature," they say, "we are condemned to failure and self-destruction." Hence the crisis in the nihilist crisis. Hence the challenge in the challenge of nihilism. This is a severe challenge, which Nietzsche rightly recognized.

It is also a challenge to which he strove to respond, and in doing so he developed fascinating insights concerning human psychology. At the same time, Nietzsche's attempt to respond to the challenge of nihilism was founded on a misapprehension. He was right in looking to Buddhism. This, after all, is the only large-scale ideology in history to have likewise denounced Being as a fiction and thus to have developed a genuinely post-theistic, post-metaphysical ethics. Like many of his contemporaries, however, Nietzsche's vision was distorted by the Schopenhauerian prism through which he contemplated Buddhism. To his eyes, Buddhist ethics appeared to be a thoroughly life-negating response to the challenge of nihilism – a nihilism of passive despair which, in the face of the nihilist crisis, failed to overcome the weak pessimistic judgment at the core of all previous ideologies and likewise judged that "life is evil." Nietzsche approved of the way the Buddha had formulated his post-metaphysical ethics in terms of a distinct vision of great health. But, for Nietzsche, what the Buddha had really propounded was an ideal of great sickness which sought to end life. To this fundamental life-negation, which lays bare the nihilism at the heart of previous predominant ideologies, Nietzsche opposed his ethics of life-affirmation.

There is no point in repeating why Nietzsche was wrong in thinking that Buddhism is life-negating, or that *amor fati* and the overcoming of compassion are diametrically opposed to *nirvāṇa* and the cultivation of compassion^{Buddhist}, respectively. Nor would there be much to gain in repeating why and how there is in fact significant complementarity between the visions of great health propounded in Nietzsche's thought and Buddhist philosophy. The latter parts of Chapters 4 and 6 provide detailed discussions of these points.

What is now required is a new, hybrid response to the challenge of nihilism – one that builds on the complementarity between Nietzsche's ethics and Buddhist philosophy to offer a new vision of great health. This is put forward as a first attempt at formulating an ethics which moves resolutely beyond the delusion of Being: an attempt I can only hope others will take up, critique, and improve upon.

Nietzsche's thought and Buddhist philosophy jointly push in a specific direction. The ethics they propound share the same fundamental structure and the same fundamental content. By way of content, the idea is essentially to grab the elephant in the room by the trunk and send it packing. The two-headed delusion of Being and self on which morals, religion, rational enquiry, etc. have been founded is not a contingent accident of human history and/or psychology. Like all delusions, it exhibits a fundamentally unhealthy take on the world. A Buddho-Nietzschean ethics thus has for its target the sickness that from the start underlies our thirst for the Stability of Being, Truth, the Good, God, etc. The goal, in short, is to achieve a state of great health in which the instable flux of evanescent, evasive becoming, which is all that the world actually contains, is no longer experienced as despairingly frustrating. The idea is not just to avoid promulgating values that rely on the fictions of Being and self, then, but to undermine these fictions by targeting their very roots in human psychology.

By way of structure, what is arrived at is a form of perfectionism formulated in terms of the figure of a distinctive "healthy type." This runs against the grain of the bulk of contemporary Anglo-American moral philosophy, which, as Taylor rightly observes, "has tended to focus on what is right to do rather than on what it is good to be, on defining the content of obligation rather than the nature of the good life."[6] Our Buddho-Nietzschean ethics, of course, is not so much concerned with a "good life" amenable to an objective description or reducible to clear criteria. Rather, it delineates the contours of a striving toward a higher health. In and of itself, it does not spell out duties, obligations and constraints.[7] As such, the evaluation grid it delivers is not concerned with evaluating actions, states of affairs, or "goods," but with determining the worth of persons. In a fashion similar to other forms of so-called virtue ethics, it is committed to the view that good actions are actions performed by good (i.e. healthy) agents, and bad actions are actions performed by bad (i.e. unhealthy) agents. Given the derivative nature of the value of actions, ethics, on this type of view, needs only to focus on what is essential, namely the status, or in this case healthiness, of agents. Our Buddho-Nietzschean response to the challenge of nihilism, accordingly, takes the form of a perfectionist virtue ethics based on the ideal of an exalted healthy type.

There are a number of things to note about what I will call *great health perfectionism*. First, it is in fact a novel strand of perfectionism, which shares little common ground with its predecessors.[8] Most perfectionist ethics

[6] Taylor, *Sources of the Self*, p. 3.

[7] This is why the outline that follows contains no normative ethics per se, only moral psychology.

[8] On perfectionism and its two major strands, "human nature perfectionism" and "objective goods perfectionism," see S. Wall, "Perfectionism," in E. N. Zalta (ed.), *Stanford Encyclopedia of Philosophy* (Fall 2008 edn). Available at: http://plato/stanford.edu/archives/fall2008/entries/perfectionism-moral.

developed over the course of history have relied on a distinctive notion of human nature. It is on this basis that a number of perfectionists (namely, Aristotle, Aquinas, Spinoza, and Marx) derive their notions of the "human good," or human goods. For a Nietzsche or a Buddha, however, the question of human nature remains open, not to say open-ended. Given their commitment to a flux worldview, neither would admit of anything so static as an immutable human nature.[9] Moreover, both Nietzsche's discussion of the complex dynamics between active and reactive forces and Buddhist therapeutic methods – namely, the cultivation of the prime virtues – suggest, each in their own way, that the individual human's character is malleable, although this may not be easy.

And that is ultimately all that matters for great health perfectionism. Indeed, at issue in Buddho-Nietzschean ethics is not so much human nature as the nature of what holds humans back. The governing metaphor is that of illness removal. It is the diagnosis of what is unhealthy that delivers what is to begin with a negatively defined *telos*, namely, the destruction of thirsting, or victory over reactive forces through self-overcoming.

Now, the human nature perfectionist might object that any form of perfectionism necessarily implies a positive idea of the Good, and that this is what is required to determine what is wrong with certain people, etc. It is far from obvious that this is required on a therapeutic model, however. When I am sick, I do not need a clear idea of what "health" is going to be like to begin enquiring as to the etiology of the symptoms I suffer from and the means of recovering from whatever illness is giving rise to these symptoms. Though *nirvāṇa* and *amor fati* are by no means purely negative concepts, then, and though much can be said about the psychology of the healthy type in Nietzsche's thought and Buddhist philosophy, these ideals do not stand for the full development of a predetermined human good based on some account of a determinate human nature. Though it is also amenable to positive descriptions, the idea of great health is first and foremost the idea of full recovery from illness, not the actualization of a predetermined good. If anything, the "good" of great health is determined in relation to the "badness" of the illness.

In this sense, great health perfectionism is also distinguished from the type of objective goods perfectionism outlined by the likes of Rawls, Parfit,

[9] In some Mahāyāna circles, the notion of "Buddha-nature" assumes the role of a human nature of sorts. The idea is that the potential for Buddhahood, or the "embryo" (*garbha*) of a Buddha's purified mind, lies at the core of every being. This development, however, is little more than a relapse into the metaphysics of Being, which Siddhārtha Gautama would have certainly condemned, from the standpoint of "ultimate truth" at the very least.

and Griffin.[10] This version of perfectionism does not rely on a view of human nature, but instead on a set of exceptional human achievements or objective goods, which the perfectionist aims to realize. Great health perfectionism, in contrast, is not geared toward the performance of particular acts (e.g. painting the Mona Lisa) or exceptional achievements setting new standards for human excellence. Here, the very idea of fixed "objective goods" is regarded with circumspection. The only (very much subjective and personal) good in a Buddho-Nietzschean ethics is recovery from illness.

What most starkly distinguishes great health perfectionism from other perfectionisms, however, is that it involves no categorical imperative. This is part of the reason the "good" of great health fails to qualify as "objective." When sick types fail to strive toward great health, they exhibit no moral failure or breach of conduct. It is certainly advisable for those who have the potential to recover from illness to progress toward great health – it is certainly "in their interest," so to speak – but there is no external standard providing an obligation for them to do so. Unlike other perfectionisms, then, a Buddho-Nietzschean ethics contains no categorical duties to oneself. If the domain of morals is the domain of categorical obligations, then great health perfectionism is simply not a form of morals. It is only an ethics. This ethics provides a clear direction for human striving, but no compulsion thus to strive.

Of course, the absence of obligations does not imply that a Buddho-Nietzschean ethics implies a moral free-for-all or apathetic laissez-faire. The perfected healthy type's actions will be regarded as good, beneficial, and admirable. Conversely, the vast majority of actions performed by foolish and deluded sick types will be deemed bad, harmful, undesirable, and despicable.[11] Moreover, if healthy types striving toward great health engage in behavior that impedes the attainment of their goal, this behavior will also be deemed bad and despicable. Committing bad acts, however, is not regarded as a moral failing, only as foolishness, or, in the naive sick type's case, as a natural, albeit unfortunate, outcome of illness. Healthy types might spontaneously try to counter or prevent such foolish action, and even preemptively to admonish the foolish person against performing such

[10] See J. Rawls, *A Theory of Justice* (Cambridge, MA: Harvard University Press, 1971), D. Parfit, "Overpopulation and the Quality of Life," in P. Singer (ed.), *Applied Ethics* (Oxford University Press, 1986), pp. 145–64, and J. Griffin, *Well-Being: Its Meaning, Measurement and Moral Importance* (Oxford: Clarendon Press, 1986).

[11] They may also be legally and/or politically condemnable, but this falls outside the relatively restrained scope of the ethics of great health which, admittedly, is prima facie entirely apolitical.

actions, but they do this because such behavior causes harm, not because it is inherently "evil."

Nevertheless, there is certainly a place for moral discourse in the ethics of great health, and even for the setting up of codes and constraints. Indeed, a key component of the healthy types' instrumentalist use of language, authority, and whatever other means may be at their disposal, is to promulgate codes of conduct that will ultimately prove beneficial to those for whom they are designed. A form of "health consequentialism"[12] will serve as a deliberative framework for perfected healthy types in this context. An important aspect of their engagement in the world will thus be to articulate various moral positions – consequentialist, deontological, or virtue-based, depending on the context – albeit with irony. Different people will hear very different things from healthy types, all of which are uttered for the ultimate purpose of preventing pointless harm and injury and also of directing those with the potential to heal themselves toward great health. These interventions will be as varied as types of people are varied. Different people may be "ill" to various degrees, and the specific manifestation of their illness, at a given time in particular, may bear sharply distinct idiosyncrasies. As such, the "spiritual diet" different people are prescribed[13] will vary considerably. From the standpoint of the healthy, however, there are no objective, categorically binding obligations, duties, or constraints. Moral discourse, like language in general, has a purely instrumental value for masters of irony like our healthy types. Even the healthy type's interventions in the lives of others, for that matter, do not proceed from some obligation to which healthy types are subject, but from their spontaneous goodwill and compassion.

The last thing to note about Buddho-Nietzschean great health perfectionism is that it is not monist. Though the fundamental illness humans suffer from has the same basic structure in all cases, and though all healthy types will thus be free of the same basic symptoms, they will not all be identical types with an identical character and behavior. Again, the key idea here is that of Buddhist ironic engagement. Different healthy types will "be" strikingly different figures in so far as they are brought to play strikingly different roles in various contexts. The idea is that they will ironically engage with the world through endless permutations in their identity and behavior. Great health involves an extraordinary level of versatility, and thus also great

[12] Cf. the virtue consequentialism of J. Driver, *Uneasy Virtue* (Cambridge University Press, 2001), or B. Bradley, "Virtue Consequentialism," *Unitas* 17(3), 2005: 282–98.

[13] I borrow the phrase "spiritual diet" from *EH* "Warum ich ein Schicksal bin" §8.

diversity among healthy types. Buddho-Nietzschean perfectionism is not a matter of making all humans identical, then, but of striving toward a state in which I can be boundlessly shifting and versatile.

It is now possible to turn to the moral psychology that underlies great health perfectionism. Here, insights can be drawn from the psychology contained in both Nietzsche's thought and Buddhist philosophy. More specifically, the ideal of the healthy type derives from a diagnosis of what is fundamentally unhealthy about human psychology. As was seen in Chapter 4, the systemic reactivity characteristic of what Nietzsche calls *décadence* can be explained, on the model of Buddhist moral psychology, as a manifestation of the primeval self-delusion. Indeed, Buddhist philosophy goes far beyond the mere critique of a unitary, abiding ego, or of any other property-bearing substance for that matter. Certainly, it denies that the very notion of something static and unchanging like a "self" or a "substance" has any purchase in a world made up exclusively of interconnected processes. But Buddhist philosophy goes further than this – "self," "thing," "substance," and "Being" are not mere fictions or illusions, they are delusions. When it comes to their belief in the self as substance and the world as a world of hypostatized "things," ordinary people are not just mistaken, but delusional. Overcoming this delusion is what great health involves.

The self-delusion is sustained through the twin pre-reflective processes of "appropriating" what is internal – or "belongs" to the self – and reifying what is external – or "belongs" to the self's horizon. I lay claim to mental and physical events that "belong to me" – on the basis of the "mine," I derive the "me" – and simultaneously interpret the world around me, with me at its center, as composed of discrete "things" whose very constitution as things reflects my concerns, fears, interests, etc. The narcissistic self-delusion thus conditions both my affective rapport with the world – systemic egotism – and my cognitive rapport to it – systemic reification of things that relate to "me" in specific ways. As Buddhist philosophy makes clear, the affective and cognitive effects of the self-delusion are really two sides of the same coin. Egotistical attraction and aversion have as their intentional objects discrete, stable "things." Conversely, the way in which I reify processes and the various meanings and values I attribute to "things" is a function of my affective states vis-à-vis these "objects." Hypostasis and reification are thus no less part of the performance of the self (via the construction of the self's self-referential horizon) than the appropriation of "my" body and mind.

In Chapter 4, I explained how such a construction of self and world results in a debilitating, enfeebling, pathological condition whereby I am both perpetually subject to dissatisfaction, anxiety, and sorrow, and endlessly prone to harmful desires, aggressive attitudes, (often unconsciously) manipulative behavior, etc. The idea, then, is that the self-delusion is ultimately what people with a genuine concern for their wellbeing (and that of those around them) will aim to recover from. In short, they will aim to attain the perfected state of great health.

While this model is broadly borrowed from Buddhist philosophy, it can be complemented with two key Nietzschean ideas. The first is the idea of reactivity. The sick type is a reactive type. The concept of reactivity brings out the paranoid-like quality of this figure's psychology. More specifically, it clarifies how self-delusion leads to perpetual suffering. In the grip of delusional narcissistic egotism, sick types continually feel targeted. When the threat of harm or disappointment appears on their horizon, sick types do not see that practically everything that happens "to them" has nothing to do with them, but is on the contrary purely accidental and arbitrary. As a result of delusional egotism, the harm will be constituted as somehow intended, the narcissistic-paranoid implication being that the sick type matters quite a bit more than s/he does. As a result of the co-arising senses of "me" and "inimical other," the sick type is thus continually reacting. Hence, among many other things, the thirst for a realm of Permanence, Peace, and Bliss – in short, Being – which is really a reaction to the countless frustrations the sick type encounters in the midst of this turbulent sea of becoming.

The second Nietzschean idea is closely connected to this. For Nietzsche, great health involves a shift in one's relationship to suffering – a shift, precisely, away from reactivity and toward activity. The idea is that the healthy type will no longer experience difficulties, resistance, and obstacles as setbacks or occasions for despair, frustration, and disillusionment. Instead of suffering such a reaction, the healthy type will instead be impelled to action. Meeting obstacles and facing difficulties, for the healthy type, will be stimulating and invigorating. The ideal of great health, then, should not simply be conceived in terms of ending suffering, as it so often is – nominally at least – in Buddhism. Certainly, the idea is to stop suffering as the sick type suffers by removing the condition for engaging with the world in a debilitating way. Beyond this, however, the idea is also to develop a rapport with the world in which difficulties and challenges become grounds for active engagement, rather than despair, frustration, and disengagement.

These two Nietzschean ideas make it possible to flesh out the psychology of great health with greater clarity. Indeed, striving toward great health involves shifting, even more generally, away from reactive/passive undergoing and toward active, creative performance. Of course, self-identification via internal appropriation and outward reification are always performed. They result from a distorting activity, albeit a delusional and, more importantly, unconscious activity. But sick types' performance of narrative identity and horizon construction is in a very real sense also undergone. Their very performance is reactive. The love of my life leaves me, say, and my identity is shattered – the very construction of my identity as "shattered" is undergone. Likewise, I am constantly only ever reacting to my environment and to the "inner" shifts among "my" physical and mental attributes.

Now, the healthy type's relation to identity is not one of ataraxic depersonalization – the idea is not to become more like people suffering from autism or late-stage Alzheimer's disease. Instead, it is one of deliberate, active self-construction. The idea is neither to neutralize the twin self-identification and reification drives (i.e. to aim for mental and physical paralysis), nor merely to "see through" the illusions and thus to withdraw into some "internal exile of the mind." Rather, the idea is to end the delusion that the "I" and reified *x, y,* and *z*'s refer to actual discrete things while continuing to engage in the performance and invention of these fictions for specific instrumental purposes, e.g. self-sustenance, endeavor prioritization, deliberation, communication, and, most importantly (as we will soon see), altruistic engagement.

The transition from sickness to health can perhaps best be described using the (vaguely Nietzschean) image of the dramatic artist. We sick types are like deluded actors in a play, convinced that we are our characters and that the props on the stage are real. Healthy types are actors who recover from the delusion that they really are their characters and that the stage world has any substantial reality, yet continue to perform a dramatic role and engage with the stage world like all the other actors. Such ironic engagement ensures not only a high level of versatility, but also a specific form of empowering (emotional) detachment. It is by virtue of such ironic distance that the healthy type puts an end to the existential suffering that characterizes the sick type's rapport with the world. In the Nietzschean idiom, ironic distance will allow healthy actors to have an aesthetic appreciation of the beauty of the play in which they have a role, instead of casting an unhealthy moral judgment on whatever is responsible for their fate. More importantly yet, ironic distance is the condition for responding to suffering – one's own and the other's – actively rather than reactively. Of course, such an ironic rapport with self and world is far easier said than done. Indeed, many reflective people might come to agree that the self is constructed and that the world is one of evanescent processes, which are then reified by the human (and animal) mind, but this alone is not enough to rid them of the feeling that they are their characters and that the stage world is real. To go from a merely intellectual understanding of these insights to genuine recovery from self-delusion requires tremendous effort. Healthy types are supremely skillful actors.

To further flesh out this Buddho-Nietzschean ideal of great health it will be necessary to address two key issues. The first relates to a perennial difficulty for Buddhist philosophy. The traditional question is: who, if there is no self, attains *nirvāṇa*? In the present context, the question can be reformulated as: who ironically performs self-identification and reification once self-delusion has been overcome, if not a previously unconstructed self? The implication in this rhetorical question, of course, is that the Buddho-Nietzschean idea of great health requires that there be a self that is not the product of a delusion. More specifically, the idea is that talking of a deliberate, active/creative construction, or performance, implies a degree of autonomy that an unconstructed self alone can possess.

First, it should be pointed out that this objection is in fact question-begging. The very idea that construction implies a constructor, performance a performer, or, more generally, action an agent, already presupposes the kind of metaphysics that is firmly rejected in Buddhist philosophy and Nietzsche's thought. Nevertheless, the objector is right to demand an account of how impersonal forces can work together to construct a person, or "self," and, even more so, of how an awareness of the impersonality of these impersonal forces can make this construction less automatic (or mechanistic) and reactive, and more deliberate and active.

With regard to this issue, the healthy type is not so different from the sick type. Specific psycho-physical elements forming a functionally autonomous subsystem are responsible for laying claim to other psycho-physical elements, which are constituted as peripheral, so to speak.[14] Though entirely composed of impersonal forces, the subsystem will, in the process of laying claim to what "belongs" to it, constitute itself as the self to which "belongs" whatever is laid claim to. Note, moreover, that this shifting subsystem's functional autonomy in no way suggests that it actually is a static self – it is simply deluded in regarding itself as such a self. What happens when great health is attained is that the subsystem recovers from this delusion. As a result, it loses its rigidity – which, I note in passing, results in much existential turmoil among sick types, especially relating to "identity crises." In gaining greater flexibility through the (lived) knowledge of its own

[14] On this point, see Siderits, *Buddhist Philosophy*, pp. 48f.

contingency and inessentiality, the shifting subsystem also gains far greater autonomy. Hence the boundless versatility of the healthy type's ironic engagement.

This explanation, however, leads to a further concern. It seems as though the passage from sickness to great health as I have described it involves going from being passively determined to being actively determinant (on self and world). But this is certainly inconsistent with Nietzsche's unequivocal commitment to strict determinism. Indeed, it seems as though no Nietzschean vision can admit of degrees of "determination," in so far as everything, for Nietzsche, is strictly determined.[15]

Two strategies can be employed to circumvent this problem. The first consists in arguing that though Nietzsche is a determinist, the reactive/active distinction does allow for various nexuses of forces being more or less determined/determinant. Healthy types, on this view, will effectively become more determinant as they progress toward great health, though even this progression and gain in "determinant-ness" will be necessary, or determined, i.e. their unavoidable fate.

The other strategy is more controversial, but also more interesting. The idea is that Nietzsche's commitment to determinism is in fact both (1) implicitly committed to a view of the universe admitting of reactive forces alone and (2) reactive in and of itself. Note that both of these critiques are launched from a firmly Nietzschean standpoint. To begin with, it is not difficult to see how determinism implies a strictly mechanistic worldview. Universal causal interrelatedness delivers a dense, impermeable cosmic block of fixed determination only in so far as causal relations are purely mechanistic. But, as Nietzsche himself points out, the domain of the mechanistic is the domain of reaction – or, more precisely, of strict proportionality between action and reaction. Strict determinism is thus a worldview that admits of reactive forces alone. If Nietzsche is sincere about the role of active, creative, dynamic form-giving forces, then strict determinism is ruled out.

Why, then, did Nietzsche so forcefully endorse a worldview that clashes with his championing of the active? I would argue that he did so out of unwitting reactivity. Nietzsche reacts to the prevalent doctrine of libertarian free will, which he sees as an instrument *décadents* use to blame their oppressors for their "deliberate" hurtful acts and to praise themselves for their disingenuously "deliberate" meekness and passivity (really an inability to retaliate). Nietzsche likewise signals that the doctrine of free will is part of

[15] *GD* v §6 and vii §§7–8.

the institutionalization of guilt, an emotion he rightly regards as deeply unhealthy.[16] The Christian doctrine of free will, in short, is a product of *ressentiment.* In a way characteristic of reactive responses, however, Nietzsche swings to the other extreme. There is no freedom whatsoever, he claims – everything is strictly determined. Nietzsche was right both to denounce the abuses of the doctrine of free will and to question whether human behavior is really as "free" as Christians, rationalists, and many theists claim. But he went too far. The ideal of great health set out here, in contrast, does admit of degrees of determination. The healthy, active type who ironically performs self-identification and reification is a more determinant type than the passive/reactive sick type.

The second key issue that needs to be addressed to flesh out our new ethics concerns the purpose of the healthy type's engagement in the world. As stated above, the healthy type continues to engage in the performance and invention of the fictions of self and "things" for instrumental purposes. This invites the question: instrumental to what purpose? After all, once great health is achieved and enfeebling suffering and anxiety are brought to an end, what else is there to strive for? What scope is there for healthy types' activity? What desires could still animate them?

These questions find their answer in Chapter 6. Self-delusion results in systemic egotism (and egoism). Conversely, recovering from self-delusion results in systemic altruism. Strictly speaking, of course, talk of self and other remains predicated on the fiction of identity – the healthy type is actually neither selfish nor unselfish, just engaged – but such talk is part of the irony in the healthy type's engagement. The main idea, in this connection, is that great health is such an empowering state that the healthy type exhibits a natural propensity spontaneously to assist others in assuaging their woes. Healthy types are thus boundlessly compassionate.

Note, however, that they are animated by a compassion that is markedly different from the emotion that commonly goes by that name. Free of egotism, healthy types will not respond to the other's woe with the implicit intention of putting an end to their own suffering. This is what sick types do. Instead, the suffering born of the healthy type's compassion will act as an invigorating stimulant to engage in compassionate actions that are genuinely geared toward the other's suffering. As in the more general case

16 Note that guilt is in fact firmly related to robust diachronic personal identity. It presupposes that I am the same person as the one who performed the act I feel guilty about. Moreover, guilt blocks compassion. Feeling guilty for a person's woe, in any way, shape or form, implies a formidably self-referential rapport with the other's suffering, which inhibits genuine compassion and may in fact lead to resentment and irritation. These observations are not Nietzsche's (or the Buddha's), but my own.

of suffering on our Nietzschean model, the shift from illness to health involves a shift away from constituting compassion-born suffering reactively – i.e. as harmful and enfeebling – and toward constituting it actively – i.e. as a stimulating preamble to the joy of victory. The victorious joy attendant upon the healthy type's compassionate action is what Buddhist texts refer to as sympathetic joy. In this way, the healthy type's practice of compassion exhibits the active/creative rapport with suffering more generally characteristic of great health. In so far as the biggest problem for most otherwise (i.e. medically) healthy people is the self-delusion itself, finally, the compassionate healthy type will be primarily concerned with nudging people in the direction of great health through acts, but also (ironic) words and injunctions.

Along with boundless strength-born compassion, the healthy type also exhibits other virtues, such as goodwill (the willingness to give happiness, not only to alleviate suffering), sympathetic joy, equanimity, generosity, fairness, etc. These are all features of an overflow of care and concern stemming from the supreme wellbeing of great health and the power and energy that attends it. Combined with compassion, these virtues will guide healthy types' behavior and determine the forms of their ironic engagement.

As is made clear in Buddhist philosophy, the advantage of articulating and gaining knowledge of the virtues of the healthy type is that it provides a certain framework for perfectionist therapy, as it were. Identifying, isolating, and combating reactive forms of response and behavior is part of the program. As suggested in both Nietzsche's thought and Buddhist texts alike, it may also be important, in this connection, for those who are far enough advanced on the path to great health to put themselves in situations in which unhealthy, or reactive, forces may gain dominion – the point being, of course, to undermine them more thoroughly. Another element, particularly emphasized in Buddhism, is the actual analysis, in meditative practice, of one's constructed identity (and of its continual construction). A key feature of the therapy, however, will also be the cultivation of those virtues that characterize the healthy mind. By learning to think and feel more like a healthy type, one already becomes healthier. The noble virtues of the healthy type, then, delineate a therapeutic program in which specific virtues are cultivated with a view to attaining great health.

A number of objections might be raised to the present attempt to develop a new, hybrid response to the challenge of nihilism. In the interests of conciseness and focus, I will close the present enquiry by considering only what I regard as the most pressing of these problems. The Buddho-Nietzschean great health perfectionism I have been propounding is susceptible to a variant of the "saintliness objection" traditionally leveled against utilitarianism.[17] The idea is that the ideal of great health, or recovering from the self-delusion, is so exceedingly ambitious that it is in fact a target that is impossible to reach. Its aim is for people to become saints of sorts. As such, it cannot inform human ethical striving, because it sets the bar so high that failure and disappointment are sure to follow.[18] Surely one should be more realistic and pragmatic than a proponent of great health perfectionism.

Now, it is perfectly possible that the ideal of great health I have been propounding is in fact unreachable. But even if it were true that this ideal were impossible for anyone to attain, this would not disqualify it as a valid goal for human striving, granted that "health" is here understood to be a matter of degree. The fact that it is impossible to produce the perfect translation of a text does not stop translators from seeking to produce the best translation they are capable of. The fact that I will never gain absolute, impeccable mastery even over my own native tongue (in this case French) does not stop me from striving toward perfection. Perfection, it would appear, is always an unreachable ideal, albeit one that provides a clear direction for human striving. This is what the ideal of great health is meant to do. Even if the ideal of "saintly" great health were unreachable – as it may very well be – it need not follow that it fails to qualify as the goal of ethical striving.

In fact, when one pauses for a moment and contemplates the scope and profundity of human foolishness and the formidable amount of harm people put themselves and one another through, it is difficult not to feel that anything short of individually and collectively striving for a bold, daring ideal would be insufficient. This is the intuition that underlies the Buddho-Nietzschean ideal of great health. Indeed, there seems to be something tragically pragmatic about the Che's war cry – *¡seamos realistas, pidamos lo imposible!*

[17] On this objection, see G. Scarre, *Utilitarianism* (London: Routledge, 1996), pp. 182f.

[18] There is of course an important difference between this objection and the traditional saintliness – or over-demandingness – objection, which attacks utilitarianism for making it a moral requirement to become a saint. Because the ethics of great health does not require that we all strive to great health, the issue cannot be about what it is reasonable to demand. Instead, the problem consists in aiming too high, in an unrealistic manner, which would presumably put many people off.

Bibliography

INDIAN SOURCES

Abhidharmakośa and *Abhidharmakośabhāṣya of Vasubandhu*, ed. P. Pradhan. Patna: Jayaswal Research Institute 1967.

Aitareyopaniṣad, in *Eighteen Principal Upaniṣads*, ed. V. P. Limaye and R. D. Vadekar. Poona: Vaidika Saṃśodhana Maṇḍala, 1958.

Aṅgutarranikāya, vols. I–VI, ed. R. Morris. London: Pāli Text Society, 1976–81.

Bodhicāryāvatāra of Śāntideva, ed. V. Bhattacharya. Calcutta: Bibliotheca Indica, Asiatic Text Society, 1960.

Bodhicāryāvatārapañjikā of Prajñākaramati, ed. L. de la Vallée Poussin. London: Asiatic Society, 1901.

Brahmasiddhi of Maṇḍanamiśra, vol. IV, ed. S. K. Sastri. Madras: Government Oriental Manuscripts Series, 1937.

Bṛhadāraṇyakopaniṣad in *Eighteen Principal Upaniṣads*, ed. V. P. Limaye and R. D. Vadekar. Poona: Vaidika Saṃśodhana Maṇḍala, 1958.

Chāndogyopaniṣad, in *Eighteen Principal Upaniṣads*, ed. V. P. Limaye and R. D. Vadekar. Poona: Vaidika Saṃśodhana Maṇḍala, 1958.

Daśabhūmikasūtra, ed. P. L. Vaidya. Darbhanga: Mithila Institute of Postgraduate Studies and Research in Sanskrit Learning, 1967.

Dhammapāda, ed. S. S. Thera. London: Pāli Text Society, 1914.

Dīghanikāya, vols. I–III, ed. T. W. R. Davids and J. E. Carpenter. London: Pāli Text Society, 1890–1911.

Kenopaniṣad in *Eighteen Principal Upaniṣads*, ed. V. P. Limaye and R. D. Vadekar. Poona: Vaidika Saṃśodhana Maṇḍala, 1958.

Madhyamakāvatāra of Candrakīrti (Sanskrit excerpts) in *Madhyamakavṛtti of Candrakīrti*, ed. L. de la Vallée Poussin. St. Petersburg: Académie Impériale des Sciences, 1903.

Madhyamakavṛtti of Candrakīrti, ed. L. de la Vallée Poussin. St. Petersburg: Académie Impériale des Sciences, 1903.

Mahāyāyanasūtrālaṃkara of Asaṅga, ed. S. V. Limaye. New Delhi: Indian Books Centre, 1992.

Majjhimanikāya, vols. I–IV, ed. V. Treckner and R. Chalmers. London: Pāli Text Society, 1888–1925.

Milindapañha, ed. V. Treckner. London: Royal Asiatic Society, 1928.

Mūlamadhyamakakārikā of Nāgārjuna, ed. J. W. de Jong. Madras: Adyar Library and Research Center, 1977.

Paramatthamañjusā of Dhammapāla, in Bhikkhu Ñāṇamoli, *The Path of Purification.* Kandry: Buddhist Publication Society, 1975.

Prasannapadā of Candrakīrti, ed. L. de la Vallée Poussin. St. Petersburg: Bibliotheca Buddhica, 1903.

Saṃyuttanikāya, vols. I–V, ed. L. Féer and R. Davids. London: Pāli Text Society, 1884–1904.

Suttanipāta of the *Khuṇḍakanikāya*, ed. D. Andersen and H. Smith. London: Pāli Text Society, 1948.

Suttanipātāṭṭhakathā of Buddhaghosa, ed. H. Smith. London: Pāli Text Society, 1966–72.

Therātherīgāthaṭṭhakathā of Dhammapāla, ed. F. L. Woodward. London: Pāli Text Society, 1980.

Triṃśikāvijñaptikārikā of Vasubandhu, in *Deux traités de Vasubandhu: Viṃśikā et Triṃśikāvijñaptikārikā*, ed. S. Lévi. Paris: Bulletins de L'École des Hautes Études, 1925.

Vigrahavyāvartanī of Nāgārjuna, ed. E. H. Johnston and A. Kunst. Delhi: Motilal Banarsidass, 1986.

Vinayapiṭaka, vol. I, ed. H. Oldenberg. London: Williams and Norgate, 1879.

Visuddhimagga of Buddhaghosa, ed. C. A. F. Rhys Davids. London: Pāli Text Society, 1975.

Yuktiṣaṣtikākārikā of Nāgārjuna, ed. C. Lindtner and R. Mahoney. Oxford: Indica et Buddhica, 2003.

WESTERN SOURCES

Abbey, R. "Descent and Dissent: Nietzsche's Reading of Two French Moralists." Doctoral dissertation, McGill University, 1994.

Nietzsche's Middle Period. Oxford University Press, 2000.

Abel, G. *Nietzsche: Die Dynamik der Willen zur Macht und die ewige Wiederkehr.* Berlin: W. de Gruyter, 1998.

Alhabari, M. *Analytical Buddhism: The Two-Tiered Illusion of the Self.* Basingstoke: Palgrave Macmillan, 2006.

"Nirvana and Ownerless Consciousness," in M. Siderits, E. Thompson, and D. Zahavi (eds.), *Self, No Self? Perspectives from Analytical, Phenomenological and Indian Traditions.* Oxford University Press, 2011, pp. 79–113.

Amadea, S. M. "Nietzsche's Thirst for India: Schopenhauerian, Brahmanist, and Buddhist Accents in Reflections on Truth, the Ascetic Ideal, and the Eternal Return," *Idealistic Studies* 34(3), 2004: 239–62.

Anquetil-Duperron, H. B. *Oupnek'hat*, 2 vols. Paris: Argentorati, 1801–2.

Appel, F. *Nietzsche contra Democracy.* Ithaca, NY: Cornell University Press, 1999.

Aristotle 1962. *Eudemische Ethik*, trans. F. Dirlmeier. Berlin: Akademie Verlag, 1962.

Arnold, D. *Buddhists, Brahmins and Belief.* New York: Columbia University Press, 2005.
Baggini, J. *Atheism: A Very Short Introduction.* Oxford University Press, 2003.
Beck, A.T. *Cognitive Therapy and the Emotional Disorders.* New York: International Universities Press, 1976.
Berkowitz, P. *Nietzsche: The Ethics of an Immoralist.* Cambridge, MA: Harvard University Press, 1995.
Berman, D. "Schopenhauer and Nietzsche: Honest Atheism, Dishonest Pessimism," in C. Janaway (ed.), *Willing and Nothingness: Schopenhauer as Nietzsche's Educator.* Oxford University Press, 1998, pp. 178–96.
Bonardel, F. *Bouddhisme et philosophie: en quête d'une sagesse commune.* Paris: Harmattan, 2008.
Bradley, B. "Virtue Consequentialism," *Unitas* 17(3), 2005: 282–98.
Breazeale, D. "Introduction," in D. Breazeale (ed.), *Untimely Meditations,* trans. R.J. Hollingdale. Cambridge University Press, 1997, pp. vii–xxxii.
Brogan, W.A. "The Central Significance of Suffering in Nietzsche's Thought," *International Studies in Philosophy* 20(1), 1988: 53–62.
Bronkhorst, J. *Greater Magadha: Studies in the Culture of Early India* II, vol. XIX. Leiden: Koninklijke Brill NV, 2007.
Brown, C.M. "Modes of Perfected Living in the Mahābhārata and the Purāṇas," in A. Fort and P. Mummes (eds.), *Living Liberation in Hindu Thought.* State University of New York Press, 1996, 157–83.
Burton, D. "Curing Diseases of Belief and Desire: Buddhist Philosophical Therapy," in C. Carlisle and J. Ganeri (eds.), *Philosophy as Therapeia.* Special issue of *Royal Institute of Philosophy Supplement* 66, 2010: 187–217.
Emptiness Appraised: A Critical Study of Nāgārjuna's Philosophy. Richmond, CA: Curzon, 1999.
Chattopadhyaya, D. "Skepticism Revisited: Nāgārjuna and Nyāya via Matilal," in P. Bilimoria and J. Mohanty (eds.), *Relativism, Suffering and Beyond: Essays in Memory of Bimal K. Matilal.* Delhi: Oxford University Press, 1997, pp. 50–68.
Clark, M. "Nietzsche, Friedrich," in *Concise Routledge Encyclopedia of Philosophy.* London: Routledge, 2000, pp. 630–1.
Nietzsche on Truth and Philosophy. Cambridge University Press, 1990.
Collins, S. *Selfless Persons: Imagery and Thought in Theravāda Buddhism.* Cambridge University Press, 1982.
Conche, M. "Nietzsche et le bouddhisme," in *Cahier du Collège International de Philosophie,* vol. IV. Paris: Osiris, 1989, pp. 125–44.
Conze, E. "Spurious Parallels to Buddhist Philosophy," *Philosophy East and West* 13(2), 1963: 105–15.
Cox, C. "From Category to Ontology: The Changing Role of *Dharma* in Sarvāstivāda Abhidharma," *Journal of Indian Philosophy* 32(5–6), 2004: 543–97.
Damasio, A. *The Feeling of What Happens: Body and Emotion in the Makings of Consciousness.* London: Heinemann, 1999.

D'Amato, M., J. Garfield, and T. Tillemans (eds.). *Pointing at the Moon: Buddhism, Logic, Analytic Philosophy*. Oxford University Press, 2009.
Danto, A. C. *Nietzsche as Philosopher*. New York: Macmillan, 2005.
Darwall, S. "Empathy, Sympathy, Care," *Philosophical Studies* 89(3), 1998: 261–82.
Dawkins, R. *The God Delusion*. Boston: Houghton Mifflin, 2006.
The Selfish Gene. Oxford University Press, 1976.
Deleuze, G. *Nietzsche et la philosophie*. Paris: Presses Universitaires de France, 1962.
De Man, P. "Nietzsche's Theory of Rhetoric," *Symposium* 28(1), 1974: 33–51.
Detwiler, B. *Nietzsche and the Politics of Aristocratic Radicalism*. Chicago University Press, 1990.
Dreyfus, G. "Self and Subjectivity: A Middle Way Approach," in M. Siderits, E. Thompson, and D. Zahavi (eds.), *Self, No Self? Perspectives from Analytical, Phenomenological and Indian Traditions*. Oxford University Press, 2011, pp. 114–56.
Driver, J. *Uneasy Virtue*. Cambridge University Press, 2001.
Droit, R.-P. *Le culte du néant: les philosophes et le Bouddha*. Paris: Seuil, 1997.
"La fin d'une éclipse?," in R.-P. Droit (ed.), *Présences de Schopenhauer*. Paris: Grasset et Fasquelle, 1989, pp. 7–23.
L'oubli de l'Inde: une amnésie philosophique. Paris: Presses Universitaires de France, 1989.
"Schopenhauer et le Bouddhisme: une 'admirable concordance'?," in E. von der Luft (ed.), *Schopenhauer*. Lewiston, NY: Edwin Mellen Press, 1988, pp. 123–38.
Ellis, A. *Reason and Emotion in Psychotherapy*. New York: Carol Publishing Group, 1991.
Figl, J. "Nietzsche's Early Encounters with Asian Thought," in G. Parkes (ed. and trans.), *Nietzsche and Indian Thought*. London: University of Chicago Press, 1991, pp. 51–63.
"Nietzsche's Encounter with Buddhism," in B. Bäumer and J. R. Dupuche (eds.), *Void and Fullness in the Buddhist, Hindu and Christian Traditions: Śūnya–pūrṇa–Pleroma*. New Delhi, D. K. Printworld, 2005, pp. 225–37.
Flanagan, O. *The Bodhisattva's Brain: Buddhism Naturalized*. Cambridge, MA: MIT Technology Press, 2011.
Fort, A. "Liberation while Living in the *Jīvanmuktiviveka*," in A. Fort and P. Mummes (eds.), *Living Liberation in Hindu Thought*. State University of New York Press, 1996, pp. 135–55.
Frazer, M. L. "The Compassion of Zarathustra: Nietzsche on Sympathy and Strength," *Review of Politics* 68(1), 2006: 49–78.
Frazier, A. M. "A European Buddhism," *Philosophy East and West* 25(2), 1975: 145–60.
Fukuyama, F. *The End of History and the Last Man*. New York: Free Press, 1992.
Gadamer, H.-G. *Wahrheit und Methode: Grundzüge einer philosophischen Hermeneutik*. Tübingen: Mohr, 1972.
Ganeri, J. *The Concealed Art of the Soul: Theories of Self and Practices of Truth in Indian Ethics and Epistemology*. Oxford University Press, 2007.

Ganeri, J. "Subjectivity, Selfhood and the Use of the Word 'I'," in M. Siderits, E. Thompson, and D. Zahavi (eds.), *Self, No Self? Perspectives from Analytical, Phenomenological and Indian Traditions*. Oxford University Press, 2011, pp. 176–92.
Gérard, R. *L'Orient et la pensée romantique allemande*. Nancy: Thomas, 1963.
Gerhardt, V. *Vom Willen zur Macht: Anthropology und Metaphysik der Macht am exemplerischen Fall Friedrich Nietzsches*. Berlin: W. de Gruyter, 1996.
Gethin, R. *The Foundations of Buddhism*. Oxford University Press, 1998.
"He Who Sees *Dhamma* Sees *Dhammas*: *Dhamma* in Early Buddhism," *Journal of Indian Philosophy* 32(4), 2004: 513–42.
Gombrich, R. F. *What the Buddha Thought*. London, Equinox, 2009.
Gowans, C. W. "Medical Analogies in Buddhist and Hellenistic Thought: Tranquility and Anger," in C. Carlisle and J. Ganeri (eds.), *Philosophy as Therapiea*. Special issue of *Royal Institute of Philosophy Supplement* 66, 2010: 11–33.
Grayling, A. C. *The Good Book: A Humanist Bible*. New York: Walker and Co., 2011.
Griffin, J. *Well-Being: Its Meaning, Measurement and Moral Importance*. Oxford, Clarendon Press, 1986.
Grimm, R. H. *Nietzsche's Theory of Knowledge*. Berlin: W. de Gruyter, 1977.
Halbfass, W. *India and Europe: An Essay in Understanding*. State University of New York Press, 1988.
Tradition and Reflection: Explorations in Indian Thought. State University of New York Press, 1991.
Hamilton, S. *Early Buddhism: A New Approach: The I of the Beholder*. Richmond, CA: Curzon, 2000.
Hamlyn, D. *Schopenhauer*. London: Routledge and Kegan Paul, 1980.
Harman, G. "Ethics and Observation," in S. Darwall, A. Gibbard, and P. Railton (eds.), *Moral Discourse and Practice*. Oxford University Press, 1997, pp. 83–8.
Explaining Value and Other Essays in Moral Philosophy. Oxford University Press, 2000.
Havas, R. *Nietzsche's Genealogy: Nihilism and the Will to Knowledge*. Ithaca, NY: Cornell University Press, 1995.
Hayes, R. P. *Diṅnāga on the Interpretation of Signs*. London: Kluwer Academic Publishers, 1989.
Heidegger, M. *Nietzsche, 4 vols*. Pfullingen: Neske, 1961.
Heine, H. *Sämtliche Werke*. Hamburg: Hoffman und Sampe, 1863.
Heller, P. *Studies on Nietzsche*. Bonn: Bouvier, 1980.
Heraclitus of Ephesus. "Fragments," in *The Art and Thought of Heraclitus*, ed. C. H. Kahn. Cambridge University Press, 1981.
Horstmann, R.-P. "Introduction," in R.-P. Horstmann and J. Norman (eds.), *Beyond Good and Evil*, trans. J. Norman. Cambridge University Press, 2002, pp. ii–xxviii.

Hulin, M. *Le principe d'égo dans la pensée indienne classique: la notion d'ahaṃkāra.* Paris: Collège de France, 1978.

Hume, D. *A Treatise of Human Nature*, ed. F. and M. Norton. Oxford University Press, 2005.

Hutter, H. *Shaping the Future: Nietzsche's New Regime of the Soul and its Ascetic Practices*. Lanham, MD: Lexington Press, 2006.

Janaway, C. *Beyond Selflessness: Reading Nietzsche's Genealogy*. Oxford University Press, 2007.

Self and World in Schopenhauer's Philosophy. Oxford: Clarendon Press, 1989.

(ed.). *Willing and Nothingness: Schopenhauer as Nietzsche's Educator*. Oxford: Clarendon Press, 1998.

Johnson, D. R. *Nietzsche's Anti-Darwinism*. Cambridge University Press, 2010.

Kant, I. *Kritik der reinen Vernunft*. Leipzig: Felix Meiner, 1926.

Kaufmann, W. *Nietzsche: Philosopher, Psychologist, Antichrist*. Princeton University Press, 1974.

Kern, H. *Der Buddhismus und seine Geschichte in Indien*. Leipzig: O. Schulze, 1882.

King, R. *Indian Philosophy: An Introduction to Hindu and Buddhist Thought*. Edinburgh University Press, 1999.

Kiowski, H. "Nietzsches Kritik an Schopenhauers Mitleidsbegriff," *Prima Philosophia* 12(1), 1999: 47–61.

Koeppen, C. F. *Die Religion des Buddhas*, 2 vols. Berlin: F. Schneider, 1857–9.

Lambrellis, D. N. "Beyond the Moral Interpretation of the World: The World as Play: Nietzsche and Heraclitus," *Philosophical Inquiry* 27(2), 2005: 211–21.

La Rochefoucauld, F. de. *Maximes et réflexions diverses*, ed. P. Kuetz. Paris: Bordas, 1966.

Leibniz, G. F. *Essai de théodicée sur la bonté de dieu, la liberté de l'homme et l'origine du mal*, ed. J. Jalabert. Paris: Aubier, 1962 [1710].

The Monadology and Other Philosophical Essays, ed. and trans. P. and A. M. Schrecker. Indianapolis, IN: Bobbs-Merrill, 1965.

Leiter, B. *Nietzsche on Morality*. London: Routledge, 2002.

Lévi-Strauss, C. *La pensée sauvage*. Paris: Plon, 1962.

López, D. S. Jr. "Do *Śrāvakas* Understand Emptiness?," *Journal of Indian Philosophy* 16(1), 1988: 65–105.

Losurdo, D. *Nietzsche, il ribelle aristocratico: biografia intellettuale e bilancio critico*. Turin: Bollati Boringhieri, 2002.

MacKenzie, M. "Enacting the Self: Buddhist and Enactivist Approaches to the Emergence of the Self," in M. Siderits, E. Thompson, and D. Zahavi (eds.), *Self, No Self? Perspectives from Analytical, Phenomenological and Indian Traditions*. Oxford University Press, 2011, pp. 239–73.

Mackie, J. L. "From *Ethics: Inventing Right and Wrong*," in S. Darwall, A. Gibbard, and P. Railton (eds.), *Moral Discourse and Practice*. Oxford University Press, 1997, pp. 89–100.

Magnus, B. *Nietzsche's Existential Imperative*. Bloomington, IN: Indiana University Press, 1978.

Martin, G. T. "Deconstruction and Breakthrough in Nietzsche and Nāgārjuna," in G. Parks (ed.), *Nietzsche and Asian Thought*. London: Chicago University Press, 1991, pp. 91–111.
Mistry, F. *Nietzsche and Buddhism: Prolegomenon to a Comparative Study*. New York: W. de Gruyter, 1981.
Moore, G. *Nietzsche, Biology and Metaphor*. Cambridge University Press, 2002.
Morrison, R. G. *Nietzsche and Buddhism: A Study in Nihilism and Ironic Affinities*. Oxford University Press, 1997.
"Nietzsche and Nirvana," in W. Santaniello (ed.), *Nietzsche and the Gods*. State University of New York Press, 2001, pp. 87–113.
Müller, M. *Beiträge zur vergleichenden Mythologie und Ethnologie*. Leipzig: Englemann, 1879.
Nagel, T. *The View from Nowhere*. Oxford University Press, 1989.
Ñāṇamoli, B. *The Path of Purification*. Kandry: Buddhist Publication Society, 1975.
Nehamas, A. *Nietzsche: Life as Literature*. Cambridge, MA: Harvard University Press, 1985.
Nicholls, M. "The Influence of Eastern Thought on Schopenhauer's Doctrine of the Thing-in-Itself," in C. Janaway (ed.), *The Cambridge Companion to Schopenhauer*. Cambridge University Press, 1999, pp. 171–212.
Nietzsche, F. W. *Nietzsche Briefwechsel*, ed. G. Colli and M. Montinari. Berlin: W. de Gruyter, 1980.
Nietzsche Werke, ed. G. Colli and M. Montinari. Berlin: W. de Gruyter, 1977.
Der Wille zur Macht, ed. E. Forster-Nietzsche and P. Gast, in *Nietzsches Werke*, vols. IX and X. Leipzig: C. G. Naumann, 1906.
Norman, K. R. "A Note on *Attā* in the *Alagaddūpama-sutta*," in *Collected Papers*, vol II. Oxford University Press, 1991, pp. 100–9.
Nussbaum, M. C. "Pity and Mercy: Nietzsche's Stoicism," in R. Schacht (ed.), *Nietzsche, Genealogy, Morality: Essays on Nietzsche's* On the Genealogy of Morals. University of California Press, 1994, pp. 139–47.
Oetke, C. "'Nihilist' and 'Non-nihilist' Interpretations of Madhyamaka," *Acta Orientalia* 57(1), 1996: 57–103.
"Remarks on the Interpretation of Nāgārjuna's Philosophy," *Journal of Indian Philosophy* 19(3), 1991: 315–23.
Oldenberg, H. *Buddha: sein Leben, seine Lehre, seine Gemeinde*. Berlin: W. Hertz, 1881.
O'Shaughnessy, B. *The Will: A Double Aspect Theory*. Cambridge University Press, 1980.
Panaïoti, A. "Anātmatā, Moral Psychology and Soteriology in Indian Buddhism," in N. Mirning (ed.), *Puṣpikā: Tracing Ancient India through Text and Traditions*. Contributions to Current Research in Indology, vol. 1. Oxford, Oxbow Books Press, forthcoming.
"Wrong View, Wrong Action in Buddhist Thought," in N. Norris and C. Balman (eds.), *Uneasy Humanity: Perpetual Wrestlings with Evils*. Oxford: Inter-Disciplinary Press, 2009, pp. 9–23.

Parfit, D. "Experiences, Subjects, and Conceptual Schemes," *Philosophical Topics* 26(1–2), 1999: 217–70.
"Overpopulation and the Quality of Life," in P. Singer (ed.), *Applied Ethics*. Oxford University Press, 1986, pp. 145–64.
Reasons and Persons. Oxford University Press, 1984.
Pearson, K. A. "For Mortal Souls: Philosophy and Therapiea in Nietzsche's *Dawn*," in C. Carlisle and J. Ganeri (eds.), *Philosophy as Therapiea*. Special issue of *Royal Institute of Philosophy Supplement* 66, 2010: 137–63.
Pippin, R. B. "Introduction," in R. B. Pippin (ed.), *Thus Spoke Zarathustra: A Book for All and None*, trans. A. Del Caro. Cambridge University Press, 2006, pp. viii–xxxv.
Priest, G. *Beyond the Limits of Thought*. Oxford University Press, 2002.
Purushottama, B. "Nietzsche as 'Europe's Buddha' and 'Asia's Superman'," *Sophia* 47(3), 2008: 359–76.
Pye, M. *Skilful Means: A Concept in Mahāyāna Buddhism*. London: Psychology Press, 2003.
Rawls, J. *A Theory of Justice*. Cambridge, MA: Harvard University Press, 1971.
Reginster, B. *The Affirmation of Life: Nietzsche on Overcoming Nihilism*. Cambridge, MA: Harvard University Press, 2006.
Rhys Davids, T. W. and W. Stede (eds.). *Pāli Text Society's Pāli–English Dictionary*. Chipstead: Pāli Text Society, 2006.
Richardson, J. *Nietzsche's New Darwinism*. Oxford University Press, 2004.
Nietzsche's System. New York: Oxford University Press, 1996.
Ricœur, P. *Soi même comme un autre*. Paris: Seuil, 1990.
Rorty, R. *Consequences of Pragmatism*. University of Minnesota Press, 1991.
Rousseau, J.-J. *Émile, ou De l'éducation*. Paris: Garnier Frères, 1967 [1762].
Ruegg, D. S. *The Literature of the Madhyamaka School of Philosophy in India*. Wiesbaden: O. Harrassowitz, 1981.
Rupp, G. "The Relationship between *Nirvāṇa* and *Saṃsāra*: An Essay on the Evolution of Buddhist Ethics." *Philosophy East and West* 21(1), 1971: 55–67.
Russell, B. *History of Western Philosophy and its Connection with Political and Social Circumstances from the Earliest Times to the Present Day*. New York: Simon and Schuster, 1945.
Sartre, J.-P. *L'être et le néant: essai d'ontologie phénoménologique*. Paris: Gallimard, 1943.
Scarre, G. *Utilitarianism*. London: Routledge, 1996.
Schechtman, M. *The Constitution of Selves*. Ithaca, NY: Cornell University Press, 1996.
Scheiffele, E. "Questioning One's 'Own' from the Perspective of the Foreign," in G. Parkes (ed.), *Nietzsche and Indian Thought*. London: University of Chicago Press, 1991, pp. 31–47.
Scheler, M. *Gesammelte Werke*, 7 vols. Bern: Francke, 1973.
Schopenhauer, A. *Sämtliche Werke*, ed. A. Hübscher. Mannheim: F. A. Brockhaus, 1988.
Schwab, R. *La Renaissance orientale*. Paris: Payot, 1950.

Siderits, M. "Buddhas as Zombies: A Buddhist Reduction of Subjectivity," in M. Siderits, E. Thompson, and D. Zahavi (eds.), *Self, No Self? Perspectives from Analytical, Phenomenological and Indian Traditions*. Oxford University Press, 2011, pp. 308–31.

Buddhism as Philosophy: An Introduction. Aldershot: Ashgate, 2007.

Buddhist Philosophy and Personal Identity: Empty Persons. Aldershot: Ashgate, 2003.

Siderits M., E. Thompson, and D. Zahavi (eds.). *Self, No Self? Perspectives from Analytical, Phenomenological and Indian Traditions*. Oxford University Press, 2011.

Sober, E. and D. S. Wilson. *Unto Others: The Evolution and Psychology of Unselfish Behaviour*. Cambridge, MA: Harvard University Press, 1998.

Soll, I. "Pessimism and the Tragic View of Life: Reconsiderations of Nietzsche's *Birth of Tragedy*," in R. C. Solomon and K. M. Higgins (eds.), *Reading Nietzsche*. Oxford University Press, 1988, pp. 104–33.

Sorabji, R. *Self: Ancient and Modern Insights about Individuality, Life, and Death*. Oxford University Press, 2006.

Spinoza, B. *A Spinoza Reader: The Ethics and Other Works*, ed. and trans. E. Curley. Princeton University Press, 1994.

Sprung, M. "Nietzsche's Trans-European Eye," in G. Parkes (ed.), *Nietzsche and Indian Thought*. London: University of Chicago Press, 1991, pp. 76–90.

Staten, H. *Nietzsche's Voice*. Ithaca, NY: Cornell University Press, 1990.

Strawson, G. "The Self," *Journal of Consciousness Studies* 6(5–6), 1997: 405–28.

Tappolet, C. "Compassion et altruisme," *Studia Philosophica* 59, 2000: 175–93.

Taylor, C. *Sources of the Self*. Cambridge, MA: Harvard University Press, 1989.

Thapar, R. *Ancient Indian Social History: Some Interpretations*. London: Sangam Books, 1984.

Ure, M. *Nietzsche's Therapy: Self-Cultivation in the Middle Works*. Lanham, MD : Lexington Press, 2008.

Vanderheyde, A. *Nietzsche et la pensée bouddhiste*. Paris: Harmattan, 2007.

Varela, F. J. *Ethical Know-How: Action, Wisdom, and Cognition*. Stanford University Press, 1999.

Viévard, L. *Vacuité (śūnyatā) et compassion (karuṇā) dans le bouddhisme madhyamaka*. Paris: Collège de France, 2002.

Wackernagel, J. *Über den Ursprung des Brahmanismus*. Basel: H. Richter, 1877.

Waldinger, R. J. *Psychiatry for Medical Students*. Washington, DC: American Psychiatric Press, 1997.

Wall, S. "Perfectionism," in E. N. Zalta (ed.), *Stanford Encyclopedia of Philosophy* (Fall 2008 edn). Available at: http://plato/stanford.edu/archives/fall2008/entries/perfectionism-moral.

Wallis, G. "The Buddha Counsels a Theist: A Reading of the *Tejjivasutta* (*Dīghanināya* 13)," *Religion* 38(1), 2008: 54–67.

Warder, A. K. *Indian Buddhism*. Delhi: Motilal Banarsidass, 1970.

Outline of Indian Philosophy. Delhi, Motilal Banarsidass, 1971.

Westerhoff, J. *Nāgārjuna's Madhyamaka: A Philosophical Introduction*. Oxford University Press, 2009.

Wicks, R. *Schopenhauer*. Oxford: Blackwell, 2008.

Williams, B. "Introduction," in B. Williams (ed.), *The Gay Science*, trans. J. Nauckhoff and A. del Caro. Cambridge University Press, 2005, pp. vii–xxii.

The Sense of the Past. Cambridge University Press, 2006.

Truth and Truthfulness. Princeton University Press, 2002.

Williams, P. *Mahāyāna Buddhism: The Doctrinal Foundations*. London: Routledge, 1989.

Willson, A. L. *A Mythical Image: The Ideal of India in German Romanticism*. Durham, NC: Duke University Press, 1964.

Wood, T. *Nagarjunian Disputations: A Philosophical Journey through an Indian Looking-glass*. University of Hawaii Press, 1994.

Young, J. *The Death of God and the Meaning of Life*. London: Routledge, 2003.

Schopenhauer. London: Routledge, 2005.

Zahavi, D. "The Experiential Self: Objections and Clarifications," in M. Siderits, E. Thompson, and D. Zahavi (eds.), *Self, No Self? Perspectives from Analytical, Phenomenological and Indian Traditions*. Oxford University Press, 2011, pp. 56–78.

Index

67672868R00146

Made in the USA
San Bernardino, CA
25 January 2018